Irish Emigration to New England Through the Port of Saint John New Brunswick, Canada 1841 to 1849

by
Daniel F. Johnson
Certified Genealogist (Canada)
P.O. Box 26025
Saint John, N.B.
Canada E2J 4M3

CLEARFIELD

Copyright © 1996 by D. F. Johnson
All Rights Reserved.

Originally published
Canada, 1996

Reprinted for
Clearfield Company, Inc. by
Genealogical Publishing Co., Inc.
Baltimore, Maryland
1997, 1998

International Standard Book Number: 0-8063-4708-2

Made in the United States of America

Daniel F. Johnson, C.G.(Canada)
P.O. Box 26025
Saint John, N.B.
Canada E2J 4M3

Printed in Canada by DanTech Enterprises Ltd.

Canadian Cataloguing in Publication Data

Johnson, Daniel F.
 Irish Emigrants & Their Vessels: Port of Saint John, N.B. Canada 1841-1849

1. New Brunswick - Irish 2. New Brunswick - History 3. New Brunswick - 19th Century Migration

Acknowledgements

In 1977 when Robert Fellows, Archivist at the Provincial Archives of New Brunswick, was compiling his book *Researching Your Ancestors In New Brunswick, Canada*, he drew my attention to a number of Emigrant lists then stowed away in archival boxes and at that time relatively unknown to researchers.

The continuing interest in Irish research, boosted by the upcoming 150th Anniversary of the Great Irish Famine and the encouragement received by the local committee members of the Irish Cultural Society has prompted the publication of these documents.

Daniel F. Johnson

Table of Contents

I. Introduction
    i. Saint John: Gateway of Irish Migration (p. 1)
    ii. Searching Irish Ancestry (p. 1)
    iii. The Emigrants of 1841 to 1849 (p. 5)

II. Emigrant Poor of Portland Parish, St. John County 1841 (p. 10)

III. The Provincial Lunatic Asylum Records 1841 (p. 12)

IV. Emigrant Poor of City of Saint John 1842
    i. Emigrants in Hospital and Parish Houses (p. 15)
    ii. Sick And Indigent Immigrants Assisted With Outdoor Relief (p. 19)
    iii. Emigrants Receiving Tickets For Passages Inland And Coastwise (p. 27)
    iv. Interments of Emigrant Poor (p.29)
    v. Emigrants in Hospital and Parish Houses (p. 30)
    vi. Sick And Indigent Immigrants Assisted With Outdoor Relief (p. 36)
    vii. Emigrants Receiving Tickets For Passages Inland And Coastwise (p. 54)
    viii. Interments of Emigrant Poor (p. 60)

V.	The Provincial Lunatic Asylum Records 1842 (p.62)
VI.	Emigrants Admitted To Alms And Work House From Vessels Arriving In 1843 (p. 64)
VII.	The Provincial Lunatic Asylum Records 1843 (p.72)
VIII.	Emigrants Admitted To Alms And Work House From Vessels Arriving In 1844 (p. 74)
IX.	Emigrants Admitted To Alms And Work House From Vessels Arriving In 1845 (p. 76)
X.	Emigrant Deaths in Hospital, Partridge Island, St. John 1846 (p. 80)
XI.	Emigrants Admitted To Alms And Work House From Vessels Arriving In 1846 (p. 80)
XII.	Emigrant Deaths in Hospital, Partridge Island, St. John 1847 (p. 94)
XIII.	Emigrants Admitted To Alms And Work House From Vessels Arriving In 1847 (p. 106)
XIV.	Emigrants Admitted To Alms And Work House From Vessels Arriving In 1848 (p. 175)
XV.	Emigrants Admitted To Alms And Work House From Vessels Arriving In 1849 (p. 184)
XVI.	Appendix
	i. Emigrant Vessel Tables 1841-1849 (p. 189)
	ii. Emigrant Vessel Footnotes (p. 207)
	iii. Emigrants of Charlotte County, N.B., 1842 (p.225)
	iv. Terrence Punch, "Be Cautious With Passenger Lists: The Envoy, 1847" (p. 233)
XVII.	Index
	i. Name Index (p. 236)

Introduction

Saint John: The Gateway of Irish Migration To New England

The importance of Saint John, New Brunswick as one of the major points of entry for Irish migration to North America has remained one of history's better kept secrets. Although the smaller Provincial ports did receive the occasional emigrant vessel, the ports of Saint John and Gross Ille, Quebec were the primary destination points of emigration to British North America. The port of Saint John is often overlooked by many North Americans of Irish descent who are better acquainted with the large ports of New York, Boston and Philadelphia.

During the years of the Irish Famine, the majority of Irish emigrants who arrived at Saint John left immediately for Boston and other New England ports. Poverty, disease and the other circumstances under which the migration took place inevitably led to the break-up of families. The almshouse documents and other public relief records contain the accounts of pregnancies among single young women, the desertions of wives by their spouses and the names of children who were orphaned by parents who succumbed to the ravages of disease. Some emigrants found employment locally while their brothers and sisters were compelled to emigrate south. Boston was a favorite destination of many emigrants. The strong connections which subsequently developed between the Irish families of Boston and Saint John are evidenced by the marriages and obituaries to be found in the New Brunswick and Massachusetts newspapers.

Searching Irish Ancestry

For years difficulties have been encountered by North American genealogists researching their Irish ancestry. Family historians have travelled to the Emerald Isle seeking an elusive ancestor who was known only to have been born *somewhere* in Ireland. These visitors soon realized that success depended upon the identification of the specific town or parish from where their ancestor migrated. Without this knowledge, the research

2   Irish Migration To New England: Port of Saint John

techniques they employed often deteriorated into a hit and miss approach where every clue, real or imagined, spawned a number of time consuming paper chases.

In recent years, a new approach to document interpretation has developed to assist genealogists. By examining all relevant records associated with emigration, facts are drawn from the broader analysis which may provide clues to specific ancestral nativity. In his landmark work, Peter Murphy, author of *Together In Exile*[1] discovered that the inhabitants of certain districts in Saint John City had migrated from the same community in Ireland. This transplanting of communities is found elsewhere in the Province of New Brunswick. By similar analysis, the nativity of some emigrants can be deduced by the vessel in which they arrived. For example, the passengers of the *Æolus* which arrived at Saint John on 31 May 1847 were the former tenants of Sir Robert Gore Booth, Bart. of Lissadell near Sligo, Ireland.

Irish Migration to the Port of Saint John, New Brunswick is a compilation of *selected* extant New Brunswick records relevant to emigration to the British colony of New Brunswick from 1841 to 1849. The records consulted were the Emigrant lists maintained by the Overseers of the Poor and the registers of admissions to the Alms House, Emigrant Hospital and the Provincial Lunatic Asylum. Extensive use was also made of the *New Brunswick Courier*, a weekly Saint John newspaper published during the 1840's. The Appendix contains tables of emigrant vessels, the information drawn from different sources such as NBC (New Brunswick Courier), A.H. (Alms House) and

---

[1] Peter Murphy, *Together In Exile* (Saint John: Lingley Printing Co., 1990)
This well referenced book contains genealogies of Saint John Irish families including Boyle, Brown, Campbell, Carroll, Cassely, Creegan, Doyle, Elmore, Feran, Finigan, Flanagan, Hanlon, Hanratty, Hoey, Johnston, Kelly, Killen, Kirk, Lowe, Magee, Markey, May, McCrink, McGuiggan, McGuire, Mills, Murphy, Oakes, Quinn, O'Reilly, Rice, Riley, Rourke, Sharkey, Small, Thompson, Toal, Traynor, Woods

Introduction 3

S.R. (ship records). The tables identify ships sailing directly to Saint John from British Ports. Like other compilations, the tables should not be considered as absolute, but a useful reference tool nevertheless.

During the years of the Irish famine, Moses H. Perley, the Emigration Agent at the Port of Saint John, published a small notice in the *New Brunswick Courier,* announcing the receipt of passenger lists which had been forwarded by mail from the emigration officers at the ports of Londonderry and Cork. Perley complained that no passenger lists were received from those vessels embarking from the smaller Irish outports. These lists were used by the officials to confirm the number of passengers aboard each vessel, but were also available to anyone looking for the names of friends and relatives.

It has been a long held belief that the passenger lists were burned in the Custom House building which was destroyed in the Great Fire of June 20, 1877, a conflagration that decimated the commercial district of the city Saint John. Another possibility, however, is that Moses Perley may have deposited these lists in his personal collection of papers, the whole of which was lost in a subsequent fire. An old vault discovered in the basement of the new Customs Building (rebuilt on the same location after the Great Fire) revealed ship manifests and passenger lists dating from 1834 to 1837.[2] Except for these few documents, it is doubtful that other passenger received at the Port of Saint have survived.

Copies of some passenger lists of vessels bound for Saint John (originating from foreign sources) have within recent years been published. In 1985 the records of the J.& J. Cooke line were compiled by Dessie Baker. *Emigrants From Derry Port,*

---

[2] The Custom House Records were deposited at the Provincial Archives of New Brunswick, P.O. Box 6000, Fredericton, N.B. E3B 5H1. where they were card indexed and microfilmed. See also *Passengers To New Brunswick* published by the Saint John Branch, New Brunswick Genealogical Society

4   Irish Migration To New England: Port of Saint John

1847-1849. The book includes the dates of booking of passengers for each vessel. In 1988 the passenger lists of both the J.& J. Cook and McCorkell Lines, 1847-1871 were published in *Irish Passenger Lists* under the direction of Brian Mitchell. Although only the year of departure is given, Mr. Mitchell includes a valuable table on pages x and xi to identify the Irish districts with the corresponding County.[3] (See also Appendix iv., Terrence M. Punch, C.G.(C) *Be Cautious With Passenger Lists: The Envoy, 1847*)

The future of Irish genealogical research, on both sides of the Atlantic Ocean, does look promising. The renewed interest of North Americans in their Irish roots has boosted tourism in Ireland. Private genealogical research centres there are consolidating their vital records and, with the use of computers, are eliminating tedious hours of research.

A careful study of New Brunswick's provincial land and church records will undoubtedly reveal new insights. Newspaper obituaries, tombstone inscriptions and other records are being catalogued and indexed every year. An example is the published series *Vital Statistics From New Brunswick Canada Newspapers*. First commenced in 1982, this project has thus extracted the births, marriages and deaths from all New Brunswick newspapers from the year 1784 to 1886. This information is available to researchers for a fee by writing to: Search And Extract (SAE) Service c/o Daniel F. Johnson, P.O. Box 26025, Saint John, N.B. Canada E2J 4M3.

An important guide to public records relevant to Irish Migration available at the Provincial Archives of New Brunswick, Fredericton, N.B. is Thomas Power's, *The Irish In Atlantic Canada*[4]

---

[3] Dessie Baker ed., *Emigrants From Derry Port, 1847-1849* (Apollo, Pa. U.S.A: Closson Press, 1985) and Brian Mitchell, *Irish Passenger Lists, 1847-1871* (Baltimore, Marland: Genealogical Publishing Co. Inc., 1988)

[4] Thomas P. Power, *The Irish In Atlantic Canada 1780-1900* (Fredericton, N.B.: New Ireland Press, 1991), *Chapter Seven*

The Emigrants of 1841-1849

The emigrants who arrived at the Port in the early 1840's were provided with more opportunities than those who came just a few years later. They were vulnerable to the diseases which plagued all vessels of that time period, but were easily accommodated upon their arrival. Alexander Wedderburn[5], the Emigration Officer at Saint John reported June 3, 1841 that typhus fever had appeared among the emigrants who had come that season, but the patients were convalescent, being comfortably lodged, provided for and attended on Partridge Island. He described the new emigrants as able bodied yeomen, many of whom had gone into the country.[6] According to the colonial returns submitted to Great Britain, passengers generally arrived in good health and a very small proportion required charitable relief. At least one-half of these emigrants left for the United States shortly after their arrival at Saint John.

Before landing in the city, the passengers were examined by medical authorities. When disease was prevalent, the ship was ordered to the Quarantine Station. The Station was located on Partridge Island, situate in the harbour a short distance from the mouth of the St. John River. The island's wind swept rocky terrain, long denuded of all but a patchwork of spruce trees and wild grasses, also supported a light house and some military works. Surrounded by the cold Atlantic waters of the Bay of Fundy, its isolation from the shores abated the fear of the spread of disease to the native populace; but the same geographical and climatic features also inhibited the operation of the Quarantine Establishment. In January 1848, Mr. Perley reported: "The island is but small and the most eligible portions are occupied by the light house, the Keeper's residence and grounds

---

[5] Alexander Wedderburn, Esq., a native of Aberdeen, Scotland and Chief Emigration Agent for New Brunswick died Saturday evening at Saint John, age 47. - June 24, 1843 N.B.C

[6] Return of Vessels From Ireland for Saint John, N.B. With Emigrants, Government Emigration Office, Saint John, June 3rd, 1841, P.A.N.B., RS555 Micro F16225-6

and the Military works. There is very scanty supply of water upon it and it is doubtful if wells would furnish a sufficient supply of good fresh water. Partridge Island is difficult to access at all times, except by the day light and in fine summer weather. In stormy weather it is positively dangerous to visit. The expense of sending supplies of fuel, straw, fresh water, provisions and stores to this Island has been very considerable during the past season, while delays frequently occurred during stormy gales, or when a heavy rain was rolling in from the Bay of Fundy or when a dense fog prevailed."[7]

In the decade preceding the *Famine Years 1845 to 1847* emigration to the Port of Saint John increased substantially. As early as 1835, the emigrants who were unable to care for themselves were sent to small parish houses in Saint John City and the adjacent community of Portland. The owners of private dwellings were reimbursed for the care of destitute families. To meet the increased demand public assistance the Lunatic Asylum was established in 1836. The following year an auxiliary hospital was opened in the city to handle victims of small pox. An auxiliary Immigration Hospital was established in 1840. Although most of the emigrants who arrived during the period preceding the *famine years* secured employment or settled within the Province of New Brunswick, the number of persons requiring public assistance increased.[8] Both Provincial and local

---

[7] Thomas P.Power, *The Irish In Atlantic Canada 1780-1900* (Fredericton, N.B.: New Ireland Press, 1991) Chapter 6, Harold E. Wright, *Partridge Island: Re-discovering the Irish Connection* pp. 127-150

[8] The following are the numbers of all the sick and distressed individuals succoured in hospitals and other parish houses and like cases of families and detached individuals partially assisted for different periods of time in the City during the eight years preceding Dec. 31st, 1842. From 1837 to 1842 the number of emigrants appears in brackets. It does not, however, include the number of emigrants succoured for six months of the year in hospitals at health station on Partridge Island. (Year, No. Individuals in Parish Houses, No. Cases of families outside): *1835*, 359, 255; *1836*, 542, 307; *1837*, 727 (419), 603 (390); *1838*, 576 (252), 466 (208); *1839*, 556 (156), 335 (117); *1840*, 694 (362), 533 (305); *1841*, 745 (353), 750 (400); *1842*, 659 (272), 1255 (720) - *New*

Introduction 7

authorities were aware of the need for a large central facility to accommodate an increasing number of destitute native to Saint John and arriving from British ports. Monica Robertson noted

"In 1839, pursuant to an act of the Legislature in 1838, tenders were called for the erection of a new county alms house on the east side of Courtenay Bay, Saint John. Like other alms houses of the period it also was to provide an infirmary for the sick, but at the date of its opening in 1842, the strain which shortly was to be placed on the new facility and its management could not be envisaged."[9]

The original register of emigrants admitted to the new Alms House is kept by the New Brunswick Museum. Their names, ages, place of nativity, vessel upon which they arrived, dates of admission, discharge or death are included herewith; categorized by the name of their vessel. Contained on the first few pages of the register are the names of individuals admitted from April 21 to August 16, 1843. Although no pages appear to be missing, the next set of persons were admitted Feb. 10, 1845.

"In 1845 and 1846 many of the destitute and ill emigrants who arrived at Saint John were cared for at the County Alms House Infirmary but in 1847, owing to the great increase in the number of emigrants stricken with fever, an emigrant hospital was erected within a stone's throw of the Alms House... The Emigrant Hospital was destroyed by fire in 1853. Fortunately the main Alms House escaped destruction and a volume of records was saved."[10]

Brunswick Courier, Saint John February 4, 1843 page 2 col. 3. - Minutes of Overseers of the Poor City of Saint John

[9] Monica Robertson, former head of the Library and Archives Department, New Brunswick Museum, Saint John: see Introduction, ed. D.F. Johnson, *The St. John County Alms And Work House*, transcription 1985.

[10] Ibid. Intro. *The St. John County Alms And Work House*.
A microfilm copy (F16225) of the original Emigrant Hospital Records may be found at the Provincial Archives of New Brunswick, Fredericton.

8   Irish Migration To New England: Port of Saint John

During the years 1845 to 1850, Moses H. Perley was the Emigration Agent at Saint John, except for a brief period in August 1849 when Thomas McAvity was temporarily assigned to assume his duties. Mr. Perley was conscientious in his responsibilities as emigration officer. He advertised for employers and publicly urged New Brunswick inhabitants to assist the emigrants to find their way about the province. He corresponded with emigration officials in Boston hoping to secure employment for the emigrants. He initiated legal proceedings against the masters of vessels for deficiency in provisions or irregular treatment of their passengers.

Among those who assisted the emigrants was Dr. James P. Collins. He had returned to Saint John from Europe after completing his medical studies to marry Miss Mary Quinn in October 1846. In the summer of 1847 he visited the Quarantine Hospital to assist the resident Health Officer, Dr. G.J. Harding. On July 2, 1847, he contracted and succumbed to typhus fever, leaving his young widow to mourn her loss. In October 1847, the New Brunswick Government provided funds to establish an Orphanage for 74 emigrant children in what was then the old Poor House building in Saint John. William Cunningham was placed in charge. The Reverend Edmond Quinn, brother-in-law of Dr. Collins, organized charitable functions to provide the necessary clothing for the orphans.

The *New Brunswick Courier* of September 24, 1847 reported: "The serious infliction upon the community of the present season of shiploads of diseased paupers[11], many of whom become Parish charges immediately upon landing and now fill our Alms Houses, hospitals, while other subsist by street begging has now become so alarming that a number of resolutions were passed at a meeting of Common Council yesterday. The New Brunswick authorities experienced other difficulties. A decline in the timber industry and its related

---

[11] Thomas P. Power, *The Irish In Atlantic Canada 1780-1900* (Fredericton, N.B.: New Ireland Press, 1991), William A. Spray, *Immigrants and Fever in New Brunswick in 1847* Chapter 5 pp. 107-126

branches, then a check to the ship-building industry and a failure of crops for the three preceding seasons had spawned a migration of native inhabitants to the United States. The local papers lamented the loss of the *young and active enterprising natives* who depart by every steamer - *"this wasting of bone and sinew."* The dismal prospect of employment and the absence of government assistance compelled most of the emigrants of 1847 to seek a future south of the border. In 1846, M.H. Perley estimated that only 1 in 8 of the arrivals remained in New Brunswick. A larger proportion of emigrants undoubtedly departed the Province the following year.

In the years following 1847, there was a substantial decrease in the number of emigrants seeking passage to Saint John. An substantial increase in the fare of passage dissuaded many of the destitute. Those who could afford passage preferred vessels which were embarking for ports in the United States. By 1850, the Government Emigration Agent at Queenstown reported that the quantity of land sown and the appearance of the potato crop in Ireland would keep numbers at home who would otherwise have emigrated that season. The port of Saint John, which had received as many as 92 passenger vessels from all Irish ports in the year 1847, reported only 29 in 1848, and 24 in 1849

Emigrant Poor of Portland Parish 1841

To His Excellency Sir Edmund Walker Head Baronet Lieutenant Governor and Commander in Chief of the Province of New Brunswick - To the Honorable the Legislative Council of the said Province and the Honorable House of Assembly convened

The Petition of the undersigned Overseers of the Poor for the Parish of Portland for the Years 1841 and 1842. Humbly Sheweth
That your Petitioners incurred a debt for the Supply of the Poor Emigrants in said Parish at that period; and that a grant by the Legislature was made that Year to reimburse them for said Expenditure but, which by some means beyond their control they did not receive.
That your Petitioners received a part of the Liabilities incurred by them by an order from the Sessions. Still leaving an amount due the Commercial Bank and several small Bills that remained unpaid when your Petitioners went out of office amounting in all to £30:0.0 Thirty Pounds
That your Petitioners feel confident that Your Excellency and Honours will not render them Liable for the Payment of a debt incurred solely for the Public Service wherein they had no Emolument whatever but on the Contrary had to perform a most arduous and Responsible duty Gratuitously (sgd) Thomas Allan, Wm Ruddock

Parish of Portland for Expenditures for aid furnished Destitute and Distressed Passenger & Emigrants
Boarding & Lodging Emigrants from 1 Jany to 31 Decr 1841: William Atlee, Alms House Keeper for Parish of Portland

Names 1841	Admitted	Disch'd
John Quin	January 1	April 4
Frederick Hughes	" 1	May 1
Margaret Wallace	" 1	June 9
Ellen Hazen	" 1	Oct. 9
Mary Cooper (child)	" 1	*died* June 4
Catharine Foster (child)	" 1	Decr 31

Names	Admitted	Disch'd
1841		
Margaret McNamara	June 10	June 31
Helen Dacey	" 17	" 23
Thomas Farry	July 3	Augt 4
Bridget Sheridan	" 5	" 12
Thomas Braden	" 5	" 25
Catherine Braden	" 5	" 25
Thomas Chittick	" 5	" 25
Mary Tracey	" 5	July 31
John McCoane	" 5	*died* July 17
Mark Miles	" 6	Augt 10
Bridget McGuire	" 6	July 16
Catharine Chittick	" 7	Augt 14
Lawrence McGowan	" 8	" 14
I. Elliott	" 10	Sep^t 17
Bridget Connelly	" 12	July 30
Tho. Connelly (child)	" 12	" 30
Wm Connelly 4 years old	" 12	" 30
Tho. Connelly 8 yrs old	" 12	" 30
Frances Connelly 10 yrs	" 12	" 30
D. Connelly 12 yrs old	" 12	" 30
Jane Black	" 13	July 29
John Black	" 14	" 29
Patrick Gallagher	" 15	Augt 19
Catharine McCoane	" 16	*died* July 27
Ann Scarlett	" 17	July 26
Robert Ford	" 20	Sep^t 7
George Porter	" 25	Augt 19
Mary McGowan	" 31	Sep^t 17
James Millar	Aug$\underline{t}$ 13	*died* Augt 25
Dan Kilney	" 13	Augt 25
Margaret O'Hara	Sep^t 18	Novr 26
Rosa Kenna	Novr 15	Decr 31

Selected Expenditures: very malignant cases of fever
June 23, 1841   Funeral Expense of Helen Dacey
July 17   "   John McCoane
July 17   "   Mary Cooper (child)
Augt 25   "   James Millar
July 2   "   John Little ... child
                "   Catharine McCoane

The Lunatic Asylum Records 1841

Record of Lunatics in the Temporary Asylum in the City of Saint John admitted in the Year 1841 - *Journals of House of Assembly 1842 Appendix, Geo. Matthew, Superintendent*

Admitted, Names, Age, Nativity, Misc.[12] dir. (direct) dis. (discharge)

Jan. 6, **Harry Bryant**, 36, Saint John, Queens Ward, St. John, dis. Feb. 26, 1841
Jan. 11, **Catharine Dillon**, 25, Galway, Ireland dir., dis. July 12, 1841
Jan. 20, **Ann Cassidy**, 39, Armagh, Ireland dir., dis. May 14, 1841
Jan. 30, **Mary McFarlan**, 40, Tyrone, Hampton Parish, N.B., remaining 1844
Jan. 30, **Thomas Ryan**, 30, Limerick, Ireland dir., dis. July 13, 1841
Feb. 2, **Jane Riggs**, 47, Portsmouth, Eng., England dir., Dukes Ward St. John, *died Aug. 24, 1842*
Feb. 4, **Timothy Madden**, 25, Roscommon, Ireland dir., dis. June 4, 1841
Feb. 3, **Mary Corker**, 50, Carlow, Queens Ward, St. John, dis. Apr. 6, 1841
Feb. 18, **Matthias Tole**, 30, Charlotte Co., Kings Ward, St. John, *died March 3, 1841*
Feb. 25, **Henry Aikin**, 40, Glasgow, Scotland dir., Sydney Ward, St. John, dis. March 17, 1841
Feb. 27, **Hazen Dowling**, 15, Westmorland, N.B., *died Feb. 20, 1843*
March 2, **James McFrederick**, 45, Donegal, Kings Ward, St. John, dis. May 20, 1842
March 12, **Mary Penrose**, 56, Dublin, U.S., Kings Ward, St. John, dis. Sept. 17, 1841
March 12, **Sarah Martin**, 28, Donegal, Kings Ward, St. John, dis. Dec. 14, 1841
March 13, **Mary Bell**, 46, Antrim, Charlotte Co., dis. Apr.

---

[12] The Province of New Brunswick is divided by counties, examples of which are ie. Carleton Co., Charlotte Co., Kings Co., Gloucester Co., St. John Co. and Westmorland Co. The Counties are composed of parishes ie. Hampton and Sussex parishes lie within Kings Co. Portland and Simonds Parish and the City of Saint John lie within St. John Co. The city of Saint John is divided by wards ie. Dukes Ward, Kings Ward, Sydney Ward and Queens Ward. Refer to Alan Rayburn, *Geographical Names of New Brunswick* (Ottawa: Surveys and Mapping Branch, Dept. of Energy, Mines and Resources, 1975)

4, 1842
March 23, **James Draper**, 50, Lancashire, Eng., Sussex, Kings Co., *died May 9, 1843*
March 25, **Mary Whalen**, 24, Clare, Ireland dir., Queens Ward, St. John, dis. Nov. 12, 1841
Apr. 1, **Charlotte F. Warner**, 20, Providence, R.I., Simonds Par., St. John, dischaged Apr. 21, 1841
Apr. 6, **John Johnston**, 50, Cumberland, Eng., Fredericton, York Co., remaining 1844
Apr. 7, **Daniel Garvin**, 26, Donegal, Ireland Dir., Simonds Parish, St. John, remaining 1844
Apr. 17, **Francis Lynn**, 35, Derry, St. Andrews, Charlotte Co., absconded Dec. 15, 1841
Apr. 25, **Elizabeth Gray**, 42, London, Queens Ward, St. John, remaining 1844
May 1, **Catharine Coyle**, 33, Roscommon, dis. Oct. 31, 1841
May 1, **John Clougher**, 28, Roscommon, United States, Charlotte Co., remaining 1844
May 4, **Thomas Walker**, 60, Scotland, Queens Ward, St. John, dis. May 13, 1841
May 11, **Bernard McCormick**, 40, Derry, Parish Simonds, Dukes Ward, St. John, dis. May 31, 1841
May 20, **Eleanor Harris**, 38, Fermanagh, Dukes Ward, St. John, dis. June 17, 1841
May 21, **Patrick Flavin**, 29, Cork, Ireland dir., Dukes Ward, St. John, dis. Nov. 3, 1841

May 22, **Timothy Gill**, 25, Yorkshire, England, U.S., Charlotte Co., remaining 1844
May 22, **Honoria Flinn**, 27, Kerry, Ireland dir., *died November 4, 1841*
May 25, **Peter Burke**, 25, Galway, United States, Charlotte Co., dis. March 6, 1843
June 9, **Christr. Bridgeon**, 33, Louth, S. Prudence, Portland Par., St. John, dis. June 15, 1841
June 14, **Ann Farnan**, 28, Derry, Ireland dir., Simonds Parish , St. John, remaining 1844
June 15, **Richard Cronin**, 35, Kerry, Woodstock, Carleton Co., *died Sept. 3, 1842*
June 24, **Richard Ryan**, 55, Tipperary, *died August 10, 1841*
June 24, **Henry Haxford**, 67, Cape Breton, Nova Scotia & Co. Gaol, dis. June 25, 1841
June 25, **John Haggerty**, 39, Cork, Liverpool, Eng., Kings Ward, St. John, dis. July 26, 1841
July 1, **Elizabeth Dunn**, 32, Cork, York Co., Kings Ward, St. John, dis. Aug. 2, 1841
July 4, **Martin Fahy**, 43, Saint John, Kings Co., dis. Apr. 25, 1842
July 8, **Eliza Murray**, 10, Cork, Oromocto, Sunbury Co., dis. May 26, 1842
July 19, **Elizabeth Todd**, 23, Tyrone, Ireland dir., Portland Parish, St. John, dis. Aug. 6, 1842

14 Irish Migration To New England: Port of Saint John

July 23, **Ellen Hays**, 32, Cork, Kings Ward, St. John, dis. Sept. 1, 1841
July 27, **James Boyle**, 37, Tyrone, Queens Ward, St. John, dis. Sept. 6, 1841
July 29, **Melinda Edgett**, 50, Kings Co., N.B., Westmorland Co., *died Oct. 15, 1841*
July 31, **Mary Tolson**, 51, Kings Co., N.B., Simonds Par. St. John, dis. Aug. 10, 1841
Aug. 2, **Rosanna McGachie**, 24, Derry, Ireland dir., Queens Ward, St. John, dis. Aug. 16, 1841
Aug. 4, **Thomas Farry**, 25, Fermanagh, Portland Parish Alms House, dis. Aug. 18, 1841
Aug. 5, **Michael J. Lowery**, 43, Derry, Queens Ward, dis. Aug. 7, 1841
Aug. 7, **John Mullen**, 28, Down, United States, Kings Ward, St. John, dis. Sept. 7, 1841
Aug. 7, **Catharine Flinn**, 22, Fermanagh, Ireland, Queens Ward, St. John, dis. Aug. 20, 1841
Aug. 13, **John Larby**, 35, Cape Breton, Bathurst, Gloucester Co., dis. Oct. 5, 1842
Aug. 13, **John McDougald**, 36, Aberdeenshire Scot, Carleton, St. John, dis. Aug. 24, 1841
Aug. 16, **Ann Clarke**, 50, Donegal, Woodstock, Carleton Co., *died 1844 consumption*
Aug. 23, **Ann Reed**, 19, Donegal, Woodstock, Carleton Co., dis. Feb. 26, 1842
Aug. 27, **James Carrol**, 29, Dublin, Marine Hospital, St. John, dis. Aug. 30, 1841
Aug. 31, **Mary Ann McCarty**, 23, Dublin, Eastport, U.S., dis. Oct. 7, 1841
Sept. 1, **Thomas Clarke**, 30, Hull, England, Miramichi, dis. Aug. 8, 1842
Sept. 23, **Ann Cairnworth**, 18, dis. Nov. 3, 1841
Sept. 26, **Thos Edmondstone**, 19, Cork, Charlotte Co. Gaol, dis. Dec. 26, 1841
Oct. 21, **Joseph Sampson**, 27, Cornwall, England, dis. Dec. 30, 1841
Nov. 1, **Mary Crowley**, 48, Cork, Ireland, Kings Ward, St. John, dis. March 30, 1843
Nov. 13, **John Carson**, 42, Fermanagh, Charlotte Co., Eloped July 31, 1842
Nov. 22, **Bridget Finn**, 27, Cork, Simonds Parish, St. John, dis. Apr. 4, 1843
Nov. 23, **Charles Theall**, 65, Old British Yorker, Westfield Par., Kings Co., *died Apr. 22, 1842*
Nov. 27, **Mansfield Cornwall**, 57, Westmorland Co., Westmorland Co., dis. May 26, 1842
Dec. 11, **Elizabeth Fletcher**, 29, Leitrim, Portland Parish, *died Dec. 18, 1841*
Dec. 12, **Alex. Bloomfield**, 17, Derry, Kings Co., dis. May 5, 1842
Dec. 31, **Mary Bannon**, 21, Fermanagh, Sidney Ward & Kings Ward, St. John, dis June 13, 1843

The Emigrant Poor
of the City of Saint John - 1842

Catalogue of Immigrants from the United Kingdom Relieved on Parish Poor Account and not charged to the Immigrant Account Year 1842 [P.A.N.B. Emigrations RS 8 Micro F7891]

      I, George Matthew, Principal Overseer of the Poor in the City and Parish of Saint John do declare and make Oath that the Abstract and detailed Statement following comprised in the Pages numbered one to Eighteen is substantially correct - and farther, that for the past two Years the large sum of Two Thousand pounds each Year has been assessed on the Inhabitants of the City and Parish of Saint John for the support of the Poor in the said Parish while at the said time one half of the whole number of Individuals assisted in Parish Poor Account consists of Immigrants from the United Kingdom as described hereinafter and of the remaining half a large proportion is comprised of Transient paupers from all parts unfairly ... themselves and of the same Parish in consequence of the ... for the Parish against such injustice. (sgd) George Matthew. Sworn before James T. Hanford, J.P. this 11th day of February 1843

      The undersigned Individuals, Immigrants from the United Kingdon (not charged on the Immigrant Account) but sustained on the Parish Poor list in the Hospital and other Parish houses in the City and Parish of Saint John by the Overseers of Poor of said Parish from the first January to the 31st December 1842. - 120 Individuals, Saint John, 31st December 1842.

Name	Age	Place of Nativity	Circumstance
Thomas Martin	71	Co. Cork	Lame & destitute
Willm McGaveron	49	Co. Fermanagh	Lame & asthmatick
Patrick May	58	Co. Kilkenny	Sick & asthmatick
Cornelius Daley	51	Co. Cork	Consumption
Timothy Ring	51	Co. Cork	Sore Legs
William Freil	76	Co. Donegal	Par blind & feeble
James White	89	Co. Tyrone	Infirm & destitute
James Johnston	48	Dumfries, Scot^d	Lame & ditto
Patrick Brennen	31	Co. Monaghan	Spinal disease

16   Irish Migration To New England: Port of Saint John

Catherine Brennen	31	Co. Monaghan	his Wife
Michael Brennen	8	Co. Monaghan	his Child
William Kelly	51	Co. Dublin	Crushed Leg
James Dixon	28	Co. Antrim	Lame & destitute
John Tolton	39	Co. Tyrone	Helpless Cripple
Samuel Clarke	40	Co. Tyrone	Distempered destitute
John Kilpatrick	56	Co. Tyrone	Sick & do
Robert Elliot	31	Cumberl[d], Eng[d]	Lame & do
John Hagarty	40	Co. Cork	Distempered Eyes
Barney Dogherty	41	Co. Donegal	lame & destitute
Niel McColgan	51	Co. Tyrone	Sick & do
James Richards	27	Plymouth, Eng[d]	Distemp & do
John Monday	53	Co. Donegal	Lame & do
John O'Donnel	45	Co. Donegal	Sick & do
Ann Hughes	63	Woolwich Eng[d]	destitute widow
Mary Murphy	78	Co. Wexford	Lame Widow
Eliz[h] Mathewson	73	Co. Cork	Destitute do
Mary Pratt	28	Manchester, Eng[d]	Sore Leg
Cath[e] Connelly	66	Co. Cork	Destitute Widow Bedridden
Jane Bryson	38	Co. Derry	ditto 1 child
Elizabeth Foley	39	Kings, Irel[d]	Destitute Widow
Deborah Johnston	76	Limerick	Destitute Widow with Cancer in Face
Mary Rairdon	56	Co. Cork	ditto consumption
Barbara Ford	47	Co. Leitrim	Dropsical
Mary Brennan	32	Co. Cork	Lame Arm with Bas[d] Ch[d] in house
Elizabeth Oliphant	31	Co. Cork	Destitute Widow 1 child
Martha Ramsay	25	Co. Donegal	Destitute Widow 2 ch[n] in house
Mary McDonough	28	Co. Tyrone	Sick and destitute
Jane Campbell	27	Co. Derry	Sick and destitute 2 ch[n]
Ann Dee	26	Co. Donegal	Destitute, Husb[d] desert[d], 2 ch[n]
Eliz[h] McCaffrey	21	Co. Antrim	do Widow 3 ch[n]
Eleanor Duffy	19	Co. Donegal	Sick & destitute
Mary Divine	39	Co. Derry	half blind Spinster
Ann Spittle	25	Co. Cork	Destitute, 2 ch[n], Husb[d] deserted
Catherine Slemons	37	Co. Tyrone	Destt[e], Husb[d] deser[d],

Rebecca Harris	15	Co. Derry	2 ch^n Sick & destitute
Elizabeth Tate	81	Co. Donegal	Destitute Widow
Elizabeth Holmes	20	Co. Derry	Destitute Husb^d deserted
William Colter	48	Sheffield, Eng^d	Lame & destitute
Cornelius Cassidy	51	Co. Dublin	Sick & destitute
Cornelius Cassidy Jr	15		doditto
Margaret Cassidy	10	do	ditto
Hugh Campbell	56	Co. Tyrone	Lame & ditto
Isabella McGuire	25	Co. Ferman^h	Sick & destitute
Daniel Foy	20	Co. Donegal	Scalded
Stephen Nelson	24	Co. Derry	Distemp^d & destitute
Patrick McHinch	36	Lancashire Eng.	do & do
Jerem^h McCann	30	Co. Donegal	do & do
Martin Furlong	57	Co. Wexford	Lame & destitute
Danl Donovan	37	Co. Cork	do do
Robt Campbell	26	Co. Donegal	do cut Foot
Frances Hays	30	Co. Limerick	Sick & destitute
Timothy Anglin	24	Co. Cork	Sore Legs
Cath^e Flaherty	32	Co. Sligo	Sick & destitute
Samuel Bentley	34	Co. Ferman^h	ditto
Edwd Swinney	35	Co. Cork	ditto & sore eyes
Thomas Quin	26	Co. Wexford	Rheumatick
Patrick Ryan	50	Co. Tipperary	
Susan McGraw	30	Co. Ferman^h	Sick & destitute. Husb^d desert^d 1 child in house
Corn^s Cassidy Jr.	15	Co. Dublin	Sick & destitute
Mich^l Murphy	54	Co. Carlow	Broken Leg
Cath^e Connolly	67	Co. Cork	Lame & destitute
John Crimmins	10½	Co. Kerry	Destitute
Hannah Meloy	34	Co. Cork	Sore Legs
Elizabeth Miller	71	Co. Donegal	ditto
Mary Pratt 2nd	30	Co. Derry	ditto
Bridget Duffy	30	Co. Ferman^h	Dest^{te} Husb^d Deserted and 2 children
Grace McCracken	42	Co. Down	Sick & destitute
John Driscol	35	Co. Cork	ditto
Dominic Foy	26	Co. Sligo	Injured while blasting
Francis McLeary	5½	Co. Monaghan	Destitute half orphan
Jane Armstrong	20	Co. Limerick	Sick & destitute
Joanna Ryan	22	Co. Cork	ditto

18   Irish Migration To New England: Port of Saint John

Ellen Welch	21	Co. Cork	Lame arm Rheumatick
Ellen Carty	29	Co. Cork	
Mary Driscol	39	Co. Cork	Destitute Widow 3 ch^n
Sarah Blair	7	Co. Antrim	do half orphan
Isabella Cook	12	Co. Donegal	Destitute
Martha McCallum	24	Co. Donegal	ditto 1 child
Elizabeth McC	25	Co. Armagh	Sick measles
Catherine Kelly 2d	30	Co. Tyrone	Destitute Widow with 3 chil^n in house
Sarah McShane	63	Co. Tyrone	Sick & destitute
Mich^l Crowley	41	Co. Cork	Lame & do
Hugh McDivitt	27	Co. Donegal	Rheumatick
Michael Dervin	30	Co. Galway	Broken Leg
Brid^t Kermerson	30	Co. Clare	Destitute, Husb^d deserted
Patrick Kermerson	10	"	her child
Ellen Kermerson	8	"	ditto
Cath^e Coveney	40	Co. Cork	Destt^e Husb^d aband^d
James Carr	35	Co. Armagh	G .. & destitute
Martha Biggers	35	Co. Derry	Sick & destitute
William Robinson	19	Devon, Eng^d	Sick Measles
Robert Parks	13½	Co. Derry	Destitute
Matthew Flinn	50	Co. Galway	Sore Legs
John Coveney	8	Co. Cork	Destitute
James McAnulty	45	Co. Derry	Sick & destitute
Mich^l Connolly	20	Co. Dublin	ditto
John Cunningham	29	Co. Galway	Lame & detitute
Michael Murphy	52	Co. Carlow	ditto
George Gibbs	34	Middlesex, Eng^d	Lame & destitute
Mich^l Connel	22	Co. Tyrone	Dropsical
Patrick Brien	54	Co. Cork	Sore Legs
Mich^l Mullen	14	Co. Derry	Distem^d & destitute
Joan^a Spillane	80	Co. Cork	Destitute Widow
Frances Walker	73	Co. Dublin	ditto
Louisa Bell	13	London	Destitute Orphan
Marg^t Welch	25	Co. Cork	Sick & destitute
Cath^e Coil	34	Co. Roscommon	ditto
Daniel Frazer	57	Perthshire, Scot^d	Destitute
Margaret Greig	37	Co. Ferman^h	Sick & destitute, Husb^d abandoned
Sarah Brady	33	Co. Antrim	Destitute, Husb^d absent
Susan^h Deering	42	Co. Donegal	Distemp^d & destitute

Port of Saint John: Emigrant Poor 1842   19

Cases of Sick and Indigent Families and Individual Immigrants from the United Kingdom assisted with **Out door Relief** in provisions & on Parish Poor Account and not charged in the Immigrant Account by the Overseers of Poor in the City during the year 1842 - 341 Families embracing 1252 Individuals Saint John, 31st December 1842 [P.A.N.B. RS 8 Microfilm F7891] - *Name, Age, Place of Nativity, No. in Family, Circumstance of disability on Admission*

Name	Age	Place	No.	Circumstance
Daniel Campbell	80	Co. Derry	2	Wife deaf, Infirm & destitute
Sarah Holman	80	Devon Eng^d	1	Destitute Widow
Mary Habertson	30	Co. Derry	2	ditto with Infant child
Marg^t Brennan	78	Co. Wexford	1	Destitute Widow
John Lemon	65	Cornwall Eng^d	2	Wife & self Infirm & destitute
Eliza Wilson	60	Bristol Eng^d	3	Destitute Widow 2 chil^n
Marg^t Stephenson	54	Co. Ferman^h	2	do do
John Scobornia	38	Falmouth Eng^d	5	do & wife & 3 child^n
Brid^t Callender	46	Co. Derry	4	Destitute widow 3 do
Marg^t Maxwell	35	Ayrshire Scot^d	6	Husband absent 5 ch^n destitute
William Creary	44	Co. Queens Ire^d	8	Sick & destitute
Mary Havelin	50	Co. Tyrone	3	Bedfast & destitute
Isaacs	35		6	Husb^d absent 5 ch^n destitute
Mary Divine	30	Co. Derry	1	Half blind spinster
Nancy Bates	43	Co. Armagh	2	Destitute widow 1 child
Marg^t Burns	38	Co. Carlow	4	ditto 3 do
Sarah Brady	32	Co. Antrim	4	Husband absent 3 do
Sarah Crawford	37	Co. Tyrone	7	Destitute widow 6 do
Eleanor Connor	36	Co. Cork	3	Husb^d deserted 2 do
Joan^a Connell	39	Co. Limerick	8	ditto 7 do
Corn^s Cassidy	51	Dublin	6	Destitute
Sarah Conway	41	Tyrone	5	do Widow 4 ch^n
Hannah Cooper	31	Monaghan	4	Husb^d deserted 2 ch^n & mother
Mary Cox	40	Ferman^h	3	ditto 2 ch^n
Ellen Carney	27	Cork	3	ditto 2 ch^n
Eliza Dele..	25	Derry	3	Destitute Widow 2 child^n
Sarah Dwyer	32	Tyrone	5	Husb^d absent 4 do
Marg^t Daley 1st	50	Cork	2	Destitute widow 1 grandch^d
Mary Fryer	53	Clare	2	Sick & dest^f widow 1 ch^d

20   Irish Migration To New England: Port of Saint John

Name	Age	Place	#	Notes
Ann Fitzgerald	40	Donegal	4	Destitute Widow 3 do
Brid^t Fullerton	26	Derry	2	Husb^d absconded 1 do
Ann Foley	36	Sligo	7	ditto 6 do
Joan^a Freeman	23	Tipperary	3	ditto 2 do
Maria Fitzgerald	40	Cork	4	Sick & destitute
Lydia Gallagher	64	Donegal	2	Destitute widow 1 child
Ellen Gillespie	47	Donegal	2	Lame & destitue widow
Nancy Hanna	32	Down	3	Destitute widow 2 child
Marg^t Hamilton	36	Cork	3	Husb^d deserted 2 do
John Hanney?	44	Tyrone	4	Lame & destitute
James Howe	51	Ferman^h	3	Sick & do
Sarah Harkin	28	Donegal	3	Dest^{te} with 2 Bast^t child^n
Ann Herbertine	42	Wexford	4	Dest^{te} widow 3 ch^n
James Laing	73	Sterling Scot^d	6	Infirm & destitute
Mary Miller	50	Donegal	2	do do
Eliz^h Miller	76	Armagh	8	Dest^{te} widow 7 child^n
John Moore	30	Monaghan	7	Destitute
Marg^t Murphy	44	Dublin	3	Dest^{te} widow 2 ch^n
Corn^s McGuire	22	Donegal	6	Destitute
Martha McGowan	56	Derry	4	do one leg^d widow 3 ch^n
Mary McCarty	32	Waterford	2	do 1 Idiot Bastard child
Jane McGachie		Antrim	4	Husb^d deserted 3 ch^n
Sarah McGraw	38	Cork	3	do 2 do
Isab^a McGarrity	28	Tyrone	3	Destitute widow 2 do
Mary McConnell	26	Tyrone	4	Husb^d deserted 3 do
Marg^t McGunagle	46	Donegal	2	Dest^{te} widow 1 do
Martha McCallum	30	Donegal	2	Dest^{te} 1 Bastard child
Mary McDade	27	Tyrone	4	Husb^d deserted 3 ch^n
Ja^s McIntire	37	Donegal	6	Sick & destitute
Ellen Newman	36	Cork	4	Dest^{te} widow 3 chil^n
Elizabeth Nelson	40	Armagh	4	do 3 do
Jane Power	65	Derry	3	do 1 do
Jane Parks	46	Derry	4	Husb^d deserted 3 do
Nich^s Rourk	40	Louth	7	Sick & destitute
Mary Reed	30	Tyrone	6	Husb^d ab^t 5 chil^n
Joan^a Spillane	81	Cork	2	Dest^{te} Widow
Frances Smith	40	Donegal	4	ditto 3 child^n
Ann Starrett	30	Donegal	4	ditto 3 do
Jane Trimble	70	Leitrim	1	Destitute widow 1 do
Jane Tuppen	33	Devon Eng^d	5	Husb^d sick 3 do
Ja^s Hennessy	50	Limerick	5	Half blind & detitute
John Sinclair	50	Greenock	7	Destitute widower
Thomas Wier	57	Sunderland Eng^d	4	Lame & destitute

Port of Saint John: Emigrant Poor 1842   21

Name	Age	Place		Condition
Elizabeth Wilson	80	Donegal	4	Destitute Widow 3 child^n
Elizabeth Ward	26	Donegal	4	Husb^d desert^d 3 do
Grace Wilson	28	Derry	2	Husb^d ab^t 1 sick child
George Wood	54	Tyrone	7	Destitute
John McGee	26	Tyrone	6	Destitute
Mary Day	50	Galway	2	Destitute Widow
Edwd McLaughlan	21	Donegal	4	Sick & destitute
Mary Donahue	25	Galway	4	Husb^d deserted 3 chil^n
Ja^s Donovan	40	Cork	7	Sick & destitute
Mary Swadler	20	Kerry	2	ditto
Mary Stevens	23	Derry	3	Husb^d ab^t 2 child^n
Ann Bazillon	50	Galloway Scotl^d	3	Destitute Widow 2 do
Mary Herrin	27	Cork	4	Husb^d in a Hospital 2 do
Mich^l Kerman	60	Ferman^h	7	Sick & destitute
Brid^t Clarke	47	Westmeath	3	Destitute Widow 2 child^n
Mich^l McGrade	37	Louth	4	Lame & destitute
Dorah Carrigan	28	Dublin	3	Husb^d ab^t 2 child^n
Ann Watkins	24	Down	1	ditto 1 do
Danl Mahony	20	North Ireland	1	Prisoner in Gaol
Hugh Campbell	28	Co. Tyrone	4	Destitute
Catherine Eagan	40	Killarney	4	do widow 3 child^n
Mary Twoomay	30	Cork	5	Husb^d deserted 4 do
Aaron McRae	51	Tyrone	2	Sick & destitute
Frances Russel	58	London	2	Destitute Widow with lame Son
Margaret Daley 2^d	22	Co. Derry	3	Husb^d ab^t 2 child^n
John Armstrong	54	Cork	10	Lame & destitute
Mary J. Beatty	34	Donegal	7	Husb^d ab^t 6 children
Sarah Mackie	23	Donegal	2	do deserted 1 ch^d
Henry McAlwee	51	Donegal	2	Lame & destitute
Elizabeth Devon	22	Waterford	5	Husb^d ab^t 4 child^n
Frances McConnel	60	Donegal	3	Destitute widow 2 do
Mary Kirkbright	30	Waterford	6	Husb^d absent 5 do
John Biggs	46	Ayrshire Scotl^d	6	Sick & destitute
Sarah Currie	39	Co. Donegal	4	Destitute widow 3 ch^n
John Stratton	32	Kerry	7	Destitute
David Brown	45	Kirkcudbright Scot^d		3Wife sick & destitute
John Jordan	40	Co. Wexford	5	Destitute
Ann Morris	56	do	2	Destitute Widow
John Livingston	60	Ferman^h	5	Destitute 3 ch^n
Mary Fox	62	Cork	2	Husb^d ab^t 1 child
Jane McHinch	29	Dublin	3	Husb^d in Hosp^l 2 child^n
Thomas Boice	38	Armagh	7	Sick & destitute

Name	Age	Origin	#	Notes
Pat McGunagle	45	Co. Tyrone	8	ditto
John Desmond	45	Cork	6	ditto
Grace McCann	43	Donegal	3	Husb[d] in Hosp[l] 2 child[n]
John McConnel	48	do	8	Destitute
John McCormick	35	Roscommon	6	Destitute
Pat McAnulty	40	Sligo	7	... but destitute
Ann Dillon	30	Donegal	2	Husb[d] ab[t] 1 child
Ann Graham	21	Tyrone	2	with Bastard ch[d] destitute
James Bell	47	Cavan	7	Destitute
Thomas Briskley	23	Cork	2	Sick & destitute
Francis Graham	48	Ferman[h]	7	Destitute
Callahan McCarty	30	Cork	5	do Widower 4 child[n]
Neil McColgan	47	Tyrone	2	Sick & destitute
Frances Sheals	40	Tyrone	1	ditto
John Dogherty	30	Donegal	5	Destitute
Mary Donovan	26	Cork	3	Sick & dest[te] widow 2 child[n]
Martin Mahony	45	Cork	6	Destitute
John Cleary	27	Ferman[h]	4	Sick & destitute
Florence McAneslin	24	Derry	3	Husb[d] ab[t] 2 child[n]
James Gibbon	45	Donegal	4	Destitute
William Parker	27	Cork	5	Destitute
Elizabeth Way	35	Queens Ire[d]	5	Sick & dest[te] Husb[d] drunkard
Michael Dunphy	48	Dublin	6	Sick & destitute
Thomas Greer	45	Donegal	7	Destitute
Cath[e] Hays	30	Limerick	2	Husb[d] in Hospital 1 ch[d]
Tho[s] Kennedy	45	Waterford	3	Destitute
Ann Watson	40	Donegal	2	Destitute widow 1 child
Thomas Healy	37	Kerry	8	Destitute
Mary Crimmins	25	do	4	ditto widow 3 child[n]
Esther White	50	Armagh	3	ditto 2 do
Daniel Swinney	24	Kerry	3	Destitute
Ellen Strattan	66	Kerry	2	do widow
Will[m] Campbell	66	Derry	2	Lame & destitute
Ann McShane	25	Tyrone	2	Destitute widow 1 child
Jane Hunter	30	Donegal	6	Husb[d] sick & destitute
James Freeborn	55	Derry	7	Destitute
Ellen Gibbon	22	Donegal	2	Husb[d] deserted 1 child
Jane Ferguson	30	Derry	5	ditto 4 do
Jane Trimble Jr.	30	Leitrim	1	Sick & destitute
Patrick Ryan	50	Tipperary	3	ditto

Port of Saint John: Emigrant Poor 1842   23

Name	Age	Origin		Status
Ann Dennison	23	Galway	2	Husband deserted 1 child
Maria Dearness	25	Birkshire England	2	do absent 1 do
Timothy Driscol	29	Co. Cork	5	Sick & destitute
Daniel Logue	27	Co. Derry	4	Destitute
James Hays	41	Cork	2	Wife sick & destitute
Joanna Mann	30	Cork	2	Destitute Widow 1 child
Samuel Matthews	50	Cornwall Eng^d	8	Sick & destitute
Mary Gorman	40	Co. Tyrone	1	ditto
Mary McCarty 3^d	23	Down	2	Husb^d deserted 1 ch^d
Mary Collins	30	Cork	5	ditto 4 child^n
Thos. McCaffrey & Saml	36	Kilkenny	2	Destitute orphans
John Carrol 2^d	50	Tyrone	5	Sick & destitute
Eleanor Harrington	24	Cork	3	Husb^d deserted 2 child^n
Mary Driscol 2nd	30	Cork	4	ditto 3 do
Frances Cramer	40	Cork	6	Husb^d absent 5 do
Hannah Meloy	34	Cork	1	Sore leg
Marg^t McMahan	25	Clare	2	Sick & destitute
Mary Murray	30	Cork	4	Husb^d deserted 3 child^n
Brid^t McGuire	23	Donegal	2	ditto 1 do
Susan McGunagle	42	Donegal	6	ditto 5 do
George Carson	30	Cork	4	Destitute
William Bowen	27	Limerick	3	Wife sick & destitute
John Farrel	47	Longford	6	Destitute
Jane Armstrong	40	Cavan	3	do widow 2 child^n
Patrick Burke	45	Galway	5	Destitute
Jere^h Donovan	43	Cork	7	do
John Cooke	60	Derry	5	do
Nicholas Rourke	50	Louth	6	sick & destitute
Ann Cassidy	40	Dublin	4	Husb^d in Hos^l 3 ch^d
Hono^a Hennessy	36	Cork	6	Husb^d deserted do
Marg^t Looney	49	Cork	3	Dest^{te} widow 2 do
Matthew Beck	38	Newcastle Eng.	6	Sick & destitute
Ann Dee	23	Donegal	2	Husb^d deserted 1 ch^d
Mary McCarty 4th & sister	19	Roscommon	2	Destitute
Bridget Nowlan	30	Co. Clare	5	Husb^d absent fam^y sick
William Hazell	30	Cork	4	Destitute
Jane Densmore	33	Co. Donegal	4	Husb^d deserted 3 child^n
John Livingston	60	Ferman^h	5	Destitute
Catherine Mahony	30	Cork	3	Sick & dest^{te}
May Foy	30	Ferman^h	4	Husb^d deserted ditto

24   Irish Migration To New England: Port of Saint John

Name	Age	County	#	Notes
Mary Quilly	28	Westmeath	2	Destitute
Catherine Conner	44	Derry	3	Husb^d deserted 3 child^n
Catherine Dogherty	40	Donegal	3	ditto 2 do
John Hagarty	40	Cork	1	Sore Eyes
Martha McClusky	25	Tyrone	1	sick & dest^{te} 4 child^n
John Livingston Jr.	18	Ferman^h	1	Destitute
Elizabeth Coleman	26	Cork	3	Husb^d deserted 2 child^n
Sarah McDermott	25	Ferman^h	1	Destitute
Mary Quinn	18	Cork	1	Sore Eyes
Mary Noonan	32	Cork	5	Husb^d deserted 4 child^n
Marg^t Fitzgerald	40	Cork	3	Dest^{te} widow 2 do
Nancy Shehan	30	Cork	2	Husb^d deserted 1 ch^d
Mary McGolrick	30	Ferman^h	3	ditto 1 ch^d & mother
Ellen Carey	30	Kerry	4	ditto 3 child^n
Henry Robinson	59	Down	1	Sick & destitute
Eliza Gamblin	26	Plymouth Eng^d	1	Dest^{te} with Inf^t Bast^d child
Edwd Clifford	23	Co. Tyrone	3	Sick & destitute
Martha Scallan	30	Wexford	3	Husb^d deserted 2 child^n
Rebecca Young	40	Donegal	4	ditto 3 do
Catherine Flaherty	34	Sligo	2	Dest^{te} with Inf^t Bast^d child
Mary Hughes	38	Sligo	2	Dest^{te} widow 1 child
Hugh Meally	52	Donegal	5	Sick & destitute
Jane Fitzgerald	24	Donegal	1	ditto
Catherine Blake	24	Donegal	2	Dest^{te} with Inf^t Bast^d child
Martin Furlong	57	Wexford	1	Lame & destitute
Mary Donovan	27	Cork	3	Dest^{te} widow 2 child^n
Mary Williams	26	Kerry	2	ditto 1 child
James Carr	35	Armagh	4	Sick & destitute
Sarah Harkin	36	Donegal	3	Destitute with 2 Bast^d child^n
James Coughlan	30	Co. Cork	3	Sick & destitute
Hugh Danlinn	46	Tyrone	5	Destitute Widower with 4 ch^d
Mary Moran	38	Roscom^n	4	Husb^d deserted 3 do
James Farrel	50	Galway	7	Destitute
George Courtney	41	Armagh	7	Lame & destitute
John Hughes	55	Tyrone	1	Destitute Old Soldier
Jane Campbell	37	Derry	3	Husb^d deserted 2 ch^n
Catherine Mahony	52	Cork	3	ditto 2 do
Eliz^h O'Harron	34	Cork	2	Destitute widow 1 ch^d

Port of Saint John: Emigrant Poor 1842

Name	Age	Origin	#	Notes
Matthias Flinn	45	Galway	2	Self & wife lame & sick
Cath^e Slemons	37	Tyrone	3	Husb^d deserted 2 ch^n
Catherine Collins	53	Donegal	1	Sick & destitute
Mary Wilson	66	Monaghan	4	Destitute widow 3 ch^n
Mich^l Crowley	41	Cork	5	Lame & destitute
Brid^t Dogherty	25	Sligo	2	Husb^d deserted 1 ch^d
Mary Sullivan	18	Cork	1	Destitute
Nancy Ryan	40	Tyrone	4	Husb^d absent 3 ch^d
James Bell	50	Tyrone	4	Destitute
Bridget Boyle	33	Derry	4	Husb^d deserted 3 ch^n
Susan Carr	32	Donegal	1	Destitute Husb^d in Hosp^l
Mary Quinn	41	Antrim	1	Sick Husb^d abent
William Gould	32	Limerick	3	Destitute
Rodger McAulay	39	Leitrim	3	ditto
Danl Lennihan	30	Cork	4	Lame & destitute
Catherine Curren	39	Donegal	5	Husb^d deserted 4 ch^n
Mich^l Jennings	45	Roscom^n	4	Destitute
Patrick Brennen	33	Monaghan	6	ditto
Pat McLaughlan	27	Leitrim	4	ditto
Grace McCracken	42	Down	1	Husb^d deserted destitute
Patrick Desmond	21	Cork	1	Destitute
Eliz^h McCaffrey	26	Antrim	1	ditto
Alice Carter	30	Limerick	4	Husb^d deserted 2 ch^n & neice
Jere^h McCann	40	Derry	4	Destitute
Mary Welsh	43	Co. Cork	1	Destitute widow
Cath^e McHiggan	38	Tyrone	1	Destitute
Brid^t Callander	45	Derry	4	Destitute widow 3 ch^n
Jane McHinch	33	Dublin	3	Hudb^d absent 2 do
Mary Driscol	29	Cork	4	Destitute widow 3 do
William Cogan	36	Cork	1	Sick & destitute
Catherine Johnston	55	Ferman^h	3	Destitute widow 2 child^n
Jane Thompson	27	Longford	1	Destitute
Brid^t McLaughlan	39	Kings Ireland	3	Husb^d ab^t 2ch^n
Garret Fitzgerald	42	Cork	1	Destitute
Thomas Holmes	74	Cork	2	Self & wife Infirm & destitute
Margaret Dunphy	40	Wexford	4	Husb^d deserted 3 ch^n
Catherine Millen	40	Tyrone	7	do absent 6 do
Matthew Gibson	38	Ayrshire, Scot^d	3	Sick & destitute
John Br...	50	Co. Kerry	1	Lame & do
Joanna O'Leary	27	do	3	Husb^d deserted 2 ch^n
Robt McDonald	28	Ferman^h	5	Destitute

26   Irish Migration To New England: Port of Saint John

Mary Mahony	35	Cork	4	Husb^d ab^t 3 ch^n
Zebulon Poland	30	Devon Eng^d	5	Destitute
Thomas Gough	43	Down	1	ditto
John Howard	46	Tipperary	4	Lame & destitute
John G. Proctor	35	Yorkshire Eng^d	1	Destitute
Ann McIver?	40	Donegal	3	Husb^d Ab^t 2 ch^n
Edward Kelly	46	Cork	4	Destitute
James Carr	32	Armagh	4	Sick & destitute
Marg^t Mahony	28	Cork	5	Husb^d absent 4 child^n
Martha Dogherty	26	Donegal	5	do 4 do
Marg^t McMahon	24	Co. Clare	1	Destitute
Patrick Heally	30	Roscom^n	4	Destitute
Margaret Bird	25	Cork	1	Destitute
Sarah Curley	20	Sligo	1	Destitute
Timothy Coleman	35	Cork	4	Destitute
Ann Herlin	40	Dublin	2	Lame & dest^{te} widow 1 child
Cath^e Brennen	32	Monaghan	5	Husb^d ab^t 4 child^n
Ann Quinn	30	Sligo	6	ditto 5 do
Cath^e McGee	27	Fermanagh	4	Husb^d deserted 3 ch^n
Cath^e Mooney	34	Sligo	1	Destitute
Mary McCallum	30	Antrim	2	Dest^{te} widow 1 ch^d
Ann McLaughlan	28	Antrim	3	Husb^d absent 2 do
William Kehoe	32	Wexford	1	Destitute
Cath^e McCormick	40	Rosscom^n	5	Husb^d ab^t 4 ch^n
John Wood	55	Cumberland Eng^d	4	Destitute
Mary Green	30	Whitehaven Eng^d	5	Husb^d ab^t 4 ch^n
Thomas Hanover	35	Devonshire Eng^d	1	Destitute Cripple
Thomas Heally	38	Co. Kerry		Destitute
Mary Glancy	24	Donegal	4	Husb^d ab^t 3 ch^n
Jane Paul	30	Derry	1	Sick & destitute
Pat O'Brien	54	Cork	1	ditto
Catherine Cook	47	Derry	2	Husb^d deserted 1 ch^d
Michael Crowley	42	Cork	4	Lame & destitute
Mary Ramsay	32	Cork	6	Husb^d in Gaol 5 ch^n
Mary Kelly	30	Cork	3	Husb^d deserted 2 do
Jane Tuppen	35	Devon Eng^d	4	Dest^{te} widow 3 do
Margaret Burns	39	Co. Carlow	3	ditto 2 do
John Harrington	32	Cork	1	Destitute
Sarah Brady	33	Antrim	4	Husb^d ab^t 3 ch^n
Thomas Kinneally	43	Waterford	4	Sick & destitute
David McKelvey	50	Antrim	4	Lame & do
Daniel Gillespie	43	Donegal	4	Destitute

Port of Saint John: Emigrant Poor 1842

John McConnell	40	Donegal	6	Frozen feet destitute
Mary Demper	34	Cork	1	Destitute
James Caulfield	37	Wexford	3	Husb^d ab^t 2 ch^n
John McIver	45	Donegal	4	Destitute
Mary Nash	28	Limerick	3	do widow 2 ch^n
Mary Donaldson	29	Donegal	5	Husb^d ab^t 4 do
Julia Quinn	20	Cork	2	ditto 1 do
Margaret Murphy	49	Co. Dublin	3	Destitute widow 2 ch^n
Charles Boyle	30	Tyrone	7	Destitute
Charles Millen		Tyrone	8	dito
Mary McCarty	32	Waterford	2	do with Imbecile Bas^d ch^d
Samuel Risk	39	Notingham Eng^d	4	Destitute
Mary Gibbon	30	Co. Tyrone	3	Husb^d Ab^t 2 ch^n
John McGee 2^d	40	Tyrone	7	Sick & destitute
Edward Haney	30	Derry	4	Destitute
Alex Jones	49	London	5	Lame & destitute
Mary Hilton	35	Limerick	7	Husb^d Ab^t 6 ch^n
Ellen Gillespy	48	Donegal	8	Lame & destitute
Davidson Kirkbride	44	Sunderl^d Eng^d	5	Sick & destitute
Cornelius Shehan	36	Waterford	3	Destitute
Patrick Allen	31	Cork	4	Sick & destitute
Jerem^h Brickly	36	Cork	6	Destitute
Jane Long	22	Derry	3	Sick Husb^d Ab^t 2 ch^n
Eliza Parish	27	Monaghan	4	Husb^d in house correc^n 3 ch^n
John Mahany	40	Kerry	5	Destitute
Patrick Leighey	38	Cork	5	Destitute

List of Passage Tickets &c for passages inland and coastwise granted to destitute Immigrants from the United Kingdom on Parish Poor Account and not charged in the Immigrant Account by the Overseers of Poor in the City during the Year 1842 - 69 Families embracing 214 Individuals, Saint John 31st December 1842 [P.A.N.B. RS 8 Microfilm F7891] *Names, Age, Nativity, Fam^y, To What Place Conveyed*

Sarah McGraw	37	Co. Cork	3	Fredericton
Joanna Mann	30	Cork	2	St. Andrews
Joann^a Donovan	43	Cork	7	St. Stephens
Frances Hays	30	Limerick	3	ditto
Nicholas Rourk	40	Louth	6	Windsor
James McAneslin	26	Derry	4	Fredericton
John Farrol	47	Longford	6	Windsor

Name	Age	County		Destination
Will[m] Hassel	30	Cork	4	St. Stephens
John Livingston Jr.	18	Ferman[h]	1	Fredericton
Jane Armstrong	40	Cavan	2	Sheffield
John Hagarty	40	Cork	1	Fredericton
John Livingston Sr.	60	Ferman[h]	5	ditto
Isabella McGarrity	28	Tyrone	2	West
Sarah McDermot	25	Ferman[h]	1	Windsor
Thomas Boyce	38	Armagh	8	ditto
Henry Robinson	59	Down	1	Fredericton
Mary Quilly	28	Westmeath	2	ditto
Joanna Freeman	24	Tipperary	2	ditto
Joan[a] Connell	40	Limerick	6	St. Stephens
Cath[e] Flaherty	34	Sligo	2	Digby
Mary Hughes	38	Sligo	2	Annapolis
Martin Furlong	57	Wexford	1	St. Andrews
Mary Donovan	27	Cork	3	Home to Ireland
George Courtney	41	Armagh	7	Windsor
Mary Sullivan	18	Co. Cork	1	Saint Stephen
Nancy Ryan	40	Tyrone	4	Halifax
Mary Quinn	41	Antrim	1	ditto
William Gould	32	Limerick	3	Annapolis
Mich[l] Jennings	45	Roscom[n]	4	Halifax
Patrick Desmond	21	Cork	4	Yarmouth
Eliz[h] McCaffrey	26	Antrim	1	Annapolis
Alice Carter	30	Limerick	4	ditto
Martha McCallum	24	Donegal	2	St. Stephens
Jerem[h] McCann	40	Donegal	4	Halifax
Mary Welch	43	Cork	1	Quoddy
Cath[e] McHiggins	38	Tyrone	1	Grand Lake
Jane McHinch	33	Dublin	3	Halifax
Sarah McDermot	26	Ferman[h]	1	Windsor
William Cogan	36	Cork	2	Liverpool Eng[d]
Jane Thompson	27	Longford	1	Windsor
Garret Fitzgerald	42	Cork	3	Halifax
Margaret Dunphy	40	Wexford	4	ditto
Ellen Gillespie	48	Donegal	1	Fredericton
Matthew Gibson	38	Ayrshire Scot[d]	3	ditto
Rob[t] McDonald	28	Co. Ferman[h]	4	Annapolis
Mary Mahany	35	Cork	4	Halifax
John Howard	46	Tipperray	4	Quoddy West
Joan[a] O'Leary	27	Kerry	3	ditto
Edward Kelly	46	Cork	6	Halifax
Marg[t] McMahon	24	Clare	1	Yarmouth

Patrick Haley	30	Roscom^n	4	L pool, L burgh & Halifax	
Margaret Bird	25	Cork	1	Yarmouth	
Sarah Curly	20	Sligo	1	ditto	
Timo^y Coleman	35	Cork	4	Cornwallis	
Ann Herlin	40	Dublin	2	L pool, L burgh & Hfx	
Ann Quinn	30	Sligo	6	Halifax	
Cath^e McGee	27	Ferman^h	4	Fredericton	
Cath^e Mooney	34	Sligo	1	Annapolis	
Roger McAulay	39	Leitrim	4	Richibucto	
Brid^t Boyle	33	Derry	5	Fredericton	
Cath^e McCormick	40	Roscom^n	5	Aylesford N.S.	
John Wood	55	Cumberland Eng^d	4	L pool, L burgh & Hfx	
Thos Hanover	35	Devon do	1	Fredericton	
Thomas Healy	38	Kerry	8	ditto	
Mary Glancy	24	Donegal	4	Westport N.S.	
Jane Vaul	30	Derry	1	Halifax	
Mary Quilly	30	Westmeath	2	Fredericton	
Cath^e McGee	26	Ferman^h	3	do	
Margaret Burns	39	Carlow	3	Quoddy West	

Emigrant Poor Interments - 1842

Deceased Indigent Immigrants from the United Kingdom interred on Parish Poor Account and not charged in the Immigrant Account by the Overseers of the Poor in the City during the Year 1842 - 18 Individuals Saint John 31st December 1842 [P.A.N.B. RS 8 Microfilm F7891]: *Date, Names, Age, Nativity, Places of Interment: Church yard of St. Malachi or Trinity*

From Hospital & other Par^h houses

Jany 4th	John O'Donnel	45	Co. Donegal	St. Malachi's	
Feby 3^d	Daniel Foy	20	Donegal	do do	
Feby 21st	Elizabeth Foley	39	Kings Ire^d	do do	
Feby 22^d	John Tolton	39	Tyrone	Trinity	
Mar^h 22^d	Rebecca Harris	15	Derry	do do	
May 4th	John Driscoll	35	Cork	St. Malachi	
May 23^d	Jane Crow	20	Limerick	Trinity	
May 26th	Sarah McShane	60	Tyrone	do do	
May 28th	James Dixon	28	Antrim	do do	
July 19th	James White	89	Tyrone	do do	
July 20th	Ja^s McAnulty	45	Derry	St. Malachi's	

30   Irish Migration To New England: Port of Saint John

From private houses in the City

Mar[h] 7th	Owen McGarrity	30	Co. Tyrone	St. Malachi
Mar[h] 24th	And[w] McMullen	30	Donegal	Trinity
Ap[l] 30th	Ellen Conner	20	Ireland	St. Malachi's
June 4th	Henry Loughery	35	Ireland	Trinity
June 14th	Joseph Carty	19	Ireland	do
June 29th	Patrick Murphy	25	Co. Louth	St. Malachi's
Sep[t] 1st	Elizabeth O'Hara	34	Cork	do

Sick & indigent Immigrants succoured in Hospitals and other Parish houses in the City (not including Hospitals at Partridge Island) by Overseer of Poor of the City & Parish of Saint John from the 1st January to the 31st December (inclusive) 1842 - 262 Individuals [P.A.N.B. Emigrations RS 8   Micro F7891: *Names, Age, Place of Nativity, Circumstance of disability on Admission*

John Daly	36	Co. Derry	Sick & destitute
Ann Daly	31	Antrim	"
Mary Daly	12	Derry	"
John Daly	10	do	"
Adam Porter	43	Down	Sick & Sore Leg
Tho[s] Hanover	35	Devon Eng[d]	Crippled by Frost
Mary Higgins	24	Donegal	Sick & destitute
Mary Higgins Jr.	4	"	"
Mary Connell	21	Co. Cork	"
Ellen Whillehan	Inf[t]	Child of do	
Mich[l] Connell	37	Co. Cork	Spinal Injury
Jere[h] O'Brien 1st	27	"	Inflamatory Fever
Garret Fitzpatrick	57	"	ruptured
Timothy Regan	61	"	Lame
Eleanor Regan	51	"	Sick & destitute
Judy Mahony	6	"	their Grand Children
David Brickley	21	"	Inflamatory Fever
Rob[t] Buchanan	20	Donegal	Sick & destitute
Jerem[h] O'Brien 2[d]	28	Cork	Inflamatory Fever
James Hennssessey	46	Waterford	Inflames Eyes
Edward Daily	24	Donegal	Inflamatory Fever
Hugh Kelly	50	Kircudbright Scot[d]	Sick & destitute
James Smith	51	Co. Down	Lame Leg
Henry Gallagher	22	Innishone	Sore Eyes
John Sterling	60	Norfolk Eng[d]	Helpless Cripple
John Bradley	38	Co. Leitrim	Inflamatory Fever
Mich[l] Cain	51	Wexford	Sick & destitute

James Duffy	64	Mayo	Infirm & destitute
Brien Doyle	49	Wicklow	Lame & destitute
Brid^t Doyle	48	"	"
Wm Wallace	20	Sligo	"
Danl Connolly	41	Leitrim	Sick & "
Corn^s Herron	29	Cork	"
Barth^w Welch	29	"	"
Jane Boyd	31	Armagh	distempered & "
Mary Quin	18	Cork	Inflamed Eyes
Marg^t Delaney	28	Kildare	Sick & destitute
Mich^l Delaney	-	child of do	"
Cathe Bowles	23	Co. Sligo	"
Sarah Lenehan	26	Roscommon	"
Marg^t Stevens	31	Cork	"
George Stevens	Inf^t	child of do	"
Marg^t McDermot	42	Co. Sligo	"
Ann McConnell	20	Derry	"
Eliza Brown	20	Cork	"
Eliza J. Brown	Inf^t	child of do	"
Mary Magnor	20	Co. Cork	Inflamatory Fever
Elizabeth Cronin	32	"	Sick & destitute
Bridget Cronin	3	"	"
Catherine Cronin	Inf^t	child of do	"
Bridget Gorman	31	Co. Clare	Sick & "
Patrick Gorman	3	Cork	"
Mary Murphy 2nd	27	Kerry	Sick & "
John Murphy	Inf^t	child of do	"
Margaret Dunn	21	Co. Tyrone	Lame Sore Foot
Bridget McGuire	18	Ferman^h	Sick & destitute
Frances Connolly	40	"	"
Francis Connolly	14	"	"
William Connolly	12	Leitrim	"
Joseph Connolly	9	"	"
Thomas Connolly	8	Ferman^h	"
Daniel Connolly	3½	"	"
Hannah Leighy	7	Kerry	deserted by Parents
Jeremiah O'Leary	6	Cork	half orphan "
Bridget McKenna	2½	Leitrim	" "
Jno McLaughlan	5½	Roscommon	Sick orphan
Ann McDermot	2 3/4	Co. Donegal	destitute half orphan
Marg^t Kennahan	4½	Donegal	Inflamatory Fever
Patrick McIntire	14	Co. Ferman^h	Sick deserted half orphan
Catherine McIntire	8 3/4	Leitrim	"

Name	Age	Origin	Condition
Terence McIntire	6	"	"
William McIntire	4	"	destitute "
Mary McIntire	11	Ferman[h]	" "
Mich[l] McCarty	5	Co. Cork	Mother in Penitenty
John Daly 2[d]	6½	"	Parents deserted
Mary Daly	27	"	"
Tho[s] Fury	13	Donegal	Sore foot
Bridget Ronan	10	Leitrim	Sick deserted half orphan
Marg[t] Clarke	23	Donegal	Sick & destitute
Sarah Brown	26		destitute
Penelope Brown	Inf[t]	child of do	destitute
Jno. Sherridan	11	Co. Donegal	Sick & destitute
Jno. Vallely	20	Cork	Lame Cut foot
Jno. Shehan	31	Cork	Frozen feet
Mich[l] Consadine	35	Co. Clare	Hurt in Eye
Joanna McCarty	14	Cork	Scalded Foot
Timothy Callaghan	22	"	Frozen Feet
Margery Crossin	19	Tyrone	Scarlet Fever
Timothy Murphy	30	Cork	Diseased Liver
Ellen Murphy	25	"	Sore Eyes
Stephen Murphy	Inf[t]	child of do	"
Tho[s] Gately	36	Co. Rocom[n]	Nearly Blind
Mary Lee	23	Limerick	Intermit[t] Fever
Margaret Lee	Inf[t]	child of do	"
Jerem[h] McCarty	35	Co. Cork	Sick & destitute
Mary McCarty	31	"	"
Mary McCarty	Inf[t]	child of do	"
Timothy Anglin	24	Co. Cork	"
Rich[d] Payden	42	Mayo	Sore Legs
Ja[s] Clarke	Inf[t]	child of do	Lame Cut Foot
Mary McAulay	11	Co. Donegal	Mother in Hospital
Ellen Stevens	12	Cork	Destitute
Mary Gamman	60	"	Sick & destitute
Corn[s] Coughlan	45	"	Sick & distressed
And[w] Bustard	28	Donegal	"
Mary Kelly	25	Limerick	Inflam[y] Fever
Frances Kelly	2	"	destitute hus[d] deserted
Alicia Kelly	Inf[t]	child of do	
Ja[s] McDonnel	27	Co. Galway	Inflamatory Fever
Elleanor Farret	23	Donegal	Inflam[y] Fever
Cathe McGuire	Inf[t]	child of do	
Bridget Gorman	34		Cancer in Breast
Mary Coughlan	40	Cork	Sick & destitute

Julia Coughlan	14	do	"
Ellen Coughlan	12½	do	"
Mary Jane Coughlan		11	Cork Sick & destitute
John Coughlan	8	do	"
Catherine Coughlan	5	do	"
James Coughlan	Inf^t	child of do	"
Catherine Burke	22	Co. Cork	Inflam^y Fever
William Crowley	25	do	"
Ellen Carty	19	do	"
Honoria Driscol	29	do	"
Mary Griffin	20	do	"
Catherine Flin	26	Leitrim	Sick & destitute
Bridget Flin	6	"	"
Thomas Flin	3½	"	"
Patrick Flin	Inf^t	child of do	"
Mary Murphy 3^d	25	Co. Cork	destitute Husb^d deserted
Denis Murphy	3	"	"
Daniel Murphy	Inf^t	child of do	"
Ellen Barry	26	Co. Cork	Houseless & destitute
Ellen Barry Jr.	Inf^t	child of do	"
Ellen Fletcher	21	Co. Ferman^h	Incurably Lame
Patrick Hyde	40	Cork	Inflam^y Fever
Judy Power	21	Limerick	"
Patrick Hyde Jr.	8	Cork	"
Patrick Burke	19	"	"
John Dalton	22	"	Dysentry
Richd Cuningham	30	Waterford	Inflam^y Fever
Ellen Cuningham	25	"	"
James Cuningham	4	"	"
Mary Cuningham	-	child of do	"
Mary Foley	27	Co. Galway	Dysentry
Patrick Sullivan	26	Cork	Inflam^y Fever
Patrick Barry	20	Co. Cork	Dysentry
Marg^t Mahoney	18	"	Sore Foot
Honoria Conway	20	"	Inflam^y Fever
Brid^t Fahy alias Kenna		17	Galway Sick & destitute
Patrick Meilen	27	Cork	Inflam^y Fever
Patrick Dooley	21	Galway	"
William Halnin	20	Cork	"
Miche Foley	20	"	"
Pat^k Callahan	22	"	"
Mary Halnin	10	Leitrim	"
Mary White 2nd	30	Cork	"

34   Irish Migration To New England: Port of Saint John

Name	Age	County	Condition
Mary Collins	24	"	destitute Hus^d deserted
Mary Collins	Inf^t	child of do	"
Judith McCarty	17	Co. Cork	Inflam^y Fever
Jerem^h Monaghan	25	Kerry	"
Ellen O'Harron	25	Tipperary	"
Mary Bryan	20	Cork	"
Marg^t O'Harron	6 mos	Tipperary	"
Jerem^h Halnin	28	Co. Cork	"
Patrick Ryan	40	Tipperary	Sick & destitute
Mary Hatherman	50	Limerick	Inflam^y Fever
Jane Constantine	26	Co. Cork	Sick & destitute
Honor^a Milbrick	25	"	Inflam^y Fever
Mary Quillon	20	Galway	Sick & destitute
Mary Herrin	27	Cork	Inflam^y Fever
Cathe Loughery	17	Donegal	Sick & destitute
William Kelly	20	Roscom^n	Dysentry
William Crocket	31	Donegal	Intermit^t Fever
Marg^t Hurley	19	Cork	Inflam^y Fever
Thos Curley	24	Sligo	"
John Hannahan	61	Limerick	Arm Broken
Patrick Mullane	20	Cork	Sore Leg
Ellen Connolly	40	"	destitute Husb^d in H. Correction
Ellen Connolly Jr	6	"	" "
Mary Connolly	Inf^t	child of do	" "
John Burke	38	Galway	Sore Leg
Patrick Brien	28	Kerry	Houseless & destitute
Ellen Brien	23	"	"
Mary Brien	2	"	"
Alex^r Shehan	30	Co. Kerry	Sore Foot
Rebecca Common	35	Leitrim	Dysentry
Richd Armstrong	Inf^t	child	Sickly Mother in L. Asy^m
Eliza Hiney	28	Co. Westmeath	Houseless & destitute
Maria Hiney	2½	"	"
Marg^t Hallaron	18	Cork	Lame Back by fall on Board Ship
Letitiae Kilpatrick	22	Antrim	Sore Leg
Marg^t Dempsey	23	Cork	Inflam^y Fever
Maurice Delay	27	"	"
Martin McHugh	30	Sligo	"
Corn^s Harrington	30	Cork	"
Timothy Scannel *	32		

* Ruptured & aditionally injured by fall on board ship

Port of Saint John: Emigrant Poor 1842   35

Cathe Murphy	25	"	Inflam^y Fever
Mary Gately	35	Roscom^n	Lame hand destitute
Patrick Gately	Inf^t	child of do	"
Cathe Supple	30	Co. Cork	Sick & disabled
Michael Supple	2 1/4	"	"
Eliza Magnor	16	"	Helpless & destitute
Thos Cunningham	35	Waterford	Inflam^y fever
Mary Gahagan	37	Donegal	sick & destitute
Honoria Sullivan	24	Cork	Inflamed Eyes
James Barry	32	Limerick	Cholera Morbis
Mary Swinney	32	Co. Cork	Dysentry
Mary Sullivan	16	"	Inflam^y Fever
Joanna Carty	26	"	Destitute Husb^d deserted
Patrick Carty	-	child of do	
Wm Vent	17	Co. Donegal	Inflam^y Fever
Honoria Collins	9	Cork	Destitute Mother deserted
Jerem^h Murphy	4	"	half orphan father deserted
Ellen Murphy	Inf^t	child of do	" "
Hugh Gelson	64	Co. Dublin	Scalded Foot
Matilda Morrow	20	Derry	Venereal distemper
Denis Hennessey	63	Clare	Sore Leg
Marg^t Blake	60	Cavan	Houseless & destitute
Mary Barry	35	Limerick	Sick & destitute
Ellen Barry 2^d	7	"	"
Catherine Barry	5	"	"
James Barry	2	"	"
Mary Owen	20	Co. Cavan	Diseased Throat
Mary Lee	12	Kerry	Inflam^y Fever
James White 2nd	30	"	Sore Legs
Mary Kelly	21	Galway	Sick & destitute
Mary Connell	29	Sligo	Destitute Husb^d deserted
Michael Connell	3	"	
Catherine Connell	Inf^t	child of do	
Elizabeth Wilby	26	Co. Cork	Inflam^y Fever
Rose Ann Ferrer	20	Monaghan	Sore Legs
Peter Connolly	20	Co. Cavan	Houseless & destitute
Mary Connolly	20	"	
Brien Connolly	Inf^t	child of do	
William Kelly	20	Roscom^n	Lame
Cathe McGaveron	25	Co. Cavan	Sick & destitute
Thomas McGaveron	2	Dublin	"
Francis McGaveron	Inf^t	child of do	"
Marg^t Finn	22	Co. Cork	Inflam^y Fever

Irish Migration To New England: Port of Saint John

Name	Age	Place	Note
Honor[a] Fitzgerald	28	"	Destitute Husb[d] deserted
Bridget Fitzgerald	8	"	"
Honoria Fitzgerald	5	"	"
Margaret Fitzgerald	3	"	"
Ellen Fitzgerald	Inf[t]	child of do	"
Ellen Muldown	26	Co. Ferman[h]	Inflam[y] Fever
George Farmer	37	Cork	Intermit[t] Fever
Dorah Gillan	34	"	Destitute Husb[d] deserted
Joseph Payton	10	"	"
Bridget McNamara	18	Clare	Sore Hand
Frances Callaghan	28	Cork	Lame inflamed Leg
Cathe Kearney	27	"	Sick & destitute
Patrick Kearney	Inf[t]	child of do	"
Ann Mellin	24	Donegal	Sick & destitute
Richard Cue	18	Co. Cork	Spinal injury
Mary Seymour	4½	St. John	destitute Parents deserted
Mary Thomas	10	Clifton	destitute Mother in L. Asy[m]
Mary O. Cain	22	Co. Derry	Sick & destitute
Marg[t] Carson	25	Tyrone	"
Cathe Cleary	44	Limerick	"
Thomas Cleary	5	"	"
James Cleary	Inf[t]	child of do	"
Ferguson Dutley	18	Aberdeen	Houseless & destitute
Elizabeth Keefe	25	Co. Cork	Sick & destitute

Sick and indigent Immigrants aided with Outdoor Relief in provisions by the Overseers of Poor in the City and Parish of Saint John from the 1st Jan[y] to the 31st Dec[r] (inclusive) 1842 - 713 families containing 2036 Individuals [P.A.N.B. Emigrations RS 8 Micro F7891 - *Names, Age, Place of Nativity, Family, Circumstance of disability*

Name	Age	Place	Fam	Note
Robert Armstrong	79	Co. Tyrone	3	Inf[m] wife & crippled son
John Bracken	40	Ferman[h]	4	Sick & destitute
Mary Carty	33	Cork	2	"
Michael Connel	43	Sligo	7	"
Eliz[h] Donaldson & sister	70	Donegal	3	Old & Infirm Spinster
Catherine Dyer	32	Sligo	2	Husb[d] dest[d] 1 child
John Dennish	27	Cork	5	Sick & destitute
Eleanor Downey	28	"	4	H[d] deserted 3 child[n]
Elizabeth Egan	22	"	3	" 2 "
Ann Flanigan	22	Leitrim	2	" 1 "
Dora Gillan	36	Cork	3	Sick & destitute

Port of Saint John: Emigrant Poor 1842   37

Name	Age	County	#	Condition
Thomas Gately	36	Roscom^n	3	Hlf blind Family sick
Jerem^h Holland	40	Cork	3	Sick & destitute
Mary Hurley	28	"	2	Inflamed Eyes
Elizabeth Hickey	28	"	3	H^d deserted Mother 1 child
Rosa Irvin	38	Ferman^h	3	Wid 2 child^n
Rosa Kindred	35	Armagh	4	Wid 3 "
Cathe Lennehan	28	Cork	2	H^d deserted 1 child
Mary Martin	35	Kings	3	Wid 2 child^n
Mary Magnor	22	Cork	2	Sick & destitute
Timothy Murphy	28	"	3	Sick Wife & 1 child
John Murphy	30	Louth	4	Wife & 2 child^n
Cathe McCaffrey	17	Tyrone	2	Sick & destitute
Brid^t McGee	33	Louth	3	Wid 2 child^n
Ellen McGarvey	44	Donegal	3	Wid 2 child^n
Mary Nagle	52	Cork	4	Wid 3 child^n
Michael Ryan	29	Tipperary	5	Sick wife & 3 child^n
Danl Sullivan	26	Kerry	3	Sick wife & 1 child
Nancy Sullivan	27	"	3	Widow Mother & child
Margaret Shey	17	Cork	2	Lame hand
Ellen Shanehan	23	"	5	H^d deserted 4 Child^n
Mary White 2^d	23	"	3	Wid sick 2 child^n
Catherine Flinn	22	Sligo	1	Destitute
Mich^l Gaveron	26	Roscom^n	4	hurt in blasting
Rach^l Dogherty	52	Tyrone	4	Wid 2 child^n home
George Brecken	36	Ferman^h	5	Sick & destitute
Barclay McElroy	14	Sligo	1	Lame Knee
Mary Burke	26	Limerick	3	2 Bast^d Child^n dest^t
Abigail Murphy	40	Cork	3	Wid & 2 child^n
Mary Pye	50	Donegal	3	Wid & 2 child^n
John Vallely	49	Armagh	5	Destitute
Corn^s Sullivan	23	Cork	3	Frozen Toes
Parick O'Brien	30	"	3	Sick & destitute
Mary McManaman	50	Donegal	4	Wid & 3 child^n
James Kenevan	40	Limerick	6	Sick & destitute
James McAulay	50	Donegal	6	"
Mary Cooper	40	Cork	5	H^d deserted 4 Child^n
Mary Pain	26	Galway	3	" 2 Child^n
Patrick Mansfield	50	Cork	7	Destitute
Ellen Morgan	30	"	3	H^d deserted 2 Child^n
Sarah Curley	20	Sligo	1	Destitute
William Jones	63	Donegal	3	Helpless Cripple
Patrick McCarty	43	Kerry	8	Destitute
Owen Flinn	25	Tipperary	4	"

38   Irish Migration To New England: Port of Saint John

Name	Age	County		Notes
Denis Whelan	24	Clare	2	Wife Sick destitute
James Adrian	35	Antrim	6	"
Jerem^h McCarty	35	Co. Cork	2	Sick & destitute
John Dwyer	35	Tipperary	5	Destitute
Alexander Taylor	22	Derry	3	"
Marg^t McCarty	26	Cork	1	"
Patrick Riley	35	Louth	6	"
Mary McLean	27	Antrim	2	H^d deserted 1 child
Alex^r Montgomery	23	Donegal	4	destitute
Cathe McKenna 1st	28	Ferman^h	6	H^d sick & destitute
Ann McAneslin	30	Derry	4	H^d ab^t deserted
Cathe McKenna 2^d	60	Kerry	2	Wid 1 child
Denis Sullivan	35	Cork	3	no English
James McAllan	34	"	5	Wife Sick
Mary Magnor 2^d	16	"	1	Destitute
Mary McCarty 2^d	22	"	2	Sick & destitute
James Smith	50	Antrim	4	Lame & "
Denis McAnulty	25	Donegal	1	Destitute
Hannah Harnet	25	Cork	5	H^d deserted 3 child^n
Mary McManus	20	Leitrim	1	Destitute
Catherine Driscol	40	Cork	4	Wife 3 child^n
George Farrel	24	Donegal	2	Sick & destitute
Thomas Lee	35	Monaghan	5	Destitute
John Bradley	35	Leitrim	1	"
Peter Duffy	45	Ferman^h	6	"
Barth^w Welch	28	Cork	1	"
Cornelius Coughlan	45	"	8	Sick & destitute
Edward Kelly	31	"	4	Destitute
Ellen Coughlan	25	"	2	Wid 1 child
Brid^t Bishopson	57	Tyrone	1	Infirm & destitute
Thomas Evans	40	Cork	6	Sick & destitute
Corn^s Lyon	41	Kerry	6	Destitute
Marg^t Bustard	58	Donegal	4	H^d deserted 3 child^n
Mary Mulharon	24	"	1	Destitute
John Small	35	Louth	6	"
Alexander Taylor	21	Derry	4	"
Marg^t Creamer	19	Waterford	1	Lame & sick
Nancy Miller	47	Down	6	Wid 5 Child^n
John Dempsey	23	Kildare	3	Destitute
Mary Slattery	28	Clare	4	H^d deserted 3 child^n
William Dorgan	30	Cork	4	Destitute
Ellen Regan	50	"	2	"
Mary Mahony	27	"	4	Wid, sister & 2 Child^n

Port of Saint John: Emigrant Poor 1842

Name	Age	County	#	Notes
Elizabeth Egan	24	"	3	H^d deserted 2 child^n
John Harrington	38	"	6	Destitute
Richd Carlin	40	Donegal	6	"
John Crowley	24	Cork	3	"
Mary McFarlin	40	Tyrone	3	Wid 2 child^n home
Mich^l McCluskey	40	Derry	6	Sick & destitute
Mary Duffy	35	Armagh	1	Destitute
James Duffy	63	Mayo	1	"
Sarah Brown	27	Durham	2	"
William Kirby	25	Co. Cork	2	"
Mary Leary	30	"	3	H^d deserted 2 child^n
Grigor Urquhart	39	London	1	Destitute
Mary O'Donnel	35	Limerick	4	Wid 3 child^n
Mary Johnston	50	Cork	4	Wid 3 "
Ellen Rairdon	57	"	2	Wid & niece destitute
Robt Buchanan	20	Donegal	1	Destitute
Danl O'Brien	26	Cork	4	"
John Rairdon	26	"	2	"
Edward Daley	24	Donegal	1	"
Brid^t McCarty	22	Co. Cork	1	Destitute
Mary Shey	20	"	1	"
Joanna Sullivan	20	"	1	"
Marg^t Donovan	35	"	2	Wid 1 child
Christopher Frame	35	Ferman^h	6	Wood^n Leg, Wife 4 Chil^n
James O'Brien	44	Cork	6	Destitute
Miche Mullen & brother & sister	12	Ferman^h	3	Destitute Hlf Orphans
Mary Broderick	25	Waterford	4	H^d deserted 2 child^n
Pat McDermot	40	Sligo	7	Detitute
John Daley & sister	21	Cork	2	"
Elizabeth Cronin	35	"	2	H^d deserted 1 child
Patrick Quin	40	Galway	3	Destitute
Patrick Carrick	42	"	1	"
Owen Quin	25	"	1	"
Thomas Conolly	23	"	1	"
Thomas Burke	23	"	1	"
Barkley Ryan	23	"	1	"
Ann Murphy	19	Cork	1	"
Marg^t Sullivan	20	"	1	"
Honoria Crowley	20	"	1	"
Wm Murphy	40	"	5	"
Thos Manyon	29	Galway	1	"
James Mitchell	40	"	1	"

William Kelly	25	"	3	"
Mary Spriggs	46	Cork	3	Wid 2 children
Cathe McGinnis	22	Kerry	1	Destitute
Mich[l] Coffee	36	"	4	"
Brid[t] Noonan	30	Galway	1	"
Brid[t] Nuckley	26	"	1	"
Patrick Manyon	30	Cork	3	Broken Arm
John Burnes	37	Co. Sligo	6	Sick & destitute
Ja[s] Manning & sister	22	Kerry	2	Destitute
Dan[l] Hannifer	30	"	4	"
Owen Sullivan	29	"	5	"
Pat Cooley	21	"	1	"
Miche Gannon	40	Galway	8	"
Thomas Tracy	40	"	7	"
Philip Monaghan	28	Meath	4	"
Mary Curtain	55	Cork	3	H[d] in U. States 2 child[n]
John Noonan	30	"	3	Sick & destitute
Brid[t] Sullivan	24	"	2	H[d] in Immig[t] Hosp[l]
Brid[t] Glenn	25	Galway	4	H[d] deserted 3 child[n]
Daniel Lynch	35	Kerry	4	Sick & destitute
Brid[t] Gately	30	Roscom[n]	1	Destitute
Mary Flinn	22	"	1	"
Denis Hays	24	Galway	1	"
Michael Carr 1st	26	"	1	"
Michael Carr 2nd	21	"	1	"
John Kenny	20	"	1	"
Rich[d] Donovan	21	Cork	4	"
John Sweeney	27	"	3	"
Corn[s] Sullivan	25	"	1	"
Denis McCarty	25	"	3	Wife sick
Catherine Flinn	27	Leitrim	2	Widdow 1 child
Bridget Dolan	20	Roscom[n]	1	Destitute
Julia Connor	38	Cork	4	H[d] in U. States 3 child[n]
Honoria Bryan	50	"	7	H[d] in Canada 6 child[n]
John Gavin	19	Galway	1	Destitute
Mich[l] Connel	25	"	1	"
John Connel	21	"	1	"
Mich[l] Heally	31	Galway	1	Destitute
William Madden	52	"	9	"
Jane Constantine	26	Cork	1	"
William Vance	70	Derry	10	Sick & destitute
Rosa Monaghan	30	"	5	H[d] absent 4 children

Name	Age	County	#	Notes
Joan[a] Murphy & 3 others	25	Cork	4	H[d] in Halifax 2 ch[d] & sister
Timothy Righley	35	Galway	5	Destitute
Martin Donahue	50	"	3	"
Peter Nighlin	27	"	5	"
John Ford	22	"	1	"
John Sullivan	25	Kerry	4	"
William Evans	37	Cork	2	"
Tho[s] Callaghan	32	Kerry	3	"
Honoria Carty	24	Cork	2	H[d] in Prison 1 child
Ellen Connolly	38	"	3	" " 2 child
James Mason	24	Derry	1	Destitute
John Fitzpatrick	26	Longford	1	"
Mich[l] Heally 2nd	30	Galway	1	"
John Carrol	22	"	1	"
Eliz[h] Irvin	32	Ferman[h]	7	H[d] absent 6 children
Timo[y] Brandon	19	Galway	1	Destitute
Marg[t] Higgins	27	"	5	H[d] in U.S. 3 child & sister
Cathe Hennessy	34	Cork	4	H[d] deserted 3 child[n]
Patrick Cahall & 2 sisters	25	Kerry	3	Destitute
Ann McMackie & sisters	17	Tyrone	2	"
Catherine Coffee	20	Galway	1	"
Sam[l] Manning	29	Cork	1	"
John Murphy	20	"	1	"
James Mullane	21	"	1	"
Mary Lovett	26	Kerry	2	H[d] deserted 1 child sick
Corn[s] Crayon	26	Co. Cork	3	Destitute
Marg[t] Barret	28	"	4	H[d] deserted 3 Child[n]
Dan[l] Shehan & Bro.	33	"	2	Destitute
Tim[y] Fitzpatrick	30	Galway	1	"
Pat Magan	30	"	1	"
Corn[s] Coughlan	45	Cork	6	"
Adam Supple	28	"	3	Wife & 1 child destitute
Arthur Keefe	21	"	1	Destitute
Mich[l] O'Donnel	49	"	6	"
Mary Hayes	36	"	1	"
Joanna Donovan	20	"	1	"
Denis McCarty & 2 others	20	"	3	"
Mary Quillen	20	Galway	1	"
Pat Sullivan	35	Cork	2	"

42 Irish Migration To New England: Port of Saint John

David Miller & Sister	21	Derry	2	"
Mary Welch	24	Galway	1	"
Jer^h Murphy Brother & Sister	21	Cork	3	"
John McGuire & Sister	25	Ferman^h	2	"
Mary Brady	34	"	2	H^d deserted 1 child
Thomas Clarke	35	Cavan	4	Destitute
Rebecca Gurrel & Sister	20	Tyrone	2	Destitute
Murty McCarty	28	Cork	3	"
Jerem^h Lane	30	"	1	"
Daniel Daley	25	"	2	"
Robt Flavin & 2 sisters	40	"	3	"
Cathe Conway & Daughter	50	"	2	Widow 1 child
Pat McDermot	35	Leitrim	3	Destitute
Mary Conway	59	Cork	4	Old Wid 3 Child^n
Mary Donovan	40	Kerry	5	H^d in U. States 4 Child^n
Joanna Kinneally	23	Cork	3	H^d deserted 2 Child^n
Ellen Shey	22	Co. Cork	4	H^d absent 2 Child
Nancy Hurley	21	"	3	H^d deserted 2 Child
Mary Coffee	30	"	3	H^d absent Mo. & 1 Child
Ellen Corcoran	32	"	3	H^d absent 2 Child^n
Marg^t Connell	42	Kerry	2	Wid 1 Daughter
Judith Mara	48	"	4	Wid 3 Children
Marg^t Kennedy	30	Galway	4	H^d deserted 3 Child^n
Marg^t Loughnane	32	"	3	H^d deserted 2 Child^n
Margaret Buke	45	"	4	Wid 3 Children
Danl Brennan	30	Kerry	7	Destitute
Ja^s Finnean	27	Cork	4	"
Ellen Hays & Sister	26	Tipperary	2	"
John McAneny	25	Limerick	1	"
Mary Callaghan	26	Cork	1	"
Joanna Healy	26	"	1	"
John Shehan	26	"	1	"
James Hasset	35	"	1	"
Mich^l Breen	25	"	3	"
Honora Buckley	22	"	1	"
Miche Glasson	37	"	4	"
Honoria Carty	24	"	3	"
Denis Brien	40	"	4	"

Port of Saint John: Emigrant Poor 1842   43

John Brien					
Brother & Sister	20	Tipperary	3	"	
John Gafney	44	Sligo	1	Lame & destitute	
John Sullivan	20	Kerry	3	Destitute	
Mich^l Sullivan	25	Cork	2	"	
John McQuid	60	Tyrone	4	"	
Joanna Kelly 1st	32	Limerick	4	"	
James McGaveron	32	Cavan	5	"	
Danl Sullivan	40	Cork	7	"	
Darby Holohan	45	Co. Cork	7	Destitute	
Michael Grady	25	"	2	"	
Patrick Brien	28	Kerry	3	"	
Jerem^h Day	30	Limerick	2	"	
Timothy Cassine	20	Kerry	1	"	
Marg^t Mahony	18	Cork	1	"	
Marg^t Talbot	40	Kerry	5	Widow 4 Children	
Frances Bustard	23	Donegal	3	" 2 "	
Marg^t Murphy 2^d	20	Cork	2	H^d deserted 1 child	
Mich^l Carter	54	Kilkenny	1	Destitute	
John Flaghan	27	Kerry	4	"	
Eliza Hiney	28	Westmeath	2	H^d in U. States 1 Child	
Mich^l Roberts	35	Cork	5	Destitute	
John Donnelly	23	Clare	2	"	
James Lee	31	Cork	4	"	
John Gorman	27	Limerick	4	"	
Patrick Welch	40	Cork	3	"	
Daniel Hogan	35	Clare	4	"	
Jane Fitzgerald	21	Donegal	1	"	
John Lacky	26	Galway	3	"	
Mary Cradock	42	Limerick	4	Wid 3 Children	
Marg^t Clansey	24	Cork	1	Destitute	
Bridget Gaveron	26	Roscom^n	3	H^d deserted 2 Child^n	
Margaret Casey	20	Cork	1	Destitute	
Thomas Wrenn	26	Leitrim	2	"	
Catherine Carey	25	Cork	2	H^d deserted 1 Child	
Mary McHugh	22	Queens Ire	2	H^d Sick	
Ellen Eaton	23	Kerry	3	H^d deserted 2 Child^n	
Marg^t Burke	25	Galway	1	Destitute	
Marg^t Harrigan	35	"	1	"	
Joanna Kelly 2nd	14	Co. Cork	1	Destitute hlf orphan	
Judith Delay	27	"	2	H^d sick	
Maria Murphy	25	Kerry	2	H^d deserted 1 child	
Mary Murphy	34	"	1	H^d in U. States	

44 Irish Migration To New England: Port of Saint John

Name	Age	County		Notes
Nancy Sullivan 2nd	24	Cork	1	Sick & destitute
Denis Rairdon	26	"	3	Destitute
Rosa Carlin	38	Donegal	6	H^d absent & 5 Child^n
Rosa McNamara	40	Galway	3	Destiute
John Lundon	25	Limerick	4	"
Mich Hoar	48	Kerry	4	"
John Coffee	40	"	4	"
Jno Whelan & Sister	28	Tipperary	2	"
John Quilty	27	"	1	"
Jane Foley	30	Cork	6	H^d deserted 5 Child^n
Mary Hay 2nd	17	Limerick	2	Destitute
Cathe Noonan	18	"	1	"
Mary Knott	36	Sligo	5	H^d in U. States 4 Child^n
Eleanor Heally	17	"	1	Destitute
Catherine Power	30	Monaghan	4	H^d deserted 3 Child^n
Hann^h Sweeney	40	Cork	6	" 5 Child^n
Catherine Verise	32	Galway	1	Widow
Marg^t Dempsey	33	Cork	1	Sick & Destitute
Mich^l Ford	28	Kerry	1	"
Stephen Callaghan	27	"	1	"
Timothy Clifford	27	"	1	"
Pat Fitzgerald	28	"	1	"
John Burke	20	"	1	"
Hann^h Sullivan	24	Cork	1	Sore Eyes "
Thos Corcoran	23	Roscom^n	6	"
Denis Callahan	19	Cork	4	"
Maurice Manni	24	Co. Kerry	1	Destitute
John Wood	21	Galway	1	"
Brid^t Mack	30	Kerry	2	H^d in Fredericton 1 ch^d
Jere^h Donahue	38	"	3	Destitute
Rosa Clifford	23	Limerick	4	H^d deserted 3 Chil^n
Cathe Golding	23	Leitrim	2	Lame & destitute
Mary Johnston	17	Ferman^h	1	Destitute
Denis O'Connor	34	Limerick	6	"
John Donellan	52	Clare	5	"
Thomas Dooley	38	Tipperary	6	"
John Cassin	36	Kerry	6	"
Danl Curren	37	"	4	"
Martin Farrel	32	Sligo	4	"
Mich^l Mahar	48	Tipperary	10	"
Richard Welch	33	Kildare	4	"
Eliz^h Harbour	40	Kerry	7	Widow & 6 Children

Port of Saint John: Emigrant Poor 1842   45

Name	Age	County		Notes
Joanna Foley	22	"	1	Destitute
Julie Griffin	20	"	1	"
Mary Fahy	27	Galway	1	"
Rebecca Common	35	Leitrim	1	"
John Power	20	Cork	1	"
Maurice Curren	25	Kerry	2	"
Mary Griffin	20	Cork	1	"
Corn^s Murphy	30	"	3	"
Martin Mullen	25	Galway	2	"
Cathe Sullivan	35	Cork	2	H^d deserted 1 Ch^d sick
John Larkin	24	Galway	3	Destitute
Ellen Shey 2^d	40	Cork	7	H^d absent 6 Children
Ellen Sullivan	25	"	1	Destitute
Mary Hurley	28	"	1	"
William Flinn	26	Tipperary	3	Destitute
James Connor	46	Kerry	5	"
John Mahegan	48	Cork	4	"
John Burke	41	Tipperary	5	"
Mary McDonough	20	Sligo	1	"
Marg^t McCarthy	25	"	1	"
Bridget Wynn	22	"	1	"
Catherine Lee	21	Leitrim	1	"
Catherine Caveny	20	"	1	"
John Shannehan	14	Cork	1	" orphan
Mary Sullivan 2^d	30	"	1	"
Cathe Murphy	22	"	3	"
Mary Crimmins 2^d	32	"	4	H^d deserted 3 Child^n
Mary McDonnel	34	Donegal	3	" 2 Child^n
Marg^t Casey	32	Cork	3	H^d in U.S. 1 Child & Sister
Elizabeth Wynn	30	Sligo	4	H^d in U. States 3 Child^n
Ann McMullin	58	Derry	4	Widow 3 Child^n
Marg^t Sullivan	25	Cork	3	H^d in U. States 2 Child^n
Jade Kohan	29	Galway	3	Sick & destitute
Mary Maghan	30	Roscom^n	1	Destitute
Brid^t McGuire	32	Cavan	6	H^d absent 5 Children
Jerem^h Connor	34	Cork	3	Sore Eyes & destitute
Joan^a Collins	32	"	5	H^d absent 4 Child^n
Catherine Darcy	23	Cavan	2	Destitute
Marg^t Dempsey	30	Kerry	4	H^d deserted 3 Child^n
Ellen Gorman	60	"	5	Widow 4 Child^n
Mary Harrington	33	Cork	3	Widow 2 "
Honor^a Sullivan 2^d	50	"	2	H^d in U. States
Ellen Connolly	60	"	1	Destitute

46   Irish Migration To New England: Port of Saint John

Name	Age	County		Notes
William Stack	40	Kerry	7	"
John Lloyd	38	Tipperary	5	Destitute
William Finn	21	"	2	"
Judy Righly & Sister	25	Limerick	2	"
Brid^t Call	19	Cork	2	"
Marg^t Blake	60	Cavan	3	Wid 2 Children
Chas Helland	25	Cork	2	Destitute
Brien Lynch	30	Cavan	4	"
Peter Connolly	20	"	3	"
Mary White	20	Cork	1	"
Joanna Carty	26	"	2	H^d deserted 1 child
Marg^t Donovan	30	"	1	Destitute
Ann Bateman	23	"	1	"
Eliza Noonan	36	Limerick	6	H^d absent 5 Children
Hugh Montague	35	Derry	4	Destitute
Alice Strelin	32	Donegal	5	H^d deserted 4 Child^n
Mary Clifford	24	Cork	1	Destitute
Honor^a Rairden	16	"	1	"
Stephen Callahan	25	Kerry	1	"
William Shey	40	"	1	"
Mich^l Connel	40	Sligo	7	Sick & destitute
Marg^t Smith	57	Derry	1	Destitute Widow
John McCarty	34	Kerry	5	"
Mich^l Foley	32	"	1	"
Pat Kavenah	21	"	1	"
James Leighy	40	Cork	7	Wife Lame & 5 Children
Pat Kelleher	23	"	2	Wife Sickly
John Hannon	31	"	6	Destitute
John Murphy	30	"	4	"
Mary Larkin	25	Galway	2	H^d absent 1 Child
James Manning	20	Kerry	2	Destitute
William Noonan	38	Limerick	7	Destitute
John Hanrahan	61	"	1	Lame Arm
Alex^r Shehan	30	Kerry	1	Destitute
Jerem^h Shey	35	"	1	" no English
Mary Barry	35	. Limerick	5	H^d Sick 3 Children
John Cranan	24	Galway	1	Destitute
Owen Gallagher	20	Donegal	1	Half Blind
Danl Kennedy & Sister	25	Tipperary	2	Destitute
Brid^t Horan	19	"	2	"
Chas Quinn	33	Donegal	4	"
Brien Scanlen	45	"	6	"

Name	Age	County	#	Notes
Marg^t Kane	21	Galway	1	"
Margaret Smith & Sister	15	Roscom.	2	"
Nancy McCane	20	Donegal	1	"
Mary Whooton	18	"	1	"
Marg^t Fee	30	Ferman^h	1	"
Patrick Keefe	32	Clare	3	"
Pat McGuire	47	Ferman^h	5	"
Murty Nowlen	40	"	5	"
John Sheridan	22	Cavan	3	"
James Spring	25	Kerry	3	"
Maurice Brian	23	"	2	"
Ja^s O'Harron	25	Tipperary	3	"
William Carrol	21	"	2	"
Jere^h Monaghan	26	Kerry	1	"
Marg^t Godsel	27	Cork	4	H^d sick & 2 children
John Ashburn	30	Kildare	1	Destitute
Marg^t Haloran	18	Cork	1	"
John Ward	24	Galway	1	"
James Irvin	22	Cork	1	"
Edward Righley	27	Co. Clare	1	Destiute
Timo^y Righley	30	Galway	1	"
John Coffee 2^d	23	Kerry	1	"
John Curtain	24	Cork	1	"
Mich^l Glenn	29	Galway	2	"
Ellen Loughnane	18	Kerry	1	Sickly & destitute
John Dolan	22	Kerry	1	Destitute
Hann^h Donahue	17	"	1	"
William Wood	35	Ferman^h	5	"
Ellen Bryne	28	Roscom^n	1	"
Cherry Looney	28	Kerry	3	"
Sarah Vance	45	Derry	4	Aged Mother & 2 Sisters
Charles Williams	45	Tyrone	5	Wife & 3 children
Judy Coughlan	24	Cork	2	H^d in U. States 1 Child
William Jones	53	Donegal	3	Lame & destitute
John Burk	38	Galway	1	Destitute
Jerry Connor	18	"	1	"
Catherine Hines	32	Sligo	3	H^d in U. States 2 Child^n
Mary Coleman	25	"	1	Destitute
Ellen Dynan	40	Cork	4	Widow 3 Children
Pat Carrol	40	"	7	Destitute
Daniel Swinney	26	"	3	"
Danl Morarity	24	Kerry	1	"

48   Irish Migration To New England: Port of Saint John

Name	Age	County	#	Notes
Ja^s Armstrong	53	Sligo	6	Wife & 4 Children
Joan^a Harrigan	16	Kerry	1	Destitute
Isabella Boyle	20	Donegal	1	"
Thomas Scanlin	26	Kerry	1	"
Thomas Welch	32	Cork	5	"
Patrick Barret	38	"	1	"
William Carrol	27	"	1	"
Frances Welch	30	Co. Cork	5	Destitute
Thomas Raidon	40	Limerick	2	"
James O'Donnel	34	"	1	"
Pat Finnigan	19	Kerry	1	"
Jerry Mullane	20	Cork	1	"
Jerry Sullivan	50	"	2	"
Cathe Mahoney	18	"	1	"
Eliza Beatty	20	Westmeath	1	Sick & destitute
Edwd Carmoney	48	Limerick	6	Destitute
Mary Halloran	17	"	1	Half orphan
Ellen Scanlen	23	"	2	H^d absent 1 child
Mary Coughlan	24	Cork	1	Sick & destitute
Debby Fahan	29	Kerry	3	H^d deserted 1 child &sister
Mary Sullivan 3^d	32	Cork	4	H^d absent 3 children
Mary Farmer	35	Kerry	4	H^d absent 3 "
Thos Ratchford	36	Meath	5	Destitute
Marg^t Callaghan	52	Limerick	3	Widow 2 Children
Pat Malone	33	Louth	3	Destitute
David Keefe	32	Cork	1	"
John Kennedy	32	Kerry	2	"
Corn^s Kennedy	22	"	1	"
Edwd Kennedy	50	Limerick	2	"
Mary Keiley	26	Cork	2	H^d absent 1 child
Matilda Morrow	20	Derry	1	distemp^d & destitute
Saml Merrick	30	Cork	3	Detitute
Wm Keyburn	22	W. Meath	1	"
Brid^t McGuire	19	Ferman^h	2	H^d absent 1 child
Timo^y Scannel	32	Cork	1	Destitute
Jerem^h Driscol	32	"	2	Sick & destitute
Ellen McCarty	49	"	5	H^d in Prison 4 Child^n
Thomas Gately	32	Roscom^n	3	Destitute
Denis Noonan	24	Limerick	2	"
Rose Ann Hassen	28	Donegal	1	"
John Hanley	27	Cork	3	"
Jane Coil	30	Donegal	1	Sickly & destitute
Mary Bresnahan	26	Kerry	3	H^d absent 2 Child^n

Port of Saint John: Emigrant Poor 1842

Name	Age	Origin		Notes
John Wallace	23	Tyrone	1	Destitute
Miche Fitzgibbon	24	Cook	1	"
James Taylor	25	Ferman^h	5	"
Brid^t Glenn 2^d	28	Galway	3	"
Mary O'Brien	44	Cork	3	"
Cathe Mahon	60	Kerry	2	Widow & G^d Child
John O'Brien	19	Cork	1	Destitute
Corn^s Mahony	30	Kerry	3	"
Danl Rairden	22	"	4	"
Ann Sullivan	26	"	3	H^d absent 2 Child^n
Honor^a McCarty	31	Cork	4	H^d deserted 3 Child^n
Ellen Fletcher	22	Ferman^h	2	Lame & Inf^m, aged mother
Patrick Rohan	36	Galway	1	Destitute
Richd Hagarty	46	Cork	7	"
David Livingstone	36	Kircudbright, Scotland	7	"
Sarah Hassen & sister	21	Derry	2	"
Mary Fitzgerald	30	Tipperary	4	"
Arthur O'Keefe	28	Cork	2	"
Patrick Bohan	29	"	4	"
Mich^l Sullivan	25	"	3	"
John Fitzgibbon & sister	24	"	2	"
Daniel Lyon	27	"	2	" Sore Eyes
William Kelly	20	Roscom^n	1	"
Brien McGaveron	50	Cavan	1	"
Brid^t Matcheson	16	Co. Clare	1	Half Orphan Destitute
Brid^t Bamson	27	Roscom^n	3	H^d deserted 2 Child^n
Wm Gorman	22	Donegal	2	Sick & destitute
Joanna Barry	25	Limerick	3	H^d deserted 2 Child^n
John Collins	30	Cork	6	Destitute
John McGachie	28	Donegal	5	"
Pat Connolly	26	Sligo	2	"
George Lahy	30	Cavan	6	"
Marg^t Bustard	59	Donegal	2	H^d deserted 1 Child
Catherine Cleary	44	Limerick	6	Widow 5 Children
Cathe McLaughlan	20	Galway	2	H^d deserted 1 Child
Hon^a Fitzgerald	28	Cork	5	H^d absent 4 Child^n
Hon^a Murphy	25	"	4	" " 3 "
Brien McGuire	60	Cavan	9	Wife & 7 Children
Cathe McGaveron	25	"	2	H^d deserted 1 Child Sick
Jerem^h Dempsey	28	Cork	1	Destitute

50   Irish Migration To New England: Port of Saint John

Name	Age	County	#	Notes
Jane Clarke & sister & brother			23	Kerry 3 "
Brid^t Ames	26	Cavan	4	Widow 3 Children
Eliza Hiney	28	W. Meath	2	H^d in U. States 1 Child
Mary Sullivan	16	Co. Cork	1	Destitute
Ellen Sullivan	19	"	1	"
Mary White 2^d	30	"	1	"
William Gloster	40	Limerick	1	"
Marg^t A. Allen	21	Belfast	1	"
Mary Finn	23	Cork	3	H^d deserted 1 Child Sick
Mary Tracy	40	"	2	H^d absent 1 Child
Ellen Courtney		Derry	1	Destitute
Mary McCarty	29	Cork	1	Sick & destitute
Chas Dogherty	10	Donegal	1	Destitute
Denis Cleary	40	Cavan	8	"
Pat Rourk	20	Cavan	3	Wife & 1 Child
Rose Curise	54	"	3	Wid 2 Children
Ellen McGowan	46	Leitrim	6	Wid 5 Children
Denis McMorrow	30	"	3	Destitute
Terrence Lee & sister	23	"	2	"
Abig^l McGourtry	23	"	1	"
Cathe Gelgowan	17	"	1	"
Marg^t Trower	20	"	1	"
Frances Kelly	27	Roscom^n	3	"
Mich^l Nowlin	23	Cavan	3	"
Edwd Callaghan	18	Derry	1	"
James Timoney	50	Leitrim	3	H^d absent 2 Children
John Kelly & sister	22	"	2	Destitute
Brien Kelly & sister	22	Ferman^h	2	"
Cathe Flinn	22	"	1	"
Brid^t Cudahy	16	Tipperary	1	"
Felix Tierney	43	Tyrone	1	"
Ann Kelly	20	Galway	1	"
Ben^j Seymore	35	Cork	3	Sick & detitute
Mary Meloy	28	Mayo	2	H^d in U. States 1 Child
Thomas Clarke	30	Hull Eng^d	1	Destitute
Patrick Clarke	30	Cavan	1	"
Susan Murray	28	Donegal	3	H^d deserted 2 Child^n
Isab^l Thompson	18	Belfast	2	" " 1 Child
Cathe Bryen	22	Cork	1	Destitute
Mary Ingram	22	Donegal	1	"
Bowen Chute	14	Kerry	1	"
Nancy McNamara	20	Clare	1	"

Port of Saint John: Emigrant Poor 1842

Name	Age	County	#	Notes
Ann Garrity	20	Galway	1	"
Mary Herring 2nd	23	Cork	1	"
Mary Bresnahan	26	Kerry	3	H^d absent 2 Child^n
Mich^l Sullivan	30	Cork	1	Sick & destitute
Mary Lahy & sister	25	"	2	Destitute
Philip Kelly	34	"	4	"
Denis Kane	23	"	4	"
Patrick Mahony	35	"	1	"
John Shey	18	Kerry	1	"
Wm Hutchinson	38	Yorkshire	6	"
Jane O'Harron	20	Cork	2	H^d deserted 1 Child
George Lahy	30	Cavan	6	Destitute
Anthony Kilroy	19	"	1	"
Henry Matthews	20	Louth	2	"
Ja^s Fitzsimons	25	Meath	1	"
Bartley Loughnan	22	Donegal	2	"
Mary McCardle & sister	26	Sligo	2	"
Eliz^h Teavens	17	Leitrim	1	"
Danl Barret	30	Cork	2	"
Thomas Daley	45	Galway	7	"
John Hurley	35	Cork	2	"
Marg^t White	25	"	1	"
Eliza Lahy	20	Cavan	5	"
Cathe Conway	35	Cork	3	Wid. 2 Children
Mary Burns	32	Sligo	5	H^d deserted 4 Ch^d
John Lynch	29	Armagh	1	Ship Wrecked
Mary Connors	17	Kerry	1	Destitute
Mary Kilkoyn	21	Sligo	1	"
John Welch	37	Kerry	9	"
Marg^t Donovan	25	Cork	1	"
Marg^t Finn	30	"	2	H^d deserted 1 Child
Corn^s McGuire	25	Donegal	6	Destitute
Mary Hurley	50	Cork	5	Destitute
Mary Callahan	25	"	1	"
Marg^t O'Donnel	21	Limerick	1	"
Brid^t Dogherty	20	Donegal	1	"
Pat Cooney & sister	28	Clare	2	Sickly & destitute
John B. Ferrar	25	London	1	Destitute
Eliza McCabe	29	Dublin	1	"
Marg^t Delay	22	Cork	1	"
Jerem^h Shehan	27	"	5	"
Brid^t Cummins	17	Galway	1	"

52   Irish Migration To New England: Port of Saint John

Name	Age	Origin		Notes
Ann Gavel	17	"	1	"
Ann Millen	24	Donegal	1	Sick & destitute
John Swinney	27	Cork	3	Destitute
Mary McArthur	29	Donegal	1	"
Mary Pye	53	Sligo	3	"
Timothy Hart	24	Cork	3	"
Cathe Seymour	24	Limerick	1	"
Denis Brien	40	Cork	4	"
Mary Murphy	27	Kerry	2	H$\underline{d}$ deserted 1 Child
Ann Boyle	25	Louth	1	Destitute
Ellen Burke	23	Cork	1	"
Mary McGaffagan	47	Donegal	1	Widow Sickly
Mary Finn	23	Cork	1	H^d deserted
Cathe McIntire	16	Donegal	1	Sickly & destitute
Matilda Morrow	20	Derry	1	distemp^d & destitute
Francis Forest	20	Cork	3	Destitute
Mary McE...	32	Derry	2	H^d dest^d 1 Child
Mary Collins	24	Cork	2	H^d deserted 1 Ch^d
Brid^t McNamara	18	Clare	1	Destitute
Cathe Supple	30	Cork	2	H^d deserted 1 Child
Joanna Donovan	20	Cork	1	Destitute
Marg^t White	25	"	1	"
Joanna Murphy	30	"	1	" no English
Mary Whelan	25	Clare	2	Sick H^d deserted
Thos Creighton	31	Glasgow	1	Destitute
Mary Connel	20	Cork	2	1 Child Bast^d
John O'Brien	50	"	2	Destitute
William Kelly	35	Down	5	"
Honoria Harnet	24	Cork	4	H^d desrted 3 Child^n
Robt Miller	26	Antrim	1	Destitute
Bridget Fahy	17	Galway	1	"
Marg^t Callahan	26	Cork	2	Wid 1 Child
Judy Murphy	28	Monaghan	1	Destitute
Mary O'Cane	22	Derry	1	Sick & destitute
Dorah Gillan	35	Cork	3	H^d desrted 2 Child^n
Laurance Hickey	38	Tipperary	6	Destitute
Sarah Gillis	40	Monaghan	5	desert^d from H^d 4 Child^n
Marg^t Connel	29	Sligo	5	H^d deserted 4 "
Rosa Irvin	40	Ferman^h	3	Wid 2 Chilren
Wm Donaldson	78	Donegal	1	helpless cripple
Mary Shey	23	Cork	1	Destitute
Marg^t Hollohan	40	Kerry	2	"
Honor^a Sullivan	20	Cork	1	"

Port of Saint John: Emigrant Poor 1842

Name	Age	County	#	Status
Joann^a Herrington	35	"	4	H^d absent 3 Child^n
Elizabeth Keefe	25	"	3	Sick & destitute
Thomas Leighy	23	Limerick	2	Destitute
Jane Fitzgerald	24	Donegal	1	"
Math^l Thomas	60	Gloucester, England	3	"
Marg^t Hennessy	45	Cork	3	Wid 2 Child^n
Sarah Evans	35	"	5	H^d absent 4 Children
Thomas Hasset	38	Kerry	4	Destitute
Margaret Dunn	28	Tyrone	5	H^d deserted 4 Ch^n
Mary Carty	32	Cork	2	" " 1 do
Jane Glenn	31	Ferman^h	1	Sick & destitute
Miche Ryan	35	Tipperary	5	" "
Mary McMaster	28	Tyrone	6	H^d absent 5 Children
Matthew Leary	25	Cork	2	Wife sick & destitute
Rose Currie	54	Cavan	3	Wid 2 Children
Mary Driscol 2nd	25	Cork	3	H^d absent 2 do
Thomas Sweetman	46	Cork	6	Sick & destitute
Honoria McCarty	50	"	4	Sick Wid 3 Child^n
Patrick Righley	39	Louth	6	Destitute
Ellen Sullivan	51	Kerry	3	Wid 2 Child^n
Owen Shey	30	Cork	5	Destitute
Mary Lyons	43	Kerry	7	H^d in Hosp 6 Child^n
John Moore	30	Monaghan	7	Destitute
Richd Hagarty	44	Cork	7	"
John Dogherty	28	"	4	"
Denis Sullivan	31	Kerry	5	Sick & destitute
Thomas Lee	36	Monaghan	6	Destitute
Mary Burke	28	Limerick	3	H^d deserted 2 Child
Honoria O'Brien	48	Cork	6	Wid 5 Children
Miche Carney	30	Clare	3	Destitute
James Leary	40	Kerry	7	"
James Smith	50	Antrim	5	Lame & destitute
Dan$\underline{l}$ Corcoran	35	Cork	5	Destitute
Cathe McKenna	69	Kerry	1	"
James McAulay	55	Donegal	6	"
John Swinney	28	Cork	3	"
Denis Sullivan 2^d	32	"	4	"
Patrick Mansfield	47	Cork	7	Detitute
Ellen Shehan alias Mary Morgan	40	"	3	Wid 2 Child^n
Patrick Quinn		"	8	Destitute

54   Irish Migration To New England: Port of Saint John

List of Passage Tickets &c for Passages inland and coastwise granted destitute Immigrants during the Year 1842 by the Overseers Poor in City - 271 cases comprising 732 Individuals, Saint John 31st December 1843 [P.A.N.B. Emigrations RS 8 Micro F7891 - *Name, Age, Nativity, Family, To what place Removed*

Name	Age	Nativity	Family	To what place Removed
Charles Hickey	34	Co. Cork	4	St. Andrews
Eliza Cagan	24	"	2	Windsor
Patrick Righley	37	Louth	6	do
J. Harrington	38	Cork	6	St. Andrews
J. Crowley	24	"	3	Fredericton
Mary Ann Duffy	25	Armagh	1	Windsor
Ann McAneslin	30	Derry	4	Fredericton
Edward Kelly	31	Cork	4	do
Eliza Brown	20	"	1	do
Mary Quinn	18	"	1	do
D. O'Brien	26	"	4	St. Andrews
John Rairdon	26	"	2	do
Edward Daley	24	Donegal	1	St. Stephen
Brid^t McCarty	22	Cork	1	Fredericton
Catherine Murphy	20	"	1	do
Mary Shey	20	"	1	do
Joanna Sullivan	20	"	1	do
Marg^t Donovan	35	"	2	do
Charles Frame	35	Ferman^h	6	do
Patrick McDermot	40	Sligo	7	do
John Daley & sister	21	Cork	2	do
Elizabeth Cronin	35	"	2	Quoddy West
Patrick Quinn	40	Galway	3	Fredericton
Patrick Carrick	42	"	1	do
Owen Quinn	25	"	1	do
J. Connolly	23	"	1	do
Thomas Burke	23	Co. Galway	1	Fredericton
B. Ryan	23	"	1	do
Catherine McGinnis	22	Kerry	1	Annapolis
Michael Coffee	36	"	4	Fredericton
Bridget Noonan	30	Galway	1	do
Bridget Buckley	26	"	1	do
R. Donovan	25	"	3	Halifax
J. Mason	24	Derry	1	Annapolis
J. Fitzpatrick	26	Longford	1	do
Patrick Cahal	25	Kerry	3	Digby

Port of Saint John: Emigrant Poor 1842

Name	Age	County	#	Destination
J. Sullivan	28	"	5	Windsor
A. Supple	28	Cork	3	Annapolis
M. O'Donnel	49	"	6	do
Corn[s] Coughlan	45	"	8	Grand Lake
Mary Hayes	30	"	1	Annapolis
Joanna Donavon	20	"	1	do
Dan[l] McCarty	25	"	3	St. Stephen
C. McCarty	26	"	1	do
Mary Quillon	20	Galway	1	Digby or Annapolis
Rebecca Gurrel	20	Tyrone	2	" "
Robert Flavin	29	Cork	3	West Quoddy
Patrick McDermot	35	Leitrim	3	do
J. Noonan	26	Cork	3	Annapolis
J. McQuidd	60	Tyrone	4	St. Stephen
J. McGaveron	35	Cavan	5	Annapolis
P. McGavan	30	"	6	do
Mary Conway	59	Cork	4	Digby
J. Cullen	25	Leitrim	1	Halifax
Patrick Brien	28	Kerry	3	do
J. Day	30	Limerick	2	Digby
Marg[t] Mahany	18	Cork	1	Digby
J. Righley	34	Galway	5	Annapolis
M. Glassin	37	Cork	4	do
Patrick Welch	40	"	3	do
J. Noonan	30	"	3	Halifax
Ja[s] Fitzgerald	21	Donegal	1	Digby
Tho[s] Wrenn & sister	26	[Latrim]	2	Peticodiac
J. London & 3 sisters	25	Limerick	4	Fredericton
P. Duff	55	"	5	Gagetown
Brid[t] Mack	30	Kerry	2	Fredericton
Jerry Donahue	38	"	3	do
J. O'Connor	34	Limerick	6	Halifax
John Donnellin	52	Clare	5	do
T. Dooley	38	Tipperary	6	do
M. Hoare	48	Kerry	4	do
T. Cassine	36	"	6	do
D. Curren	27	"	5	do
Mich[l] Farrel	32	Sligo	4	Yarmouth
J. Gorman	26	Limerick	4	do
M. Mahar	48	Tipperary	10	St. Andrews
Elizabeth Harbour	40	Kerry	8	do
Joanna Foley	23	"	1	do

56   Irish Migration To New England: Port of Saint John

Julia Griffin	20	"	1	do
Mary Foley	27	Galway	1	Halifax
Rebecca Common	35	[Latrim]	1	St. Stephen
John Leekey	26	Galway	3	Quoddy West
William Flinn	26	Tipperary	3	Cornwallis
James Conner	46	Kerry	5	Annapolis
Mich[l] Brien	35	Cork	3	do
Mary McDonough	20	Sligo	1	do
Marg[t] McCarthy	25	Co. Sligo	1	Annapolis
Bridget Wynn	22	"	1	do
Catherine Lee	21	[Latrim]	1	Digby
Catherine Caveny	20	"	1	do
Mary Lovett	26	Kerry	2	West Quoddy
William Stack	40	"	7	St. Andrews
J. Lloyd	38	Tipperary	5	do
William Finn	21	"	2	do
Judith Righley	25	Limerick	2	do
Bridget Call	19	Cork	2	do
Mary Ann White	20	"	1	do
Margaret Donovan	30	"	1	do
Ann Bateman	23	"	1	do
Ellen Shey	40	"	7	Fredericton
Mary Clifford	24	"	1	do
Honoria Rairdon	16	"	1	do
J. Callahan	25	Kerry	1	do
John McCarty	34	"	5	Halifax
Mich[l] Falvy	32	"	1	do
Patrick Kavanah	21	"	1	do
James Leighey	40	Cork	7	do
Patrick Kellahan	23	"	2	do
John Hannon	31	"	6	do
John Murphy	30	"	4	Annapolis
Mary Larkin	25	Galway	2	St. Stephen
William Noonan	38	Limerick	7	Halifax
Alex[r] Shehan	30	Kerry	1	do
Margaret Fee	30	Ferman[h]	1	Digby
Patrick Keefe	32	Clare	3	Annapolis
Patrick McGuire	47	Ferman[h]	5	do
Murty Nowlin	40	Ferman[h]	5	Annapolis
John Sheridan	22	Cavan	3	do
James Spring	25	Kerry	3	do
Maurice Brian	23	"	2	do
James O'Harron	25	Tipperary	3	do

Port of Saint John: Emigrant Poor 1842   57

William Carrol	21	"	2	do
Mary Coleman	25	Sligo	1	do
Patrick Carrol	40	Cork	7	Halifax
Daniel Swinney	26	"	3	do
James Armstrong	53	Sligo	6	St. David
Daniel Hogan	35	Cork	4	Annapolis
John Mahegan	48	"	4	do
John Flaghan	27	Kerry	4	do
Joseph Eaton	32	"	4	Maitland N.S.
Isabella Boyle	20	Donegal	1	Halifax
P. McLaughlan	27	[Latrim]	4	Maitland N.S.
Thomas Welch	32	Cork	1	Annapolis
Frances Welch	30	"	5	Halifax
Patrick Barret	38	"	1	Annapolis
William Carrol	27	"	1	do
Thomas Rairdon	40	Limerick	2	do
Ellen Scanlin	23	"	2	St. Andrews
Thomas Corcoran	23	Roscom^n	6	do
John Burke	41	Tipperary	5	do
Patrick Malone	33	Louth	3	Annapolis
David Keefe	22	Cork	1	do
John Kennedy	32	Kerry	2	do
Cornelius Kennedy	22	"	1	do
Edward Kennedy	50	Limerick	2	Halifax
Mary Keily	26	Cork	2	Yarmouth
Samuel Merrick	30	Co. Cork	3	Halifax
Eliza Beatty	20	Westmeath	1	do
William Keyburn	22	"	1	do
Bridget McGuire	19	Ferman^h	2	Fredericton
Timothy Scannel	32	Cork	1	St. Stephen
John Hanley	27	"	3	Halifax
Jane Coil	30	Donegal	1	Fredericton
Mary Bresnahan	26	Kerry	3	Annapolis
John Wallace	23	Tyrone	1	Quoddy West
Frances Bustard	23	Donegal	3	Back to Ireland
Miche Fitzgibbon	24	Cork	1	St. Andrews
Ellen Harrington	25	"	3	Fredericton
James Taylor	25	Ferman^h	5	Annapolis
John O'Brien	19	Cork	1	Halifax
Corn^s Mahany	30	Kerry	3	do
Daniel Rairdon	22	"	4	do
John Collins	30	Cork	6	do
Ann Sullivan	26	Kerry	3	St. Andrews

Name	Age	Origin		Destination
Mary Sullivan 2^d	30	Cork	1	St. Stephen
Judy Rohan	29	Galway	3	do
Ellen Fletcher	22	Ferman^h	2	Halifax
Patrick Rohan	36	Galway	1	St. Stephen
David Livingston	36	Kircudbright, Scotland	7	Peticodiac
George Lahey	30	Co. Cavan	6	do
Richd Carlin	36	Donegal	7	Liverpool N.S.
Sarah Hassen	21	Kerry	1	Fredericton
Mary Hassen	27	"	1	do
Mary Fitzgerald	30	Tipperary	4	Halifax
Arthur O'Keefe	28	Cork	2	do
John Fitzgibbon	24	"	2	do
Daniel Lyon	27	Co. Cork	2	Halifax
William Kelly	20	Roscom^n	1	Annapolis
James Lee	30	Cork	4	Quoddy West
Bridget Matcheson	16	Clare	1	Annapolis
William Gorman	22	Donegal	2	Liverpool N.S.
John McGachie	28	"	5	Liverpool N.S.
Patrick Connolly	26	Sligo	2	St. Stephen
Richd Donovan	25	Cork	4	Liverpool N.S.
Jer^h Driscol	32	"	2	Halifax
Jer^h Dempsey	28	"	2	do
Jane Chute	23	Kerry	3	do
Mary Sullivan	16	Cork	1	Hampton N.B.
Ellen Sullivan	19	"	1	St. Stephen
Mary White 2nd	30	"	1	Halifax
Mary Ann Allen	21	Belfast	1	Yarmouth
Charles Quinn	33	Donegal	4	Digby
Mary Tracy	40	Cork	2	Halifax
Ellen Courtney	50	Derry	1	do
Peter Connolly	21	Cavan	3	Lpool Lburgh or Halifax
Charles Dougherty	16	Donegal	1	Annapolis
Denis Cleary	40	Cavan	8	Lpool Lburgh or Halifax
Patrick Burke	20	"	3	" "
Ellen McGowan	46	[Latrim]	7	" "
Denis McMorrow	30	"	4	" "
Terrence Lee	23	"	2	" "
Abigail McGantry	23	"	1	" "
Cathe Gilgoure	17	"	1	" "
Marg^t Trower	20	"	1	" "
Margaret Kane	22	Galway	1	Yarmouth
Michael Nowlin	23	Cavan	3	Liverpool N.S.

Port of Saint John: Emigrant Poor 1842

Name	Age	County	#	Destination
Edward Callahan	18	Co. Derry	1	Liverpool N.S.
John Kelly	22	[Latrim]	2	"
Brien Kelly	22	"	2	Yarmouth
Catherine Flinn	22	Ferman[h]	1	Halifax
Bridget Condahy	16	Tipperary	1	Lpool, Lburgh or Halifax
Felix Tierney	43	Tyrone	7	St. Andrews
Mary Meloy	28	Mayo	2	"
Mary O'Brien	44	Cork	2	Halifax
Isabella Thompson	18	Belfast	2	Quoddy West
Catherine Bryan	22	Cork	1	Yarmouth
Mary Ingram	22	Donegal	1	do
Eliza Hiney	30	Westmeath	2	do
Bowen Chute	14	Kerry	1	do
Nancy McNamara	20	Clare	1	do
Ann Garrity	20	Galway	1	do
Mary Bresnahan	36	Kerry	3	Windsor
Miche Sullivan	30	Cork	1	St. Stephen
Mary Lahey	25	Cork	2	Lpool, Lburgh or Halifax
Phillip Kelly	34	"	4	" "
Denis Kane	23	"	4	" "
Patrick Mahaney	35	"	1	" "
John Shey	18	Kerry	1	St. Stephen
Jane O'Harron	20	Cork	2	do
George Leighy	30	Cavan	1	Fredericton
Anthony Kilroy	19	"	1	do
Henry Matthews	30	Louth	2	Annapolis
Ja[s] Fitzsimmons	25	Meath	1	do
Batley Loughlane	22	Donegal	2	Liverpool N.S.
Mary McCardle	26	Sligo	2	Lpool, Lburgh or Halifax
Elizabeth Fevans	17	[Latrim]	1	" "
Danniel Basset	30	Co. Cork	2	Fredericton
Thomas Daley	45	Galway	7	St. Andrews
Jerem[h] Murphy	29	Cork	5	Fredericton
Mary Connor	17	Kerry	1	Yarmouth
Mary Kilkoyn	21	Sligo	1	do
Mary Callahan	25	Cork	1	St. Stephen
Marg[t] O'Donnel	21	Limerick	1	Yarmouth
Patrick Cooney	28	Clare	2	St. Stephen
John B. Farrar	25	London	1	Halifax
W[m] Hutchinson	38	Yorkshire	6	Peticodiac
Ann Cavil	17	Galway	1	St. Stephen
John Swinney	37	Cork	3	Fredericton
Mary McArthur	29	Donegal	1	Halifax

60   Irish Migration To New England: Port of Saint John

Mary Pye	53	Sligo	3	do
Timothy Hart	24	Cork	3	St. Stephen
John Welch	37	Kerry	9	Truro N.S.
Ann Boyle	25	Louth	1	Fredericton
Ellen Burke	23	Cork	1	Annapolis
Mary McGaffagon	47	Donegal	1	St. Stephen
Mary Finn	23	Cork	1	"
Mary McEwe	38	Derry	2	Yarmouth
Brid^t McNamara	18	Clare	1	"
Martin McHugh	25	Sligo	3	Quoddy West
Joanna Donavan	20	Cork	1	St. Stephen
Margaret White	25	"	1	"
Joanna Murphy	30	"	1	"
Thomas Creighton	31	Glasgow	1	Fredericton
John O'Brien	50	Co. Cork	3	Halifax
William Kelly	35	Down	5	Lpool, Lburgh or Halifax
Patrick Mahany	25	Galway	6	" "
Bridget Fahy alais Kennedy	17	Galway	1	Quoddy
Margaret Higgins	27	"	4	Fredericton
Laurance Hickey	38	Tipperay	6	Halifax or Lpool
Jane Fitzgerald	24	Donegal	1	Gagetown
Nathe Thomas	60	[Gloster], England	3	Fredericton

Deceased indigent Immigrants [intered] at the Expense of the Overseers of the Poor of the City during the Year 1842 [P.A.N.B. Emigrations RS 8 Micro F7891

Name	Age	Nativity	Place of Interment
From Hospitals & other Parish houses:			
Joseph Connolly	9	[Latrim]	St. Malachys Church Yard
Jane Boyd	31	Armagh	Trinity Church Yard
Eliza J. O'Brien	Inf^t	Child	do
Jerem^h O'Brien	28	Co. Cork	do
Mary Lee	23	Limerick	St. Malachys Church Yard
Patrick Gorman	3	Cork	do
Mary E. McCarty	Inf^t	Child	Trinity Church Yard
Andrew Bustard	28	Co. Donegal	do
Daniel Connelly	4	[Latrim]	St. Malachys Church Yard
John McLaughlin	6	"	Trinity Church Yard
William Crowley	25	Cork	do
Patrick Hyde	40	"	do

Mary Gannivan	60	"		St. Malachys Church Yard
Catherine Burke	22	"		do
George Stevens	Inf^t	Child		do
Ann McDermot	3	Co. Donegal		Trinity Church Yard
Catherine Cronin	Inf^t	Child		do
Patrick Barry	20	Co. Cork		St. Malachys Church Yard
Patrick Dooley	21	Galway		Trinity Church Yard
Patrick Ryan	40	Tipperary		do
Mary Hatherman	50	Limerick		St. Malachys Church Yard
Bridget McKennah	3	[Latrim]		Trinity Church Yard
Margaret Lee	Inf$\underline{t}$	Child		St. Malchys Church Yard
Thomas Flinn	3	Co. [Latrim]		do
Mary Cunningham	1½	Welsford		Trinity Church Yard
John Daulton	22	Co. Cork		Trinity Church Yard
Honoria Melerick	25	"		do
John Sterling	60	Norfolk Eng^d		
Morris Delay	27	Co. Cork		St. Malachys Church Yard
Francis Callahan	28	"		do
Ellen Murphy	1½	"		Trinity Church Yard

From Private houses in the City:

Mary Crowley	2½	Co. Cork	St. Malachys Church Yard
Thomas McGachie	4	Derry	Trinity Church Yard
Bridget Keefe	2	Cork	St. Malachys Church Yard
Mich^l Slattery	Inf^t	Child	do
Michael Kennevan	Inf^t	Child	do
William Morgan	16	Co. Cork	do
John O'Donnel	25	Limerick	Trinity Church Yard
Patrick Driscol	5	Cork	St. Malachys Church Yard
Joanna Murphy	2	"	do
Morgan Clifford	28	Limerick	Trinity Church Yard
Sarah Birmingham	24	"	do
Catherine Crowley	Inf^t	Child	St. Malachys Church Yard
Marg^t McAllen	Inf^t	Child	do
Julia Barret	Inf^t	Child	do
John Finn	Inf^t	Child	do
Rachel Armstrong	Inf^t	Child	Trinity Church Yard
Honoria Sullivan	3	Co. Cork	St. Malachys Church Yard
Cathe McMahan	60	Clare	do

The Lunatic Asylum 1842

Record of Lunatics in the Temporary Asylum in the City of Saint John admitted in the Year 1842 - *Journals of House of Assembly 1843 Appendix, Geo. Matthew, late Superintendent* dates of admission, discharge, death, age, native place, last residence

Thomas Partelow — admitted Jan. 1, 1842 dis. Mar. 27, 1843; 39, Saint John, Sydney Ward, St. John

Edwd McLaughlan — admitted Jan. 4, 1842 dis. Feb. 12, 1842; 40, Derry, Dukes Ward, St. John

Matthew Teat — admitted Jan. 6, 1842 remaining 1844; 29, Saint John, Kings Co.

Perez Cogan — admitted Jan. 10, 1842 dis. Feb. 22, 1842; 40, Cork, Dukes Ward, St. John

Ann Cassidy — admitted Jan. 13, 1842 dis. Sept. 21, 1842; 40, Armagh, Charlotte Co.

John Gillan — admitted Jan. 17, 1842 dis. May 6, 1842; 34, Antrim, Portland Parish, St. John

Robert Murkersu — admitted Jan. 18, 1842 dis. July 31, 1842; 44, Aughternrety, Scotland, Grand Manan

Denis McAnully — admitted Feb. 10, 1842 dis. Mar. 7, 1842; 25, Donegal, York Co.

Lucy Dennis — admitted Feb. 19, 1842 dis. Oct. 8, 1842; 20, Fredericton, Portland Parish, St. John

Grigor Urquhart — admitted Mar. 18, 1842 dis. May 18, 1842; 39, London, Pictou, N.S.

Thomas Mulcahy — admitted March 24, 1842 remaining 1844; 36, Kilkenny, Portland Parish, St. John

Catherine Heally — admitted Mar. 26, 1842 dis. Apr. 20, 1842; 17, Cork, Portland Parish, St. John

Elizabeth Lavery — admitted March 27, 1842 remaining 1844; 37, Armagh, Charlotte Co.

Eliza Gamblin — admitted Apr. 8, 1842 dis. June 1, 1842; 26, Plymouth, Kings Co.

William Divine — admitted Apr. 11, 1842 dis Jan. 5, 1843; 24, Derry, Simonds Par., St. John

Elizabeth McGee — admitted Apr. 16, 1842 remaining 1844; 46, Fermanagh, Queens Ward, St. John

Martha Hunter — admitted Apr. 22, 1842 eloped Apr. 26, 1842; 24, Derry, Kings Ward, St. John

Marian Hopper — admitted May 9, 1842 dis. May 17, 1842; 28, Leith, Scot., Queens Ward, St. John

Robert Buchanan — admitted May 23, 1842 dis. May 26, 1842; 20, Donegal, Kings Ward, St. John

Theresa J. Sharpe — admitted May 31, 1842 *died June 27, 1842*; 6,

Mary Holloran	Portland, Kings Co. admitted June 3, 1842 dis. June 4, 1842; 27, Donegal, Sydney Ward, St. John
John B. Power	admitted June 6, 1842 dis. July 11, 1842; 20, Cork, Ireland direct
Diana Armstrong	admitted July 4, 1842 dis. Aug. 5, 1842; 30, Louth, Ireland direct
William Ray	admitted July 4, 1842 remaining 1844; 30, Waterford, Ireland direct & P.E.I.
Francis Lynn	admitted July 8, 1842 eloped Nov 13, 1843; 36, Derry, Charlotte Co.
Jeremiah Shey	admitted July 11, 1842 dis. July 18, 1842; 35, Kerry, Ireland direct
John Goodwin	admitted July 13, 1842 dis. Mar. 27, 1843; 20, Saint John, Kings Ward, St. John
John Russell	admitted July 16, 1842 dis. Oct. 19, 1842; 51, Is. Guernsey, Northumberland
John G. Proctor	admitted July 31, 1842 dis. Aug. 31, 1842; 35, Yorkshire, U.S.A. & York Co.
Thomas Gough	admitted Aug. 4, 1842 dis. Aug. 27, 1842; 42, Down, York Co.
Mary Gamage	admitted Aug. 7, 1842 dis. Aug. 16, 1842; 36, Limerick, Windsor, N.S.
William Gloster	admitted Aug. 8, 1842 dis. Aug. 16, 1842; 20, Limerick, Ireland direct & U.S
Mary Whelan	admitted Aug. 12, 1842 dis. Aug. 29, 1842; 25, Clare, Queens Ward, St. John
Mary Kinnear	admitted Aug. 23, 1842 *died 1844 of chronic dysentry*; 50, Westmorland, Westmorland.
Richard Fielding	admitted Sep. 10, 1842 dis. Oct. 10, 1842; 25, Kilkenny, Ire, Charlotte Co.
Robert Duncan	admitted Oct. 7, 1842 dis. July 8, 1843 sent home to Scotland; 32, Ayrshire, U.S. & Charlotte Co.
Jane Thomas	admitted Oct. 13, 1842 *died 1844 of cancer of the womb*; 35, Limerick, England direct
John Cosh	admitted Oct. 26, 1842 dis. Jan 5, 1843; 39, Tyrone, England direct
John Kilpatrick	admitted Nov. 16, 1842 dis. Mar. 22, 1843; 56, Tyrone, Queens Ward, St. John
Peter Clarke	admitted Dec. 8, 1842 eloped Jan. 9, 1843; 52, Woodstock, Carleton Co.
John Gallagher	admitted Dec. 27, 1842 dis. May 6, 1843; 57, Tyrone, Nova Scotia & Kings Co.
Catherine Collins	admitted Dec. 29, 1842 dis. Jan. 16, 1843; 54, Donegal, Kings Co.
William Johnston	admitted Dec. 31, 1842 dis. Mar. 27, 1843; 52, Philadelphia, U.S. & York Co.

Emigrants in the Alms And Work House For City & County of St. John, N.B.

Register of Admissions to the new Alms and Work House, East Side, Courtenay Bay from the Portland Alms House, City Infirmary including age, place of nativity, from which Parish and Circumstance from April 21st, 1843 to August 10th, 1843 [Original Admission Book, New Brunswick Museum, Saint John]

George Fawcet, 63, Donegal, Ire., admitted Apr. 21, 1843 from Portland Alms House, destitute and infirm, *transfer to record book Aug. 16, 1843*

Isabella Fawcet, 52, Leitrim, Ire., admitted Apr. 21, 1843 from Portland Alms House, destitute and infirm, *transfer to record book Aug. 16, 1843*

Michael Wilson, 38, Waterford, Ire., admitted Apr. 21, 1843 from Portland Alms House, destitute and lame, discharged July 7, 1843 by order of commissioners.

William Coleman, Waterford, Ire., admitted Apr. 21, 1843 from Portland Alms House, discharged Aug. 16, 1843 by his own wishes

Patrick Russel, 63, Cork, Ire., admitted Apr. 21, 1843 from Portland Alms House, to infirmary June 22 to July 12 except Sunday, *transfer to record book Aug. 16, 1843*

James White, 60, St. John, N.B., admitted Apr. 21, 1843 from Portland Alms House, destitute and invalid, discharged May 8, 1843, removed to infirmary

James McWade, 25, Tyrone, Ireland, admitted Apr. 21, 1843 from Portland Alms House, destitute and healthy, *transfer to record book Aug. 16, 1843* by his own wishes

Henry Dalton, 36, Plymouth, England, admitted Apr. 21, 1843 from Portland Alms House, blind, discharged June 26, 1843, left on his own accord

Isabella Laird, 71, Donegal, Ire., admitted Apr. 21, 1843 from Portland Alms House, *transfer to record book Aug. 16, 1843*

Harriet Atkins, 42, Sussex, Eng., admitted Apr. 21, 1843 from Portland Alms House, discharged Aug. 10, 1843 on her own accord

Port of Saint John: Alms & Work House Records 1843   65

Mary Sheridan, 70, Waterford, Ire., admitted Apr. 21, 1843 from Portland Alms House, discharged June 15, 1843, left

Mary Jones, 28, Cardigan, Wales, admitted Apr. 21, 1843 from Portland Alms House, destitute and lazy, discharged June 16, 1843, left premises on her own

Agness Taylor, 18, Greenock, Scot., admitted Apr. 21, 1843 from Portland Alms House, idiot, *transfer to record book Aug. 16, 1843*

Rosana McCoy, 25, Donegal, Ire., admitted Apr. 21, 1843 from Portland Alms House, discharged Aug. 16, 1843 by order of commissioners

Hugh McCoy, 2, admitted Apr. 21, 1843 from Portland Alms House, *transfer to record book Aug. 16, 1843*

John McCoy, 4, New Brunswick, admitted Apr. 21, 1843 from Portland Alms House, *transfer to record book Aug. 16, 1843*

Margaret Boyd, 20, Cavan, Ire., admitted Apr. 21, 1843 from Portland Alms House, discharged June 27, 1843, went to Boston

James Boyd, 1 1/3 year, Cavan, Ire., admitted Apr. 21, 1843 from Portland Alms House, discharged June 27, 1843, went to Boston with mother

Jane Hunter, 3, New Brunswick, admitted Apr. 21, 1843 from Portland Alms House, *transfer to record book Aug. 16, 1843*

Sellia McDonald, 6, admitted Apr. 21, 1843 from Portland Alms House, discharged May 30, 1843, taken away by mother

Edwd. McDonald, 4, admitted Apr. 21, 1843 from Portland Alms House, discharged May 30, 1843, taken away by mother

Cather. McDonald, 1 2/3, admitted Apr. 21, 1843 from Portland Alms House, discharged May 30, 1843, taken away by mother

William Densmore, 10, cripple, admitted Apr. 21, 1843 from Portland Alms House, *transfer to record book Aug. 16, 1843*

John Densmore, 8, admitted Apr. 21, 1843 from Portland Alms House, discharged Aug. 10, 1843, sent to Geo. Trowe? P. Lancaster to be a farmer

Mary Stewart, 74, Greenock, Scot., admitted Apr. 26, 1843, from Simonds, one eye, discharged June 12, 1843,

Infirmary 12 days, finally left

Mary Dowds, admitted Apr. 25, 1843, from Portland, discharged May 1, 1843, taken away by Patrick Dowds by order of J. Gallagher

Margaret Dowds, admitted Apr. 25, 1843, from Portland, discharged May 1, 1843, taken away by Patrick Dowds by order of J. Gallagher

Bridget Dowds, admitted Apr. 25, 1843, from Portland, discharged May 1, 1843, taken away by Patrick Dowds by order of J. Gallagher

James Dowd, admitted Apr. 25, 1843, from Infirmary, discharged April 27, 1843, sent to mother at Infirmary

Garret Fitzpatrick, 60, Ireland, admitted Apr. 29, 1843, from City Infirmary, *transfer to record book Aug. 16, 1843*

William Freal, 72, Donegal, Ire., admitted Apr. 29, 1843, from City Infirmary, *transfer to record book Aug. 16, 1843*

Gabriel Cane, 76, Hungary, admitted Apr. 29, 1843, from City Infirmary, *transfer to record book Aug. 16, 1843*

Bryant Doyle, admitted Apr. 29, 1843, from City Infirmary, discharged June 27, 1843,

removed to Infirmary till June 7

Elizabeth Currey, 55, Quebec, admitted Apr. 29, 1843, from City Infirmary, *transfer to record book Aug. 16, 1843*, Infirmary 12 days finally left

Mary Brenen, 30, Cork, Ire., admitted Apr. 29, 1843 from City Infirmary, *transfer to record book Aug. 16, 1843*, Infirmary 12 days finally left

John Brenen, 5, St. John, N.B., *transfer to record book Aug. 16, 1843*, mother here also

Mary Timms, Lanca, Ire., admitted Apr. 29, 1843 from City Infirmary, discharged May 15, 1843, sent to Infirmary

Hannah Dee, 20, Ireland, admitted Apr. 29, 1843 from City Infirmary, discharged June 27, went to Boston

Dennis Dee, 1/3, admitted Apr. 29, 1843 discharged June 27, 1843, went with mother

Elizabeth George, 6, Calais, admitted Apr. 29, 1843 from Infirmary, *transfer to record book Aug. 16, 1843*

William Roney, 12, N.B., admitted Apr. 29, 1843 from Infirmary, healthy, *transfer to record book Aug. 16, 1843*

Turrents McIntyre, 10, Ireland,

Port of Saint John: Alms & Work House Records 1843   67

admitted Apr. 29, 1843, bound to Elisha Fowler of Norton, K.C. When of age to get 2 common suits, 1 holiday suit & yoke 2 old steers

William McIntyre, 8, Ireland, admitted Apr. 29, 1843, *transfer to record book Aug. 16, 1843*

John Golding, 7, N.B., admitted Apr. 29, 1843, discharged June 15, 1843, taken away by mother

James H. Golding, 5, N.B., admitted Apr. 29, 1843, discharged June 15, 1843, taken away by mother

Margaret Jordon, 6, admitted Apr. 29, 1843, discharged June 13, 1843, taken away by Cathr. Jordon

Morris Herren, 10 mos., admitted Apr. 29, 1843, died June 14, 1843, buried in the premises

Enora M. Lachey, 5, admitted Apr. 29, 1843, *transfer to record book Aug. 16, 1843*, discharged May 1, 1843, taken by father by order of J. Gallagher.

James Dowd, admitted Apr. 29, 1843

Hannah Leary, 9, admitted Apr. 29, 1843, *transfer to record book Aug. 16, 1843,*

Ellen O'Neil, 3, admitted Apr. 29, 1843, *transfer to record book Aug. 16, 1843*

Mary Mcarty, 12, admitted Apr. 29, 1843, *transfer to record book Aug. 16, 1843,*

Donald Mcarty, 6, admitted Apr. 29, 1843, *transfer to record book Aug. 16, 1843,*

Mary A. Daley, 4, St. John, N.B., admitted Apr. 29, 1843, discharged May 9, 1843, taken away by Wm Shannohan & Julia Daily to Boston to father

Catherine Kelley, 40, Tyrone, Ire., admitted May 2, 1843 from City Infirmary, *transfer to record book Aug. 16, 1843*, sent to Infirmary

Hugh Kelley, 5, St. John, N.B., admitted May 2, 1843 from City Infirmary, *transfer to record book Aug. 16, 1843*

John Kelley, 3½, St. John, N.B., admitted May 2, 1843 from City Infirmary, *transfer to record book Aug. 16, 1843*

Catherine Kelley, 2½, St. John, N.B., admitted May 2, 1843 from City Infirmary, *transfer to record book Aug. 16, 1843*

Ellen Barrey, admitted May 2, 1843 from City Infirmary, discharged May 31, 1843, taken away by Patrick Barrey.

Each shirt & Scotch homespun dress

James Barrey, admitted May 2, 1843 from City Infirmary, discharged May 31, 1843

Catherine Barrey, admitted May 2, 1843 from City Infirmary, discharged May 31, 1843

Ewd. Dunahue, admitted May 3, 1843, discharged May 4, left with consent

Mary Brymer, 70, Derry, Ire., admitted May 5, 1843 from Portland, *transfer to record book Aug. 16, 1843*, sent to Infirmary

Bernard Dougherty, 37, Donegal, Ire., admitted May 6, 1843 from City Infirmary, *transfer to record book Aug. 16, 1843*

Mary Conner, 20, Ireland, admitted May 6, 1843, discharged June 27, 1843, went to Boston

Ellen Conner, 1½, St. John, N.B., admitted May 6, 1843 from City Infirmary, discharged June 27, 1843, went to Boston with mother

Mary Blake, 60, Donegal, Ire., admitted May 6, 1843 from City Infirmary, *transfer to record book Aug. 16, 1843*, went to Boston

Ellen McCarty, 21, Donegal, Ire., admitted May 6, 1843 from City Infirmary, discharged June 27, 1843, went to Boston

Mary A. McCarty, 5 mos., St. John, N.B., admitted May 6, 1843 from City Infirmary, discharged June 28, 1843, went to Boston with mother

Nicholas Wise, 54, St. John, N.B., admitted May 10, 1843 from City Infirmary, discharged May 31, 1843, sent to Infirmary

Elizabeth Dunion, 23, Cork, Ire., admitted May 10, 1843 from City Infirmary, May 29, 1843, by order of commissioners

John Dunion, 3, St. John, N.B., admitted May 10, 1843 from City Infirmary, discharged May 29, 1843, went with mother Elizabeth

Catherine Dunion, 8 mos., St. John, N.B., admitted May 10, 1843 from City Infirmary, discharged May 29, 1843, went with mother Elizabeth

Ellen McLauclan, 27, Down, Ire., admitted May 10, 1843 from City Infirmary, *transfer to record book Aug. 16, 1843*, by order of commissioners

Hugh McLauclan, 1¼, Pisarico N.B., admitted May 10, 1843 from City Infirmary

Port of Saint John: Alms & Work House Records 1843

Allecia Forsythe, 41, Tyrone, Ire., admitted May 10, 1843 from County St. John, *transfer to record book Aug. 16, 1843*, by order of commissioners

Fanny Forsythe, 8½, Tyrone, Ire., admitted May 10, 1843 from County St. John, *transfer to record book Aug. 16, 1843*

George Forsythe, 6½, Tyrone, Ire., admitted May 10, 1843 from County St. John, discharged July 17, 1843

Wm Forsythe, 3, St. John, N.B., admitted May 10, 1843 from County St. John, *transfer to record book Aug. 16, 1843*

Ths. M. McCarty, 63, Cork, Ire., admitted May 11, 1843 from City Infirmary, discharged June 14, 1843, went to Boston

Caroline Hachay, 19, Dublin, Ire., admitted May 11, 1843 from St. John, *transfer to record book Aug. 16, 1843*, at Infirmary 22 May to 31st July

Catherine Collings, 54, Donegal, Ire., admitted May 11, 1843 from Portland, discharged July 11, 1843, left

Michael Murphy, 60, Carlow, Ire., admitted May 11, 1843 from City Infirmary, *transfer to record book Aug. 16, 1843*

Thomas Partelow, 40, St. John, N.B., admitted May 11, 1843 from St. John, *transfer to record book Aug. 16, 1843*

Timothy Ring, 55, Cork, Ire., admitted May 15, 1843 from Infirmary, *transfer to record book Aug. 16, 1843*

Emily Oakley, 30, London, England, admitted May 20, 1843 from St. John, discharged May 30, 1843, left

Eliezer Oakley, 7, Birmingham, England, admitted May 20, 1843 from St. John, discharged July 3, 1843, taken away by mother

Patrick Ryon, 50, Tipperary, Ire., admitted May 22, 1843 from St. John

Ellen Ryon, 40, Tipperary, Ire., admitted May 22, 1843 from St. John, discharged July 25, 1843, sent to Infirmary

Thomas Ryon, 3½, St. John, N.B., admitted May 22, 1843 from St. John, discharged July 25, 1843, went with mother to Infirmary

Mary A. Ryon, 9 mos., St. John, N.B., admitted May 22, 1843 from St. John, discharged July 25, 1843, went with mother to Infirmary

Thomas Eastcock, 43, Oxfordshire, Eng., admitted

May 23, 1843 from Infirmary, discharged June 2, 1843, sent to Infirmary

James Oakley, 38, London, Eng., admitted May 25, 1843, from St. John, healthy, discharged May 30, 1843, left for Boston

Daniel Fraser, Scotland, admitted May 29, 1843 from Infirmary, *transfer to record book Aug. 16, 1843*

Mary A. Driskil, 3½, St. John, N.B., admitted June 3, 1843 from St. John, discharged June 28, 1843, sent to Infirmary to mother

William Kelly, 50, Dublin, Ire., one leg, admitted June 11, 1843 from Infirmary, *transfer to record book Aug. 16, 1843*

William Donoldson, 74, Donegal, Ire., cripple, admitted June 15, 1843 from Infirmary, *transfer to record book Aug. 16, 1843*

Susan McGraugh, 32, Fermanagh, Ire., admitted June 15, 1843 from Infirmary, discharged Aug. 15, 1843, by order of commissioners, infirm June 22 to July 22

Patrick Quin, 60, Tyrone, Ire., one eye, admitted June 22, 1843 from Infirmary, *transfer to record book Aug. 16, 1843*

Thomas Gately, 33, Roscommon, Ire., admitted July 4, 1843 from Infirmary, *transfer to record book Aug. 16, 1843*, by order of commissioners

Mathew Rairdon, admitted July 12, 1843 from Infirmary, discharged July 14, 1843, got employment

Mary Gately, admitted July 21, 1843 from Infirmary, *transfer to record book Aug. 16, 1843*, by order of commissioners

Patrick Gately, admitted July 21, 1843 from Infirmary, *transfer to record book Aug. 16, 1843*

Fanny Forsythe, 8½, Tyrone, Ire., admitted July 26, 1843 from St. Martins, discharged July 31, 1843, went to Mr. J. Marsters

Thomas Ryon, 3½, St. John, N.B., admitted July 27 from Infirmary, *transfer to record book Aug. 16, 1843*, by order of commissioners

M.A. Ryon, 9 mos., St. John, N.B., admitted July 27 from Infirmary, *transfer to record book Aug. 16, 1843*, by order of commissioners

John Barber, Isle of Jersey, admitted July 28 from Infirmary, discharged July 29, 1843, got employment

Port of Saint John: Alms & Work House Records 1843

Thomas Wier, 56, London, Eng., admitted July 28 from Infirmary, *transfer to record book Aug. 16, 1843*, by order of commissioners

Ellen Ryon, 40, Tipperary, Ire., admitted July 31 from Infirmary, *transfer to record book Aug. 16, 1843, by order of commissioners*

Eliza - , infant, St. John, N.B., *transfer to record book Aug. 16, 1843*

Jane MacMullen, healthy, admitted Aug. 3, 1843 from Infirmary, *transfer to record book Aug. 16, 1843*, by order of commissioners

Wm McMullen, 7 mos., St. John, N.B., healthy, admitted Aug. 3, 1843 from Infirmary, *transfer to record book Aug. 16, 1843*

John Brown, 47, Kerry, Ire., admitted Aug. 4, 1843 from Infirmary, *transfer to record book Aug. 16, 1843*

Dorah Patton, 34, Bandon, Ire., healthy, admitted Aug. 5, 1843 from Infirmary, *transfer to record book Aug. 16, 1843*, by order of commissioners

Joseph Patton, 8, Bandon, Ire., healthy, admitted Aug. 5, 1843, *transfer to record book Aug. 16, 1843*

Elizabeth Patton, 4, New Brunswick, healthy, admitted Aug. 5, 1843, *transfer to record book Aug. 16, 1843*

William Roney, 12, New Brunswick, healthy, admitted Aug. 5, 1843, *transfer to record book Aug. 16, 1843*

Saml Clarke, 50, Tyrone, Ire., admitted Aug. 8, 1843, *transfer to record book Aug. 16, 1843*

Thos. O'Bryan, 90, Tyrone, Ire., healthy, admitted Aug. 9, 1843 from Portland, *transfer to record book Aug. 16, 1843*

Willm McGoveren, 50, Ferman^h, Ire., admitted Aug. 10, 1843 from St. John, *transfer to record book Aug. 16, 1843*

Mary Seymores, admitted Aug. 16, 1843, *transfer to record book Aug. 16, 1843*

The Lunatic Asylum 1843

Record of Lunatics in the Temporary Asylum in the City of Saint John admitted in the Year 1843
Journals of House of Assembly 1844 Appendix, Geo. Matthew, late Superintendent - dates of admission and discharge, age, nativity, last residence

Ann McConnel	admitted Jan. 1, 1843 dis. June 1, 1843; 21, Derry, Ireland direct
Susan McGraw	admitted Jan. 1,1843 dis. June 3, 1843; 31, Fermanagh, Simonds Parish, St. John
Ann Cassidy	admitted Jan. 11, 1843 dis. April, 19, 1843; 52, Dublin, Charlotte Co.
Mary Gahagan	admitted Jan. 12, 1843 dis. Feb. 3, 1843; 48, Donegal, Ireland direct
James Dogherty	admitted Jan. 17, 1843 dis. Mar. 11, 1843; 21, Saint John, Queens Ward, St. John
Dorah Gillan	admitted Feb. 9, 1843 dis. Mar. 20, 1843; 34, Cork, Queens Ward, St. John
John Gillan	admitted Feb. 13, 1843 eloped Aug. 9, 1843; 35, Antrim, Kings Co.
Margaret O'Donnel	admitted Feb. 13, 1843 dis. May 27, 1843; 26, Fermanagh, Queens Ward, St. John
Jane Fitzgerald	admitted Feb. 22, 1843 dis May 19, 1843; 25, Donegal, Queens Co.
William Ellison	admitted March 1, 1843; 53, Down, Simond Parish, St. John
John Carter	admitted March 7, 1843 dis. Aug. 29, 1843; 36, Sligo, York Co.
Rowland Bunting	admitted March 18, 1843 dis. Apr. 21, 1843; 14, Charlotte N.B., Kings Co.
Benjamin Seymore	admitted March 24, 1843 dis. Nov. 25, 1843; 35, Cork, Kings Ward, St. John
Mercy Robson	admitted March 25, 1843; 25, Sackville, N.B., Westmorland Co.
Francis Aikin	admitted March 28, 1843 dis. Apr. 15, 1843; 36, Donegal, Dukes Ward, St. John
Andrew Kircil	admitted April 26, 1843 dis. Oct. 19, 1843; 45, Armagh, Charlotte Co.
Charlotte Hector	admitted May 14, 1843; 20, York Co., York Co. (col)
Nathan Godsoe	admitted May 23, 1843 dis. Sept. 6, 1843; 45,

Port of Saint John: Lunatic Asylum 1843   73

William Smith	Portland Parish, N.B., Queens Ward, St. John admitted May 29, 1843 *died May 31, 1843*; 60, Cavan, United States & Charlotte
Mary Ann Colman	admitted June 11, 1843 dis. July 15, 1843; 25, Dublin, Queens Ward, St. Joh
Joseph Lawrence	admitted June 17, 1843; 23, Westmorland Co. , Westmorland Co.
William Lloyd	admitted June 19, 1843 *died Oct. 20, 1843*; 50, Halifax, N.S., Kent Co.
Isaac Miller	admitted June 30, 1843; 74, Cornwallis, N.S., York Co.
William Anderson	admitted July 17, 1843; 25, Saint John, Sydney Ward, St. John
Francis Roden	admitted July 25, 1843 dis. Nov. 27, 1843; 33, Derry, Portland Parish
William J. Emslie	admitted July 28, 1843; 20, Saint John, Kings Ward, St. John
Catherine Reed	admitted Aug. 7, 1843; 39, Sackville, N.B., Westmorland Co.
Cornelius Crowley	admitted Aug. 10, 1843 dis. Sept. 10, 1843; 31, Cork, Portland Parish
Rebecca Lawrence	admitted Aug. 24, 1843 dis. Nov. 4, 1843; 18, Sackville, N.B., Nova Scotia & Eastport, U.S.
Maria McFarlan	admitted Aug. 24, 1843; 37, Sackville, N.B., Westmorland Co.
Grace Shelton	admitted Aug. 26, 1843 dis. Sept. 25, 1843; 70, Philadelphia, U.S., Kings Co.
Henry Robinson	admitted Sept. 13, 1843; 60, Down, Carleton Co.
Elizabeth McLardy	admitted Sept. 15, 1843 dis. Oct. 17, 1843; 65, Renfrewshire, Scot., Kings Ward, St. John
John Dunn	admitted Sept. 19, 1843 dis. Nov. 1, 1843; 35, Yorkshire, England, Portland Parish
James S. Stewart	admitted Sept. 25, 1843; 16, Saint John, Sydney Ward, St. John
Malvinia James	admitted Sept. 29, 1843; 31, State of Maine, U.S., United States direct
L. Magnus Westerberg	admitted Oct. 3, 1843; 34, Gottenberg, Sweden, United States direct
Alex. Lawrence	admitted Oct. 12, 1843 dis. Oct. 27, 1843; 56, Aberdeen, Scotland, Kings Co.
James Quinlan	admitted Nov. 3, 1843; 27, Kilkenny, Gloucester Co.
John Tyke	admitted Nov. 4, 1843; 50, Longford, Kent Co.
Patrick Donnelly	admitted Nov. 4, 1843; 43, Derry, Kent Co.

John Miller   admitted Nov. 4, 1843; 41, Derry, Dukes Ward, St. John
Eliza Ballentine   admitted Nov. 8, 1843; 19, Saint John, Kings Ward, St. John
Sarah A. Carleton   admitted Nov. 10, 1843; 25, Tyrone, Ireland direct
James Young   admitted Nov. 17, 1843; 45, St. Stephen, N.B., Charlotte Co.
C. Burr   admitted Dec. 23, 1843; 19, Kingsclear, York Co., York Co. (alias Debois)
Charles Carrol   admitted Dec. 27, 1843; 39, Kilkenny, Portland Parish

Emigrants Admitted to the Alms House Saint John From Vessels Arriving in 1844

Asia sailed from Derry, Ire., landed at Saint John, June 10, 1844
Elizabeth McBride, 19, R.C., Derry, Ire., adm. to Alms House Feb. 10, 1845, dis. May 13, 1845

Clio, sailed from Cork, Ire., landed at Saint John June 9, 1844
Ann O'Sullivan, 8 mos., R.C., Alms House, adm. May 1, 1845 died May 30, 1845

Gen. Parkhill, sailed from Liverpool, England, landed at New York Oct. 22, 1844
John Carberry, 18, Prot., Leitrim, Ire., adm. July 2, 1845, dis. July 16, 1845, taken away by mo.

John Francis sailed from Cork, Ire., landed at Saint John June 20, 1844, adm. to Alms House Feb. 10, 1845
Nancy Buckley, widow, 30, R.C., Cork, Ire.
Jane Buckley, 5, R.C., Cork, Ire.
John Buckley, 2 mos., R.C., Alms House, mother came in *John Francis*
Mary Harrington, 23, R.C., Cork, Ire.
Cath. Harrington, R.C., Alms House, died Oct. 17, 1845, mother came in *John Francis*

Nancy sailed from Liverpool, England, landed at Halifax, N.S. Oct. 15, 1844
John Dalton, 29, Prot., Kilkenny, Ire., adm. to Alms House Apr. 15, 1845, dis. July 3, 1845

Sovereign, sailed from Newry, Ire., landed at Saint John Sept. 2, 1844

James Coleman, 24, R.C., Down, Ire., adm. July 14, 1845 dis. Aug. 29, 1845

Thorney Close sailed from Donegal, Ire., landed at Saint John July 8, 1844.
Margt. Morrow, 24, R.C., Donegal, Ire., adm. to Alms House Feb. 10, 1845, dis. Apr. 29, 1845
Margt. Morrow jr., 15 mos., Donegal, Ire., adm. to Alms House Feb. 10, 1845, dis. Apr. 29, 1845

Mrs. Margt. Reilley, 32, Prot., Fermanagh, Ire., adm. to Alms House May 27, 1845
Arthur Reilly, 3 mos., Prot., Saint John, N.B., adm. to Alms House May 27, 1845, died Aug. 24, 1845, mother came in ***Thorney Close***

Emigrants Admitted to the Alms House Saint John From Vessels Arriving in 1845

Albion, sailed from Cork, Ire., landed at Saint John, May 28, 1845
Thos. Healy, 23, R.C., Cork, Ire., adm. June 30, 1845 dis. July 2, 1845

Ann, sailed from Donegal, Ire., landed at Saint John May 27, 1845
Unity Caulfield, 24, R.C., Donegal, Ire., adm. July 5, 1845 dis. Aug. 6, 1845
Biddy Donnell, 23, R.C., Donegal, Ire., adm. July 8, 1845 dis. Sept. 30, 1845
Bridget Divers, 19, R.C., Donegal, Ire., adm. July 12, 1845 dis. Aug. 25, 1845
Bridget Kennedy, 25, R.C., Donegal, Ire., adm. July 16, 1845 dis. Aug. 5, 1845
James Higgins, 23, R.C., Donegal, Ire., adm. July 17, 1845 dis. Aug. 1, 1845
Mrs. Hannah Higgins, 22, R.C., Donegal, Ire., adm. July 17, 1845 dis. Aug. 1, 1845

Ann, sailed from Limerick, Ire., landed at Saint John Aug. 21, 1845
Bridget Lawler, 28, R.C., Clare, Ire., adm. Aug. 26, 1845 dis. Sept. 25, 1845
Eli Lawlor, 18, R.C., Clare, Ire., adm. Aug. 26, 1845 dis. Sept. 30, 1845

Caroline, sailed from Ballyshannon, Ire., landed at Saint John, June 10, 1845
Margt. Lennan, 17 years 6 mos., Methodist, Fermanagh, Ire., adm. May 5, 1846

Clyde, sailed from Liverpool, England, landed at Saint John January 2, 1845, adm. to Alms House February 10, 1845: all Prebyterian, Galloway, Scotland, dis. Feb. 20, 1845
Mrs. Jane Kelly, 31, widow
Elizabeth Kelly, 12 Jane Kelly, 7
Robt. Kelly, 14, Henry Kelly, 10
Wm Kelly, 9, Anthony Kelly, 4½
Alexander Kelly, 2

Dominica, sailed from Cork, Ire., landed at Saint John June 5, 1845
Mary Warren, 28, R.C., Cork, Ire., adm. July 5, 1845 dis. Aug. 18, 1845
Norrie Cunningham, 30, R.C., Cork, Ire., adm. July 15, 1845 dis. Aug. 5, 1845
Martin Joyce, 26, Prot., Cork, Ire., adm. July 17, 1845 dis. July 23, 1845
Ellen Smith, 23, R.C., Cork, Ire., adm. July 19, 1845 dis. Nov. 1, 1845
Johanna Sweeney, 21, R.C.,

Port of Saint John: Alms & Work House 1845 77

Cork, Ire., adm. March 21, 1846

Eliza Ann, sailed from Cork, Ire., landed at Saint John May 21, 1845
Mrs. Bridget Sweeney, 30, R.C., Waterford, Ire., adm. June 20, 1845 dis. July 13, 1845
John Lawton, 26, R.C., Cork, Ire., adm. June 25, 1845 dis. Aug. 4, 1845
John Carty, 28, R.C., Waterford, Ire., adm. June 25, 1845 dis. Aug. 25, 1845
Hanora Heaney, 26, R.C., Cork, Ire., adm. Aug. 22, 1845 dis. Aug. 25, 1845
Wm Murphy, 53, R.C., Cork, Ire., adm. Dec. 4, 1845, Alms House Feb. 10, 1846 adm. Feb. 10, 1846 dis. Apr. 2, 1846

Eliza Gillis, sailed from Galway, Ire., landed at Saint John July 23, 1845
Mary A. Mealey, 15, R.C., Galway, Ire., adm. Aug. 24, 1845 dis. Aug. 25, 1845
Patk. Hardiman, 19, R.C., Galway, Ire., adm. Sept. 16, 1845 dis. Oct. 8, 1845
Catharine Krian, 22, R.C., Galway, Ire., adm. Oct. 17, 1845, Alms House Feb. 10, 1846
Hannah O'Brien, 23, R.C., Bandon, Cork, Ire., adm. Nov. 20, 1845 dis. Dec. 27, 1845
Lewis Carey, 3 mos., R.C., Alms House, adm. Nov. 29, 1845, mo. came in *Eliza Gillis* dis. Apr. 5, 1846
Cath. Carey, 22, R.C., Galway,

Ire., adm. Feb. 10, 1846 dis. April 1, 1846

Governor Douglas, 1845
Mary Cain, 17, R.C., Cork, Ire., adm. June 17, 1846 dis. Nov. 21, 1846

Jane, sailed from Cork, Ire., landed at Saint John July 1845
James O'Connell, 12 years 3 mos., R.C., Cork, Ire., adm. Feb. 13, 1846 dis. March 11, 1846

John Esdaile, sailed from South Shields, England, landed at Saint John May 10, 1845
Saml. Baird, 23, Prot., Gloucester, England, adm. April 6, 1846

John Wesley, sailed from Cork, Ire.; landed at Saint John May 22 (23), 1845
Cath. McArty, 19, R.C., Cork, Ire.. adm. May 24, 1845 dis. Sept. 2, 1845
Wm Geaney, 24, R.C., Cork, Ire., adm. June 10, 1845, dis. July 2, 1845
Ellen Collins, 27, R.C., Cork, Ire., adm. May 12, 1846

Lady Mary Fox, sailed from Cork, Ire., landed at Saint John June 3(5), 1845
Mary Lovett, 22, R.C., Kerry, Ire., adm. June 9, 1845 dis. Aug. 18, 1845
Tim Connolly, 32, R.C., Cork, Ire., adm. June 18, 1845 dis. Aug. 1, 1845

Margt. Sullivan, 20, R.C., Cork, Ire., adm. Feb. 7, 1846 died March 21, 1846
- Sullivan, Alms House, adm. March 12, 1846 died May 7, 1846. mo. came in *Lady Mary Fox*

Lord Fitzgerald, sailed from Galway, Ire., landed at Saint John June 9, 1845
Ellen Manion, 23, R.C., Galway, Ire., adm. June 15, 1845 dis. Aug. 5, 1845, adm. Jan. 5, 1846 dis. Jan. 31, 1846
Mary Brown, 32, R.C., Galway, Ire., adm. June 24 died July 10, 1845
Margt. Lalley, 24, R.C., Galway, Ire., adm. June 27, 1845, Alms House Feb. 10, 1846
Richd. Bateman, 5 mos., R.C., Alms House, adm. Feb. 10, 1846, mo. came *Lord Fitzgerald*
Judy Dooley, 20, R.C., Galway, Ire., adm. Oct. 16, 1846 dis. Nov. 21, 1846

Mary, sailed from Cork, Ire., landed at Saint John June 23, 1845
Mrs. Margt. Baker, 22, R.C., Cork, Ire., adm. Oct. 6, 1845 dis. Nov. 11, 1845
Mrs. Kearns, 47, R.C., Cork, Ire., adm. Oct. 7, 1845 died Oct. 17, 1845

New Zealand, sailed from Derry, Ire., landed at Saint John July 1845
Cath. Strawbridge, 17, R.C., Donegal, Ire., adm. Sept. 10, 1845 dis. Oct. 28, 1845
Mary I. Cuthbert, 19, Presbyterian, Derry, Ire., adm. May 6, 1846 dis. May 30, 1846

Pallas, sailed from Cork, Ire., landed at Saint John 1845
John Crowley, 28, R.C., Cork, Ire., adm. Feb. 26, 1846 dis. March 31, 1846

Pons Ælii, sailed from Cork, Ire., landed at Saint John, June 1, 1845
Roger Conner, 25, R.C., Cork, Ire., adm. June 5 dis. June 17, 1845

Redwing, sailed from Galway, Ire, landed at Saint John May 27, 1845
Ann Eagan, 29, R.C., Galway, adm. May 30, 1845 dis. July 19, 1845
Ellen Eagan, 30, R.C., Galway, Ire., adm. Apr. 17, 1846 dis. May 7, 1846
Mrs. Byrnes, 30, R.C., Galway, Ire., adm. Sept. 22, 1846 died Dec. 10, 1846

Sarah, sailed from Cork, Ire., landed at Saint John June 1845
Mrs. Eliz. Power, 19, R.C., Cork, Ire., adm. Aug. 30, 1845 dis. Jan. 20, 1846

St. Lawrence, sailed from Cork, Ire., landed in Saint John May 21, 1845
Margt. Hornett, 26, R.C., Cork, Ire., adm. Dec. 2, 1845 dis. Dec. 27, 1845

Peter Sullivan, 22, R.C., Cork, Ire., adm. Jan. 20, 1846, dis. March 5, 1846

Thorney Close, sailed from Donegal, Ire., landed at Saint John, June 13, 1845
Edwd. Haggarty, 18, R.C., Donegal, Ire., adm. July 26, 1845 dis. Sept. 6, 1845
Mrs. Margt. McGowan, 21, R.C., Donegal, Ire., adm. Aug. 30, 1845 dis. Sept. 3, 1845
Mrs. Mary Armstrong, 24, R.C., Leitrim, Ire., Sept. 20, 1845, Alms House Feb. 10, 1846
Emily Armstrong, 4 mos., R.C., Alms House, admin Feb. 10, 1846

Triumph, sailed from Cork (Castletown), Ire., landed at Saint John May 27, 1845
Jerry Sullivan, 14, R.C., Cork, Ire., adm. June 3, 1845, dis. Sept. 12, 1845
Mary O'Brien, 20, R.C., Cork, Ire., adm. Feb. 10, 1846 dis. May 30, 1846

Venilia, sailed from Derry, Ire., landed at Saint John May 23, 1845
Robert Howie, 19, Presbyterian, Donegal, Ire., adm. Alms House May 24, 1845, Alms House, Feb. 10, 1846, age 20
Dennis Lynchigan, 18, R.C., Donegal, Ire., adm. June 4, 1845, Alms House Feb. 10, 1846, age 19, dis. March 11, 1846
Mary McLaughlin, 21, R.C., Donegal, Ire., adm. June 16, 1845 dis. Sept. 30, 1845
John Porter, 24, R.C., Donegal, Ire., adm. June 25, 1845 dis. Aug. 4, 1845

Wakefield, sailed from Newry, Ire., landed at Saint John July 27, 1845
Mary McMahon, 21, R.C., Down, Ire., adm. March 21, 1846 dis. June 15, 1846
Wm McMahon, Alms House, adm. Apr. 15, 1846 dis. June 15, 1846. Mo. came in *Wakefield*

Warrior, sailed from Drogheda, Ire., landed in Saint John June 13, 1845
Rosa McArron, 25, R.C., Meath, Ire., adm. Dec. 5, 1845, died Jan. 8, 1846

Emigrant Deaths in Hospital Partridge Island, Saint John 1846

Return of passengers who have died in hospital at Partridge Island, June of 1846 to date signed by G.I. Harding, M.D., Health Officer, Partridge Island, June 24th 1846.[1]

1846
May 19   Grace McGowan, age 19, *Envoy*, Londonderry, fever
May 26   Dennis McCarthy, age 25, *Albion*, Cork, fever
May 27   George Thomas, age 55, *Albion*, Cork, fever
June 6   Rose O'Neils, age 56, *Envoy*, Londonderry, fever
June 12   Mary Daily, age 30, *Sir Jas. McDonnell*, Tralee, inflammation of bowels
June 13   John Connell, age 30, *Martha*, Cork, fever
June 15   Hannah McLaughlin, age 40, *Envoy*, Londonderry, relapsed with inflammation of bowels after fever.
June 16   Cornelius Kelly, age 58, *Coxon*, Cork, paralysis from inflammation of the brain in consequence of fever on board the ship.

Emigrants Admitted to the Alms House Saint John From Vessels Arriving in 1846

Alarm, sailed from Cork, Ire., landed at Saint John May 14, 1846
Julia Colter, 20, R.C., Cork, Ire., adm. July 29, 1846 dis. Aug. 14, 1846
Mary Clelan, 21, R.C., Cork, Ire., adm. Apr. 15, 1847

Albion, sailed from Cork, Ire., landed at Saint John May 20, 1846
Tim Conohan, 21, R.C., Kerry, Ire., adm. May 21, 1846 dis. July 10, 1846
Mrs. Julia Mahony, 23, R.C., Cork, Ire., adm. May 23, 1846 dis. June 13, 1846
Jerry Mahony, 8 mos., R.C.,

---

[1] P.A.N.B., Emigration Micro. F7891

Cork, Ire., adm. May 23, 1846 dis. June 12, 1846
Julia Hayes, 22, R.C., Cork, Ire., adm. May 23, 1846 dis. July 4, 1846
Wm Neville, 26, R.C., Cork, Ire., adm. May 25, 1846 died Aug. 21, 1846
Aeneas Dealey, 12, R.C., Cork, Ire., adm. May 25, 1846 dis. Oct. 9, 1846
Mrs. Bridget McColliff, 24, R.C., Cork, Ire., adm. May 29, 1846 dis. June 24, 1846
Jerry McColliff, 7 mos., R.C., Cork, Ire., adm. May 29, 1846 died May 29, 1846
Ellen Carrol, 22, R.C., Cork, Ire., adm. June 1, 1846 dis. June 22, 1846
Mrs. Bridget Dougan, 32. R.C., Cork, Ire., adm. June 3, 1846 died June 7, 1846
Joanna Dougan, 10 mos., R.C., Cork, Ire., adm. June 3, 1846 dis. June 12, 1846, taken away by father
Wm Pine, 22, R.C., Cork, Ire., adm. June 3, 1846 dis. July 7, 1846
Richd. Keoffe, 23, R.C., Cork, Ire., adm. June 4, 1846 dis. July 4, 1846
Wm Bryant, 22, R.C., Cork, Ire., adm. June 5, 1846 dis. July 10, 1846
Joanna Foley, 18, R.C., Cork, Ire., adm. June 5, 1846 dis. June 22, 1846
Mrs. Ellen Hooley, 29, R.C., Cork, Ire., adm. June 6, 1846 dis. July 28, 1846
John Hooley, 8 mos., R.C., Cork, Ire., adm. June 6, 1846 died June 14, 1846, mo. in ho.
Mrs. Ann Hooley, 24, Prot., Cork, Ire., adm. June 8, 1846 dis. June 9, 1846 adm. June 20, 1846 dis. June 30, destitute, two children husband deserted
John Hooley, 3 years 6 mos., Prot., Cork, Ire., adm. June 8, 1846 dis. July 9, 1846
Wm Hooley, 6 mos., Prot., Cork, Ire., adm. June 8, 1846 dis. June 20, 1846
Patk. Mahony, 27, R.C., Cork, Ire., adm. June 8, dis. June 15, 1846
Tim Conohan, 21, R.C., Kerry, Ire., adm. July 17, 1846 dis. Feb. 2, 1847
Richd. Keoffe, 23, R.C., Cork, Ire., adm. Aug. 6, 1846 dis. Sept. 1, 1846
Ellen Barret, 19, R.C., Cork, Ire., adm. Sept. 4, 1846 dis. Sept. 28, 1846
Mrs. Ellen Healey, 37, R.C., Cork, Ire., adm. Oct. 1, 1846 dis. Dec. 28, 1846
Patk. Healey, 1 month, R.C., Boston, adm. Oct. 1, 1846 dis. Dec. 28, 1846, mo. came in *Albion*
Patk. Healey, 30, R.C., Cork, Ire., adm. Nov. 7, 1846 dis. Dec. 28, 1846

Alexander, sailed from Derry, Ire., landed at Saint John June 23, 1846
Sally Ferry, 37, R.C., Derry, Ire., adm. June 30, 1846 dis. Aug. 15, 1846 adm. Nov. 14, 1846, Alms House, adm. Feb. 20, 1847

Nancy McCahy, 22, Prot., Derry, Ire., July 4, 1846 dis. July 14, 1846
Ellen McColgan, 20, R.C., Donegal, Ire., adm. Aug. 19, 1846 dis. Aug. 29, 1846 adm. Sept. 2, 1846 dis. Oct. 12, 1846
Wm McLaughlin, 20, R.C., Derry, Ire., adm. Aug. 27, 1846 dis. Sept. 13, 1846 adm. Sept. 24, 1846 dis. Nov. 2, 1846

Ann Wise, sailed from Sligo, Ire., landed at Saint John June 24(25) 1846
Mrs. Bridget McDonough, 40, R.C., Sligo, Ire., adm. Aug. 25, 1846, Alms House Feb. 20, 1847
Wm McDonough, 18, R.C., Sligo, Ire., adm. Aug. 25, 1846, Alms House Feb. 20, 1847 died March 25, 1847
Jno. McDonough, 4, R.C., Sligo, Ire., adm. Aug. 25, 1846, Alms House Feb. 20, 1847, age 4 years 6 mos., dis. May 27, 1847

Aulaby, sailed from Cork, Ire., landed at Saint John June 30, 1846
Michl. Coughlan, 40, R.C., Cork, Ire., adm. July 8, 1846 dis. Aug. 1, 1846
Laurence Donovan, 27, R.C., Cork, Ire., adm. July 27, 1846 dis. Aug. 8, 1846
Honora Donovan, 22, R.C., Cork, Ire., adm. July 27, 1846 dis. Aug. 15, 1846

Bremn?, sailed from Cork, Ire., landed at Saint John July 9, 1846
Mary Driscol, 25, R.C., Cork, adm. July 20, 1846 dis. Aug. 20, 1846

British Queen, sailed from Newry, Ire., landed at Saint John June 19, 1846
Rose McCullough, 15, R.C., Tyrone, Ire., adm. Dec. 30, 1846 died Jan. 4, 1846

Brothers, sailed from Bantry, Ire., landed at Saint John, May 11, 1846
Julia Connel, 18, R.C., Cork, Ire., adm. June 16, 1846 dis. Oct. 5, 1846
Ellen McArty, 23, R.C., Cork, Ire., adm. June 17, 1846 dis. July 20, 1846
Mrs. Norrie Collins, 32, R.C., Cork, Ire., adm. July 13, 1846 dis. Sept. 29, 1846
Mary Collins, 1 year 3 mos., R.C., Cork, Ire., adm. July 13, 1846, died Sept. 8, 1846
Jno. Collins, 3 years 6 mos., R.C., Cork, Ire., adm. July 13, 1846, died Aug. 31, 1846
Margaret Conner, 22, R.C., Cork, Ire., adm. Apr. 26, 1847
Margaret Cronin, 22, R.C., Cork, Ire., adm. Apr. 26, 1847 dis. May 13, 1847

Catharine, sailed from Killala, Ire., landed at Yarmouth, N.S. Oct. 1846
Mrs. Nancy Killane, 34, R.C., Mayo, Ire., adm. Dec. 1, 1846 dis. Dec. 9, 1846
Mary Killane, 9, R.C., Mayo, Ire., adm. Dec. 1, 1846 dis. Dec. 9, 1846

Bridget - , 7, R.C., Mayo, Ire., adm. Dec. 1, 1846 dis. Dec. 9, 1846

Jno. Killane, 4 years 6 mos., R.C., Mayo, Ire., adm. Dec. 1, 1846 dis. Dec. 9, 1846

Michl. Killane, 2, R.C., Mayo, Ire., adm. Dec. 1, 1846 dis. Dec. 9, 1846

Widow Finan, 40, R.C., Mayo, Ire., adm. Dec. 4, 1846 dis. Dec. 9, 1846

Jno. Finan, 12, R.C., Mayo, Ire., adm. Dec. 4, 1846 dis. Dec. 9, 1846

Biddy McInnes, 10, R.C., Mayo, Ire., adm. Dec. 4, 1846 dis. Dec. 9, 1846

Charles, sailed from Youghal, Ire., landed at Saint John June 29, 1846

Cath. Lane, 19, R.C., Kerry, Ire., adm. Aug. 14, 1846 dis. Oct. 24, 1846

Michl. Murray, 30, R.C., Waterford, Ire., adm. Aug. 15, 1846 dis. Aug. 20, 1846

Ellen Dunn, 16, R.C., Cork, Ire., adm. Aug. 25, 1846 dis. Sept. 30, 1846

Bridget Lane, 22, R.C., Cork, Ire., adm. Aug. 30, 1846 dis. Sept. 30, 1846

Edwin Doyle, 30, R.C., Waterford, Ire., adm. May 7, 1847 dis. June 30, 1847

Chieftain, sailed from Derry, Ire., landed at Saint John Aug. 2, 1846

Mary Flanagan, 26, R.C., Clare, Ire., adm. Sept. 24, 1846 dis. Jan. 26, 1847

Sarah O'Brien, 27, R.C., Clare, Ire., adm. Oct. 21, 1846 dis. Dec. 1, 1846

Catherine Deveney, 30, R.C., Galway, Ire., adm. Apr. 16, 1847

Conservative, sailed from Dublin, Ire., landed at Yarmouth, N.S. Jan. 28, 1846

John Cunningham, 23, R.C., Louth, Ire., adm. June 6, 1846

Coxon, sailed from Cork, Ire., landed at Saint John May 19, 1846

Jerry Keilley, 10, R.C., Cork, Ire., adm. June 5, 1846 dis. June 9, 1846

John Conden, 26, R.C., Cork, Ire., adm. June 6, 1846, ran away June 8, 1846 adm. June 28, 1846 dis. Aug. 22, 1846

James Murphy, 30, R.C., Waterford, Ire., adm. June 27, 1846 dis. Aug. 1, 1846

Mrs. Ellen Herrick, 32, R.C., Cork, Ire., adm. July 22, 1846 dis. Aug. 7, 1846

Jno. Herrick, 9 mos., R.C., Cork, Ire., adm. July 22, 1846 dis. Aug. 7, 1846

Cath. Donovan, 10, R.C., Cork, Ire., adm. July 22, 1846 dis. Aug. 7, 1846

Mary Murphy, 26, R.C., Cork, Ire., adm. Aug. 1, 1846 dis. Aug. 24, 1846

Honora Driscol, 24, R.C., Cork, Ire., adm. Aug. 6, 1846 dis. Sept. 2, 1846

James Murphy, 30, R.C., Waterford, Ire., adm. Aug. 8,

84 Irish Migration To New England: Port of Saint John

1846 died Aug. 15, 1846
Joanna Heron, 22, R.C., Cork, Ire., adm. Aug. 24, 1846 dis. Feb. 8. 1847

Creole, sailed from Londonderry, Ire., landed at Saint John May 28, 1846
Jane Lynn, widow, 38, Prot., Fermanagh, Ire., adm. May 18, 1846
Thos. Lynn, 7, Prot., Fermanagh, Ire., adm. May 18, 1846. Mo. in Ho. Fa. dead.
Jno. Lynn, 9 mos., Prot., Saint John, N.B., adm. May 18, 1846. Mo. in Ho. Fa. dead. Mo. came in *Creole*
Rose Harkins, 38, R.C., Donegal, Ire., adm. Sept. 12, 1846 dis. Sept. 14, 1846
Jas. Harkins, 3, R.C., Donegal, Ire., adm. Sept. 12, 1846 dis. Sept. 14, 1846
Wm Harkins, 9 mos., R.C., Donegal, Ire., adm. Sept. 12, 1846 dis. Sept. 14, 1846

Danube, sailed from Ballyshannon, Ire., landed at Saint John Aug. 14, 1846
Chas. McHugh, 26, Prot., Donegal or Bally-shannon, Ire., adm. Aug. 17, 1846 dis. Oct. 14, 1846 adm. Oct. 26, Alms House Feb. 20, 1847 dis March 30, 1847
Thos. Mehan, 23, R.C., Donegal, Ire., adm. Aug. 18, 1846 dis. Oct. 30, 1846
Mary Dever, 20, R.C., Donegal, Ire., adm. Aug. 20, 1846 dis. Oct. 24, 1846
Eleanor Dunlevy, 18, R.C.,

Donegal, Ire., adm. Aug. 24, 1846 dis. Sept. 6, 1846
Mary Byrne, 21, R.C., Donegal, Ire., adm. Nov. 16, 1846, Alms House Feb. 20, 1847
Jno. Boyle (Jno. Byrne), Alms House, adm. Dec. 4, 1846, Alms House, Feb. 20, 1847, mo. came in *Danube*
Margaret Byrne, 21, R.C., Donegal, Ire., adm. Feb. 20, 1847 dis. March 11, 1847

Dealy (Daley), sailed from Bantry, Cork, Ire., landed at Saint John, May 12 (13), 1846
Jeremiah Donahue, 20, R.C., Cork, Ire., adm. May 18, 1846 dis. June 26, 1846
William Mahony, 22, R.C., Cork, Ire., adm. July 15, 1846 dis. Sept. 18, 1846
William Mahony Jr., 1, R.C., Cork, Ire., adm. July 15, 1846 died July 25, 1846
Jno. Leary, 21, R.C., Cork, Ire., adm. July 17, 1846 dis. Sept. 18, 1846
Honora Hurley, 22, R.C., Cork, Ire., adm. Aug. 10, 1846, Alms House Feb. 20, 1847 adm. Feb. 20, 1847
Mary Sullivan, 23, R.C., Cork, Ire., adm. Aug. 17, 1846 dis. Sept. 12, 1846
Cath. Sullivan, 3 weeks, R.C., Cork, Ire., adm. Aug. 17, 1846 died Aug. 23, 1846
Joanna Foley, 32, R.C., Cork, Ire., adm. Aug. 20, 1846 dis. Sept. 26, 1846
Bidy Foley, 6, R.C., Cork, Ire., adm. Aug. 20, 1846 dis. Sept. 26,

1846
Norrie Foley, 2, R.C., Cork, Ire., adm. Aug. 20, 1846 dis. Sept. 26, 1846
Patk. Carthy, 27, R.C., Cork, Ire., adm. Aug. 24, 1846 dis. Sept. 29, 1846
Johanna Hurley, R.C. Alms House, adm. Oct. 14, 1846, Alms House Feb. 20, 1847, age 4 mos., mo. came in *Daley*
Eugene Sullivan, 27, R.C., Cork, Ire., adm. Dec. 6, 1846 dis. Jan. 18, 1847
Ann Morris, 21, Prot., Bandon, Cork, Ire., adm. Jan. 15, 1847 dis. Feb. 7, 1847

Envoy, sailed from Londonderry, Ire., landed at Saint John, May 22, 1846
Marjory Doherty, 18, R.C., Derry, Ire., adm. May 25, 1846 dis. June 29, 1846
Philip McGavigan, 21, R.C., Derry, Ire., adm. May 25, 1846 dis. June 15, 1846
Wm McGonigal, 24, R.C., Donegal, Ire., adm. May 22, 1846 dis. July 27, 1846
Thos. Stewart, 28, Presby., Derry, Ire., adm. June 1, 1846 dis. July 15, 1846
Ann Stewart, 15, Presby., Derry, Ire., adm. June 1, 1846 dis. June 24, 1846
Ann McGilly, 18, R.C., Derry, Ire., adm. June 1, 1846 dis. Aug. 8, 1846
Ann Campbell, 30, R.C., Tyrone, Ire., adm. June 1, 1846 dis. July 10, 1846
Hugh Taylor, 22, Prot., Antrim, Ire., adm. June 1, 1846, dis. June 20, 1846
Wm Dougherty, 23, R.C., Donegal, Ire., adm. June 2, 1846 dis. June 29, 1846
Chas. McQuade, 20, R.C., Tyrone, Ire., adm. June 3, 1846 dis. June 22, 1846
Jno. Thomson, 18, Presby., Derry, Ire., adm. June 3, 1846 dis. Aug. 25, 1846
Mary Jane Thomson, 16, Presby., Derry, Ire., adm. June 3, 1846 dis. June 22, 1846
Ellen Cain, 20, R.C., Derry, Ire., adm. June 3, 1846 dis. June 25, 1846
Ann Muldoon, 24, R.C., Fermanagh, Ire., adm. June 3, 1846 dis June 29, 1846
Sarah O'Hara, 26, R.C., Tyrone, Ire., adm. June 3, 1846 dis. Aug. 2, 1846
Rebecca I. King, 17, Prot., Derry, Ire., adm. June 4, 1846 dis. July 9, 1846
Ann Edwards, 21, Presby., Donegal, Ire., adm. June 4, 1846 dis. July 4, 1846
Danl Duffy, 18, R.C., Donegal, Ire., adm. June 5, 1846 dis. June 15, 1846
Neill Duffy, 20, R.C., Donegal, Ire., adm. June 5, 1846 dis. June 15, 1846
John Tonor, 17, R.C., Derry, Ire., adm. June 5, 1846 dis. July 4, 1846
John Jackson, 24, Prot., Tyrone, Ire., adm. June 5, 1846 dis. Aug. 10, 1846
Jas. Doherty, 19, R.C., Derry, Ire., adm. June 6, 1846 dis. June 22,

86 Irish Migration To New England: Port of Saint John

1846
Jane Stuart, 22, Presby., Derry, Ire., adm. June 6, 1846 dis. June 24, 1846
Elizabeth Cook, 21, Prot., Donegal, Ire., adm. June 7, 1846 dis. June 24, 1846
Rose Ann Haragan, 19, R.C., Derry, Ire., adm. June 8, 1846 dis. June 22, 1846
Patk. Hanley, 22, R.C., Tyrone, Ire., adm. June 8, 1846 dis. Sep. 16, 1846
Thos. Hanley, 14, R.C., Tyrone, Ire., adm. June 8, 1846 dis, Aug. 24, 1846
Mrs. Isabella Phillips, 21, Prot., Tyrone, Ire., adm. June 10, 1846 dis. June 24, 1846
Jane McGarigle, 18, Prot., Donegal, Ire., adm. June 12, 1846 dis. July 14, 1846
Mary McGarigle, 18, Prot., Donegal, Ire., adm. June 12, 1846 dis. July 9, 1846
Sarah Stuart, 19, Presby., Derry, Ire., adm. June 12, 1846 dis. July 4, 1846
James Proctor, 20, Prot., Derry, Ire., June 12, 1846 dis. July 1, 1846
Chas. Wilson, 20, Prot., Tyrone, Ire., adm. June 15, 1846 dis. Aug. 1, 1846
Andw. Wilson, 18, Prot., Tyrone, Ire., adm. June 15, 1846 dis. July 27, 1846
Jane Wilson, 14, Prot., Tyrone, Ire., adm. June 15, 1846 dis. July 27, 1846
Mary I. Ewing, 17, Presb., Donegal, Ire., adm. June 15, 1846 dis. July 2, 1846

Mrs. Charlotte Jackson, 19, Presby., Tyrone, Ire., adm. July 2, 1846 dis. Aug. 17, 1846
- McLellan, Alms House, adm. July 18, 1846 died July 25, 1846, mo. came in *Envoy*
Rosanna McAvity (or Roseanna McArney), 25, R.C., Derry, Ire., adm. July 27, 1846, Alms House Feb. 20, 1847
Patk. Lynch, 23, R.C., Derry, Ire., adm. Sept. 1, 1846 dis. Sept. 26, 1846
Jno. Thomson, 18, Presb., Derry, Ire., adm. Sept. 24, 1846 dis. Oct. 3, 1846

Faugh-a-Ballagh, sailed from Dublin, Ire., landed at Saint John June 30, 1846
Mary Conner, 16, R.C., Westmeath, Ire., adm. July 2, 1846 dis. Aug. 3, 1846
Michl. Monohan, 20, R.C., Cavan, Ire., adm. Aug. 17, 1846 dis. Sept. 7, 1846

George Ramsay, sailed from Kinsale, Ire., landed at Saint John May 25, 1846
Jno. Donovan, 32, R.C., Kinsale, Ire., adm. Nov. 17, 1846 died Dec. 28, 1846

Harriet, sailed from Derry, Ire., landed at Saint John June 2, 1846
Mrs. Bridget Swift, 38, R.C., Fermanagh, Ire., adm. June 6, 1846 dis. Aug. 21, 1846
Cath. Swift, 14, R.C., Fermanagh, Ire., adm. June 6, 1846 died July 2, 1846

Port of Saint John: Alms & Work House 1846   87

John Curry, 22, Prot., Tyrone, Ire., adm. June 10, 1846 died Sept. 16, 1846
Ellen McAffrey, 21, R.C., Tyrone, Ire., adm. June 18, 1846 died July 1, 1846
Ellen Hanna, 18, Presby., Tyrone, Ire., adm. July 9, 1846 dis. Aug. 17, 1846
Sarah O'Donnell, 22, R.C., Donegal, Ire., adm. Sept. 15, 1846 dis. Oct. 13, 1846
Mary Devlin, 20, R.C., Tyrone, Ire., adm. Oct. 6, 1846 dis. Dec. 2, 1846
Henry Devlin, 1 month, R.C., Saint John, adm. Oct. 6, 1846 died Nov. 14, 1846, mo. came in *Harriet*
David Curry, 20, Prot., Tyrone, Ire., adm. Nov. 11, 1846 dis. Jan. 5, 1847

Harry King, sailed from Kerry, Ire., landed at Saint John July 1, 1846
Mrs. Joanna Hussey, 40, R.C., Kerry, Ire., adm. July 27, 1846 dis. Nov. 1, 1846
Mary Hussey, 16, R.C., Kerry, Ire., adm. July 27, 1846 dis. Nov. 1, 1846
Alice Hussey, 9, R.C., Kerry, Ire., adm. July 27, 1846 dis. Nov. 1, 1846
Thos. Hussey, 7, R.C., Kerry, Ire., adm. July 27, 1846 dis. Nov. 1, 1846
Humphrey Sullivan, 20, R.C., Cork, Ire., adm. Aug. 19, 1846 dis. Sept. 2, 1846

John Begg, sailed from Galway, Ire., arrived at Saint John June 2, 1846
Biddy Head, 24, R.C., Galway, Ire., adm. Oct. 12, 1846 dis. Jan. 11, 1847
Jno. Head, Alms House, adm. Oct. 12, 1846 died Dec. 13, 1846, mo. came in *John Begg*

John Francis, sailed from Cork, Ire., landed at Saint John June 3, 1846
Wm Murphy, 26, R.C., Cork, Ire., adm. June 8, 1846 dis. Oct. 5, 1846
Tim Dogan, 30, R.C., Cork, Ire., adm. June 10, 1846 dis July 1, 1846
Ellen Leary, 23, R.C., Cork, Ire., adm. June 11, 1846 died July 11, 1846
John Hayes, 28, R.C., Cork, Ire., adm. June 22, 1846 dis. July 27, 1846

Lady Napier, sailed from Westport, Ire., landed at Saint John June 23, 1846
Anthony Byrne, 30, R.C., Mayo, Ire., adm. June 24, 1846 dis. June 25, 1846
Mrs. Mary Burne, 26, R.C., Mayo, Ire., adm. June 24, 1846 dis. June 25, 1846
Mary Byrne Jr., 5, R.C., Mayo, Ire., adm. June 24, 1846 dis. June 25, 1846

Leviathan, sailed from Cork, Ire., landed at Saint John Sept. 20, 1846
Jeremiah Healey, 20, R.C., Cork, Ire., adm. Oct. 1, 1846 dis. Nov. 2, 1846 adm. Dec. 8, 1846, Alms

House Feb. 20, 1847, dis. Apr. 22, 1847

Linden, sailed from Galway, Ire., landed at Saint John June 13, 1846
Mrs. Cath. Folara, 40, R.C., Galway, Ire., adm. July 11, 1846 dis. Sept. 11, 1846
Biddy Cain, 40, R.C., Clare, Ire., adm. Feb. 20, 1847 dis. Feb. 26, 1847

Londonderry, sailed from Derry, Ire., landed at Saint John November 1846
John McCutcheon, 25, Prot., Tyrone, Ire., adm. Apr. 15, 1847 dis. Apr. 21, 1847

Lord Glenelg, sailed from Cork, Ire., landed at Saint John June 3, 1846
Joanna Guiney, 20, R.C., Limerick, Ire., adm. June 13, 1846 dis. June 22, 1846
James Keating, 22, R.C., Cork, Ire., adm. June 20, 1846 dis. July 10, 1846
Mrs. Ellen Dunane, 28, R.C., Cork, Ire., adm. Aug. 24, 1846 dis. Sept. 27, 1846
Mrs. Mary Keating, 24, R.C., Cork, Ire., adm. Apr. 7, 1847

Martha, sailed from Cork, Ire., landed at Saint John June 4, 1846
Margt. McArty, 22, R.C., Kerry, Ire., adm. June 6, 1846 dis. July 9, 1846
Joanna Learey, 20, R.C., Kerry, Ire., adm. June 8, 1846 dis. July 9, 1846
Lawrence Sullivan, 22, R.C., Cork, Ire., adm. June 13, 1846 died June 16, 1846
Ellen Moore, 19, R.C., Kerry, Ire., adm. June 13, 1846 dis. July 9, 1846
Julia Riley, 22, R.C., Cork, Ire., adm. June 13, 1846 dis. Sept. 2, 1846
Mrs. Sullivan, 26, R.C., Cork, Ire., adm. June 16, 1846 dis. July 29, 1846
Michl. Sullivan, 26, R.C., Cork, Ire., adm. June 16, 1846 dis. July 20, 1846
Edwd. Fitzgerald, 27, R.C., Fermanagh, Ire., adm. June 16, 1846 dis. Aug. 3, 1846
Mrs. Ellen Welch, 26, R.C., Cork, Ire., adm. June 17, 1846 dis. July 4, 1846
Mrs. Mary Sullivan, 32, R.C., Cork, Ire., adm. June 25, 1846 dis. July 4, 1846
Patk. Leary, 20, R.C., Kerry, Ire., adm. June 27, 1846 dis. dis. Aug. 17, 1846
Margt. Conohan, 19, R.C., Kerry, Ire., adm. June 29, 1846 dis. Aug. 10, 1846
John Splahan, 25, R.C., Cork, Ire., adm. July 1, 1846 dis. July 27, 1846
James Moreley, 22, R.C., Cork, Ire., adm. July 21, 1846 dis. Oct. 9, 1846
Michl. Sullivan, 26, R.C., Cork, Ire., adm. Aug. 14, 1846 dis. Aug. 18, 1846
Ann Sullivan, 18, R.C., Kerry, Ire., adm. Nov. 9, 1846, Alms House Feb. 20, 1847, dis. March 24,

1847, adm. May 18, 1847, age 19, dis. May 27, 1847.

Mary, sailed from Cork, Ire., landed at Saint John May 20, 1846
Mary Tobin, 20, R.C., Kerry, Ire., adm. July 25, 1846 dis. Oct. 24, 1846
Wm Tobin, 30, R.C., Cork, Ire., adm. Sept. 22, 1846 died Nov. 1, 1846

Mary Campbell (Mary Kemble), sailed from Derry, Ire., landed at Saint John July 20, 1846
Mrs. Maria Stewart, 28, Prot., Derry, Ire., adm. July 21, 1846 dis. Oct. 7, 1846 adm. Oct. 22, Alms House, adm. Feb. 20, 1847
Sophia Stewart, 10, Derry, Ire., adm. July 21, 1846 dis. Nov. 14, 1846 adm. Apr. 24, 1847, age 11.
Eliza McDermott, 15, Presby., Donegal, Ire., adm. Apr. 6, 1847

Midas
Mrs. Margt. Joyce, 28, R.C., Galway, Ire., adm. Aug. 22, 1846 died Sept. 13, 1846

Ocean, sailed from Cork, Ire., landed at Saint John June 6, 1846
Richd. Murray, 23, R.C., Cork, Ire., adm. July 20, 1846 dis. Aug. 4, 1846 adm. Jan. 15, 1847 dis. Feb. 11, 1847
Bridget Bryant, 24, R.C., Cork, Ire., adm. July 29, 1846 dis. Aug. 20, 1846
Wm Bryant, 24, R.C., Cork, Ire., adm. July 31, 1846 dis. Aug. 20, 1846
Edwd. Gleeson, 27, R.C., Cork, Ire., adm. Sept. 1, 1846 Oct. 31, 1846

Pallas, sailed from Cork, Ire., landed at Saint John May 22, 1846
Cath. Roach, 19, R.C., Cork, Ire., adm. May 26, 1846 dis. Sept. 7, 1846, adm. Oct. 22, 1846 dis. Nov. 9, 1846
Edmund Barrett, 27, R.C., Cork, Ire., adm. May 30, 1846 dis. Aug. 8, 1846, adm. Aug. 20, 1846 dis. Oct. 12, 1846
Margt. Sullivan, 20, R.C., Cork, Ire., adm. June 1, 1846, dis. July 6, 1846
Sarah Knowles, 35, R.C., Cork, Ire., June 11, 1846 died June 24, 1846
David Crowley, 20, R.C., Cork, Ire., adm. June 26, 1846 dis. Aug. 3, 1846
Edward Clelan, 30, R.C., Cork, Ire., adm. Aug. 31, 1846 dis. Oct. 31, 1846
Cath. Shehan, 20, R.C., Cork, Ire., adm. Sept. 12, 1846 dis. Sept. 28, 1846
Biddy McArney, R.C., Alms House, Sept. 15, 1846, mo. came in *Pallas*
Mary Landrigan, 36, R.C., Fermh., Ire., adm. Sept. 20, 1846 dis. Nov. 9, 1846
John Welch, 20, R.C., Cork, Ire., adm. Jan. 19, 1847, Alms House, Feb. 20, 1847, dis. Apr. 26, 1847

Pons Ælii, sailed from Berehaven, Ire., landed at Saint John June

16, 1846
Thomas Baker, 23, Prot., Cork, Ire., adm. July 13, 1846, died Aug. 7, 1846

Princess, sailed from Cork, Ire., landed at Saint John May 16, 1846
Dan Mahony, 52, R.C., Cork, Ire., adm. Aug. 1, 1846 dis. Aug. 14, 1846
Mich. McAnarney, 26, R.C., Killarney, Ire., adm. Aug. 5, 1846 dis. Aug. 8, 1846
Julia Griffin, 19, R.C., Cork, Ire., adm. Aug. 31, 1846 dis. Sept. 8, 1846
Princess Royal, sailed from Cork, Ire., landed at Saint John June 3(5), 1846
John Fitzgerald, 21, R.C., Limerick, Ire., adm. Oct. 13, 1846 dis. Oct. 14, 1846 adm. Jan. 19, 1847, age 22, Alms House Feb. 20 dis. June 5, 1847
Mrs. Margaret Fitzgerald, 22, R.C., Limerick, Ire., adm. May 22, 1847, taken away by husband

Racer, sailed from Dingle, Ire., landed at Saint John June 29, 1846
Mary Shea, 19, R.C., Kerry, Ire., adm. June 29, 1846, dis. Oct. 7, 1846
Joanna Hannifin, 21, R.C., Kerry, Ire., adm. June 29, 1846 dis. Aug. 17, 1846
Betty Murphy, 55, R.C., Kerry, Ire., adm. June 30, 1846 dis. Aug. 20, 1846
Tim Harragan, 21, R.C., Kerry, Ire., adm. June 30, 1846 dis.

Aug. 1, 1846
Peggy Harragan, 20, R.C., Kerry, Ire., adm. June 30, 1846 dis. Aug. 17, 1846
Moris Fitzgerald, 20, R.C., Kerry, Ire., adm. June 30, 1846 dis. July 27, 1846
James Kilday, 25, R.C., Kerry, Ire., adm. July 1, 1846 dis. Aug. 3, 1846
Patk. Moran, 20, R.C., Kerry, Ire., adm. July 1, 1846 dis. July 28, 1846
Mary Conner, 20, R.C., Kerry, Ire., adm. July 1, 1846 dis. Aug. 3, 1846
Ellen Sullivan, 18, R.C., Kerry, Ire., adm. July 1, 1846 dis. Aug. 1, 1846
Mary Bowler, 22, R.C., Kerry, Ire., adm. July 2, 1846 dis. July 24, 1846
Joanna Kennedy, 22, R.C. Kerry, Ire., adm. July 2, 1846 dis. Sept. 2, 1846
Mrs. Mary Kennedy, 30, R.C., Kerry, Ire., adm. July 2, 1846 dis. July 16, 1846
Eleanor Fielding, 68, R.C., Kerry, Ire., adm. July 2, 1846 died July 11, 1846
Mrs. Joanna Shea, 30, R.C., Kerry, Ire., adm. July 2, 1846 dis. July 16, 1846
Patk. Kennedy, 25, R.C., Kerry, Ire., adm. July 2, 1846 dis. July 24, 1846
Ellen Kennedy, 8, Kerry, Ire., adm. July 2, 1846 dis. July 24, 1846
Joanna Kennedy, 2, Kerry, Ire., adm. July 2, 1846 dis. July 14, 1846

Mary Connor, 22, R.C., Kerry, Ire., adm. July 4, 1846 dis. July 26, 1846

Joanna Harrigan, 25, R.C., Kerry, Ire., adm. July 6, 1846 dis. July 26, 1846

Mrs. Mary Sullivan, 30, R.C., Kerry, Ire., adm. July 7, 1846 dis. Aug. 20, 1846

Mich. Sullivan, 1 year 6 mos., Kerry, Ire., adm. July 8, 1846 dis. Aug. 27, 1846

Patk. Shea, 2, Kerry, Ire., adm. July 8, 1846 dis. July 28, 1846

Mrs. Mary Hannifin, 30, R.C., Kerry, Ire., adm. July 9, 1846 dis. July 16, 1846

Danl. Hannifin, 42, R.C., Kerry, Ire., adm. July 9, 1846 died July 17, 1846

Peggy McArty, 45, R.C., Kerry, Ire., adm. July 13, 1846 dis. Aug. 1, 1846

Mary Kennedy, 28, R.C., Kerry, Ire., adm. July 17, 1846 dis. Sept. 6, 1846

Mrs. Cath. Laing, 45, R.C., Kerry, Ire., adm. July 17, 1846 dis. Aug. 12, 1846

Patk. Doyle, 22, R.C., Kerry, Ire., adm. July 18, 1846 dis. July 20, 1846

Michl. Fitzgerald, 22, R.C., Kerry, Ire., adm. July 18, 1846 dis. July 20, 1846

James Kennedy, 14, R.C., Kerry, Ire., adm. July 21, 1846 dis. Aug. 14, 1846

John Finnigan, 33, R.C., Kerry, Ire., adm. July 25, 1846 dis. Sept. 12, 1846

Mrs. Mary Finnigan, 30, R.C., Kerry, Ire., adm. July 25, 1846 dis. Sept. 12, 1846

Michl. Conner, 12, R.C., Kerry, Ire., adm. July 25, 1846 dis. Aug. 10, 1846

Thos. Sullivan, 35, R.C., Kerry, Ire., adm. July 27, 1846 dis. Aug. 20, 1846

Mary McArty, 19, R.C., Kerry, Ire., adm. Aug. 22, 1846 dis. Sept. 4, 1846

Recovery, sailed from Sligo, Ire., landed at Saint John June 18

Mrs. Cath. Reilley, 23, R.C., Mayo, Ire., adm. Sept. 3, 1846, Alms House Feb. 27, 1847

John Coan, 20, R.C., Galway, Ire., adm. Dec. 26, 1846 dis. Jan. 4, 1847

Regina, sailed from Baltimore, Ire., landed at Saint John June 2, 1846

Dennis Hayes, 18, R.C., Cork, Ire., adm. June 8, 1846, dis. Sept. 26, 1846

Dennis Spillane, 18, R.C., Cork, Ire., June 16, 1846 dis. Aug. 14, 1846

John Lavis, 18, R.C., Cork, Ire., adm. Sept. 9, 1846 dis. Sept. 17, 1846

James Leavis, 16, R.C., Cork, Ire., adm. Sept. 22, 1846 died Oct. 12, 1846

Renewal, sailed from Berehaven, Ire., landed at Saint John June 20, 1846

John Sullivan, 16, R.C., Cork, Ire., adm. July 24, 1846 dis. Aug. 1, 1846

John Hawkes, 17, R.C., Cork,

92   Irish Migration To New England: Port of Saint John

Ire., adm. Aug. 18, 1846 dis. Sept. 17, 1846 adm. Oct. 27, 1846 dis. Jan. 22, 1846

Renewal, sailed from Baltimore, Ire., landed at Saint John, Oct. 17, 1846
Ellen Glenhorn, 20, R.C., Cork, Ire., adm. Feb. 8, 1847, Alms House, Feb. 20, 1847
Ellen Leahorn, 22, R.C., Cork, Ire., adm. Feb. 20, 1847 dis. March 24, 1847
Mary Donovan, 23, R.C., Cork, Ire., adm. Apr. 13, 1847

Richard Parker, sailed from Cork, Ire., landed at Saint John June 29, 1846
Mary Mahony, 30, R.C., Cork, Ire., adm. July 15, 1846 dis. Aug. 9, 1846
Michl. Delay, 33, R.C., Cork, Ire., adm. July 20, 1846 dis. Aug. 5, 1846
Deborah Regan, 23, R.C., Kerry, Ire., adm. July 25, 1846 dis. Aug. 20, 1846
John Conway, 28, R.C., Cork, Ire., adm. July 25, 1846 dis. Aug. 12, 1846
Mary Horn, 22, R.C., Kerry, Ire., adm. July 25, 1846 dis. Aug. 17, 1846
Danl. Horne, 21, R.C., Cork, Ire., adm. July 27, 1846 dis. Aug. 14, 1846
Mrs. Mary O'Neill, 30, R.C., Cork, Ire., adm. July 29, 1846 dis. Aug. 20, 1846
Joanna O'Neill, 2, R.C., Cork, Ire., adm. July 29, 1846 dis. Aug. 20, 1846

Chas. McArty, 30, R.C., Cork, Ire., adm. Aug. 1, 1846 dis. Aug. 8, 1846

Sir James McDonnell, sailed from Cork, Ire., landed at Saint John May 19 (20), 1846
Thos. Kirby, 5, Kerry, Ire., adm. June 5, 1846 dis. July 28, 1846, uncl. and aunt in Ho., Jas. & Cath. Sullivan
James Sullivan, 26, R.C., Kerry, Ire., adm. June 5, 1846 dis. July 28, 1846
Cath. Sullivan, 40, R.C., Kerry, Ire., adm. June 5, 1846 dis. July 28, 1846

Themis, sailed from Bantry, Ire., landed at Saint John June 21, 1846
Margt. McArty, 20, R.C., Kerry, Ire., adm. July 25, 1846 dis. Aug. 20, 1846
Peter O'Brien, 28, R.C., Cork, Ire., adm. Aug. 19, 1846 dis. Sept. 26, 1846

Victoria, sailed from Youghal, Ire., landed at Saint John June 28, 1846
Jas. Crawford, 6, R.C., Cork, Ire., adm. July 17, 1846, adm. Feb. 20, 1847, age 7, dis. Apr. 9, 1847
Robt. Crawford, 4, R.C., Cork, Ire., adm. July 17, 1846, adm. Feb. 20, 1847, age 4 years 6 mos., dis. June 28, 1847
Patk. Delaney, 20, R.C., Galway, Ire., adm. Sept. 1, 1846 dis. Oct. 13, 1846
Edwd. Hannen, 23, R.C., Galway, Ire., adm. Sept. 1, 1846 dis. Oct.

13, 1846
Patk. Delaney, 20, R.C., Galway, Ire., adm. Oct. 19, 1846 dis. Dec. 22, 1846

Virgilia, sailed from Derry, Ire., landed at Saint John June 2(3), 1846
Geo. Campbell, 26, Presby., Donegal, Ire., adm. June 11, 1846 dis. Oct. 10, 1846
Ann Jane McLellan, 21, Presby., Derry, Ire., adm. July 17, 1846 dis. Oct. 24, 1846
Tim Foley, 32, R.C., Cork, Ire., adm. Aug. 6, 1846 dis. Sept. 29, 1846
Michl. Foley, 32, R.C., Cork, Ire., adm. Aug. 20, 1846 dis. Sept. 19, 1846
Jno. Foley, 4, R.C., Cork, Ire., adm. Aug. 20, 1846 dis. Sept. 19, 1846
Mrs. Dorah Cumming, 22, R.C., Cork, Ire., adm. Dec. 8, 1846 dis. Jan. 4, 1846
Wm Cumming, Alms House, adm. Dec. 11, 1846 dis. Jan. 4, 1846, *mo. came in Virgilia*
John Byrne, 2 mos., R.C., Alms House, Feb. 20, 1847, mo. came in Virgilia dis. March 11, 1847

Warrior, sailed from Drogheda, Ire., landed at Saint John May 30, 1846
Edwd. Fitzsimmons, 18, R.C., Louth, Ire., adm. Aug. 22, 1846 dis. Oct. 28, 1846

Wellington, sailed from Galway, Ire., landed at Saint John, June 4, 1846
Mrs. Mary Mullins, 25, R.C., Galway, Ire., adm. Apr. 30, 1847 died May 16, 1847
Margaret Mullins, 4 mos., R.C., Portland, N.B., adm. Apr. 30, 1847, mo. came in *Wellington*

Woodland Castle, sailed from Cork, Ire., landed at Saint John June 1, 1846
Mrs. Ellen Moore, 44, R.C., Cork, Ire., adm. June 4, 1846 dis. June 8, 1846
Richd. Moore, 20, R.C., Cork, Ire., adm. June 4, 1846 dis. June 9, 1846
Joanna Scanlan, 25, R.C., Cork, Ire., adm. June 8, 1846 dis. June 15, 1846
Patk. Scanlan, 1 year 6 mos., R.C., Cork, Ire., adm. June 8, 1846 dis. June 15, 1846
Dennis Killenan, 24, R.C., Cork, Ire., July 25, 1846 dis. Aug. 12, 1846

Emigrant Deaths in Hospital Partridge Island, Saint John 1847

Passengers of the Barque **Aldebaran**, Barres cleared Sligo, Ireland March 22 arrived Saint John Sunday May 16, 1847 who died in Hospital Partridge Island, Saint John as reported in New Brunswick Courier.

From 7th May to 2nd July

Andrew Devitt, 50
Michael Gillan, 18
John McCalee, 32
Philip Ford, 20
Mary Kelly, 27
James Kilmartin, 40
John McManus, 33
William Rafter, 50
Mary Harrington, 8
John Dougan, 60
Conly Tummany, 23
Larky McCue, 25
Bartley Mantan, 30
John Murray, 26
Patrick Culgin, 28
Honora Bray, 26
Barbara Preston, 60
Mary Gunning, 9 m.
Bernard Kelley, 30
Thomas Rafter, 30
Mary Shea, 2
Peter Cooper, 35
Sarah Brannan, 25
Charles Layman, 30
Mary McGee, 30
Patrick Maloney, 20
Mary Mack, 8
Michael Mullaney, 20
Con. Corragan, 10
Thomas Judge, 40

Mary Maloney, 25
Catherine Fox, 20
Margaret Morrison, 25
Michael Kennon, 20
Peggy Sullivan, 1½
Mary Mann, 25
James Dyer, 27
Michael Lahey, 30
Jerry Cronin, 27
Martin Clarke, 22
Mary Morrisey, 25
Patrick McDermote, 10
John Rafter, 30
Ann Boyce, 6
Unity Gray, 23
Jerry McManus, 4
Mary Learey, 3
Mary Harrington, 30
Catherine Rafter, 25
John Martin, 15
Mary Operan, 9
Mary Harrington, 9
Jerry Sullivan, 10
Winny Conley, 40
Michael Clifford, 23
Bridget Doherty, 23
James McGee, 4
John Green, 22
Patrick Conley, 40
Honora McGee, 25
Bridget Coil, 18

Henry Dogan, 18
Catherine Allan, 12
Lawrence Morin, 30
Thomas Dougan, 13
Francis Gillespie, 13
John Morrison, 23
Charles Flynn, 24
Owen Coughlin, 10
Rody McMorrisy, 33
Ann Gill, 36

Month of July
Nona McManus, 40
Thomas Parat, 60
Winney Parat, 13
John McLynn, 50
Martha Jolly, 22
Hugh Dugan, 33
Thomas Dugan, 19
Ann Coleman, 5.

since 31st July to 7th Aug.
John Gillespie, 14

Passengers of Brig **Midas**, Stitt, left Galway, Ireland arrived Saint John Wednesday May 5th, 1847 who died in Hospital Partridge Island, Saint John as reported in New Brunswick Courier.

From 7th May to 2nd July
John Shaughnessy, age 30; Martin Walsh, age 18

From 10th to 17th Sept
Mary Beatty, 4

During the week ending 11 Sept. 1847
Mary Cameron, 12
John King, 5 mos.

From 24th Sept. to 1st Nov.
Pat. Badger, 31
Thomas Corcannon, 16; Laurence Foy, 57
Pat. Jennings, 5
Pat. Killigan, 32

Passengers of Barque **Mary Harrington**, Montgomery, left Donegal, Ireland arrived Saint John Wednesday May 12th, 1847 who died in Hospital Partridge Island, Saint John as reported in New Brunswick Courier.

From 7th May to 2nd July
Patrick Kerigan, 20

96   Irish Migration To New England: Port of Saint John

Passengers of **Governor Douglas**, Clark, left Baltimore, Ireland April 28th arrived Saint John Monday May 31st, 1847 who died in Hospital Partridge Island, Saint John as reported in New Brunswick Courier.

From 7th May to 2nd July
James McGinnis, 25
Margaret Haley, 5
Hurly Sullivan, 35
John Neil, 34
Mary Nickolson, 30
Patrick Ranney, 42
John Quinn, 22
Daniel Lynch, 22
Mary McNeely, 26

Month of July
John Nicholson, 60
Will Danner, 50
Mary Shannon, 3
Mary Nicholson, 45
Charles Coram, 21
Jerry Hollin, 5

Passenger of **Ocean**, left Baltimore, Ireland April 28th arrived Saint John Friday May 28th, 1847 who died in Hospital Partridge Island, Saint John as reported in New Brunswick Courier.

From 7th May to 2nd July   Mary Rafter, 32

Passengers of Barque **Amazon**, Hays, left Liverpool, England, April 23rd, arrived Saint John Tuesday May 25th, 1847 who died in Hospital Partridge Island, Saint John as reported in New Brunswick Courier.

From 7th May to 2nd July
Winfred Cummidy, age 46
Briget Marven, 25
Ann Duggan, 2 1/2
Mary Hobin, 27
Rachel Gypsum, 22
Norry Sullivan, 30
Charles McGuire, 8
James Gibson, 30
Patrick McDonagh, 25
Patrick McDonough, 20
Catherine Curryan, 16
Martin Aikin, 16

John Coffee, 40
Catherine Owen, 56
Thomas McGraugh, 30
Bernard Morin, 4
William Kennedy, 50
James Gill, 4
Joseph Martin, 2
Margaret Craig, 40
William Kennedy, 35
Margaret McDonough, 3 mos.
Margaret Low, 50
John Moran, 50
George Corr, 33

Francis W. Mullin, 45
Alexander Taylor, 38
William Barret, 31
Ellen Kennedy, 60

Month of July
Thomas Moran, 5
Mary Costello, 26
Mary Corryan, 32
John Corrigan, 16
Cath Hautagan, 22
Jane Partan, 20

Pat. McCarlan, 28
Edward McMullan, 5 mos.
James Looney, 20
Owen Corrigan, 52
John Craig, 14
John Johnstone, 25
Razo Balin, seaman, 21
Margaret Mullin, 24
James Rooney, 15
Patrick Lausay, 45
Mick McGrath, 30
Timothy Connor, 25

Passengers of **Inconstant**, left Cork, Ireland, April 20th arrived Saint John May 22nd, 1847 who died in Hospital Partridge Island, Saint John as reported in New Brunswick Courier.

From 7th May to 2nd July
Ellen McCarty, 20

Catherine Hennisay, 25
Ellen McCarty, 25

Passengers of **Perserverance**, Callaghan, left Cork, Ireland April 30th arrived Saint John Thursday June 24th, 1847 who died in Hospital Partridge Island, Saint John as reported in New Brunswick Courier.

From 7th May to 2nd July
Robert Hues, 60
John McCarty, 40
Catherine O'Harrin, 55
Catherine O'Herrin, 50
Daniel Aherrin, 53
Ellen Morrison, 15
Patrick Murray, 40
John Craig, 19
John Linesa, 33
Constantia Breslin, 20

Month of July
Daniel O'Harran, 10
Mary Durigan, 30
Jerry Olman, 40
Mrs. Keefe, 26
Francis Mann, 31
Michael Savage, 40
Betsy Murray, 20

Passengers of **Hannah**, Shaw, left Sligo, Ireland April 30th arrived Saint John Saturday July 3rd, 1847 who died in Hospital Partridge Island, Saint John reported in New Brunswick Courier.

From 7th May to 2nd July
John Foley, 23
John McCugle, 32
Month of July
Michael Baran, 45

Mary McGowan, 28
Martin Maloney, 50
Daniel Garnet, 28
Catherine Dowd, 35
John Porthan, 38

Passenger of Barque **Marchioness of Clydesdale**, Ferguson left Londonderry, Ireland arrived Saint John Monday May 17th, 1847 who died in Hospital Partridge Island, Saint John as reported in New Brunswick Courier.

From 7th May to 2nd July
Charles Duffy, age 40

Passengers of **Pallas**, Hall, left Cork, Ireland arrived Saint John Saturday May 22nd, 1847 who died in Hospital Partridge Island, Saint John as reported in New Brunswick Courier.

From 7th May to 2nd July
Peter Ryan, 22
Jerry Cronin, 30
Jerry Crummins, 25
Timothy Crummins, 25
Margaret Carty, 25
Mary Carty, 20
Mary Hickey, 25
Mary Harrison, 54
Mary Harrington, 50
Andrew Mannian, 40
Capt. Hall, 45
Daniel Linehan, 25
Catherine Donahough, 39
Jerry Harrigan, 60

Mary Clance, 20
Patrick Keefe, 25

Month of July
Mary Harrigan, 60
Mary Marrygan 49
Will Gillespie, 54
Thos. O'Connor, 15
James Power, 25
Thomas Clarke, 54
Daniel Sullivan, 23
Jerry Harrington, 57
Margaret Glancy, 16,
Mary Ryan, 21

Passengers of **Sir Charles Napier**, Sear, left Londonderry, Ireland arrived Saint John Sunday May 23rd, 1847 who died in Hospital Partridge Island, Saint John as reported in New Brunswick Courier.

From 7th May to 2nd July
John Mitchel, 18
Hugh Boyce, 60

Month of July
Thos Boyer, 12
Will Boyer, 6

Passengers of Brig **Thorney Close**, James Horan, left Donegal, Ireland arrived Saint John Sunday May 23rd, 1847 who died in Hospital Partridge Island, Saint John as reported in New Brunswick Courier.

From 7th May to 2nd July
Barbara Preston, age 65
Mary Tummany, 26
Andrew Tait, 35
James Lynch, 40
Bernard Higgins, 25
Michael Mahir, 26
Ellen Catten, 28

Month of July
John McShannon, 24
Edward McGiness, 20
Charles Cotton, 21
Patk. Campbell, 15
Eleanor Karan, 23
Ann McGrath, 25

Passengers of Brig **Mary**, left Cork, Ireland arrived Saint John Tuesday May 25th, 1847 who died in Hospital Partridge Island, Saint John as reported in New Brunswick Courier.

From 7th May to 2nd July
Michael Cronin, 28
Thomas Ford, 30
Johanna Leary, 12
Bridget Hurly, 16

James Lynch, 36.
Margaret Coughlin, 25.

Month of July
Ellen Donaghue, 27

Passengers of Brig **Dealy**, Stirratt, left Bantry, Ireland arrived Saint John Friday May 28th, 1847 who died in Hospital Partridge Island, Saint John as reported in New Brunswick Courier.

From 7th May to 2nd July
Bridget Conny, age 10
Catherine Collins, age 20
Ellen Haley, 17

Month of July
Rachael Kingston, 33

Passengers of **Æolus**, Michael Driscoll, left Sligo, Ireland arrived Saint John Monday May 31st, 1847 who died in Hospital Partridge Island, Saint John reported in New Brunswick Courier.

100   Irish Migration To New England: Port of Saint John

From 7th May to 2nd July Patrick Crade, 7
Sally Toher, 18 Biddy Kilbride, 15
David Henry, 55 Mary Hartt, 25
Unity Burns, 11 Mary McLoughlin, 40

Passengers of Barque **Malvinia**, Chantley, left Baltimore, Ireland May 9th arrived Saint John July 3rd, 1847 who died in Hospital Partridge Island, Saint John as reported in New Brunswick Courier.

From 7th May to 2nd July *Month of July*
James Carney, 26 Ellen Ryan, 21

Passengers of Brig **Friends**, left Waterford, Ireland (via St. John's, Nfld.) who died in Hospital Partridge Island, Saint John as reported in New Brunswick Courier.

From 7th May to 2nd July *Month of July*
William Conner Jane Reardon, 32
 Winfred Kennedy, 14

Passengers of Schr. **Sally**, Tooling, left Cork, Ireland, May 13th, 1847 arrived Saint John Monday July 5th, 1847 who died in Hospital Partridge Island, Saint John as reported in New Brunswick Courier.

Month of July
John Quinn, 37
Mary Cochrane, 30

Passengers of **Caledonia**, left Cork, Ireland arrived Saint John May 13th, 1847 who died in Hospital Partridge Island, Saint John as reported in New Brunswick Courier.

7th May to 2nd July Will Ligam, 4
Anne McManus, 50 James Lunney, 28
Month of July *31st July to 7th Aug.*
Ellen Wiseman, 25 Dennis Honlahan, 3

Passengers of Brig **Ruby**, Ellenwood (Ellingwood), left Sligo, Ireland, May 8th arrived Saint John Sunday June 20th, 1847 who died in Hospital Partridge Island, Saint John as reported in New Brunswick Courier.

Month of July
Pat Kennedy, 40
Mary Long, 59

Passengers of **David**, Yorke, left Galway, Ireland (via Halifax, N.S.) arrived Saint John Monday May 31st, 1847 who died in Hospital Partridge Island, Saint John as reported in New Brunswick Courier.

24th Sept. to 1st Nov.
Pat. Connor, 18 mos.

Mary Naughton, 3 mos.
Pat. Nathen, 39.

Passengers of Brigt. **Kingston**, Mason, cleared Cork, Ireland May 20th, arrived Saint John Thursday July 22nd, 1847 who died in Hospital Partridge Island, Saint John as reported in New Brunswick Courier.

Month of July
Mary Sullivan, 5

Passengers of Brig **Bache McEvers**, Betty, cleared Cork, Ireland May 22nd arrived Saint John Sunday July 4th, 1847 who died in Hospital Partridge Island, Saint John as reported in New Brunswick Courier.

Month of July
Mick McCarty, 24
Mary Kelly 21
Eliza Noonan, 65
Margaret McCarty, 21

Mary Hogan, 26
Pat Connor, 56
Carty Sullivan, 14
31st July to 7th Aug.
Eliza Latta, 30

Passengers of **Garland**, cleared Cork, Ireland May 28th arrived Saint John Thursday June 24th, 1847 who died in Hospital Partridge Island, Saint John as reported in New Brunswick Courier.

102   Irish Migration To New England: Port of Saint John

Month of July
George Hisan, 21

Passengers of **John Clarke**, Robert Disbrow, cleared Londonderry, Ireland May 21st, arrived Saint John Wednesday June 30th, 1847 who died in Hospital Partridge Island, Saint John as reported in New Brunswick Courier.

Month of July
Pat. Doherty, 25

Betsey Johnston, 31
Sarah Calvin, 10

Passengers of **Ambassadress**, Bannerman, cleared Liverpool, England May 27th arrived Saint John Sunday July 4th, 1847 who died in Hospital Partridge Island, Saint John as reported in New Brunswick Courier.

Month of July
Sarah Cassidy, age 20
Martin Speed, 4
Daniel McDougal, 25
Edward Looney, 24
Mick Sullivan, 5

Margaret Rooney, 26
Ellen Garr, 24
31st July to 7th Aug.
John Burns, 21
Catherine Ryan, 40

Passengers of Barque **Royal Mint**, Williams, cleared Liverpool, England May 30th arrived Saint John Sunday July 18th, 1847 who died in Hospital Partridge Island, Saint John as reported in New Brunswick Courier.

Month of July
Mick Callaghan, 20
Jim Murphy, 40
Nich Carrel, 26

John Ford, 13
William Cherry, seaman, 50
31st July to 7th Aug.
John Irving, 36

Passengers of Brig **Gem**, Murray, cleared Galway May 28th arrived Saint John Wednesday June 30th, 1847 who died in Hospital Partridge Island, Saint John as reported in New Brunswick Courier.

Month of July
Thos Barker, 30.

31st July to 7th Aug.
John Burke, 30

Port of Saint John: Patrige Island Deaths 1847

Passenger of Barque **Linden**, York, left Galway, Ireland, arrived Saint John Monday June 14th, 1847 who died in Hospital Partridge Island, Saint John as reported in New Brunswick Courier.

prior 26th June
Margaret Neil, 30

Passengers of Brig **Seraph**, Mather, left Cork, Ireland (via Boston) arrived Saint John Tuesday July 6th, 1847 who died in Hospital Partridge Island, Saint John as reported in New Brunswick Courier.

Month of July
John Treagh, 50
Thos. Blackson, 26
Will Pine, 30

31st July to 7th Aug.
Daniel Clark, 32
John Maguire, 26

Passengers of Brig **Magnes**, left Galway, Ireland, June 3rd arrived Saint John Saturday July 24th, 1847 who died in Hospital Partridge Island, Saint John reported in New Brunswick Courier.

31st July to 7th August
Patrick Wallace, 50
Andrew Gwynn, 30
6th to 20th August
Michael Carry, 37
20th to 27th August
Mary Haynes, 25
Mary Butin, 30
Norah Healey, 6
Catherine Gilligan, 8
Week ending 3rd Sept.
Patrick Wallace, 12
William Beatty, 4

Peter Larkin, 30
Michael Cilcannon, 3
Week ending 11th Sept.
Judy Wallis, 7
Thomas Keenan, 25
Catherine Cunningham, 22
10th Sept. to 17th Sept.
Catherine Wallace, 12
Mary Wallace, 9
17th Sept. to 25th Sept.
James Kenny, 12
24th Sept. to 1st Nov.
Judy Wallace, 40

Passengers of Brig **Trafalgar**, Younghusband left Cork, Ireland June 5th, arrived Saint John Thursday July 15th, 1847 who died in Hospital Partridge Island, Saint John as reported in New Brunswick Courier.

Irish Migration To New England: Port of Saint John

Month of July 1847
John Mahony, 15 mos.
John Bryan, 26
Ellen Bryan, 50
John Lane, 30
Robert Driscoll, 24

John Land, 50
Honor Fitzgerald, 24
Thos. Stubs, seaman, 20
31st July to 7th August
Eliza Lean, 18

Passengers of Barque **Ward Chipman**, Bilton left Cork, Ireland, June 12th, arrived Saint John Thursday July 22nd, 1847 who died in Hospital Partridge Island, Saint John as reported in New Brunswick Courier.

31st July to 7th August
John Crowley, 70
James Dahy, 3

Daniel Buckley, 19
John Quin, 25
Catherine Ryan, 25

Passsengers of **Very Rev. Theobold Matthew**, Yorke, left Galway, Ireland, arrived Saint John Saturday July 3rd, 1847 who died in Hospital Partridge Island, Saint John as reported in New Brunswick Courier.

Month of July
Will Kain, 23
Patrick Quinn, 26

Passengers of **Blanch**, Green left Donegal, Cork, arrived Saint John Tuesday July 6th, 1847 who died in Hospital Partridge Island, Saint John as reported in New Brunswick Courier.

Month of July
Francis McArthur, 28

31st July to 7th August
Mary Mahon, 30

Passengers of Brig **Alice**, left Galway, Ireland July 8th, arrived Saint John August 20th, 1847 who died in Hospital Partridge Island, Saint John as reported in New Brunswick Courier.

6th August to 20th August
John Lowrey, 7
Week ending 3rd Sept.
Bridget Connor, 4

10th Sept. to 17th Sept.
Michael Mahon, 37

Passengers of Barque **Bethel**, Mosher, left Galway, Ireland, July 15th, arrived Saint John Sunday August 29th, 1847 who died in Hospital Partridge Island, Saint John as reported in New Brunswick Courier.

10th Sept. to 17th Sept.
Catherine Kinney, 47
John Hober, 29
Daniel Murray, 2.
Week ending 11 Sept.
Nancy Vaughan, 28
Joseph Conway, 29
Patrick Welsh, 22
Week ending 24th Sept.
Mary Finley
Bridget Connell, 37
Pat. Maloney, 27
Nancy Lonevan, 35
Sarah Jackson, 53

Timothy Dermond, 25
Bartholomew Connell, 52
William Flanagan
24th Sept. to 1st Nov.
Bridget Deering, 3
James Deering, 2
Ellen Fallasy
Michael Jackson, 53
William Kirby, 22
John Kenny 52
Richard Morley, 50
Mary McCormack, 7
Edward Welsh, 9 mos.

Passengers of Schr. **Lord Fitzgerald**, Yorke left Galway, Ireland July 23rd arrived Saint John September 9th, 1847 who died in Hospital Partridge Island, Saint John as reported in New Brunswick Courier.

10th Sept. to 17th Sept.
Michael Carrington, 37
Week ending 24th Sept.
Patrick Madden, 73
Mary Coff, 52
Bridget Haik, 1
Mary Madden, 27
Mary Hear, 27

24th Sept. to 1st Nov.
Michael Hennehey, 8
Peggy Laughlin, 26
Thos. Malone, 11 mos.
Patrick McLaughlin, 31
Patrick Sexton, 55
Mary Walsh, 27

Emigrants Admitted to the Alms House Saint John From Vessels Arriving in 1847

Although the Emigrant Hospital was located within proximity of the Alms House complex, Courtenay Bay, Saint John, it was a separate institution with its own records. *(see Immigration, PANB, RS555 B1c microfilm F16226)* A comparison of the Emigrant Hospital Records 1847-1849 with the Alms & Work House Records for the same period revealed considerable duplication in names, ages, and places or origin. The following is a consolidation of the records of both the Emigrant Hospital and Alms & Work House Records. In the case where an emigrant appears in both of these institutions, the Emigrant Hospital is identified with the dates of admission, discharge or death. Otherwise, the information is solely derived from the Alms & Work House Records.

Abeona, sailed from Cork, Ire., arrived at Saint John July 13, 1847
John Sullivan, 30, R.C., adm. July 20, 1847 died Aug. 6, 1847
Geo. Patterson, 21, Prot. Cork, Ire., adm. July 21, 1847 dis. Aug. 18, 1847
John Lane, 7, Prot., Cork, Ire., adm. Aug. 16, 1847 dis. Aug. 17, 1847 adm. Aug. 17, 1847 dis. Aug. 19, 1847
William Leane, 18, Prot., Cork, Ire., adm. Aug. 16, 1847 dis. Aug. 31, 1847
Henry Leane, 14, Prot., Cork, Ire., adm. Aug. 16, 1847 dis. Aug. 31, 1847
Allice Leane, 9, Prot., Cork, Ire., adm. Aug. 16, 1847 dis. Aug. 17, 1847 adm. Aug. 17, 1847 dis. Aug. 19, 1847

Mrs. Desmond, 55, R.C., Cork, Ire., adm. Aug. 17, 1847 died Aug. 21, 1847
Catherine Desmond, 7, R.C., Cork, Ire., adm. Aug. 17, 1847 dis. Sept. 3, 1847
Johanna Desmond, 7 mos., R.C., Cork, Ire., adm. Aug. 17, 1847 died Aug. 25, 1847
Patrick Desmond, 16, R.C., Cork, Ire., adm. Aug. 17, 1847 dis. Sept. 3, 1847
Judy Doran, 40, R.C., Donegal, Ire., adm. Aug. 17, 1847 dis. Aug. 26, 1847
Denis Desmond, 50, R.C., Cork, Ire., adm. Aug. 21, 1847 died Aug. 24, 1847
Eliza Leane, 9, Cork, Ire., adm. Aug. 27, 1847 dis. Sept. 2, 1847
Ellen Desmond, 18, R.C., Cork, Ire., adm. Sept. 24, 1847

Alice Lane, 11, Prot.,Cork, Ire., adm. Sept. 25, 1847
Mary Callaghan, 19, R.C., Cork, Ire., adm. Sept. 27, 1847
Owen Steel, 50, R.C., Cork, Ire., Cork, Ire., adm. March 20, 1848 dis. Aug. 5, 1848 adm. Aug. 7, 1848 dis. Dec. 31, 1848 adm. Emigrant Hospital Aug. 7, 1848, destitute, dis. Dec. 31, 1848
Nicholas Moran, 5, R.C., Tyrone, Ire., adm. March 20, 1848 dis. May 6, 1848 adm. Emigrant Hospital May 1, 1848, fever
Honora Maguire, 2, Sligo, Ire., adm. March 20, 1848
Mary Moran, 3, Tyrone, Ire., adm. March 20, 1848 died Apr. 1, 1848

Adeline (Adelaide), sailed from Cork, Ire., arrived at Saint John Aug. 3, 1847
John Donovan, 23, R.C., Cork, Ire., adm. Aug. 17, 1847
Jerry Kennedy, 30, R.C., Cork, Ire., adm. Aug. 26, 1847
Dan Donovan, 23, R.C., Cork, Ire., adm. Sept. 1, 1847
Mary Coan, 10, R.C., Kerry, Ire., adm. Sept. 3, 1847 died Sept. 18, 1847
Mary Connell, 18, Cork, Ire., adm. March 20, 1848 died March 6, 1848

Aeolus, sailed (second voyage) from Sligo arrived at Saint John Nov. 1st, 1847
Ed. McAnn, 30, R.C., Sligo, Ire., adm. March 20, 1848 died Apr. 12, 1848
And. Tumony, 14, R.C., Sligo, Ire., adm. March 20, 1848 died March 28, 1848
Mich. Kilmartin, 18, R.C., Sligo, Ire., adm. March 20, 1848 died June 5, 1848 adm. Emigrant Hospital May 1, 1848
Thos. Kilmartin, 15, R.C., Sligo, Ire., adm. March 20, 1848 dis. July 13, 1848 adm. Emigrant Hospital May 1, 1848, destitute
Pat. Kilmartin, 54, R.C., Sligo, Ire., adm. March 20, 1848 dis. July 19, 1848 adm. Emigrant Hospital May 1, 1848, destitute
James Duffy, 25, R.C., Sligo, Ire., adm. March 20, 1848 dis. Aug. 7, 1848 adm. Emigrant Hospital May 1, 1848, destitute
Martin Rourk, 30, R.C., Sligo, Ire., adm. March 20, 1848 dis. July 12, 1848 adm. Emigrant Hospital May 1, 1848
Pat McMurray, 14, R.C., Sligo, Ire., adm. March 20, 1848 dis. March 31, 1848
James McMurray, 40, R.C., Sligo, Ire., adm. March 20, 1848 died March 21, 1848
Pat Pye, 20, R.C., Sligo, Ire., adm. March 20, 1848 died March 21, 1848
Tom Pye, 50, R.C., Sligo, Ire., adm. March 20, 1848 dis. Apr. 18, 1848 adm. May 13, 1848 dis. July 21, 1848 adm. Emigrant Hospital May 13, 1848, destitute
Wm Pye, 23, R.C., Sligo, Ire., adm. March 20, 1848 dis. Apr. 18, 1848 adm. May 13, 1848 dis. July 21, 1848 adm. Emigrant Hospital May 13, 1848, destitute
Dominick Flanagan, 22, R.C., Sligo, Ire., adm. March 20, 1848 dis. Dec. 31, 1848 adm. Emigrant

Hospital May 1, 1848, destitute Æneas Harkins, 19, R.C., Sligo, Ire., adm. March 20, 1848 died March 28, 1848
Francis Cronin, 66, R.C., Sligo, Ire., adm. March 20, 1848 dis. July 3, 1848 adm. Emigrant Hospital May 1, 1848, destitute
Pat McLaughlin, 15, R.C., Sligo, Ire., adm. March 20, 1848 dis. Oct. 17, 1848 adm. Emigrant Hospital May 1, 1848, destitute
James Kilcoin (James Kilcolin), 24, R.C., Sligo, Ire., adm. March 20, 1848 dis. Dec. 4, 1848 adm. Emigrant Hospital May 1, 1848, fever
Dan. Carolane, 65, R.C., Sligo, Ire., adm. March 20, 1848 dis. May 15. 1848 adm. Emigrant Hospital May 1, 1848, fever
Thomas Carolane 18, R.C., Sligo, Ire., adm. March 20, 1848 dis. May 15, 1848 adm. Emigrant Hospital May 1, 1848, fever
James McSharry, 15, R.C., Sligo, Ire., adm. March 20, 1848 dis. Apr. 7, 1848
Ned Leonard, 50, R.C., Sligo, Ire., adm. March 20, 1848 dis. May 13, 1848 adm. Emigrant Hospital May 1, 1848, fever
Jas. Moohan, 32, R.C., Sligo, Ire., adm. March 20, 1848 dis. Oct. 17, 1848 adm. Emigrant Hospital May 1, 1848, destitute
Jas. Williamson, 23, R.C., Sligo, Ire., adm. March 20, 1848 dis. Apr. 17, 1848
John Gallagher, 22, R.C., Sligo, Ire., adm. March 20, 1848 dis. July 19, 1848 adm. Emigrant Hospital May 1, 1848, destitute

Michl. Meloy, 20, R.C., Sligo, Ire., adm. March 20, 1848 dis. Mar. 29, 1848
Thos. Pye, 16, R.C., Sligo, Ire., adm. March 20, 1848 dis. Apr. 25, 1848
John Pye, 40, R.C., Sligo, Ire., adm. March 20, 1848 dis. May 3, 1848 adm. Emigrant Hospital May 1, 1848, destitute
Wm Pye, 21, R.C., Sligo, Ire., adm. March 20, 1848 dis. May 3, 1848 adm. Emigrant Hospital May 1, 1848, destitute
Alex. Walker, 20, Prot., Sligo, Ire., adm. March 20, 1848 dis. July 12, 1848 adm. Emigrant Hospital May 1, 1848, destitute
Tim Mooney, 18, R.C., Sligo, Ire., adm. March 20, 1848 dis. Apr. 19, 1848
Ed Rafter, 32, R.C., Sligo, Ire., adm. March 20, 1848 dis. May 8, 1848 adm. Emigrant Hospital May 1, 1848, fever
Tom McSharry, 24, R.C., Sligo, Ire., adm. March 20, 1848 dis. Apr. 20, 1848
Pat McGee, 25, R.C., Sligo, Ire., adm. March 20, 1848 dis. Apr. 17, 1848
Henry McKever (Henry McEver), 25, R.C., Sligo, Ire., adm. March 20, 1848 dis. May 8, 1848 adm. Emigrant Hospital May 1, 1848, destitute
Michl. Laden. 60, R.C., Sligo, Ire., adm. March 20, 1848 dis. March 25, 1848
John Kilgallon, 40, R.C., Sligo, Ire., adm. March 20, 1848 dis. Apr. 17, 1848
Martin Duffy, 48, R.C., Sligo, Ire.,

adm. March 20, 1848 dis. Apr. 14, 1848
Martin Duffy jr., 18, R.C., Sligo, Ire., adm. March 20, 1848 dis. Apr. 14, 1848
John Mullen, 50, R.C., Sligo, Ire., adm. March 20, 1848 dis. July 19, 1848 adm. Emigrant Hospital May 1, 1848, destitute
Pat. Harrison, 20, R.C., Tyrone, Ire., adm. March 20, 1848 dis. May 16, 1848 adm. Emigrant Hospital May 1, 1848, destitute
Mich. Harkins, 15, R.C., Sligo, Ire., adm. March 20, 1848 dis. Apr. 10, 1848
Martin Hartt, 15, R.C., Sligo, Ire., adm. March 20, 1848 dis. Apr. 10, 1848
Pat McAnn, 4, R.C., Sligo, Ire., adm. March 20, 1848 dis. Sept. 11, 1848 adm. Emigrant Hospital May 1, 1848, destitute
Jno. McKendra, 12, R.C., Sligo, Ire., adm. March 20, 1848 died May 2, 1848 adm. Emigrant Hospital May 1, 1848, destitute
Thos. Duffy, 5, R.C., Sligo, Ire., adm. March 20, 1848 died Apr. 23, 1848
Pat. Gill, 10, R.C., Sligo, Ire., adm. March 20, 1848 died March 21, 1848
Michl. McMurray, 10, R.C., Sligo, Ire., adm. March 20, 1848 dis. March 29, 1848
John McMurray, 5, R.C., Sligo, Ire., adm. March 20, 1848 dis. March 29, 1848
Hugh McMurray, 3, R.C., Sligo, Ire., adm. March 20, 1848 dis. March 29, 1848
Roger Carolane, 12, R.C., Sligo, Ire., adm. March 20, 1848 dis. May 15, 1848 adm. Emigrant Hospital May 1, 1848, destitute
Pat McSharry, 13, R.C., Sligo, Ire., adm. March 20, 1848 dis. Apr. 7, 1848
Thos. Rafter, 9, R.C., Sligo, Ire., adm. March 20, 1848 dis. May 24, 1848 adm. Emigrant Hospital May 1, 1848, destitute
Francis Rafter, 5, R.C., Sligo, Ire., adm. March 20, 1848 dis. May 24, 1848 adm. Emigrant Hospital May 1, 1848, destitute
John Duffy, 13, R.C., Sligo, Ire., adm. March 20, 1848 dis. Apr. 14, 1848
Jas. Harkins, 5, R.C., Sligo, Ire., adm. March 20, 1848 dis. Apr. 10, 1848
Allen Hartt, 5, R.C., Sligo, Ire., adm. March 20, 1848 dis. March 20, 1848
Mrs. Ellen Johnston, 40, Sligo, Ire., adm. March 20, 1848 dis. May 25, 1848
Hanna Kelly, 22, Sligo, Ire., adm. March 20, 1848 dis. Aug. 3, 1848
Ellen McGowan, 16, Sligo, Ire., adm. March 20, 1848 dis. Oct. 24, 1848 to Philadelphia
Kitty Laughlin, 30, Sligo, Ire., adm. March 20, 1848 dis. July 11, 1848
Mary Laughlin, 18, Sligo, Ire., adm. March 20, 1848 dis. Apr. 23, 1848
Cath. Rooney, 20, Sligo, Ire., adm. March 20, 1848 dis. March 29, 1848
Mary Harrison, 20, Sligo, Ire., adm. March 20, 1848 dis. May 29, 1848

Mary Rourk, 18, Sligo, Ire., adm. March 20, 1848 dis. May 18, 1848 returned May 26, 1848
Betty Corigan, 30, Sligo, Ire., adm. March 20, 1848 dis. Apr. 13, 1848
Margt. Corritt, 17, Sligo, Ire., adm. March 20, 1848 dis. May 18, 1848
Mary Kilmartin, 20, Sligo, Ire., adm. March 20, 1848 dis. May 18, 1848
Mrs. Biddy Kilmartin, 40, Sligo, Ire., adm. March 20, 1848 dis. Sept. 6, 1848
Cath. Rourk, 19, Sligo, Ire., adm. March 20, 1848 dis. May 18, 1848 adm. July 7, 1848, age 20, dis. Aug. 8, 1848
Ann O'Neill, 20, Sligo, Ire., adm. March 20, 1848 dis. Apr. 17, 1848
Nelly Healey, 20, Sligo, Ire., adm. March 20, 1848 dis. June 22, 1848
Ann McKendra, wid., 50, Sligo, Ire., adm. March 20, 1848 dis. Apr. 19, 1848
Ann McKendra, jr., 15, Sligo, Ire., adm. March 20, 1848 dis. May 22, 1848
Mrs. Biddy Duffy, 35, Sligo, Ire., adm. March 20, 1848 dis. June 20, 1848
Mary McCann, 29, Sligo, Ire., adm. March 20, 1848 dis. Sept. 11, 1848 adm. Dec. 16, 1848, age 30
Mrs. Ann Pye, 50, Sligo, Ire., adm. March 20, 1848 dis. Aug. 7, 1848
Cath. Campbell, 19, Sligo, Ire., adm. March 20, 1848 dis. July 5, 1848
Biddy Campbell, 15, Sligo, Ire., adm. March 20, 1848 dis. July 5, 1848
Mary Flanagan, wid., 45, Sligo, Ire., adm. March 20, 1848
Kitty Flanagan, 20, Sligo, Ire., adm. March 20, 1848
Elsi Gillan, wid., 40, Sligo, Ire., adm. March 20, 1848 dis. Aug. 1, 1848
Mrs. Mary Cronan, 50, Sligo, Ire., adm. March 20, 1848 dis. July 3, 1848
Libby Cronan, 14, Sligo, Ire., adm. March 20, 1848 dis. May 17, 1848
Cath. Fox, 19, Sligo, Ire., adm. March 20, 1848 dis. Apr. 18, 1848
Bridget Gillen, 40, Sligo, Ire., adm. March 20, 1848 dis. May 16, 1848
Nancy McGowan, 16, Sligo, Ire., adm. March 20, 1848 dis. May 16, 1848
Ann Rooney, 40, Sligo, Ire., adm. March 20, 1848 dis. May 13, 1848
Mary Healey, wid., 40, Sligo, Ire., adm. March 20, 1848 dis. March 21, 1848
Nelly McMurray, 50, Sligo, Ire., adm. March 20, 1848 dis. March 31, 1848
Mary Pye, 22, Sligo, Ire., adm. March 20, 1848 dis. Apr. 18, 1848
Ann Pye, 15, Sligo, Ire., adm. March 20, 1848 dis. July 21, 1848
Mrs. Nancy Pye, 40, Sligo, Ire., adm. March 20, 1848 dis. Aug. 3,

Port of Saint John: Alms House 1847

1848
Mary Harkins, 20, Sligo, Ire., adm. March 20, 1848 dis. Apr. 18, 1848
Biddy Harkins, 15, Sligo, Ire., adm. March 20, 1848 dis. May 9, 1848
Mrs. Mary Mullen, 50, Sligo, Ire., adm. March 20, 1848 dis. July 19, 1848
Kitty Carolane, 21, Sligo, Ire., adm. March 20, 1848 dis. May 15. 1848
Mary Carolane, 19, Sligo, Ire., adm. March 20, 1848 dis. May 15, 1848
Mary Carolane, 17, Sligo, Ire., adm. March 20, 1848 dis. July 26, 1848
Cath. McGaugh, 14, Sligo, Ire., adm. March 20, 1848 dis. July 7, 1848
Wid. McSharry, 32, Sligo, Ire., adm. March 20, 1848 died Apr. 7, 1848
Nelly Moran, 40, Sligo, Ire., adm. March 20, 1848 dis. Aug. 1, 1848
Sally Conners, 15, Sligo, Ire., adm. March 20, 1848 died Apr. 3, 1848
Honor Kilmartin, 52, Sligo, Ire., adm. March 20, 1848 dis. July 11, 1848
Peggy Kilmartin, 21, Sligo, Ire., adm. March 20, 1848 dis. Aug. 6, 1848
Betty Duffy, 42, Sligo, Ire., adm. March 20, 1848 dis. Apr. 14, 1848
Biddy Duffy, 23, Sligo, Ire., adm. March 20, 1848 dis. Apr. 17, 1848 adm. Apr. 19, 1848 dis. May 18, 1848
Kitty Duffy, 15, Sligo, Ire., adm. March 20, 1848 dis. Apr. 14, 1848
Winni Moohan, 40, Sligo, Ire., adm. March 20, 1848 dis. Oct. 17, 1848
Biddy Moohan, 23, Sligo, Ire., adm. March 20, 1848 dis. June 7, 1848, sent to Boston
Mary Kilgallon, 50, Sligo, Ire., adm. March 20, 1848 dis. Apr. 17, 1848
Ellen Mulloy, 38, Sligo, Ire., adm. March 20, 1848 dis. July 5, 1848
Cath. Williamson, 23, Sligo, Ire., adm. March 20, 1848 dis. Apr. 24, 1848
Mrs. Winni Rafter, 20, Sligo, Ire., adm. March 20, 1848 dis. May 24, 1848
Biddy Gallagher, 19, Sligo, Ire., adm. March 20, 1848 dis. May 15, 1848
Mrs. Ann McKever, 40, Sligo, Ire., adm. March 20, 1848 dis. June 12, 1848
Mary McSharry, 26, Sligo, Ire., adm. March 20, 1848 dis. June 7, 1848
Ann Gallagher, 30, Sligo, Ire., adm. March 20, 1848 dis. July 8, 1848
Biddy Leaden, 22, Sligo, Ire., adm. March 20, 1848 dis. Apr. 11, 1848
Honor Leaden, 20, Sligo, Ire., adm. March 20, 1848 dis. Apr. 28, 1848
Catherine Leaden, 18, Sligo, Ire., adm. March 20, 1848 dis. March 23, 1848
Mrs. Matilda Magee, 24, Sligo, Ire., adm. March 20, 1848 dis.

Apr. 24, 1848
Ann Foley, 30, Sligo, Ire., adm. March 20, 1848 dis. Apr. 20, 1848
Biddy Leaden, 60, Sligo, Ire., adm. March 20, 1848 dis. Apr. 24, 1848
Honor Leaden, 20, Sligo, Ire., adm. March 20, 1848 dis. Apr. 24, 1848
Mary Leaden, 18, Sligo, Ire., adm. March 20, 1848 dis. March 23, 1848
Hanna Leaden, 16, Sligo, Ire., adm. March 20, 1848 dis. March 23, 1848
Cath. Mooney, 40, Sligo, Ire., adm. March 20, 1848 dis. Apr. 3, 1848
Mary Ann Mooney, 16, Sligo, Ire., adm. March 20, 1848 dis. May 6, 1848
Grace Duffy, 62, Sligo, Ire., adm. March 20, 1848 died Jan. 7, 1849
Margt. Mullen, 15, Sligo, Ire., adm. March 20, 1848 dis. June 22, 1848
Biddy Gillin, 20, Sligo, Ire., adm. March 20, 1848 dis. July 20, 1848
Cath. Gillin, 18, Sligo, Ire., adm. March 20, 1848 dis. May 18, 1848 adm. June 13, 1848 dis. July 10, 1848
Biddy Harkins, 38, Sligo, Ire., adm. March 20, 1848 dis. Apr. 10, 1848
Mary Harrison, 21, Sligo, Ire., adm. March 20, 1848 dis. Apr. 10, 1848
Bridget Hartt, 35, Sligo, Ire., adm. March 20, 1848 dis. Apr. 10, 1848
Eliz. Johnston, 4 years 6 mos., Sligo, Ire., adm. March 20, 1848 dis. May 25, 1848
Margt. Johnston, 7, Sligo, Ire., adm. March 20, 1848 dis. May 25, 1848
Mary McGuire, 32, Sligo, Ire., adm. March 20, 1848
Ellen McCann, 6, Sligo, Ire., adm. March 20, 1848 dis. Sept. 11, 1848 adm. Dec. 16, 1848
Biddy Kilmartin, 13, Sligo, Ire., adm. March 20, 1848 died Apr. 23, 1848
Margt. Gill, 13, Sligo, Ire., adm. March 20, 1848 dis. Aug. 3, 1848
Hanora Cronin, 12, Sligo, Ire., adm. March 20, 1848 died March 21, 1848
Margt. Cronin, 10, Sligo, Ire., adm. March 20, 1848 died March 23, 1848
Biddy Healey, 12, Sligo, Ire., adm. March 20, 1848 dis. March 21, 1848
Mary Mullen, 12, Sligo, Ire., adm. March 20, 1848 dis. May 17, 1848
Ann Mullen, 3, Sligo, Ire., adm. March 20, 1848 dis. June 22, 1848
Peggy Carolane, 11, Sligo, Ire., adm. March 20, 1848 dis. Apr. 16, 1848
Betty Kilmartin, 10, Sligo, Ire., adm. March 20, 1848 dis. May 17, 1848
Cath. McSharry, 10, Sligo, Ire., adm. March 20, 1848 dis. Apr. 7, 1848
Mary Duffy, 9, Sligo, Ire., adm. March 20, 1848 dis. Apr. 14, 1848

Kitty Moohan, 12, Sligo, Ire., adm. March 20, 1848 dis. Oct. 17, 1848
Biddy Moohan, 10, Sligo, Ire., adm. March 20, 1848 dis. Oct. 17, 1848, sent to Boston
Nelly McKever, 4, Sligo, Ire., adm. March 20, 1848 dis. June 12, 1848
Mary Harkins, 9, Sligo, Ire., adm. March 20, 1848 dis. Apr. 10, 1848
Mary Hartt, 11, Sligo, Ire., adm. March 20, 1848 dis. Apr. 10, 1848
Ellen Hartt, 5, Sligo, Ire., adm. March 20, 1848 dis. Apr. 10, 1848
Kitty Laden, 20, Sligo, Ire., adm. March 28, 1848 dis. May 16, 1848
Mary Laden, 16, Sligo, Ire., adm. March 28, 1848 dis. May 16, 1848
Tom Pye (Thos. Pye), 15, R.C., Sligo, Ire., adm. May 17, 1848 dis. July 21, 1848 adm. Emigrant Hospital May 17, 1848, bowel comp.
Pat Green, 40, R.C., Sligo, Ire., adm. May 17, 1848 dis. July 12, 1848 adm. Emigrant Hospital May 17, 1848, sprain
Brian McSharry (Barney McSharry), 22, R.C., Sligo, Ire., adm. May 18, 1848 dis. June 7, 1848 adm. Emigrant Hospital May 18, 1848
Mary McGowan, 4, Sligo, Ire., adm. May 22, 1848 dis. May 31, 1848
Mary Rourk, 18, Sligo, Ire., adm. May 22, 1848 dis. July 26, 1848

Mary McKendra, wid., 50, Sligo, Ire., adm. May 22, 1848 dis. July 31, 1848
Kitty Garvan, 17, Sligo, Ire., adm. May 22, 1848 dis. June 21, 1848
Hanna McSharry (Hanna Foley), 20, Sligo, Ire., adm. May 22, 1848 dis. Aug. 1, 1848
Mic. McGowan, 38, R.C., Leitrim, Ire., adm. May 22, 1848 dis. May 31, 1848 adm. Emigrant Hospital May 25, 1848, destitute adm. June 2, 1848, destitute, dis. July 2, 1848
Pat Higgins, 20, R.C., Sligo, Ire., adm. May 30, 1848 dis. July 8, 1848 adm. Emigrant Hospital June 1, 1848, fever
Ann McGuire, 30, R.C., Fermanagh, Ire., adm. Sept. 20, 1848 dis. Oct. 24, 1848 adm. Nov. 3, 1848 died Nov. 13, 1848
Pat Kilbride, 40, R.C., Sligo, Ire., adm. Oct. 28, 1848 dis. Dec. 31, 1848 adm. Emigrant Hospital Oct. 28, 1848, destitute, dis. Dec. 31, 1848
John Kilbride, 8, R.C., Sligo, Ire., adm. Oct. 28, 1848 dis. Dec. 31, 1848 adm. Emigrant Hospital Oct. 28, 1848, destitute, dis. Dec. 31, 1848
John Gallagher, 5, R.C., Sligo, Ire., adm. Oct. 30, 1848 dis. Dec. 31, 1848, mo. dead fa. deserted adm. Emigrant Hospital Oct. 30, 1848, destitute, dis. Dec. 31, 1848
Mary McAnn, 2 years 6 mos., R.C., Sligo, Ire., adm. Dec. 16, 1848
Pat. McCann, 4, R.C., Sligo, Ire., adm. Dec. 16, 1848

Æolus, sailed from Sligo, Ire., arrived at Saint John June 9, 1847

Denis Calone, 24, R.C., Sligo, Ire., adm. June 24, 1847 dis. Aug. 24, 1847

Dan Donovan, 22, R.C., Cork, Ire., adm. June 26, 1847, dis. July 6, 1847

Paddy Carthy, 30, R.C., Sligo, Ire., adm. June 26, 1847, dis. July 6, 1847

Denis Connor, 27, R.C., Sligo, Ire., adm. June 29, 1847 dis. July 12, 1847

John Keavlahan, 19, R.C., Sligo, Ire., adm. June 29, 1847 died Aug. 17, 1847

Allan Dowling, 22, R.C., Cork, Ire., adm. June 29, 1847 dis. July 12, 1847

James Currie, 40, Prot., Sligo, Ire., adm. June 29, 1847 dis. July 13, 1847

Mrs. Margaret Currie, 48, Prot., Sligo, Ire., adm. June 29, 1847 dis. July 12, 1847

Nancey Focher (Nancey Forker), 15, R.C., Sligo, Ire., adm. June 29, 1847 dis. July 12, 1847

Margaret Burke, 17, R.C., Sligo, Ire., adm. June 30, 1847

Mary Hennigan, 20, R.C., Sligo, Ire., adm. July 1, 1847 dis. July 11, 1847

Mrs. Smith, 32, R.C., Sligo, Ire., adm. July 1, 1847 dis. July 8, 1847

John Smith, 1 year 9 mos., R.C., Sligo, Ire., adm. July 1, 1847 dis. July 8, 1847

Mary McGlone, 17, R.C., Sligo, Ire., adm. July 1, 1847 dis. Aug. 11, 1847

Michael McGlone, 19, R.C., Sligo, Ire., adm. July 1, 1847

Patrick Connors, 28, R.C., Sligo, Ire., adm. July 1, 1847 dis. July 7, 1847

Brian Calone, 22, R.C., Sligo, Ire., adm. July 1, 1847 dis. Aug. 24, 1847

Mrs. Mary Cumming, 24, R.C., Sligo, Ire., adm. July 2, 1847, dis. Aug. 25, 1847

Biddy Cumming, 1 year 9 mos., R.C., Sligo, Ire. adm. July 2, 1847

Denis Curney, 40, R.C., Sligo, Ire., adm. July 2, 1847, dis. Aug. 25, 1847

Francis Warrant, 5, adm. July 3, 1847, died July 18, 1847

Owen Focher (Owen Forker), 35, R.C., Sligo, Ire., adm. July 3, 1847, dis. July 12, 1847

Mrs. Mary Focher (Mrs. Mary Forker), 26, R.C., Sligo, Ire., adm. July 3, 1847, dis. July 11, 1847

Teady Galoon, 17, R.C., Sligo, Ire., adm. July 3, 1847, dis. July 17, 1847

Mary Galoon, 16, R.C., Sligo, Ire., adm. July 5, 1847, dis. July 12, 1847

Nancy Kilbride, 39, R.C., Sligo, Ire., adm. July 6, 1847, died July 25, 1847

John Kilbride, 9, R.C., Sligo, Ire., adm. July 6, 1847, dis. July 29, 1847, taken by father

Eliza Gillin, 50, R.C., Sligo, Ire., adm. July 7, 1847, dis. July 17, 1847

Winni Gillin, 20, R.C., Sligo, Ire., adm. July 7, 1847, dis. July 17, 1847

Port of Saint John: Alms House 1847   115

Catherine Gillin, 18, R.C., Sligo, Ire., adm. July 7, 1847, dis. July 17, 1847
Ellen Gillin, 12, R.C., Sligo, Ire., adm. July 7, 1847, dis. July 17, 1847
Jane Gillin, 6, R.C., Sligo, Ire., adm. July 7, 1847, dis. July 17, 1847
Ellen Foley, 22, R.C., Sligo, Ire., adm. July 7, 1847, dis. July 11, 1847
Cath. Ann O'Conner, 7 years 6 mos., R.C., Alms House, adm. July 7, 1847, dis. July 17, 1847
Owen Keavlahan, 80, R.C., Sligo, Ire., adm. July 7, 1847, died July 20, 1847
John Galoon, 20, R.C., Sligo, Ire., adm. July 7, 1847 dis. July 17, 1847
Nelly Galoon, 15, R.C., Sligo, Ire., adm. July 8, 1847 dis. July 17, 1847
Martin Galoon, 18, R.C., Sligo, Ire., adm. July 8, 1847 dis. July 17, 1847
Owen Galoon, 12, R.C., Sligo, Ire., adm. July 8, 1847 dis. July 17, 1847
Thomas Galoon, 8, R.C., Sligo, Ire., adm. July 8, 1847 dis. July 17, 1847
James McGaloon, 60, R.C., Sligo, Ire., adm. July 8, 1847
Mary Kilbride, 18, R.C., Sligo, Ire., adm. July 8, 1847 died Aug. 6, 1847
Mary Gilroy, 47, R.C., Sligo, Ire., adm. July 8, 1847 died July 28, 1847
Mary Gilroy, 12, R.C., Sligo, Ire., adm. July 8, 1847 died July 28, 1847
Biddy Gilroy, 10, R.C., Sligo, Ire., adm. July 8, 1847 dis. Aug. 25, 1847
Hugh McGloun, 13, R.C., Sligo, Ire., adm. July 8, 1847 dis. July 17, 1847
James McGloun, 9, R.C., Sligo, Ire., adm. July 8, 1847 dis. July 17, 1847
Mary Crann, 27, R.C., Sligo, Ire., adm. July 9, 1847
Catherine Crann, 7, R.C., Sligo, Ire., adm. July 9, 1847 dis. July 12, 1847
Mary Crann, 2, R.C., Sligo, Ire., adm. July 9, 1847 dis. July 12, 1847
Mary Hartt, 5., R.C., Sligo, Ire., adm. July 9, 1847
James McGowan, 30, R.C., Sligo, Ire., adm. July 10, 1847
Nathl. Hood, 20, Prot., Sligo, Ire., adm. July 10, 1847 dis. July 12, 1847
Biddy Conlie, 25, R.C., Sligo, Ire., adm. July 10, 1847
Patrick Maylone (Patrk. Maglone), 22, R.C., Sligo, Ire., adm. July 16, 1847
Adam Johnston, 49, Prot., Sligo, Ire., adm. July 17, 1847 adm. March 20, 1848 dis. May 25, 1848 adm. Emigrant Hospital May 1, 1848
Thos. Johnson, 16, Prot., Sligo, Ire.,, adm. July 21, 1847
Robt. Johnson, 13, Prot., Sligo, Ire.,, adm. July 21, 1847
Charles Johnson, 9, Prot., Sligo, Ire.,, adm. July 21, 1847
Eliza Johnson, 4 years 6 mos., Prot., Sligo, Ire.,, adm. July 21,

116 Irish Migration To New England: Port of Saint John

1847
Margaret Johnson, 7, Prot., Sligo, Ire.,, adm. July 21, 1847 died Sept. 28, 1847
William Johnston, 22, Prot., Sligo, Ire., adm. Aug. 22, 1847
Mary Anne Johnston, 14, Prot., Sligo, Ire., adm. Aug. 22, 1847 dis. Aug. 26, 1847
Edward McGowen, 6, R.C., Sligo, Ire., adm. Sept. 1, 1847, dis. Sept. 4, 1847
Mary McGowen, 14, R.C., Sligo, Ire., adm. Sept. 1, 1847, dis. Sept. 4, 1847
Margaret McGowen, 30, R.C., Sligo, Ire., adm. Sept. 1, 1847, dis. Sept. 4, 1847
Cecilla McGowen, 18, R.C., Sligo, Ire., adm. Sept. 1, 1847, dis. Sept. 4, 1847
Ellen McGowen, 8, R.C., Sligo, Ire., adm. Sept. 1, 1847
Bridget McDonnell, 18, R.C., Sligo, Ire., adm. Sept. 23, 1847
Mich. Malone, 19, R.C., Sligo, Ire., adm. Sept. 23, 1847
Pat Focher (Pat Forker), 10, R.C., Sligo, Ire., adm. Sept. 24, 1847
Pieacey Costello, 25, R.C., Sligo, Ire., adm. Sept. 24, 1847
Pat Clancey, 50, R.C., Sligo, Ire., adm. Sept. 24, 1847
John Johnston, 17, Prot., Sligo, Ire., adm. March 20, 1848 dis. May 23, 1848 adm. Emigrant Hospital May 1, 1848

Albatross, sailed from Liverpool, England, landed at Boston, Mass. Apr. 26, 1847
Thomas Mantle, 49, R.C., Clare, Ire., adm. May 10, 1847 died May 14, 1847

Aldebaran, sailed from Sligo, Ire., arrived at Saint John June 18, 1847
John Finan, 20, R.C., Sligo, Ire., adm. June 26, 1847 dis. July 7, 1847
James Brannen, 55, R.C., Mayo, Ire., adm. Sept. 23, 1847
Cath. Brannen, 12, R.C., Mayo, Ire., adm. Sept. 23, 1847
James Brennan, 54, R.C., Mayo, Ire., adm. March 20, 1848 dis. March 21, 1848

Amazon, sailed from Liverpool, England, arrived at Saint John June 18, 1847
John Enright, 22, R.C., Cork, Ire., adm. June 20, 1847 died July 11, 1847
Thos. May, 20, R.C., Sligo, Ire., adm. June 23, 1847 dis. July 17, 1847 adm. July 23, 1847 died Aug. 20, 1847
Margaret Sullivan, 15, R.C., Kerry, Ire., adm. June 26, 1847
Thos. Bowes, 30, R.C., Tipperary, Ire., adm. June 27, 1847 dis. July 17, 1847
Edward Keary, 21, R.C., Cork, Ire., adm. June 30, 1847
John Coburt, 26, R.C., Cork, Ire., adm. July 2, 1847, dis. July 31, 1847
Mathew Flinn, 30, R.C., Waterford, Ire., adm. July 3, 1847, dis. July 12, 1847
Isabella McMullin, 30, R.C., Fermanagh, Ire., adm. July 5, 1847, dis. Aug. 3, 1847
Alexander McMullin, 26, R.C.,

Port of Saint John: Alms House 1847 117

Fermanagh, Ire., adm. July 5, 1847, dis. Aug. 3, 1847
Francis McMullin, 2, R.C., Fermanagh, Ire., adm. July 5, 1847, dis. Aug. 3, 1847
Mary Carr, 1 year 3 mos., R.C., Fermanagh, Ire., adm. July 5, 1847, dis. Aug. 3, 1847
Catherine Carr, 1 month, R.C., Quarantine Station, adm. July 5, 1847 dis. Aug. 3, 1847
John Conoroy, 21, R.C., Waterford, Ire., adm. July 6, 1847
Micheal Warren, 20, R.C., Roscommon, Ire., adm. July 6, 1847, dis. Sept. 1, 1847
Thomas Foy (Thomas Toy), 25, R.C., Mayo, Ire., adm. July 7, 1847, died Aug. 10, 1847
Hanora Hopkins, 21, R.C., Mayo, Ire., adm. July 14, 1847 dis. Aug. 24, 1847
Elizabeth Flaherty, 34, R.C., Kings Co., Ire., adm. July 7, 1847
Matt. Flynn, 30, R.C., Waterford, Ire., adm. July 20, 1847
Mary Cavanagh, 40, R.C., Wicklow, Ire., adm. July 24, 1847 died July 28, 1847
Catherine Cavanagh, 5, R.C., Wicklow, Ire., adm. July 24, 1847
Mary Cavanagh, 3, R.C., Wicklow, Ire., adm. July 24, 1847 died Aug. 1, 1847
Matt Murphy, 23, R.C., Cork, Ire., adm. Aug. 3, 1847
Ellen McCarthy, 20, R.C., Cork, Ire., adm. Sept. 8, 1847
Mary Sullivan, 16, R.C., Kerry, Ire., adm. Sept. 21, 1847

Ambassadress, sailed from Liverpool, England arrived Saint John July 13, 1847
Matt. Malady, 30, R.C., Kings Co., Ire., adm. July 16, 1847 dis. Sept. 20, 1847
Anne McGarragin, 19, R.C., Louth, Ire., adm. July 16, 1847 dis. Aug. 4, 1847
Charlotte Mathews, 27, Prot., Kings Co., Ire., adm. July 16, 1847 died July 18, 1847
Thos. Mathews, 2 years 6 mos., 27, Prot., Kings Co., Ire., adm. July 16, 1847 died Aug. 8, 1847
George Mathews, 2 mos., Prot., Kings Co., Ire., adm. July 16, 1847 died July 28, 1847
John Butler, 1 year 6 mos., R.C., Cork, Ire., adm. July 16, 1847 died Aug. 2, 1847
Mary Redmond, 20, R.C., Kings Co., Ire., adm. July 16, 1847 died July 23, 1847
John Tivnan, 17, R.C., Kings Co., Ire., adm. July 16, 1847 died Sept. 12, 1847
Mrs. Anne McGarrahan, 26, R.C., Leitim, Ire., adm. July 19, 1847 dis. Aug. 4, 1847
Mary McGarrahan, 6, R.C., Leitim, Ire., adm. July 19, 1847 died July 30, 1847
Michael Foley, 24, R.C., Leitrim, Ire., adm. July 19, 1847
Thomas Fleming, 22, R.C., Mayo, Ire., adm. July 19, 1847 dis. July 27, 1847
Michl. Herron, 20, R.C., Galway, Ire., adm. July 19, 1847
Patt. Herron, 15, R.C., Galway, Ire., adm. July 19, 1847
John Herron, 13, R.C., Galway, Ire., adm. July 19, 1847
Mary Herron, 11, R.C., Galway,

Ire., adm. July 19, 1847 died Aug. 16, 1847
Biddy Herron, 9, R.C., Galway, Ire., adm. July 19, 1847 died Aug. 29, 1847
Eliza Herron, 7, R.C., Galway, Ire., adm. July 19, 1847 died Sept. 13, 1847
And. Mills, 21, R.C., Cork, Ire., adm. July 20, 1847
Owen Dealy, 46, R.C., Donegal, Ire., adm. July 21, 1847 dis. July 21, 1847
Wm Barnan, 57, R.C., Kings Co., Ire., adm. July 21, 1847 died July 29, 1847
Margaret Barnan, 22, R.C., Kings Co., Ire., adm. July 21, 1847
Libby Barnan, 18, R.C., Kings Co., Ire., adm. July 21, 1847
Catherine Barnan, 16, R.C., Kings Co., Ire., adm. July 21, 1847
Anne Barnan, 13, R.C., Kings Co., Ire., adm. July 21, 1847
Alli Barnan, 11, R.C., Kings Co., Ire., adm. July 21, 1847 died July 30, 1847
Biddy Barnan, 6, R.C., Kings Co., Ire., adm. July 21, 1847 died July 27, 1847
Catherine Munn, 28, R.C., Donegal, Ire., adm. July 21, 1847 died July 25, 1847
Michl. Spann, 45, R.C., Kings Co., Ire., adm. July 21, 1847 dis. Sept. 17, 1847
Mrs. Margaret Span, 42, Kings Co., Ire., adm. July 21, 1847 dis. Sept. 17, 1847
Michl. Donald, 2, R.C., Tipperary, Ire., adm. July 21, 1847 died July 27, 1847
John Donald, 32, R.C., Tipperary, Ire., adm. July 21, 1847 dis. Sept. 8, 1847
Julia Donnell, 32, R.C., Tipperary, Ire., adm. July 21, 1847 dis. Sept. 17, 1847
Margaret Donnell, 4, R.C., Tipperary, Ire., adm. July 21, 1847 died Aug. 14, 1847
Margaret Maine, 1 week, R.C., Sligo, Ire., adm. July 21, 1847 died Aug. 21, mo. came in *Ambassadress*
Heny. Devitt, 19, R.C., Fermanagh, Ire., adm. July 21, 1847 died Aug. 17, 1847
John Roche, 21, R.C., Waterford, Ire., adm. July 21, 1847
Stephen McGuiggan, 20, R.C., Louth, Ire., adm. July 22, 1847 died Aug. 4, 1847
Mich. Wade, 24, R.C., Galway, Ire., adm. July 22, 1847 dis. July 29, 1847
Edwd. Goslin, 41, Prot., Germany, adm. July 22, 1847 dis. Aug. 1, 1847
Mrs. Jane Goslin, 40, Prot., Germany, adm. July 22, 1847 dis. Aug. 1, 1847
Pauline Goslin, 8, Prot., Germany, adm. July 22, 1847 dis. Aug. 1, 1847
Jane Goslin, 5, Prot., Germany, adm. July 22, 1847 dis. Aug. 1, 1847
Nancy Mahony, 25, R.C., Tipperary, Ire. adm. July 23, 1847
Mary O'Neil, 35, R.C., Armagh, Ire., adm. July 23, 1847, died Aug. 1, 1847
Owen O'Neill, 35, R.C., Armagh, Ire., adm. July 23, 1847
Geo. O'Neill, 11, R.C., Armagh,

Ire., adm. July 23, 1847
Jno. O'Neill, 9, R.C., Armagh, Ire., adm. July 23, 1847
Patk. O'Neill, 7, R.C., Armagh, Ire., adm. July 23, 1847
Margaret O'Neil, 5, R.C., Armagh, Ire., adm. July 23, 1847 dis. Oct. 6, 1847
James Farrel, 40, R.C., Tipperary, Ire., adm. July 23, 1847 died Aug. 21, 1847
Thomas Clare, 30, R.C., Kilkenny, Ire., adm. July 23, 1847 adm. July 24. 1847, dis. Aug. 24, 1847
James Clifford, 18, R.C., Kerry, Ire., adm. July 23, 1847
Heny. McBride, 40, R.C., Fermanagh, Ire., adm. July 23, 1847 dis. Aug. 2, 1847
Anne Belford, 19, Prot., Kings Co., Ire., adm. July 24, 1847
John - , 16, R.C., Kilkenny, Ire., adm. July 24, 1847 dis. Sept. 17, 1847
Patk. McNamara, 25, R.C., Tipperary, Ire., adm. July 24, 1847
James McHugh, 19, R.C., Cavan, Ire., adm. July 26, 1847 dis. Aug. 20, 1847
Thos. McHugh, 9, R.C., Cavan, Ire., adm. July 26, 1847 died July 29, 1847
Rose McHughes, 32, R.C., Cavan, Ire., adm. July 26, 1847 died Aug. 22, 1847
Mary McHughes, 12, R.C., Cavan, Ire., adm. July 26, 1847 dis. Aug. 21, 1847
Lilly McHughes, 4, R.C., Cavan, Ire., adm. July 26, 1847 died Aug. 14, 1847
Sarah Conway, 28, Derry, Ire., adm. July 27, 1847
Johanna Conway, 30, R.C., Cork, Ire, adm. July 27, 1847 dis. Aug. 31, 1847
Bernard Cassidy, 23, R.C., Leitrim, Ire., adm. July 27, 1847
Thomas Fleming, 40, R.C., Waterford, Ire., adm. July 27, 1847 died July 29, 1847
Fanny Doyle, 19, R.C., Sligo, Ire., adm. July 27, 1847 dis. Aug. 7, 1847
Peter Caulfield, 21, R.C., Kings Co., Ire., adm. July 27, 1847 dis. Aug. 12, 1847
John Mulholland, 9, R.C., Tyrone, Ire., adm. July 27, 1847 dis. Aug. 23, 1847
Adelaide Carey, 13, R.C., Kings Co., Ire., adm. July 28, 1847 dis. Aug. 6, 1847
Kearn Lantry, 30, R.C., Kings Co., Ire., adm. July 28, 1847 dis. Sept. 1, 1847
Wenie Lantry, 25, R.C., Cork, Ire., adm. July 28, 1847 dis. Sept. 1, 1847
Thomas Redmond, 24, R.C., Clare, Ire., adm. July 28, 1847 died Sept. 1847
Bridget Sullivan, 25, R.C., Cork, Ire., adm. July 28, 1847
Danl. Regan, 27, R.C., Cork, Ire., adm. July 29, 1847
Patk. Hanniming, 50, R.C., Kings Co., Ire., adm. July 30, 1847 died July 31, 1847
Andw. Mulholland, 33, R.C., Tyrone, Ire., adm. July 30, 1847 dis. Aug. 9, 1847
Jane Mulholland, 35, R.C., Tyrone, Ire., adm. July 30, 1847
John Keller, 7, R.C., Kings Co.,

Ire., adm. July 30, 1847 dis. Aug. 5, 1847
Bridget Keller, 30, R.C., Kings Co., Ire., adm. July 30, 1847 dis. Aug. 4, 1847
Catherine Keller, 3, R.C., Kings Co., Ire., adm. July 30, 1847 dis. Aug. 5, 1847
Peter Reilley, 13, R.C., Louth, Ire., adm. July 30, 1847 dis. Aug. 24, 1847
Fanny McEwe, 20, R.C., Cavan, Ire., adm. July 30, 1847 dis. Aug. 21, 1847
James Foley, 37, R.C., Sligo, Ire., adm. July 31, 1847, dis. Aug. 12, 1847
Bridget Foley, 29, R.C., Sligo, Ire., adm. July 31, 1847, dis. Aug. 12, 1847
James Foley, jr., 10, R.C., Sligo, Ire., adm. July 31, 1847, dis. Aug. 12, 1847
Michl. Foley, 8, R.C., Sligo, Ire., adm. July 31, 1847, dis. Aug. 12, 1847
John Foley, 1 year 6 mos., R.C., Sligo, Ire., adm. July 31, 1847, dis. Aug. 12, 1847
Catherine Wallace, 27, R.C., Tipperary, Ire., adm. Aug. 2, 1847 dis Aug. 25, 1847
Mrs. Margaret Mitchel, 60, R.C., Galway, Ire., adm. Aug. 3, 1847 died Aug. 19, 1847
Pat Mitchell, 10, R.C., Galway, Ire., adm. Aug. 3, 1847 dis. Aug. 24, 1847
And. Mitchell, 12, R.C., Galway, Ire., adm. Aug. 3, 1847 dis. Aug. 24, 1847
James McHugh, 19, R.C., Cavan, Ire., adm. Aug. 4, 1847 dis. Aug. 23, 1847
Judy Clifford, 24, R.C., Kerry, Ire., adm. dis. Aug. 26, 1847
Anne Murphy, 24, R.C., Galway, Ire., adm. Aug. 5, 1847
Mary Hughes, 19, R.C., L.Pool, Eng., adm. Aug. 6, 1847
Catherine Coffey, 16, R.C., Tipperary, Ire., adm. Aug. 6, 1847 died Sept. 9, 1847
Judy Coffey, 14, R.C., Tipperary, Ire., adm. Aug. 6, 1847 died Sept. 17, 1847
Anne Killmartin, 24, R.C., Sligo, Ire., adm. Aug. 7, 1847 dis. Aug. 31, 1847
Matth. McNamara, 4, R.C., Tipperary, Ire., adm. Aug. 9, 1847, died Sept. 13, 1847
Margaret McNamara, 40, R.C., Tipperary, Ire., adm. Aug. 9, 1847 adm. March 20, 1848 dis. Aug. 1, 1848
Margaret Coan, 40, R.C., Galway, Ire., adm. Aug. 10, 1847 died Aug. 27, 1847
Mary Coan, 15, R.C., Galway, Ire., adm. Aug. 10, 1847
Dennis Coan, 52, R.C., Galway, Ire., adm. Aug. 10, 1847 died Aug. 20, 1847
Dennis Coan Jr., 13, R.C., Galway, Ire., adm. Aug. 10, 1847
John Coan, 2, R.C., Galway, Ire., adm. Aug. 10, 1847 died Sept. 13, 1847
Peter Carr, 18, Down, Ire., adm. Aug. 11, 1847
John McKenna, 23, R.C., Tyrone, Ire., adm. Aug. 13, 1847 dis. Aug. 16, 1847
Sarah Berne, 25, R.C., Roscommon, Ire., adm. Aug. 14,

Port of Saint John: Alms House 1847

1847 dis. Aug. 31, 1847
Ellen Berne, 23, R.C., Roscommon, Ire., adm. Aug. 14, 1847 dis. Aug. 31, 1847
Mary Kelley, 19, R.C., Galway, Ire., adm. Aug. 21, 1847 dis. Sept. 28, 1847
Catherine Mitchell, 9, R.C., Galway, Ire., adm. Sept. 4, 1847
Biddy Mitchel, 12, R.C., Galway, Ire., adm. Sept. 4, 1847
Mary Mitchel, 6, R.C., Galway, Ire., adm. Sept. 4, 1847
Cate Mitchel, 9, R.C., Galway, Ire., adm. Sept. 4, 1847
Michl. Mitchel, 4, R.C., Galway, Ire., adm. Sept. 4, 1847
James O'Connor, 26, R.C., Clare, Ire., adm. Sept. 4, 1847 died Sept. 6, 1847
Austen Conners, 3, R.C., Clare, Ire., adm. Sept. 6, 1847
Catherine Langan, 19, R.C., Mayo, Ire., adm. Sept. 18, 1847 adm. Sept. 29, 1847, age 20
Mary Shaughnesy, 9, R.C., Clare, Ire., adm. Sept. 28, 1847
Henry Gallagher, 8 mos., R.C., Donegal, Ire., adm. Sept. 29, 1847
Mary Gallagher, 21, R.C., Donegal, Ire., adm. Sept. 29, 1847
Michl. Hearne, 20, R.C., Galway, Ire., adm. March 20, 1848 dis. June 29, 1848 adm. Emigrant Hospital May 1, 1848
Patk. Hearne, 20, R.C., Galway, Ire., adm. March 20, 1848 dis. Dec. 31, 1848 adm. Emigrant Hospital May 1, 1848, age 15
John Roche, 21, R.C., Waterford, Ire., adm. March 20, 1848 dis.

Apr. 19, 1848
Patk. McNamara, 25, R.C., Tipperary, Ire., adm. March 20, 1848 died Apr. 29, 1848
John McDonough, 18, Galway, Ire., adm. March 20, 1848 dis. May 9, 1848
Arthur Maguigan, 50, R.C., Louth, Ire., adm. March 20, 1848 dis. Apr. 18, 1848
Mrs. Margt. McGuigan, 44, Louth, Ire., adm. March 20, 1848 dis. Apr, 18, 1848
Julia Coffee, 16, R.C., Tipperary, Ire., adm. Dec. 29, 1848

Anne, sailed from Kinsale, Ire. arrived June 25, 1847
Libby Murray, 50, R.C., Cavan, Ire., adm. Aug. 4, 1847 died Aug. 31. 1847

Æneas, sailed from Cork, Ire., arrived at Saint John July 1, 1847
Richd. Leary, 19, R.C., Cork, Ire., adm. July 14, 1847 dis. Aug. 3, 1847
Maurice Nehel, 50, R.C., Cork, Ire., adm. Aug. 26, 1847 died Sept. 14, 1847
Mary Neagle, 2, R.C., Cork, Ire., adm. Aug. 26, 1847 died Sept. 6, 1847
Elizabeth Neil, 45, R.C., Cork, Ire., adm. Aug. 26, 1847 died Sept. 9, 1847
Mary Lee, 22, R.C., Cork, Ire., adm. Sept. 20, 1847
Wm Lee, 50, R.C., Cork, Ire., adm. Sept. 22, 1847 adm. March 20, 1848 died Sept. 11, 1848 adm. Emigrant Hospital May 1, 1848, fever

Irish Migration To New England: Port of Saint John

Aulaby,
Michl. Sullivan, 30, R.C., Kerry, Ire., adm. March 20, 1848 dis. March 31, 1848

Bache McEvers, sailed from Cork, Ire., arrived Saint John July 20, 1847
Johanna Crowley, 25, R.C., Waterford, Ire., adm. July 24, 1847 died July 29, 1847
John Crane, 30, R.C., Kerry, Ire., adm. July 24, 1847 died Aug. 7, 1847
Michl. Neville, 18, R.C., Waterford, Ire., adm. July 24, 1847 dis. Sept. 18, 1847
Michl. Crowley, 24, R.C., Cork, Ire., adm. Aug. 5, 1847
Patk. Leary, 25, R.C., Cork, Ire., adm. Aug. 5, 1847 adm. Aug. 10, 1847
Michl. Garret, 25, R.C., Cork, Ire., adm. Aug. 6, 1847
Tim Murray, 29, R.C., Cork, Ire., adm. Aug. 7, 1847 died Aug. 7, 1847
Catherine Neville, 40, R.C., Waterford, Ire., adm. Aug. 10, 1847 dis. Aug. 26, 1847
Mary Neville, 17, R.C., Waterford, Ire., adm. Aug. 10, 1847 dis. Aug. 26, 1847
Mary Donovan, 28, R.C., Cork, Ire., adm. Aug. 16, 1847 dis. Aug. 26, 1847
Hanora Donovan, 5, R.C., Cork, Ire., adm. Aug. 16, 1847
Jerry Donovan, 9, R.C., Cork, Ire., adm. Aug. 16, 1847
William Donovan, 4 mos., R.C., Cork, Ire., adm. Aug. 16, 1847 died Aug. 18, 1847
Bridget Donovan, 7, R.C., Cork, Ire., adm. Aug. 16, 1847
William Donovan, 35, R.C., Cork, Ire., adm. Aug. 16, 1847
Michael Nevin, 19, R.C., Waterford, Ire.. adm. Aug. 31, 1847
John Haly, 30, R.C., Cork, Ire., adm. Sept. 11, 1847
Michael Haley, 10, R.C., Cork, Ire., adm. Sept. 11, 1847

Berbice,
Pat Ford, 20, R.C., Galway, Ire., adm. Sept. 14, 1847

Bethel, sailed from Galway, Ire., arrived Saint John Sept. 7, 1847
Mary Genley, 18, R.C., Galway, Ire., adm. Sept. 16, 1847 dis. Sept. 25, 1847
Pat Genley, 19, R.C., Clare, Ire., adm. Sept. 16, 1847
James O'Brien, 16, R.C., Clare, Ire., adm. Sept. 16, 1847
Michael Willis, 30, R.C., Clare, Ire., adm. Sept. 16, 1847
Thomas Walsh, 31, R.C., Clare, Ire., adm. Sept. 16, 1847
Michael Walsh, 24, R.C., Clare, Ire., adm. Sept. 16, 1847
Hanora Dunn, 25, R.C., Galway, Ire., adm. Sept. 17, 1847
Mary Gaynor, 20, R.C., Galway, Ire., adm. Sept. 17, 1847
John Moran, 22, R.C., Clare, Ire., adm. Sept. 17, 1847
John Cooke, 35, R.C., Galway, Ire., adm. Sept. 17, 1847
Margt. Lynch, 24, R.C., Clare, Ire., adm. Sept. 18, 1847
Denis Fye, 30, R.C., Galway, Ire., adm. Sept. 19, 1847

Mary Bochan, 5, R.C., Galway, Ire., adm. Sept. 21, 1847 died Sept. 25, 1847
Bridget Bochan, 3, R.C., Galway, Ire., adm. Sept. 21, 1847
Cath. Brochan, 20, R.C., Galway, Ire., adm. Sept. 21, 1847
Laurence Bochan, 7, R.C., Galway, Ire., adm. Sept. 21, 1847
Margt. Dolan, 30, R.C., Galway, Ire., adm. Sept. 21, 1847
David Melowney, 24, R.C., Clare, Ire., adm. Sept. 21, 1847
Peggy Kearney, 27, R.C., Clare, Ire., adm. Sept. 27, 1847
Biddy Finigan, 16, R.C., Galway, Ire., adm. Sept. 29, 1847
Wm McNamara, 40, R.C., Galway, Ire., adm. March 20, 1848 dis. March 25, 1848
Mich. Lennan, 25, R.C., Clare, Ire., adm. March 20, 1848 dis. May 8, 1848 adm. Emigrant Hospital May 1, 1848, destitute
Jno. Regan, 6, R.C., Cork, Ire., adm. March 20, 1848 dis. May 17, 1848 adm. Emigrant Hospital May 1, 1848, destitute
Nancy Hogan, 24, Clare, Ire., adm. March 20, 1848 dis. May 1, 1848
Mich. Melvin, 57, R.C., Galway, Ire., adm. Apr. 18, 1848, dis. Apr. 18, 1848
Pat Melvin, 12, R.C., Galway, Ire., adm. Apr. 18, 1848, dis. Apr. 18, 1848
Peggy Melvin, 42, Galway, Ire., adm. Apr. 18, 1848, dis. Apr. 18, 1848
Ellen Melvin, 10, Galway, Ire., adm. Apr. 18, 1848, dis. Apr. 18, 1848

Judy Melvin, 5, Galway, Ire., adm. Apr. 18, 1848, dis. Apr. 18, 1848

Blanche,
Sarah McCoughel, 21, R.C., Donegal, Ire., adm. Aug. 19, 1847 dis. Aug. 24, 1847
Catherine Hegarty, 17, R.C., Donegal, Ire., adm. Sept. 17, 1847
Michael Wade, 24, R.C., Kerry, Ire., adm. Sept. 17, 1847 adm. March 20, 1848 dis. Apr. 4, 1848

Bloomfield, sailed from Galway, Ire., arrived Saint John, Aug. 7, 1847
Wm King, 34, R.C., Mayo, Ire., adm. Aug. 11, 1847
Patk. King, 30, R.C., Mayo, Ire., adm. Aug. 11, 1847
Margaret King, 4, R.C., Mayo, Ire., adm. Aug. 11, 1847 died Aug. 31, 1847
Mary King, 2, R.C., Mayo, Ire., adm. Aug. 11, 1847
Edwd. Martin, 30, R.C., Mayo, Ire., adm. Aug. 11, 1847
Austin Conners, 24, R.C., Clare, Ire., adm. Aug. 11, 1847
Hanora Nevin, 30, R.C., Mayo, Ire., adm. Aug. 11, 1847 died Aug. 24, 1847
Biddy Nevin, 2, R.C., Mayo, Ire., adm. Aug. 11, 1847 died Sept. 3, 1847
Margt. Flemming, 24, R.C., Waterford, Ire., adm. Aug. 11, 1847 dis. Aug. 24, 1847
Mrs. Biddy Fennety, 40, R.C., Cork, Ire., adm. Aug. 12, 1847 died Aug. 16, 1847

124 Irish Migration To New England: Port of Saint John

Margaret Fennety, 12, R.C., Cork, Ire., adm. Aug. 12, 1847 dis. Sept. 28, 1847
Danl. Kelley, 12, R.C., Cork, Ire., adm. Aug. 12, 1847 dis. Aug. 17, 1847
Charles Daly, 79, R.C., Cork, Ire., adm. Aug. 12, 1847 dis. Aug. 21, 1847
John Ford, 43, R.C., Galway, Ire., adm. Aug. 12, 1847 died Sept. 21, 1847
Danl. Connelly, 30, R.C., Cork, Ire., adm. Aug. 12, 1847
Patrick Maguinas, R.C., Cork, Ire., adm. Aug. 13, 1847 died Aug. 13, 1847
Pat Hegan, 21, R.C., Mayo, Ire., adm. Aug. 14, 1847 dis. Aug. 17, 1847
Catherine Loughen, 30, R.C., Galway, Ire., adm. Aug. 17, 1847, died Aug. 26, 1847
Mary Loughen, 10, R.C., Galway, Ire., adm. Aug. 17, 1847
Michael Loughen, 6, R.C., Galway, Ire., adm. Aug. 17, 1847
John Loughen, 4, R.C., Galway, Ire., adm. Aug. 17, 1847
James Loughen, 1, R.C., Galway, Ire., adm. Aug. 17, 1847, died Aug. 26, 1847
John Loughen, 30, R.C., Galway, Ire., adm. Aug. 17, 1847
John Heffron, 20, R.C., Galway, Ire., adm. Aug. 24, 1847. dis. Sept. 16, 1847
Biddy Heffron, 16, adm. Aug. 24, 1847
John Clementy, 40, 40, R.C., Derry, Ire., adm. Aug. 24, 1847
Patrick Egan, 21, R.C., Mayo, Ire., adm. Aug. 28, 1847 died Sept. 13, 1847
Mary Fennety, 14, R.C., Mayo, Ire., adm. Sept. 2, 1847
Anthony Flaherty, 34, R.C., Galway, Ire., adm. Sept. 2, 1847 dis. Sept. 9, 1847
John Loughlan, 29, R.C., Galway, Ire., adm. Sept. 5, 1847
Michl. Loughen, 11, R.C., Galway, Ire., adm. Sept. 5, 1847
John Loughen, 6, R.C., Galway, Ire., adm. Sept. 5, 1847
Margaret Daly, 40, R.C., Galway, Ire., adm. Sept. 11, 1847
Pat King, 30, R.C., Mayo, Ire., adm. March 20, 1848 dis. Apr. 3, 1848
Mrs. Mary King, 25, Mayo, Ire., adm. March 20, 1848 dis. Apr. 3, 1848
Emily Martin, 27, Down, Ire., adm. May 22, 1848 dis. July 31, 1848
Jno. Welch, 3, R.C., Mayo, Ire., adm. July 13, 1848 dis. Jan. 1, 1849 adm. Emigrant Hospital July 13, 1848, destitute, dis. Dec. 31, 1848
Bridget Welch, 5, R.C., Mayo, Ire., adm. July 13, 1848

British Merchant, sailed from Cork, Ire., arrived at Saint John Aug. 15, 1847
Cornelius Kelly, 7, R.C., Cork, Ire., adm. Aug. 15, 1847
James McAvity, 6 mos., R.C., Kerry, Ire., adm. Aug. 15, 1847 died Aug. 28, 1847
Daniel Talvey, 28, R.C., Cork, Ire., adm. Aug. 15, 1847 dis. Aug. 24, 1847
Jerry McCarthy, 24, R.C., Cork,

Port of Saint John: Alms House 1847   125

Ire., adm. Aug. 15, 1847
Margaret McCarthy, 13, R.C., Kerry, Ire., adm. Aug. 15, 1847 dis. Sept. 23, 1847
Mary Carthy, 40, R.C., Cork, Ire., adm. Aug. 16, 1847 dis. Aug. 31, 1847
Catherine Hennesy, 14, R.C., Kerry, Ire., adm. Aug. 16, 1847 dis. Aug. 31, 1847
Michael Barry, 35, R.C., Kerry, Ire., adm. Aug. 16, 1847
Mary Sullivan, 38, R.C., Cork, Ire., adm. Aug. 17, 1847 died Sept. 1, 1847
Ellen Long, 25, R.C., Cork, Ire., adm. Aug. 17, 1847 dis. Aug. 23, 1847
Matt Long, 30, R.C., Cork, Ire., adm. Aug. 17, 1847 died Aug. 23, 1847
Hanora Harrington, 19, R.C., Cork, Ire., adm. Aug. 17, 1847
James Neil, 23, R.C., Cork, Ire., adm. Aug. 17, 1847 dis. Sept. 18, 1847
John Hooley, 20, R.C., Cork, Ire., adm. Aug. 18, 1847 dis. Aug. 24, 1847
Thomas Cremins, 36, R.C., Tipperary, Ire., adm. Aug. 18, 1847 died Aug. 24, 1847
Patrick Cremmins, 14, R.C., Tipperary, Ire., adm. Aug. 18, 1847 dis. Aug. 24, 1847
Denis Donovan, 28, R.C., Cork, Ire., adm. Aug. 18, 1847 dis. Aug. 23, 1847
John McCarthy, 23, R.C., Cork, Ire., adm. Aug. 18, 1847 dis. Aug. 31, 1847
Edmond Walsh, 30, R.C., Waterford, Ire., adm. Aug. 19, 1847 dis. Aug. 19, 1847
Edmond Staunton, 28, R.C., Cork, Ire., adm. Aug. 19, 1847 dis. Aug. 19, 1847
Jerry Sullivan, 30, R.C., Cork, Ire., adm. Aug. 21, 1847 died Aug. 31, 1847
John Holtan, 30, R.C., Cork, Ire., adm. Aug. 21, 1847
Johanna White, 12, R.C., Cork, Ire., adm. Aug. 21, 1847
Mary White, 10, R.C., Cork, Ire., adm. Aug. 21, 1847
Ellen McCarthy, 30, R.C., Cork, Ire., adm. Aug. 21, 1847 died Aug. 29, 1847
John McCarthy, 1 years 6 mo., R.C., Cork, Ire., adm. Aug. 21, 1847 dis. Sept. 1, 1847
Patrick Donovan, 4, R.C., Cork, Ire., adm. Aug. 21, 1847 died Sept. 10, 1847
John Sullivan, 22, R.C., Cork, Ire., adm. Aug. 21, 1847 dis. Sept. 9, 1847
James McGrory, 24, R.C., Donegal, Ire., adm. Aug. 21, 1847 dis. Aug. 23, 1847
Jeremiah Donovan (Jerry Donovan), 19, R.C., Cork, Ire., adm. Aug. 22, 1847 dis. Sept. 9, 1847 adm. Sept. 27, 1847
James McDonagh, 21, R.C., Galway, Ire., adm. Aug. 22, 1847
Mary Callaghan, 18, R.C., L.Pool, Eng., adm. Aug. 22, 1847
Fanny McCarthy, 28, R.C., Cork, Ire., adm. Aug. 24, 1847 dis. Sept. 14, 1847
Julia McCarthy, 36, R.C., Cork, Ire., adm. Aug. 25, 1847 dis. Sept. 23, 1847
Mary Sullivan, 26, R.C., Cork, Ire.,

adm. Aug. 25, 1847 dis. Sept. 23, 1847 *
James Donovan, 34, R.C., Cork, Ire., adm. Aug. 25, 1847 died Sept. 7, 1847
Pat Allen, 33, R.C., Cork, Ire., adm. Aug. 26, 1847 died Aug. 29, 1847
Walter Bennett, 34, R.C., Cork, Ire., adm. Aug. 30, 1847
John Ryan, 30, R.C., Cork, Ire., adm. Sept. 2, 1847 dis. Sept. 12, 1847
James Cotter, 34, R.C., Cork, Ire., adm. Sept. 2, 1847
Ellen Lynch, 23, R.C., Waterford, Ire., adm. Sept. 7, 1847
Catherine Keshane, 23, R.C., Cork, Ire., adm. Sept. 11, 1847
Martin Ryan, 33, R.C., Tipperary, Ire., adm. Sept. 22, 1847
Honor Smeddy, 20, R.C., Cork, Ire., adm. Sept. 29, 1847
Jerry McArty, 24, R.C., Cork, Ire., adm. Mar. 20, 1848 dis. Apr. 15, 1848
Dennis Donovan, 12, R.C., Cork, Ire., adm. March 20, 1848 dis. Apr. 16, 1848
Joanna Lewis, 18, Limerick, Ire., adm. March 20, 1848 dis. Aug. 3, 1848
Winni Ryan, 40, Tipperary, Ire., adm. March 20, 1848 dis. Apr. 16, 1848
Bridget Ryan, 5, Tipperary, Ire., adm. March 20, 1848 dis. May 3, 1848

British Queen, sailed from Derry, Ire., arrived Saint John July 19, 1847
Pat Allen, 33, R.C., Cork, Ire.,
adm. Aug. 13, 1847 dis. Aug. 24, 1847
Jane Murdock, 21, R.C., Derry, Ire., adm. Sept. 11, 1848
Margaret Murdock, 4, R.C., Derry, Ire., adm. Sept. 11, 1848

Buksa?,
Mary Warren, 1 year 6 mos., R.C., Cork, Ire., adm. Aug. 22, 1847 dis. Aug. 30, 1847
John Warren, 6 mos., R.C., Cork, Ire., adm. Aug. 22, 1847 died Aug. 30, 1847
Hanora Warren, 25, R.C., Cork, Ire., adm. Aug. 23, 1847 dis. Aug. 30, 1847

Caledonia, sailed from Liverpool, England, arrived at Saint John May 25, 1847
Mrs. Jane Donnelly, 25, R.C., Kildare, Ire., adm. June 3, 1847
Michl. Donelly, 30, R.C., Kildare, Ire., adm. June 3, 1847, dis. July 5, 1847
Dan Donelly, 2 years 6 mos., R.C., Kildare, Ire., adm. June 3, 1847, dis. July 5, 1847
Peter Donelly, 1 year 4 mos., R.C., Kildare, Ire., adm. June 3, 1847, dis. July 5, 1847
Wilm. McLoon, 53, R.C., Tyrone, Ire., adm. June 11, 1847, dis. June 12, 1847, adm. June 18, 1847, age 54
Bernd. McLoon, 13, R.C., Tyrone, Ire., adm. June 11, 1847, dis. June 12, 1847, adm. June 18, 1847 dis. Aug. 23, 1847
Thos. McLoon, 12, R.C., Tyrone, Ire., adm. June 11, 1847, dis. June 12, 1847 adm. June 18,

Port of Saint John: Alms House 1847

1847
Wilm. McLoon, 6, R.C., Tyrone, Ire., adm. June 11, 1847, dis. June 12, 1847 adm. June 18, 1847
Mary McLoon, 3, R.C., Tyrone, Ire., adm. June 11, 1847, dis. June 12, 1847, adm. June 18, died Aug. 19, 1847
Thos. Haneberry, 29, R.C., Galway, Ire., adm. June 23, 1847 died June 25, 1847

Caledonia, sailed from Cork, Ire., arrived July 13, 1847
Michael Donelly, 30, R.C., Kildare, Ire., adm. July 8, 1847 dis. Aug. 12, 1847
Bridget Shifna, 27, R.C., Donegal, Ire., adm. July 20, 1847 dis. July 29, 1847
Elen Keating, 11, R.C., Waterford, Ire., adm. July 20, 1847 dis. Aug. 11, 1847
Catherine Keating, 9, R.C., Waterford, Ire., adm. July 20, 1847 dis. Aug. 11, 1847
Michl. Mahony, 24, R.C., Kerry, Ire., adm. July 29, 1847 dis. Aug. 31, 1847
Thos. McLoon, 12, R.C., Tyrone, Ire., adm. Sept. 22, 1847
Wm McLoon, 54, R.C., Tyrone, Ire., adm. Sept. 22, 1847
Danl. Donelly, 3 years 3 mos., R.C., Kildare, Ire., adm. March 20, 1848 dis. Jan. 1, 1849 adm. Emigrant Hospital May 1, 1848, destitute
Peter Donelly, 2, R.C., Kildare, Ire., adm. March 20, 1848 dis. Jan. 1, 1849 adm. Emigrant Hospital May 1, 1848, destitute

Mrs. Jane Donelly, 25, Kildare, Ire., adm. March 20, 1848

Caroline, sailed from Cork, Ire., arrived at Saint John July 13, 1847
Bridget Shefna, 10, R.C., Donegal, Ire., adm. July 20, 1847 dis. July 29, 1847
Dan Gilmartin, 22, R.C., Leitrim, Ire., adm. Aug. 22, 1847 dis. Aug. 31, 1847
Mary Kennedy, 20, Tipperary, Ire., adm. March 20, 1848 dis. May 14, 1848

Chieftain, sailed from Galway, Ire., arrived Saint John July 5, 1847
Hannora Fenney, 40, R.C., Galway, Ire., adm. July 13, 1847 died Aug. 17, 1847
Bridget Fenney, 11, R.C., Galway, Ire., adm. July 13, 1847
Michael Finarty, 9, R.C., Galway, Ire., adm. July 13, 1847
Martin Finarty, 3 years 6 mos.R.C., Galway, Ire., adm. July 13, 1847 died Sept. 13, 1847
Johanna Laughlin, 60, R.C., Clare, Ire., adm. July 13, 1847, died Aug. 20, 1847
James Noen, 25, R.C., Galway, Ire., adm. July 15, 1847 died Aug. 4, 1847
Eliza Maley, 9, R.C., Galway, Ire., adm. July 15, 1847
Mary Turdum, 50, R.C., Galway, Ire., adm. July 16, 1847 died July 28, 1847
Mary Heron, 50, R.C., Galway, Ire., adm. July 16, 1847 dis. July 20, 1847

Mary Daly, 19, R.C., Cork, Ire., July 26, 1847, dis. Aug. 2, 1847
Biddy Dugan, 26, R.C., Cork, Ire., adm. July 26, 1847
Ellen McBemore, 50, Scotland, adm. July 26, 1847 dis. July 28, 1847
Mary Fitzpatrick, 40, R.C., Clare, Ire., adm. July 26, 1847 dis. Aug. 2, 1847
Mary Devaly, 19, R.C., Cork, Ire., adm. Aug. 4, 1847
John Conners, 30, R.C., Clare, Ire., adm. Aug. 10, 1847 died Sept. 4, 1847
Edwd. Connell, 9, R.C., Galway, Ire., adm. Aug. 11, 1847
Jerry Scanlan, 30, R.C. Cork, Ire., adm. Aug. 11, 1847 dis. Sept. 7, 1847
Tim Scanlan, 9, R.C. Cork, Ire., adm. Aug. 11, 1847
John Scanlan, 2, R.C. Cork, Ire., adm. Aug. 11, 1847 died Sept. 5, 1847
Jeremiah Delaney, 30, R.C. Cork, Ire., adm. Aug. 11, 1847
Catherine Brown, 28, R.C., Galway, Ire., adm. Aug. 11, 1847 dis. Sept. 18, 1847
Michael Milon, 50, R.C., Galway, Ire., adm. Aug. 17, 1847
Michael Malone, 45, R.C., Galway, Ire., adm. Aug. 22, 1847
Sarah Burke, 40, R.C., Galway, Ire., adm. Sept. 2, 1847
John Bourke, 9, R.C., Galway, Ire., adm. Sept. 2, 1847
Mrs. Ellen Linane, 23, R.C., Clare, Ire., adm. Sept. 9, 1847
Bridget Linane, 7, R.C., Clare, Ire., adm. Sept. 9, 1847
Francis Lenan, 30, R.C., Clare, Ire., adm. Sept. 13, 1847
Mary Walsh, 29, R.C., Galway, Ire., adm. Sept. 15, 1847
Margaret Walsh, 2, R.C., Galway, Ire., adm. Sept. 15, 1847 dis. Sept. 17, 1847
John Walsh, 5, R.C., Galway, Ire., adm. Sept. 15, 1847
Jno. Flaherty, 40, R.C., Galway, Ire., adm. Sept. 22, 1847
Michl. Holland, 10, R.C., Galway, Ire., adm. Sept. 23, 1847
Jno. Holland, 8, R.C., Galway, Ire., adm. Sept. 23, 1847
Martin Holland, 4, R.C., Galway, Ire., adm. Sept. 23, 1847
Nancy Holland, 30, R.C., Galway, Ire., adm. Sept. 23, 1847
Cath. Ferguson, 12, R.C., Galway, Ire., adm. Sept. 23, 1847
Mary Ferguson, 30, R.C., Galway, Ire., adm. Sept. 23, 1847
Pat Flaherty, 17, R.C., Galway, Ire., adm. March 20, 1848 dis. March 29, 1848
Pat Flaherty, 16, R.C., Galway, Ire., adm. March 20, 1848 dis. May 19, 1848 adm. Emigrant Hospital May 1, 1848, destitute
Mary Curley, 22, Galway, Ire., adm. March 20, 1848 dis. June 16, 1848
Margt. Flaherty, 15, Galway, Ire., adm. March 20, 1848 dis. July 27, 1848
Brid. Malone, 20, Clare, Ire., adm. March 20, 1848 dis. Apr. 6, 1848
Brian King, 36, R.C., Galway, Ire., adm. May 4, 1848 dis. Dec. 31, 1848 adm. Emigrant Hospital May 4, 1848, bowel comp.
Pat King, 5, R.C., Galway, Ire., adm. May 4, 1848 died Nov. 14,

Port of Saint John: Alms House 1847   129

1848 adm. Emigrant Hospital May 4, 1848, bowel comp.
- King, R.C., Emigrant Hopital, adm. May 9, 1848 died Nov. 15, 1848, fa. & mo. in ho., mo. came in *Chieftain*, adm. Emigrant Hospital May 4, 1848, St. John, delicate
Ann King, 13, R.C., Galway, Ire., adm. Oct. 24, 1848

Coronation,
Mary Barnes, 38, Antrim, Ire., adm. March 20, 1848 dis. March 26, 1848
Mary Barnes, 39, Prot., Liverpool, Eng., adm. Sept. 5, 1848 dis. Nov. 25, 1848

Coxon,
Mary Corkeran, 20, R.C., Cork, Ire., adm. Sept. 14, 1847 adm. Sept. 23, 1847

Creole,
John Kirk, 1, R.C., Tyrone, Ire., adm. Sept. 19, 1847
Anne Kirk, 7, R.C., Tyrone, Ire., adm. Sept. 19, 1847 adm. March 20, 1848 dis. July 3, 1848
Catherine Kirk, 30, R.C., Tyrone, Ire., adm. Sept. 19, 1847, adm. March 20, 1848 dis. July 3, 1848

Cushlamachree, sailed from Galway, Ire., arrived at Saint John Aug. 16, 1847
Randle McDonnell, 55, Roscommon, Ire., adm. Aug. 26, 1847
John Trahee, 55, R.C., Cork, Ire., adm. Aug. 26, 1847 died Sept. 18, 1847

Biddy Tracy, 5, R.C., Galway, Ire., adm. Sept. 4, 1847 dis. Sept. 7, 1847
Mrs. Judy Tracy, 40, R.C., Galway, Ire., adm. Sept. 4, 1847
Michael Tracy, 30, R.C., Galway, Ire., adm. Sept. 4, 1847 dis. Sept. 7, 1847
Edward Murphy, 48, R.C., Cork, Ire., adm. Sept. 4, 1847 dis. Sept. 16, 1847
John Sallory, 27, R.C., Galway, Ire., adm. Sept. 17, 1847 died Sept. 19, 1847
David Goggin, 22, R.C., Cork, Ire., adm. March 20, 1848 died Dec. 27, 1848 adm. Emigrant Hospital May 1, 1848
John Meloy, 13, R.C., Galway, Ire., adm. March 20, 1848 dis. May 17, 1848 adm. Emigrant Hospital May 1, 1848, destitute

David,
Martin Foley, 30, R.C., Galway, Ire., adm. March 20, 1848 dis. May 22, 1848 adm. Emigrant Hospital May 1, 1848, destitute
Pat Madden, 3 years 6 mos., R.C., Cork, Ire., adm. July 25, 1848 dis. Sept. 5, 1848 adm. Emigrant Hospital July 25, 1848, destitute, dis. Sept. 5, 1848
Bridget Madden, 19, R.C., Galway, Ire., adm. July 25, 1848 dis. Sept. 5, 1848

Dealy (Daley), sailed from Cork, Ireland, arrived at Saint John June 18, 1847
Mary Sullivan, 22, R.C., Cork, Ire., adm. June 19, 1847 died July 4, 1847

Margaret Horgan, 30, R.C., Cork, Ire., adm July 5, 1847, died July 12, 1847
Mrs. Anne Connell, 40, R.C., Sligo, Ire., adm. July 17, 1847
Catherine Toomey, 28, R.C., Cork, Ire., adm. July 14, 1847 dis. July 27, 1847
Mary Donnell, 10, R.C., Limerick, Ire., adm. July 21, 1847 died Aug. 18, 1847
Margaret Sweeney, 17, R.C., Cork, Ire., adm. July 26, 1847 adm. Aug. 4, 1847 dis. Aug. 13, 1847
Mary Donovan, 20, R.C., Cork, Ire., adm. Aug. 2, 1847 died Aug. 20, 1847
Jerry Sullivan, 19, Cork, Ire. (not listed in Alms House Records) adm. Emigrant Hospital July 24, 1848, fever, dis. Aug. 6, 1848

Eliza, sailed from Waterford, Ire. arrived Saint John June 21, 1847
Patrick Tierny, 34, R.C., Cork, Ire. adm. July 14, 1847
Julia Cain, 17, R.C., Waterford, Ire., adm. July 20, 1847 dis. Aug. 2, 1847
Catherine Donovan, 20, R.C., Waterford, Ire., adm. July 27, 1847
Thos. Clancy, 22, R.C., Waterford, Ire., adm. July 28, 1847
Michl. Ryan (Michl. Regan), 18, R.C., Waterford, Ire., July 29, 1847
Mary Haly, 2, R.C., Waterford, Ire., adm. Sept. 7, 1847 died Sept. 9, 1847
Mary Haly, 28, R.C., Waterford, Ire., adm. Sept. 7, 1847

Eliza Ann, sailed from Galway, Ire., arrived June 21, 1847
Mary Mulherrin, 25, R.C., Galway, Ire., adm. July 6, 1847, died Sept. 7, 1847
Michl. Hahar, 22, R.C., Galway, Ire., adm. July 22, 1847 died Aug. 22, 1847
Fergus O'Brien, 20, R.C., Galway, Ire., adm. July 23, 1847
Edward Hickson, Prot., Kerry, Ire., adm. Aug. 17, 1847
Patt. Flynn, 19, R.C., Galway, Ire., adm. Sept. 19, 1847

Eliza McArthy, sailed from Cork, Ire., arrived June 18, 1847
Margaret Forester, 19, R.C., Clare, Ire., adm. July 19, 1847 dis. Aug. 9, 1847

Eliza Parker, sailed from Waterford, Ire., arrived at Saint John June 21, 1847
Jno. Ryan, 57, R.C., Waterford, Ire., adm. Aug. 5, 1847 died Aug. 26, 1847
Catherine Riggin, 20, R.C., Waterford, Ire., adm. Aug. 24, 1847
Joanna Leary, 70, R.C., Cork, Ire., adm. Sept. 21, 1847
Hannah Coleman, 12, R.C., Cork, Ire., adm. Sept. 22, 1847 dis. Sept. 26, 1847
Eliza Coleman, 5, R.C., Cork, Ire., adm. Sept. 22, 1847 dis. Sept. 26, 1847
Betty Moore, 16, Cork, Ire., adm. March 20, 1848 dis. March 25, 1848

Port of Saint John: Alms House 1847

Elizabeth Cremns, sailed from Youghal, Ire., arrived July 13, 1847
Margaret Cordey, 16, R.C., Antrim, Ire., adm. Aug. 4, 1847 died Aug. 18, 1847
Johanna Manning, 6 mos., R.C., Kerry, Ire., adm. Aug. 4, 1847 dis. Aug. 16, 1847

Elizabeth Grimmer, sailed from Waterford, Ire., arrived Saint John June 21, 1847
Saml. McNutt, 18, R.C., Donegal, Ire., adm. Aug. 5, 1847 died Aug. 15, 1847

Elizabeth Mary, sailed from Cork, Ire., arrived July 22, 1847
John Donovan, 29, R.C., Waterford, Ire., adm. Aug. 11, 1847

Ella, sailed from Cork, Ire., arrived Saint John June 18, 1847
Mary Callaghan, 35, R.C., Cork, Ire., adm. June 28, 1847 dis. Aug. 5, 1847
Patrick Falvey, 25, R.C., Kerry, Ire., adm. June 28, 1847 dis. July 26, 1847
Tim Driscoll, 20, R.C., Cork, Ire., adm. July 3, 1847, dis. Aug. 2, 1847
Mary Reily, 30, R.C., Cork, Ire., adm. July 3, 1847
Michael Hannon, 26, R.C., Cork, Ire., adm. July 8, 1847 died Aug. 6, 1847
Patrick Kilbride, 44, R.C., Sligo, Ire., adm. July 3, 1847 dis. July 25, 1847
Peter Gilroy, 19, R.C., Sligo, Ire., adm. July 8, 1847, dis. Aug. 25, 1847
James Gilroy, 16, R.C., Sligo, Ire., adm. July 8, 1847, dis. Aug. 25, 1847
Mary Kidney, 22, R.C., Cork, Ire., adm. July 13, 1847 died July 30, 1847
Matt. Reiley, 30, R.C., Cork, Ire., adm. July 22, 1847 dis. Aug. 16, 1847
Johanna Murphy, 19, R.C., Cork, Ire., adm. July 23, 1847 dis. Aug. 24, 1847
Mary Murphy, 23, R.C., Cork, Ire., adm. July 23, 1847 dis. Aug. 24, 1847
Tim Sullivan, 30, R.C.,Cork, Ire., adm. July 27, 1847 dis. Aug. 10, 1847
Peggy Mannen, 23, R.C., Cork, Ire., adm. July 31, 1847 died Aug. 2, 1847
Patrick Nevin, 38, R.C., Tipperary, Ire., adm. Aug. 30, 1847 dis. Sept. 1, 1847
Darby Liester, 32, Clare, Ire., adm. Aug. 31, 1847
Wenifred Loughan, 30, R.C., Galway, Ire., adm. Sept. 4, 1847 died Sept. 17, 1847
Judy Loughen, 3, R.C., Galway, Ire., adm. Sept. 5, 1847
Pat Loughen, 40, R.C., Galway, Ire., adm. Sept. 11, 1847
Edward Hogan, 7, R.C., Cork, Ire., adm. Sept. 13, 1847
John Hogan, 15, R.C., Cork, Ire., adm. Sept. 13, 1847
Mrs. Norry Hogan, 42, R.C., Cork, Ire., adm. Sept. 13, 1847
Mary Hogan, 17, R.C., Cork, Ire., adm. Sept. 13, 1847

132 Irish Migration To New England: Port of Saint John

Hanna Hogan, 10, R.C., Cork, Ire., adm. Sept. 13, 1847
Ellen Hogan, 4, R.C., Cork, Ire., adm. Sept. 13, 1847
John Bourke, 35, R.C., Galway, Ire., adm. Sept. 13, 1847
James Malone, 30, R.C., Clare, Ire., adm. Sept. 13, 1847
Dan Donovan, 22, R.C.,Cork, Ire., adm. Sept. 17, 1847
Pat. Grogan, 17, R.C., Galway, Ire., adm. Sept. 19, 1847
Pat. McDonell, 20, R.C., Galway, Ire., adm. Sept. 23, 1847
Mary Murphy, 19, R.C., Clare, Ire., adm. Sept. 24, 1847
Pat. Murphy, 22, R.C., Clare, Ire., adm. Sept. 24, 1847 adm. March 20, 1848 dis. July 6, 1848 (ship *Ella*) adm. Emigrant Hospital May 1, 1848 (ship *Ellis*)
Jno. Bodkin, 20, R.C., Galway, Ire., adm. Sept. 24, 1847
Martin Malone, 21, R.C., Clare, Ire., adm. Sept. 24, 1847 adm. March 20, 1848 died Apr. 5, 1848
Pat Nevin, 38, R.C., Tipperary, Ire., adm., Sept. 28, 1847
Jno. Burke, 35, R.C., Galway, Ire., adm. Sept. 28, 1847
Thos. Ryan, 29, R.C., Galway, Ire., adm. March 20, 1848 dis. June 26, 1848 (ship *Ella*) adm. Emigrant Hospital May 1, 1848, lame (ship *Ellis*)
Thos. McDonough, 23, R.C., Galway, Ire., adm. March 20, 1848 dis. May 24, 1848 (ship Ella) adm. Emigrant Hospital May 1, 1848, lame (ship *Ellis*)
Terry Grimes, 30, R.C., Galway, Ire., adm. March 20, 1848 died Apr. 9, 1848

John Hegan, 47, R.C., Cork, Ire., adm. March 20, 1848 dis. Apr. 22, 1848
John Hegan jr., 14, R.C., Cork, Ire., adm. March 20, 1848 dis. May 8, 1848 adm. Emigrant Hospital May 1, 1848, destitute
Pat Lyons, 5, R.C., Galway, Ire., adm. March 20, 1848 dis. Apr. 19, 1848
Edward Hogan, 6, R.C., Cork, Ire., adm. March 20, 1848 dis. May 8, 1848 adm. Emigrant Hospital May 1, 1848, destitute
Cecelia Grimes, 40, Galway, Ire., adm. March 20, 1848
Margt. Grimes, 6, Galway, Ire., adm. March 20, 1848

Ellen,
Jno. Hogan, 15, Cork, Ire., adm. March 20, 1848 dis. March 26, 1848

Ellis, sailed from Cork, arrived June 18, 1847
Dan Donovan, 22, R.C., Cork, Ire., adm. March 20, 1848 dis. June 22, 1848 adm. Emigrant Hospital May 1, 1848, lame
Pat. Murphy, 22, R.C., Clare, Ire., adm. Sept. 24, 1847 adm. March 20, 1848 dis. July 6, 1848 (ship *Ella*) adm. Emigrant Hospital May 1, 1848 (ship *Ellis*)
Thos. Ryan, 29, R.C., Galway, Ire., adm. March 20, 1848 dis. June 26, 1848 (ship *Ella*) adm. Emigrant Hospital May 1, 1848, lame (ship *Ellis*)

Energy, sailed from Londonderry, Ire., arrived August 10, 1847

Port of Saint John: Alms House 1847 133

Pat McLynch, 12, Donegal, Ire.

Envoy, sailed from Londonderry, Ire., arrived at Saint John Aug. 16, 1847
James Doherty, 20, R.C., Derry, Ire., adm. Aug. 10, 1847
William Griffin, 25, Prot., Donegal, Ire., adm. Aug. 15, 1847 dis. Sept. 14, 1847
Henry Glass, 20, R.C., Derry, Ire., adm. Aug. 19, 1847 dis. Aug. 28, 1847 adm. Aug. 31, 1847
Pat McGlinche, 14, R.C., Donegal, Ire., adm. Aug. 20, 1847
Hugh Logue, 60, R.C., Donegal, Ire., adm. Aug. 21, 1847
Ellen Bar, 16, Derry, Ire., adm. Aug. 25, 1847
Susan Doran, 38, R.C., Donegal, Ire., adm. Sept. 6, 1847
James Gallagher, 20, R.C., Fermanagh, Ire., adm. Sept. 12, 1847
Nicholas Carney, 33, R.C., Fermanagh, Ire., adm. Sept. 12, 1847
Widow Coleman, 46, R.C., Cork, Ire., adm. Sept. 21, 1847 dis. Sept. 26, 1847
Biddy Doherty, 19, R.C., Derry, Ire., adm. Sept. 21, 1847 dis. Sept. 27, 1847

Fanny,
Ann Mullin, 22, R.C., Kerry, Ire., adm. Dec. 12, 1848

Francis, 1847 (possibly *John Francis*, 1848)
Alex. Donovan, 27, Cork, Ire., adm. July 11, 1848 dis. July 22, 1848

Friends, sailed from Waterford, Ire., arrived at Saint John June 18, 1847
Harriett Phelan, 28, R.C., Tipperary, Ire., adm. June 26, 1847 dis. July 15, 1847

Garland, sailed from Cork, Ire., arrived Saint John July 1, 1847
Peggy Murphy, 14, R.C.,Cork, Ire., adm. July 16, 1847
Thos. Mitchell, 16, R.C., Galway, Ire., adm. July 28, 1847 dis. Aug. 24, 1847
Danl. Mahony, 45, R.C., Cork, Ire., adm. July 28, 1847 dis. Aug. 28, 1847
Dan Mahony, jr., 5, R.C., Cork, Ire., adm. July 28, 1847 dis. Aug. 28, 1847

Gem, sailed from Galway, Ire. arrived Saint John
Jane Kelly, 26, R.C., Queens Co., Ire., adm. July 1 1847, dis. July 15, 1847
Julia Kelly, 9 mos., R.C, Queens Co., Ire., adm. July 1 1847, dis. July 15, 1847
Ellen Broderick, 35, R.C., Galway, Ire., adm. Aug. 26, 1847
Ellen Broderick, 30, R.C., Galway, Ire., adm. Sept. 20, 1847
Mary Fitzgerald, 22, R.C., Kerry, Ire., adm. Sept. 22, 1847
Michl. Naulty, 1, R.C., Galway, Ire., adm. March 20, 1848 dis. Apr. 16, 1848
Margt. Naulty, 7, Galway, Ire., adm. March 20, 1848 dis. March 30, 1848

Gem of London,
Biddy Broderick, 20, R.C., Galway, Ire., adm. Sept. 12, 1847
Mary Dillan, 22, R.C., Galway, Ire., adm. Sept. 14, 1847

Glory, sailed from Cork, Ire., arrived Saint John Aug. 12, 1847
Dennis Garavan, 20, R.C., Cork, Ire., adm. Aug. 6, 1847

Governor Douglas, sailed from Berehaven, Ire., arrived at Saint John June 21, 1847
Patrick Sullivan, 20, R.C., Cork, Ire., adm. June 21, 1847 dis. July 27, 1847
Mrs. Judy Shea, 24, R.C., Cork, Ire., adm. June 21, 1847 dis. July 2, 1847
Bridget Carney, 16, R.C., Cork, Ire., adm. June 21, 1847 dis. July 7, 1847
Judy Carney, 18, R.C., Cork, Ire., adm. June 21, 1847 dis. July 7, 1847
Hanora Murphy, 15, R.C., Cork, Ire., adm. June 21, 1847 dis. July 5, 1847
Jerry Kelly, 20, R.C., Cork, Ire., adm. June 22, 1847 dis. July 7, 1847
Jerry Sullivan, 34, R.C., Cork, Ire., adm. June 22, 1847 dis. July 7, 1847
Denis Sullivan, 40, R.C., Cork, Ire., adm. June 23, 1847 dis. July 5, 1847
Daniel Murphy, 30, R.C., Cork, Ire., adm. June 24, 1847 dis. July 7, 1847
Jerry Neil, 28, R.C., Cork, Ire., adm. June 25, 1847 dis. Aug. 9, 1847
Owen McCarthy, 25, R.C., Kerry, Ire., adm. June 25, 1847 dis. Aug. 9, 1847
James Leary, 26, R.C., Cork, Ire., adm. June 28, 1847
Michael Green, 23, R.C., Cork, Ire., adm. June 28, 1847 dis. July 7, 1847
Patrick McCarthy, 40, R.C., Cork, Ire., adm. June 29, 1847 died June 30, 1847
John Riordan, 20, R.C., Cork, Ire., adm. July 1, 1847 dis. July 27, 1847
Hugh Connors, 24, R.C., Sligo, Ire., adm. July 1, 1847 dis. July 12, 1847
Michael Shea, 31, R.C., Cork, Ire., adm. July 3, 1847, dis. July 5, 1847
Mary Dougan, 20, R.C., Cork, Ire., adm. July 6, 1847, died Aug. 15, 1847
Michl. Green, 25, R.C., Cork, Ire., adm. Aug. 5, 1847, dis. Sept. 8, 1847
Michael Murphy, 5, R.C., Mayo, Ire., adm. Sept. 7, 1847
Peggy Murphy, 30, R.C., Mayo, Ire., adm. Sept. 7, 1847 dis. Sept. 8, 1847
Mary Murphy, 7, R.C., Mayo, Ire., adm. Sept. 7, 1847 dis. Sept. 8, 1847

Gowrie, sailed from Cork, Ire. arrived at Saint John Aug. 12, 1847
James Shoughereau, 26, R.C., Kerry, Ire., adm. Aug. 16, 1847
James Drescool, 35, R.C., Cork, Ire., adm. Aug. 16, 1847

Jas. Shaughereux, 26, R.C., Cork, Ire., adm. March 20, 1848 dis. July 4, 1848 adm. Emigrant Hospital May 1, 1848, fever

Hannah, sailed from Sligo, Ire., arrived at Saint John July 5, 1847
Mrs. Mary Finn, 25, R.C., Sligo, Ire., adm. June 29, 1847
Mary Finn jr., 3, R.C., Sligo, Ire., adm. June 29, 1847
Mrs. Margt. McGlown, 27, R.C., Mayo, Ire., adm. July 3, 1847
Martin McGloun, 22, R.C., Mayo, Ire., adm. July 5, 1847
John Boyle, 35, R.C., Sligo, Ire., adm. July 5, 1847, dis. July 21, 1847
Henry Boyle, 11, R.C., Sligo, Ire., adm. July 5, 1847
James Boyle, 16, R.C., Sligo, Ire., adm. July 5, 1847, dis. July 21, 1847
Mary Branna, 7 years 6 mos., R.C., Roscommon, Ire., adm. July 7, 1847
John Finny, 20, R.C., Galway, Ire., adm. July 9, 1847
James Maloone, 31, R.C., Leitrim, Ire., adm. July 9, 1847
Mary Malone, 4, R.C., Leitrim, Ire., adm. July 9, 1847 died Aug. 15, 1847
Catherine Brennin, 27, R.C., Roscommon, Ire., adm. July 9, 1847 died July 17, 1847
Kitty Crann, 35, R.C., Roscommon, Ire., adm. July 9, 1847
Mary Crann (Mary Brannan), 7 years 6 mos., R.C., Roscommon, Ire., adm. July 9, 1847
Hanna Crann, (Hanna Brannan), 1 week, adm. July 9, 1847, died July 27, 1847
Mary O'Gara, 19, R.C., Sligo, Ire., adm. July 9, 1847
Mrs. Mary Somers, 28, R.C., Sligo, Ire., adm. July 9, 1847
John Tivnan, 10, R.C., Sligo, Ire., adm. July 10, 1847, dis. July 26, 1847
John Malone, 6, R.C., Leitrim, Ire., adm. July 10, 1847 died Aug. 15, 1847
Bartholomew Somers, 2, R.C., Sligo, Ire., adm. July 10, 1847 dis. Aug. 2, 1847
Ann McManus, 20, R.C., Sligo, Ire., adm. July 10, 1847
Mrs. Malone, 35, R.C., Lietrim, Ire., adm. July 12, 1847
Darby Crain, 38, R.C., Roscommon, Ire., adm. July 13, 1847 died Sept. 5, 1847
John Moran, 31, R.C., Roscommon, Ire., adm. July 13, 1847 dis. Aug. 31, 1847
Mary Langin, 22, R.C., Sligo, Ire., adm. July 15, 1847 dis. Aug. 4, 1847
Owen Tivnan, 11, R.C., Sligo, Ire., adm. July 16, 1847
James McManus, 9, R.C., Sligo, Ire., adm. July 19, 1847 died Aug. 4, 1847
Patk. McManus, 7, R.C., Sligo, Ire., adm. July 19, 1847 died July 27, 1847
Mary McKilline, 32, R.C., Mayo, Ire., adm. July 27, 1847 died Sept. 1, 1847
Michl. Kilrayan, 5, R.C., Sligo, Ire., adm. July 29, 1847 died Aug. 10, 1847
Rose Kilryan, 28, R.C., Sligo, Ire.,

adm. July 29, 1847 dis. Aug. 26, 1847
Ellen Learey, 5, R.C., Cork, Ire., adm. July 29, 1847 died Aug. 16, 1847
Bridget Clancy, 24, R.C., Roscommon, Ire., adm. Aug. 7, 1847 dis. Sept. 21, 1847
Mary Tyner (Mary Fyner) 20, R.C., Cork, Ire., adm. Aug. 7, 1847 dis. Sept. 28, 1847
Margaret Maglone, 30, R.C., Mayo, Ire., adm. Sept. 13, 1847
Thomas Hogan, 26, R.C., Mayo, Ire., adm. Sept. 17, 1847
Mary Nevin, 40, R.C., Tyrone, Ire., adm. Sept. 21, 1847

Hannah Kerr,
Ann Godfray, 21, Prot., Derry, Ire., adm. Sept. 25, 1847

Harriet,
Frs. Ellis, 35, R.C., Donegal, Ire., adm. March 20, 1848 dis. Apr. 19, 1848

Helen Anne, sailed from Kinsale, Ire., arrived at Saint John July 10, 147
Denis Sullivan, 21, R.C., Cork, Ire., adm. July 10, 1847 dis. July 18, 1847

Highland Mary, sailed from Cork, Ire., arrived at Montreal 1847
John Sullivan, 58, R.C., Kerry, Ire., adm. Nov. 29, 1848
Jno. Sullivan Jr., 15, R.C., Kerry, Ire., adm. Dec. 6, 1848

Huron,
Mary Moran, 40, Tyrone, Ire.,

adm. March 20, 1848 dis. May 6, 1848

Inconstant, sailed from Cork, Ire., arrived at Saint John May 31 (June 5), 1847
Mary Cotter, 20, R.C., Cork, Ire., adm. June 3, 1847 died June 10, 1847
Jerry Crowley, 40, R.C., Cork, Ire., adm. June 4, 1847 died June 4, 1847
Ellen Sullivan, 28, R.C., Cork, Ire., adm. June 5. 1847 died June 5, 1847
Geo. Tape, 25, Prot., Cork, Ire., adm. June 5, 1847 adm. Mar. 20, 1848 dis. Dec. 31, 1848. adm. May 1, 1848 to Emigrant Hospital for general debility
Ellen Tape, 23, Prot., Cork, Ire., adm. June 5, 1847
Ellen Hooley, 23, R.C., Cork, Ire., adm. June 5, 1847
Thos. Demery, 23, R.C., Cork, Ire., adm. June 5, 1847 dis. Aug. 18, 1847
Dan Murphy, 30, R.C., Cork, Ire., adm. June 5, 1847 dis. July 20, 1847
Michl. Harrigan, 30, R.C., Cork, Ire., adm. June 7, 1847 died June 17, 1847
Dennis Quinlan, 20, R.C., Cork, Ire., adm. June 7, 1847 dis. June 28, 1847
Johanna Quinlan, 18, R.C., Cork, Ire., adm. June 7, 1847 dis. July 15, 1847
Mary Carney, 20, R.C., Cork, Ire., adm. June 8, 1847 dis. Aug. 1, 1847
Mrs. Jane Flynn, 50, R.C., Cork,

Port of Saint John: Alms House 1847

Ire., adm. June 8, 1847
Wm McArty, 29, R.C., Cork, Ire., adm. June 8, 1847 adm. Mar. 20, 1848 dis. July 11, 1848 adm. May 1, 1848 to Emigrant Hospital for general debility
Johanna Carney, 27, R.C., Cork, Ire., adm. June 9, 1847 dis. July 17, 1847
Mary Sullivan, 2 years 6 mos., R.C., Cork, Ire., adm. June 11, 1847
Judy Sullivan, 8 mos., R.C., Cork, Ire., adm. June 11, 1847
Mrs. Jane Sullivan, 23, R.C., Cork, Ire., adm. June 12, 1847 dis. July 27, 1847
John Sullivan, 23, R.C., Cork, Ire., adm. June 12, 1847 dis. July 27, 1847
Mary Donaley, 26, R.C., Cork, Ire., adm. June 16, 1847
Mary Donaley, 9 mos., R.C., Cork, Ire., adm. June 16, 1847
Eliza Lahy (Eliza Lalry), 20, Prot., Cork, Ire., adm. June 16, 1847 dis. Aug. 2, 1847
Ellen Sexton, 30, R.C., Cork, Ire., adm. June 17, 1847 dis. July 17, 1847
Johanna Walsh, 26, R.C., Cork, Ire., adm. June 18, 1847 dis. July 20, 1847
Mrs. Eliza Tape, 25, Prot., Cork, Ire., adm. June 18, 1847
Annie Tape, 3, Prot., Cork, Ire., adm. June 18, 1847
John Tape, 1, Prot., Cork, Ire., adm. June 18, 1847
Ellen Dalton, adm. June 19, 1847 died June 21, 1847
Catherine Allen, 24, R.C., Cork, Ire., June 21, 1847 dis. Aug. 9, 1847, adm. Aug. 24, 1847 dis. Sept. 2, 1847
Edward Desmond, 29, R.C., Cork, Ire., adm. June 23, 1847
Nancy Hurley, 25, R.C., Cork, Ire., adm. June 24, 1847 dis. July 11, 1847
Thomas Hurley, 3 years 6 mos., R.C., Cork, Ire., adm. June 24, 1847 dis. July 11, 1847
Daniel Sullivan, 25, R.C., Cork, Ire., adm. July 1, 1847 died July 20, 1847
John Tape, 30, Prot., Cork, Ire., adm. July 7, 1847
Mary Carney, 24, R.C., Cork, Ire., adm. Aug. 15, 1847
Dennis Donahy, 25, R.C., Cork, Ire., adm. July 24. 1847 died Sept. 16, 1847
Cath. McArty, 8, Cork, Ire., adm. Apr. 14, 1848 dis. Apr. 16, 1848
And. Desmond, 29, R.C., Cork, Ire., adm. July 5, 1848 dis. Aug. 8, 1848 adm. Emigrant Hospital July 5, 1848, fever, dis. Aug. 8, 1848

James,
Nancy Leary, 22, R.C., Cork, Ire., adm. Aug. 24, 1847 dis. Sept. 25, 1847

James Reddin, sailed from Liverpool, England
Gerald Gallagher, 27, R.C., Dublin, Ire., adm. June 22, 1847
Jerald Gallagher, 27, R.C., Wexford, Ire., adm. March 20, 1848 dis. May 16, 1848, adm. May 30, 1848 dis. June 26, 1848 adm. Emigrant Hospital May 30, 1848, bruise

Jane, sailed from Limerick, Ire., arrived in Saint John Aug. 5, 1847
Stephen Kilmartin, 30, R.C., Galway, Ire., adm. July 31, 1847 dis. Aug. 31, 1847
Judy Killmartin, 28, R.C., Galway, Ire., adm. July 31, 1847 died Aug. 28, 1847
Peggy Killmartin, 5, R.C., Galway, Ire., adm. July 31, 1847 dis. Aug. 13, 1847
Cate Killmartin, 1, R.C., Galway, Ire., adm. July 31, 1847 died Aug. 18, 1847
Judy Brien, 19, R.C., Cork, Ire., adm. July 31, 1847 dis. Sept. 25, 1847
Catherine Magee, 30, R.C., Fermanagh, Ire., adm. Aug. 1, 1847 dis. Aug. 16, 1847
Peter Gillane, 24, R.C., Galway, Ire., adm. Aug. 4, 1847
James Cassidy, 55, R.C., Clare, Ire., adm. Aug. 11, 1847
Anne Capels, 24, R.C., Limerick, Ire., adm. Aug. 20, 1847 died Sept. 7, 1847
James Sheley, 45, R.C., Limerick, Ire., adm. Sept. 7, 1847
Edward Sheley, 12, R.C., Limerick, Ire., adm. Sept. 7, 1847
Edmund Shehey, 12, R.C., Limerick, Ire., adm. March 20, 1848 dis. Apr. 25, 1848
Robt. Sehey, 10, R.C., Limerick, Ire., adm. March 20, 1848 dis. Apr. 25, 1848
James Sheyhey, 8, R.C., Limerick, Ire., adm. March 20, 1848 dis. Apr. 25, 1848
Mary Shehey, 19, Limerick, Ire., adm. March 20, 1848 dis. Apr. 18, 1848
Margt. Shehey, 14, Limerick, Ire., adm. March 20, 1848 dis. Apr. 29, 1848
Bridget Campbell, 24, Derry, Ire., adm. March 20, 1848 dis. Apr. 19, 1848

Jane & Mary,
Jerry Donovan, 20, R.C., Cork, Ire., adm. Sept. 1, 1847 adm. March 20, 1848 dis. Apr. 14, 1848

John Begg,
Peter Galoone, 24, R.C., Galway, Ire. adm. July 13, 1847
Stephen Kilmartin, 30, R.C., Galway, Ire., adm. July 14, 1847 dis. Aug. 30, 1847
Thos. Spellman, 29, R.C., Galway, Ire., adm. March 20, 1848 dis. May 17, 1848 adm. Emigrant Hospital May 1, 1848, Iritis (vessel *Thos. Begg*)

John Clarke, sailed from Londonderry, Ire., arrived at Saint John July 3, 1847
William McColgan, 18, R.C., Donegal, Ire., adm. July 5, 1847, dis. July 26, 1847
John Lowrey, 19, Preby., Donegal, Ire., adm. July 6, 1847, died Aug. 14, 1847
John Reily, 16, R.C., Donegal, Ire., adm. July 10, 1847 dis. July 23, 1847
John Mohan, 27, R.C., Donegal, Ire., adm. July 14, 1847 died July 18, 1847
Hugh McDade, 28, R.C., Derry, Ire., adm. July 14, 1847 died July

Port of Saint John: Alms House 1847

16, 1847
Dan Haggerty, 31, R.C., Donegal, Ire., adm. July 19, 1847 dis. July 26, 1847
Mary Doherty, 20, Donegal, Ire., adm. March 20, 1848
Jos. White, 27, Prot., Tyrone, Ire., adm. May 13, 1848 died Nov. 29, 1848 adm. Emigrant Hospital May 13, 1848, fever
David Harper, 27, Preby., Derry, Ire., adm. Aug. 3, 1848 dis. Aug. 14, 1848 adm. Emigrant Hospital Aug. 3, 1848, dysentry, dis. Aug. 14, 1848

John Wesley, sailed from Baltimore, Ire., arrived at Saint John
Mrs. Cate Hegarty, 40, R.C., Cork, Ire., adm. July 3, 1847

John S. DeWolfe, sailed from Killala, Ire., arrived at Saint John Aug. 14, 1847
Pat Hughes, 22, R.C., Mayo, Ire., adm. Aug. 14, 1847 died Aug. 17, 1847
Thomas Hanigan, 18, R.C., Mayo, Ire., adm. Aug. 15, 1847 dis. Sept. 29, 1847
Peggy Kelly, 20, R.C., Mayo, Ire., adm. Aug. 17, 1847
Ellen Harrison, 30, R.C., Mayo, Ire., adm. Aug. 17, 1847 died Sept. 23, 1847
Denis Harrison, 20, R.C., Mayo, Ire., adm. Aug. 17, 1847
Martin Walsh, 22, R.C., Mayo, Ire., adm. Aug. 17, 1847 dis. Aug. 27, 1847
Martin May, 32, R.C., Mayo, Ire., adm. Aug. 19, 1847 died Sept.

19, 1847
John Goldin, 17, R.C., Mayo, Ire., adm. Aug. 19, 1847 died Aug. 27, 1847
Patrick Broderick, 28, R.C., Mayo, Ire., adm. Aug. 20, 1847
Domenick Scanlin, 24, R.C., Mayo, Ire., adm. Aug. 20, 1847 dis. Aug. 26, 1847
Biddy Murphy, 22, R.C., Mayo, Ire., adm. Aug. 20, 1847 dis. Aug. 25, 1847
Tom Geohen, 30, R.C., Mayo, Ire., adm. Aug. 22, 1847 dis. Aug. 26, 1847
Pat Kelly, 22, R.C., Mayo, Ire., adm. Aug. 24, 1847 dis. Aug. 26, 1847 adm. Sept. 1, 1847
John McKeane, 22, R.C., Mayo, Ire., adm. Aug. 24, 1847
Mary Meirn, 22, R.C., Mayo, Ire., adm. Aug. 25, 1847 dis. Aug. 26, 1847
Catherine Meirn, 48, R.C., Mayo, Ire., adm. Aug. 25, 1847 dis. Aug. 26, 1847
Margt. McKinny, 18, R.C., Mayo, Ire., adm. Aug. 25, 1847
James Merrin, 30, R.C., Mayo, Ire., adm. Aug. 25, 1847 dis. Aug. 26, 1847
Bridget Maurice, 22, R.C., Mayo, Ire., adm. Aug. 26, 1847 dis. Sept. 2, 1847
John O'Hara, 1 year 6 mos., R.C., Mayo, Ire., adm. Aug. 27, 1847 dis. Sept. 4, 1847
Richard O'Hara, 40, R.C., Mayo, Ire., adm. Aug. 27, 1847 dis. Sept. 4, 1847
Mary O'Hara, 30, R.C., Mayo, Ire., adm. Aug. 27, 1847 dis. Sept. 4, 1847

John Duffy, 24, R.C., Mayo, Ire., adm. Aug. 27, 1847
Margaret Duffy, 2 years 6 mos., R.C., Mayo, Ire., adm. Aug. 27, 1847 dis. Sept. 25, 1847
Mrs. Molly Hussey, 60, R.C., Sligo, Ire., Aug. 28, 1847
Paddy Hosey, 56, R.C., Sligo, Ire., Aug. 28, 1847
Biddy Hester, 33, R.C., Mayo, Ire., Aug. 28, 1847
Mary Hester, 17, R.C., Mayo, Ire., Aug. 28, 1847
Anne Moore, 45, Mayo, Ire., Aug. 28, 1847 died Aug. 30, 1847
Phelix O'Neil, 15, R.C., Sligo, Ire., adm. Aug. 28, 1847
Martin Flinn, 30, R.C., Mayo, Ire., adm. Aug. 28, 1847
Pat Kennedy, 24, R.C., Mayo, Ire., adm. Sept. 2, 1847
Brid. Murphy, 22, R.C., Mayo, Ire., adm. Sept. 6, 1847 died Sept. 8, 1847
Margaret McKenna, 24, R.C., Mayo, Ire., adm. Sept. 8, 1847
Michael Brelian, 27, R.C., Mayo, Ire., adm. Sept. 8, 1847 dis. Sept. 17, 1847
Mary O'Brien, 37, R.C., Mayo, Ire., adm. Sept. 12, 1847
Mary Hasted, 30, R.C., Mayo, Ire., adm. Sept. 15, 1847
Thomas Walsh, 3, R.C., Mayo, Ire., adm. Sept. 17, 1847
Biddy Walsh, 1, R.C., Mayo, Ire., adm. Sept. 17, 1847 died Sept. 22, 1847
Biddy Walsh, 24, R.C., Mayo, Ire., adm. Sept. 17, 1847
Mary Flannegan, 23, R.C., Galway, Ire., adm. Sept. 17, 1847 adm. March 20, 1848, age 24, dis. May 9, 1848
Ellen Burke, 28, R.C., Mayo, Ire., adm. Sept. 17, 1847 adm. March 20, 1848 dis. Aug. 5, 1848
Pat. Rearney, 14, R.C., Mayo, Ire., adm. Sept. 17, 1847
Charles Rooney, 69, R.C., Sligo, Ire., adm. Sept. 18, 1847
Pat Hosey, 60, R.C., Sligo, Ire., adm. Sept. 18, 1847
John Walsh, 9, R.C., Mayo, Ire., adm. Sept. 19, 1847
Margaret Larken, 20, R.C., Mayo, Ire., adm. Sept. 19, 1847
Thos. Mendugh, 22, R.C., Mayo, Ire., adm. Sept. 23, 1847
Pat Durkin, 14, R.C., Mayo, Ire., adm. Sept. 23, 1847
John Gorcan, 75, R.C., Mayo, Ire., adm. Sept. 23, 1847
Pat Kelly, 4, R.C., Mayo, Ire., adm. Sept. 24, 1847
Tom Kelly, 6 mos., R.C., Mayo, Ire., adm. Sept. 24, 1847
Pat. Kelly, 41, R.C., Mayo, Ire., adm. Sept. 24, 1847 adm. March 20, 1848 dis. June 26, 1848 adm. Emigrant Hospital May 1, 1848, destitute
Mrs. Cath. Kelly, 30, R.C., Mayo, Ire., adm. Sept. 24, 1847 adm. March 20, 1848 dis. June 28, 1848
James Durkin, 16, R.C., Mayo, Ire., adm. March 20, 1848 dis. March 29, 1848
Tim Healey, 42, R.C., Mayo, Ire., adm. March 20, 1848 dis. May 29, 1848 adm. Emigrant Hospital May 1, 1848, dystenty
John Brown, 40, R.C., Mayo, Ire., adm. March 20, 1848 dis. May 29, 1848 adm. Emigrant Hospital

Port of Saint John: Alms House 1847 141

May 1, 1848, dystentry
Anthony Healey, 11, R.C., Mayo, Ire., adm. March 20, 1848 dis. May 29, 1848 adm. Emigrant Hospital May 1, 1848, destitute
John Healey, 9, R.C., Mayo, Ire., adm. March 20, 1848 dis. May 29, 1848 adm. Emigrant Hospital May 1, 1848, destitute
Margt. Gillespie, 35, Mayo, Ire., adm. March 20, 1848 dis. Apr. 13, 1848
Biddy Healey, 32, Mayo, Ire., adm. March 20, 1848 dis. Apr. 29, 1848
Margt. Hartt, 16, Mayo, Ire., adm. March 20, 1848 dis. Apr. 18, 1848
Kitty Brown, 30, Mayo, Ire., adm. March 20, 1848 dis. May 29, 1848
Biddy Kearney, 12, Mayo, Ire., adm. March 20, 1848 dis. March 29, 1848
Mary Healey, 8, Mayo, Ire., adm. March 20, 1848 dis. May 29, 1848
Biddy Healey, 6, Mayo, Ire., adm. March 20, 1848 dis. May 29, 1848
Kitty Healey, 9 mos., Mayo, Ire., adm. March 20, 1848 dis. May 29, 1848

Kingston, sailed from Cork, Ire., arrived at Saint John July 22, 1847
Thomas Conners, 31, R.C. Tipperary, Ire., adm. July 23, 1847 died Sept. 17, 1847
Thomas Conners, 4, R.C. Tipperary, Ire., adm. July 23, 1847 died Sept. 1, 1847
James Conners, 2, R.C. Tipperary, Ire., adm. July 23, 1847 died Aug. 28, 1847
Margaret Connor, 40, R.C. Tipperary, Ire., adm. July 23, 1847 dis. Sept. 26, 1847
Mary Connor, 6, R.C. Tipperary, Ire., adm. July 23, 1847
Mary Donovan, 25, R.C., Cork, Ire., adm. July 29, 1847
John Lehane, 20, R.C., Cork, Ire., adm. Aug. 3, 1847 died Aug. 29, 1847
Mrs. Delany, 40, R.C., Cork, Ire., adm. Aug. 11, 1847 dis. Aug. 18, 1847
Edward Delaney, 1 year 4 mos., Cork, Ire., adm. Aug. 11, 1847
Tim McMahon, 30, R.C., Tipperary, Ire., adm. Aug. 11, 1847 adm. Sept. 5, 1847
Mich. Collins, 15, R.C., Cork, Ire., adm. Aug. 11, 1847
Abby Collins, 8, R.C., Cork, Ire., dis. Aug. 18, 1847
John O'Mara, 36, R.C., Tipperary, Ire., adm. Aug. 13, 1847
Edward O'Mara, 12, R.C., Tipperary, Ire., adm. Aug. 13, 1847
John O'Mara, 8, R.C., Tipperary, Ire., adm. Aug. 13, 1847
Brien O'Mara, 2, R.C., Tipperary, Ire., adm. Aug. 13, 1847 died Sept. 14, 1847
Murria O'Mara, 6, R.C., Tipperary, Ire., adm. Aug. 13, 1847
Nancy McMahon, 25, R.C., Tipperary, Ire., adm. Aug. 13, 1847
John McCarthy, 17, R.C., Cork, Ire., adm. Aug. 16, 1847 died Aug. 28, 1847

Tim Larkin, 20, R.C., Kerry, Ire., adm. March 20, 1848 dis. May 8, 1848 adm. Emigrant Hospital May 1, 1848, destitute
Bridget O'Mara, 14, Tipperary, Ire., adm. March 20, 1848 dis. Apr. 22, 1848

Lady Bagot, sailed from New Ross, Ire., arrived in Saint John July 19
Patk. Murphy, 36, R.C., Wexford, Ire., adm. July 21, 1847 died Aug. 1, 1847
Laurence Murphy, 20, R.C., Wexford, Ire., adm. July 26, 1847 dis. Sept. 16, 1847
Patk. Murphy, 14, R.C., Wexford, Ire., adm. July 26, 1847 dis. Sept. 6, 1847 adm. Sept. 11, 1847 dis. Sept. 16, 1847
James Powers, 19, R.C., Wexford, Ire., adm. July 27, 1847 dis. Aug. 16, 1847 adm. Aug. 17, 1847
Henry McBrine, 40, R.C., Fermanagh, Ire., adm. July 27, 1847 dis. Aug. 3, 1847
Catherine Murphy, 32, R.C., Waterford, Ire., adm. July 28, 1847
Michl. Murphy, 10, R.C., Waterford, Ire., adm. July 28, 1847
Mary Murphy, 38, R.C., Waterford, Ire., adm. July 28, 1847 dis. Sept. 8, 1847
Ellen Murphy 1, R.C., Waterford, Ire., adm. July 28, 1847 died Aug. 12, 1847
Ellen Grey, 15, Derry, Ire., adm. July 29, 1847 dis. Sept. 13, 1847
Bridget Bulger, 40, R.C., Wexford, Ire., adm. July 30, 1847
Mary Duggan, 17, R.C., Wexford, Ire., adm. July 30, 1847 dis. Aug. 4, 1847
Mary Morrison, 21, Cavan, Ire., adm. July 30, 1847
Catherine Quigly, 19, R.C., Wexford, Ire., adm. July 31, 1847 dis. Aug. 10, 1847
Michl. Bulger, 33, R.C., Wexford, Ire., adm. Aug. 2, 1847 died Aug. 28, 1847
Margaret Bulger, 8, R.C., Wexford, Ire., adm. Aug. 2, 1847 died Aug. 28, 1847
Margaret Gorman, 25, R.C., Wexford, Ire., adm. Aug. 4, 1847 died Sept. 11, 1847
Mary Casey, 64, R.C., Wexford, Ire., adm. Aug. 4, 1847 died Aug. 15, 1847
Mrs. Alia Murphy, 30, R.C., Waterford, Ire., adm. Aug. 17, 1847 died Sept. 1, 1847
Ally Powers, 30, R.C., Tipperary, Ire., adm. Aug. 25, 1847
Patrick Powers, 6, R.C., Tipperary, Ire., adm. Aug. 25, 1847
Thomas Casey, 28, R.C., Wexford, Ire., adm. Aug. 25, 1847 dis. Sept. 1, 1847 adm. Sept. 8, 1847 died Sept. 10, 1847
John Lee, 40, R.C., Galway, Ire., adm. Aug. 25, 1847 dis. Sept. 1, 1847
William Casey, 31, R.C., Wexford, Ire., adm. Sept. 14, 1847
Jno. Murphy, 24, R.C., Carlow, Ire., adm. May 4, 1848 dis. July 17, 1848 adm. Emigrant Hospital May 4, 1848, fever

Port of Saint John: Alms House 1847

Lady Caroline, 1847
Eliz. Laughlin, 23, Prot., Down, Ire., adm. Aug. 28, 1848 dis. Oct. 4, 1848

Lady Constable, arrived at P.E.I., 1847
Michael Neil (Michl. Neal), 30, R.C., Queens Co., Ire., adm. July 7, 1847, dis. Aug. 20, 1847 adm. March 20, 1848 dis. Apr. 19, 1848

Lady Fox,
Mathew Kennedy, 32, R.C., Clare, Ire., adm. Sept. 18, 1847

Lady Napier,
Bridget Fehin, 19, R.C., Mayo, Ire., adm. Sept. 24, 1847
Mich. Meenan, 25, R.C., Tyrone, Ire., adm. March 20, 1848 dis. March 29, 1848
Mich. Meenan, 5, R.C., Tyrone, Ire., adm. March 20, 1848 dis. March 29, 1848
Biddy Meenan, 27, Tyrone, Ire., adm. March 20, 1848 dis. March 29, 1848
Ann Meenan, 10, Tyrone, Ire., adm. March 20, 1848 dis. March 29, 1848

Lady Sale, sailed from Sligo, Ire., arrived at Saint John Aug. 16, 1847
Patrick McGovern, 15, R.C., Sligo, Ire., adm. Sept. 16, 1847
Anne McGowan, 18, R.C., Sligo, Ire., adm. Sept. 18, 1847
Bridget Galone, 19, R.C., Sligo, Ire., adm. Sept. 18, 1847
Mary Noon, 16, R.C., Sligo, Ire., adm. Sept. 21, 1847
Winni Rooney, 9, R.C., Sligo, Ire., adm. Sept. 22, 1847
Tim Rooney, 55, R.C., Sligo, Ire., adm. Sept. 22, 1847
James Rooney, 20, R.C., Sligo, Ire., adm. Sept. 22, 1847
Jno. Scanlan, 25, R.C., Sligo, Ire., adm. Sept. 22, 1847
Wm Gillin, 30, R.C., Sligo, Ire., adm. Sept. 22, 1847
Owen Golderick, 50, R.C., Sligo, Ire., adm. Sept. 22, 1847
Pat Golderick, 16, R.C., Sligo, Ire., adm. Sept. 22, 1847
Mich. McLaughlin, 23, R.C., Sligo, Ire., adm. Sept. 22, 1847
Jno. Gilmartin, 70, R.C., Sligo, Ire., adm. Sept. 23, 1847
Owen Kilmartin, 25, R.C., Sligo, Ire., adm. Sept. 23, 1847
Bridget Kilmartin, 16, R.C., Sligo, Ire., adm. Sept. 23, 1847
Cath. Healey, 52, R.C., Sligo, Ire., adm. Sept. 24, 1847
Brian Haley, 14, R.C., Sligo, Ire., adm. Sept. 24, 1847
Ann Perin, 20, R.C., Sligo, Ire., adm. Sept. 24, 1847
Mary Doherty, 20, R.C., Sligo, Ire., adm. Sept. 24, 1847
Cath. Conway, 25, R.C., Sligo, Ire., adm. Sept. 24, 1847
James Conray, 27, R.C., Sligo, Ire., adm. Sept. 24, 1847 adm. March 20, 1848 died May 12, 1848 adm. Emigrant Hospital May 1, 1848, fever, bowel comp.
Mary Brannen, 9, R.C., Sligo, Ire., adm. Sept. 25, 1847
Ann Brannen, 21, R.C., Sligo, Ire., adm. Sept. 25, 1847
Pat Gibbon, 26, R.C., Sligo, Ire.,

adm. Sept. 25, 1847
Frs. McGlown, 20, R.C., Sligo, Ire., adm. Sept. 25, 1847
Mich. Finn, 20, R.C., Sligo, Ire., adm. Sept. 25, 1847
James Gardner, 18, R.C., Sligo, Ire., adm. Sept. 25, 1847
Mary Gardner, 30, R.C., Sligo, Ire., adm. Sept. 25, 1847
Margt. McNulty, 18, R.C., Sligo, Ire., adm. Sept. 25, 1847
Biddy Foley, 14, R.C., Sligo, Ire., adm. Sept. 25, 1847
Mary Foley, 13, R.C., Sligo, Ire., adm. Sept. 25, 1847
Cath. Hartt, 19, R.C., Sligo, Ire., adm. Sept. 25, 1847
Susan Doherty, 13, R.C., Sligo, Ire., adm. Sept. 25, 1847 dis. Sept. 27, 1847
Ann Burke, 19, R.C., Sligo, Ire., adm. Sept. 27, 1847
Biddy Gilloon, 21, R.C., Sligo, Ire., adm. Sept. 27, 1847
Sally Kilmartin, 20, R.C., Sligo, Ire., adm. Sept. 27, 1847
Margt. Gallagher, 30, R.C., Sligo, Ire., adm. Sept. 27, 1847 died Sept. 28, 1847
Frs. Golderick (Frs. McGolderick), 17, R.C., Sligo, Ire., adm. Sept. 27, 1847 adm. March 20, 1848 dis. May 8, 1848 adm. Emigrant Hospital May 1, 1848, destitute
Wm Gilmartin, 15, R.C., Sligo, Ire., adm. Sept. 27, 1847
Thos. Gilmartin, 20, R.C., Sligo, Ire., adm. Sept. 27, 1847
Jno. McGlown, 15, R.C., Sligo, Ire., adm. Sept. 27, 1847
Dan Feehely, 28, R.C., Sligo, Ire., adm. Sept. 27, 1847
Matt Kelly, 54, R.C., Sligo, Ire., adm. Sept. 27, 1847
Matt Kelly jr., 14, R.C., Sligo, Ire., adm. Sept. 27, 1847
James Kelly, 10, R.C., Sligo, Ire., adm. Sept. 27, 1847
Owen Kelly, 6, R.C., Sligo, Ire., adm. Sept. 27, 1847
Chas. Kearney, 20, R.C., Sligo, Ire., adm. Sept. 28, 1847 adm. March 20, 1848 dis. Apr. 4, 1848
Manus Foley, 20, R.C., Sligo, Ire., adm. Sept. 28, 1847
Terrence Costello, 15, R.C., Sligo, Ire., adm. Sept. 29, 1847
Pat Magowan, 15, R.C., Sligo, Ire., adm. Sept. 29, 1847
John Conolly, 20, R.C., Sligo, Ire., adm. March 20, 1848 dis. June 19, 1848 adm. Emigrant Hospital May 1, 1848, destitute
John Gunnin, 30, R.C., Sligo, Ire., adm. March 20, 1848 dis. June 7, 1848 adm. Emigrant Hospital May 1, 1848, destitute
Owen Lenahan, 20, R.C., Sligo, Ire., adm. March 20, 1848 dis. Sept. 20, 1848 adm. Oct. 4, 1848 dis. Oct. 9, 1848 adm. Emigrant Hospital May 1, 1848, destitute
Pat. Harkins, 17, R.C., Sligo, Ire., adm. March 20, 1848 dis. July 19, 1848 adm. Emigrant Hospital May 1, 1848, fever
Pat. Cassidy, 21, R.C., Sligo, Ire., adm. March 20, 1848 dis. Apr. 12, 1848
Pat Finnigan, 16, R.C., Sligo, Ire., adm. March 20, 1848 dis. May 19, 1848 adm. Emigrant Hospital May 1, 1848, fever
Jas. Gillan, 60, R.C., Sligo, Ire., adm. March 20, 1848 dis. May 16, 1848 adm. Emigrant Hospital

May 1, 1848, destitute
Jno. Kilbride (John Kilbride), 8, R.C., Sligo, Ire., adm. March 20, 1848 dis. May 10, 1848 adm. May 12, 1848 dis. Sept. 20, 1848 returned Oct. 28, 1848 adm. Emigrant Hospital May 1, 1848, destitute adm May 12
Tom Cassidy, 1 year 3 mos., R.C., Sligo, Ire., adm. March 20, 1848 dis. Apr. 14, 1848
Ann Branley, 14, Sligo, Ire., adm. March 20, 1848 dis. Oct. 20, 1848
Mary Gunnin, 30, Sligo, Ire., adm. March 20, 1848 dis. June 7, 1848
Peggy Kilmartin, 22, Sligo, Ire., adm. March 20, 1848 dis. June 7, 1848
Bridget Harkins, wid., 40, Sligo, Ire., adm. March 20, 1848 died Apr. 14, 1848
Wid. Carleton, 46, Sligo, Ire., adm. March 20, 1848 dis. May 13, 1848
Sally Carleton, 22, Sligo, Ire., adm. March 20, 1848 dis. Apr. 25, 1848
Mary Foley, wid., 40, Sligo, Ire., adm. March 20, 1848 dis. Apr. 22, 1848
Margt. Harkins, 60, Sligo, Ire., adm. March 20, 1848 dis. July 11, 1848 returned July 14, 1848
Bridget Gallagher, 19, Sligo, Ire., adm. March 20, 1848 dis. May 13, 1848
Ellen Gallagher, 17, Sligo, Ire., adm. March 20, 1848 dis. May 19, 1848
Mary Moran, 20, Sligo, Ire., adm. March 20, 1848 dis. Aug. 1, 1848
Peggy Gill, 50, Sligo, Ire., adm.

March 20, 1848 dis. Aug. 13, 1848
Mary Cassidy, 30, Sligo, Ire., adm. March 20, 1848 dis. Apr. 14, 1848
Cecilia Clancy, 52, Sligo, Ire., adm. March 20, 1848 dis. Apr. 29, 1848
Ann Kearny, 14, Sligo, Ire., adm. March 20, 1848 dis. Apr. 17, 1848
Mary McGolderick, 35, Sligo, Ire., adm. March 20, 1848 dis. March 27, 1848
Biddy McGolderick, 22, Sligo, Ire., adm. March 20, 1848 dis. May 26, 1848
Cath. Gunnin, 4, Sligo, Ire., adm. March 20, 1848 dis. June 7, 1848
Winni Kilmartin, 20, Sligo, Ire., adm. March 20, 1848 dis. May 1, 1847
Mary McGolderick, 5, Sligo, Ire., adm. March 20, 1848 died March 1848
Michl. Feeney, 29, R.C., Sligo, Ire., adm. March 23, 1848 dis. May 25, 1848 adm. Emigrant Hospital May 1, 1848, destitute
Brian O'Rourk, 70, R.C., Sligo, Ire., adm. March 30, 1848 died May 12, 1847 adm. Emigrant Hospital May 1, 1848, fever
Ann Kearns, 15, Sligo, Ire., adm. Apr. 26, 1848 dis. June 26, 1848
Jas. Condray, 27, R.C., Sligo, Ire., adm. May 1, 1848 died May 12, 1848
Pat Kilbride, 40, R.C., Sligo, Ire., adm. May 12, 1848 dis. Sept. 20, 1848 adm. Emigrant Hospital May 12, 1848, destitute
Peggy Harkins, 60, Sligo, Ire.,

adm. July 14, 1848 dis. July 19, 1848
Bridgt Costello (Biddy Costello), 22, R.C., Sligo, Ire., adm. Nov. 15, 1848 adm. Sept. 5, 1848 dis. Sept. 28, 1848
Aaron Surahan, 20, Sligo, Ire. (not listed in Alms House Records) adm. Emigrant Hospital Oct. 4, 1848, scrofulous, dis. Oct. 9, 1848

Lelia,
Tom Folan, 15, R.C., Galway, Ire., adm. July 24, 1847

Leviathan,
John Connelly, 35, R.C., Galway, Ire., adm. June 25, 1847 dis. July 20, 1847

Leviathan, sailed from Baltimore, Ire., arrived Saint John August 20, 1847
Danl. Daly, 30, R.C., Cork, Ire., adm. Aug. 31, 1847 dis. Sept. 3, 1847
Mrs. Mary Savage, 26, R.C., Kerry, Ire., adm. Sept. 22, 1847 adm. March 20, 1848 dis. Apr. 19, 1848
Owen Savage, 32, R.C., R.C., Cork, Ire., adm. Sept. 22, 1847 adm. March 20, 1848 dis. Apr. 19, 1848

Linden, sailed from Galway, Ire., arrived at Saint John June 18
Nailon Conway, 40, R.C., Clare, Ire., adm. June 24, 1847 died July 24, 1847
Patrick Sullivan, 20, R.C., Cork, Ire., adm. June 25, 1847

John Conners, 22, R.C., Galway, Ire., adm. June 25, 1847 died Sept. 16, 1847
Mathew Finarty, 30, R.C., Galway, Ire., adm. June 30, 1847
Michl. Hesson, 21, R.C., Galway, Ire., adm. June 30, 1847 died July 22, 1847
Mary Manogue, 20, R.C., Clare, Ire., adm. July 1, 1847 dis. Sept. 23, 1847
Mrs. Mary Kelly, 20, R.C., Clare, Ire., adm. July 2 1847, dis. July 24, 1847
Cate Lyons, 25, R.C., Clare, Ire., adm. July 2, 1847, died July 17, 1847
Tim Donovan, 30, R.C., Clare, Ire., adm. July 2, 1847, died July 4, 1847
Darby Consadin (Darby Consader), 25, R.C., Clare, Ire., adm. July 2, 1847, dis. July 17, 1847 adm. July 24, 1847 died July 25, 1847
Patrick Curlin (Patrick Coslin), 26, R.C., Galway, Ire., adm. July 2, 1847, dis. Aug. 1, 1847
Michael King, 11, R.C., Galway, Ire., adm. July 3, 1847, dis. Aug. 2, 1847
Edmond Cole, 27, R.C., Galway, Ire. adm. July 3, 1847
Michael Costello, 27, R.C., Galway, Ire., adm. July 3, 1847, dis. Aug. 5, 1847
Bridget Dealy, 20, R.C., Clare, Ire., adm. July 5, 1847, dis. Aug. 14, 1847
Mrs. Mary Manion, 30, R.C., Galway, Ire., adm. July 5, 1847, died July 5, 1847
John Donovan, 33, R.C., Clare,

Port of Saint John: Alms House 1847

Ire., adm. July 5, 1847 died July 9, 1847
Michael Connor, 25, R.C., Galway, Ire., adm. July 5, 1847
Edward Walsh, 40, R.C., Mayo, Ire., adm. July 6, 1847, died
Brian Folan, 26, R.C., Galway, Ire., adm. July 6, 1847, died Aug. 19, 1847
John McDonagh, 24, R.C., Galway, Ire., adm. July 6, 1847 adm. Emigrant Hospital June 1, 1848, fever, dis. July 31, 1848
Bridget Burk, 20, R.C., Galway, Ire., adm. July 6, 1847, dis. July 20, 1847
Patrick Nailon, 19, R.C., Clare, Ire., adm. July 7, 1847, dis. Sept. 7, 1847
Bat. Kelly, 25, R.C., Clare, Ire., adm. July 8, 1847 dis. July 20, 1847
John Fitzgerald, 29, R.C., Cork, Ire., adm. July 9, 1847
Lawrence McMahon, 25, R.C., Clare, Ire., adm. July 10, 1847 dis. July 23, 1847
Mary Joyce, 16, R.C., Galway, Ire., adm. July 10, 1847 dis. Aug. 21, 1847
Ann Costello, 16, R.C., Galway, Ire., adm. July 10, 1847, dis. Aug. 5, 1847
Mary Hopkins, 22, R.C., Mayo, Ire., adm. July 11, 1847
John Marr, 28, R.C., Galway, Ire., adm. July 12, 1847 died July 28, 1847
Mrs. Margaret King, 30, R.C., Galway, Ire., adm. July 13, 1847
Hannora Lennan, 22, R.C., Galway, Ire., adm. July 14, 1847 dis. Aug. 2, 1847
Michl. Sullivan, 21, R.C., Galway, Ire., adm. July 14, 1847 dis. July 27, 1847
Martin Heron, 21, R.C., Galway, Ire., adm. July 16, 1847 died Aug. 2, 1847
Thos. Selor, 27, R.C., Galway, Ire., adm. July 16, 1847 died July 21, 1847
Mary Burns, 24, R.C., Clare, Ire., adm. July 28, 1847 dis. Sept. 8, 1847
Margt. Connelly, 50, R.C., Galway, Ire., adm. Aug. 5, 1847
Margaret Connelly, 7, R.C., Galway, Ire., adm. Aug. 5, 1847
John Donahue, 24, R.C., Kerry, Ire., adm. Aug. 5, 1847
Margaret King, 35, R.C., Galway, Ire., adm. Aug. 7, 1847 dis. Aug. 20, 1847
Patk. Curlin, 27, R.C., Galway, Ire., adm. Aug. 9, 1847
Edwd. Pole, 27, R.C., Galway, Ire., adm. Aug. 9, 1847 died Aug. 16, 1847
Mich. King, 8, R.C., Galway, Ire., adm. Aug. 9, 1847 dis. Aug. 20, 1847
Denis Dunlevy, 40, R.C., Mayo, Ire., adm. Aug. 12, 1847 died Aug. 16, 1847
Patrick Coomie, 26, R.C., Galway, Ire., adm. Aug. 18, 1847
Michael Connor, 24, R.C., Galway, Ire., adm. Aug. 18, 1847
Joanna Nealon, 20, R.C., Clare, Ire., adm. Aug. 18, 1847 adm. March 20, 1848 dis. July 31, 1848
Patrick Henrey, 24, R.C., Galway, Ire., adm. Aug. 18, 1847
Sally Finny, 2, R.C., Galway, Ire.,

adm. Aug. 27, 1847
Mrs. Nelly Finny, 22, R.C., Galway, Ire., adm. Aug. 27, 1847
Michael Ring, 11, R.C., Galway, Ire., adm. Aug. 30, 1847
John McConnell, 51, R.C., Dublin, Ire., adm. Aug. 30, 1847
Mathew Sullivan, 30, R.C., Kerry, Ire., adm. Aug. 30, 1847
Thomas Walsh, 1, R.C., Clare, Ire., adm. Sept. 4, 1847
Mary Walsh, 26, R.C., Clare, Ire., adm. Sept. 4, 1847 dis. Sept. 17, 1847
John Murphy, 3 years 6 mos., R.C., Cork, Ire., adm. Sept. 4, 1847
Martin Foy, 23, R.C., Galway, Ire., adm. Sept. 21, 1847
Jno. Flaherty, 40, R.C., Galway, Ire., adm. Sept. 22, 1847
Joanna Nevin, 20, R.C., Clare, Ire., adm. Sept. 27, 1847
Margt. Costello, 16, R.C., Galway, Ire., adm. Sept. 28, 1847
Mary Manogue, 25, R.C., Galway, Ire., adm. Sept. 28, 1847 adm. March 20, 1848 dis. May 13, 1848
Biddy Welch, 20, Wicklow, Ire., adm. March 20, 1848 dis. May 29, 1848
John McDonough, 24, R.C., Galway, Ire., adm. May 30, 1848 dis. July 31, 1848
Peter Manion, 25, R.C., Galway, Ire., adm. July 14, 1848 dis. July 26, 1848
Pat Connory, 14, Galway, Ire. (not listed in Alms House Records) adm. Emigrant Hospital June 1, 1848, fever, dis. Aug. 8, 1848
Pat Conolly, 35, Galway, Ire. (not listed in Alms House Records) adm. Emigrant Hospital June 22, 1848, fever, dis. Dec. 31, 1848
Tim Kerley, 6, Cork, Ire. (not listed in Alms House Records) adm. Emigrant Hospital July 6, 1848, bowel comp., dis. July 18, 1848
Conor Sexton, 55, Clare, Ire. (not listed in Alms House Records) adm. Emigrant Hospital July 31, 1848, fever, died Oct. 13, 1848

Londonderry, left Derry, Ire., arrived at Saint John Aug. 21, 1847
Robert Mercer, 19, R.C., Donegal, Ire., adm. Aug. 25, 1847
Thomas McColgan, 17, R.C., Derry, Ire., adm. Sept. 3, 1847 dis. Sept. 4, 1847
Mary McQuaid, 22, R.C., Derry, Ire., adm. Sept. 14, 1847
Hugh Ward, 30, R.C., Donegal, Ire., adm. March 20, 1848 dis. June 7, 1848 adm. Emigrant Hospital May 1, 1848, destitute
Neil Ward, 4, R.C., Donegal, Ire., adm. March 20, 1848 dis. Sept. 5, 1848 adm. Emigrant Hospital May 1, 1848, destitute
John Ward, 2, R.C., Donegal, Ire., adm. March 20, 1848 dis. Sept. 5, 1848 adm. Emigrant Hospital May 1, 1848, destitute
Mrs. Mary Wade, 30, Donegal, Ire., adm. March 20, 1848 dis. Apr. 25, 1848
Mary McDade, 20, Donegal, Ire., adm. March 20, 1848 dis. May 9, 1848
Rose Toner, 30, Tyrone, Ire.,

adm. March 20, 1848
Rose Ward, 7, Donegal, Ire., adm. March 20, 1848 dis. Sept. 5, 1848
Nancy Ward, 5 years 6 mos., Donegal, Ire., adm. March 20, 1848 dis. Sept. 5, 1848
Fanny Ward, 8, Donegal, Ire., adm. March 20, 1848 dis. Sept. 5, 1848
Jas. McGinn, 30, R.C., Tyrone, Ire., adm. May 5, 1848 dis. May 19, 1848 adm. Emigrant Hospital May 5, 1848, consumption, adm. June 22, 1848, consumption, died July 12, 1848
Dominick Gallagher (not listed in Alms House Emigrant Book), 22, Donegal, Ire., adm. Emigrant Hospital May 1, 1848, bowel comp. dis. July 24, 1848

Lord Fitzgerald, sailed from Galway, Ire., arrived at Saint John Sept. 17, 1847
Lawrence Fahey, 20, R.C., Galway, Ire., adm. Sept. 17, 1847
Biddy Madden, 2 years 6 mos., R.C., Galway, Ire., adm. Sept. 21, 1847
Peggy Madden, 30, R.C., Galway, Ire., adm. Sept. 21, 1847
Michl. Kelly, 30, R.C., Clare, Ire., adm. Sept. 21, 1847
Winni Fahey, 15, R.C., Galway, Ire., adm. Sept. 24, 1847
Jno. McNamara, 19, R.C., Clare, Ire., adm. Sept. 24, 1847 adm. Emigrant Hospital June 1, 1848, fever dis. June 26, 1848
Cath. Quinn, 20, R.C., Galway, Ire., adm. Sept. 26, 1847
Pat Conway, 30, R.C., Galway, Ire., adm. Sept. 27, 1847
Nancy Nailon, 25, R.C., Clare, Ire., adm. Sept. 28, 1847
And. Crow, 23, R.C., Clare, Ire., adm. Sept. 29, 1847 adm. Emigrant Hospital June 1, 1848, fever dis. June 22, 1848
Biddy Griffin, 24, Mayo, Ire., adm. March 20, 1848 dis. Apr. 26, 1848
Cath. Cuff, 28, Galway, Ire., adm. March 20, 1848 dis. Oct. 2, 1848
Bridget Lynch, 21, Galway, Ire., adm. March 20, 1848 died Apr. 22, 1848

Lotus, Liverpool, England, 1847
James Keoffe, 36, R.C., Clare, Ire., adm. Oct. 3, 1848 dis. Dec. 31, 1848 adm. Emigrant Hospital Oct. 3, 1848, sore eyes, dis. Dec. 31, 1848

Magnes, sailed from Galway, Ire., arrived at Saint John Aug. 4, 1847
James McMahon, 22, R.C., Clare, Ire., adm. Aug. 4, 1847 dis. Aug. 17, 1847
Peggy Roach, 20, R.C., Clare, Ire., adm. Aug. 5, 1847 dis. Sept. 3, 1847
Mary Carney, 22, R.C., Clare, Ire., adm. Aug. 5, 1847
Peter Murphy, 24, R.C., Clare, Ire., adm. Aug. 5, 1847 died Aug. 15, 1847
Patk. Kennan, 30, R.C., Clare, Ire., adm. Aug. 5, 1847 dis. Aug. 29, 1847
Pat Burns (Pat Byrne) 24, R.C., Clare, Ire., adm. Aug. 11, 1847
Darby Grady, 26, R.C., Galway,

150 Irish Migration To New England: Port of Saint John

Ire., adm. Aug. 16, 1847 died Aug. 30, 1847
Thos. Sherry, 27, R.C., Clare, Ire., adm. Aug. 20, 1847
Ellen Shannon, 21, R.C.,Clare, Ire., adm. Aug. 21, 1847 dis. Sept. 7, 1847
Patrick Rhodes, 25, R.C., Clare, Ire., adm. Aug. 31, 1847
Mrs. Mary Rhodes, 22, R.C., Clare, Ire., adm. Aug. 31, 1847
Mich. Killmartin, 22, R.C., Clare, Ire., adm. Sept. 1, 1847 dis. Sept. 15, 1847
Judy McCarthy, 12, R.C., Cork, Ire., adm. Sept. 2, 1847
Mrs. Kitty Casey, 30, Cork, Ire., adm. Sept. 2, 1847
James Casey, 8, Cork, Ire., adm. Sept. 2, 1847
John Casey, 30, Cork, Ire., adm. Sept. 2, 1847
Sarah Bradley, 20, R.C., Derry, Ire., adm. Sept. 2, 1847 dis. Sept. 6, 1847
James Kearns, 16, R.C., Clare, Ire., adm. Sept. 2, 1847
Wm Connell, 30, R.C., Galway, Ire., adm. March 20, 1848 dis. May 29, 1848 adm. Emigrant Hospital May 1, 1848, destitute
Mary Kearney, 22, Clare, Ire., adm. March 20, 1848 dis. July 5, 1848
Kate Welch, 27, Galway, Ire., adm. March 20, 1848 dis. Apr. 17, 1848

Malvina, sailed from Baltimore, Ire., arrived at Saint John July 2, 1847
Catherine Carney, 20, R.C., Cork, Ire., adm. July 5, 1847, died July 23, 1847
Dan Hegarty, 26, R.C., Cork, Ire., adm. July 5, 1847 dis. July 17, 1847
Mary Driscoll, 30, R.C., Cork, Ire., adm. July 6, 1847, dis. July 20, 1847
Denis Daly, 25, R.C., Cork, Ire., adm. July 10, 1847 dis. Aug. 12, 1847
Mrs. Mary Hegarty, 35, R.C., Cork, Ire., adm. July 13, 1847 died Aug. 8, 1847
John Heggarty, 10, R.C., Cork, Ire., adm. July 13, 1847 adm. Aug. 3, 1847, age 11, died Sept. 7, 1847
Ellen Donnelly, 27, R.C., Cork, Ire., adm. July 16, 1847 died July 20, 1847
Mary Hurley, 23, R.C., Cork, Ire., admin July 17, 1847 dis. Sept. 13, 1847
Mrs. Johanna Carney, 30, R.C., Cork, Ire., adm. July 18, 1847 dis. Aug. 11, 1847
Dennis Dealey, 24, R.C., Cork, Ire., adm. July 20, 1847
Patk. Haggerty, 37, Cork, Ire., adm. Aug. 2, 1847 dis. July 29, 1847
James Kelly, 20, R.C., Cork, Ire., adm. March 20, 1848 dis. March 29, 1848

Marchioness of Clydesdale, sailed from Derry, Ireland, arrived at Saint John May 1847
Beckey McMonegal, 17, Prot., Donegal, Ire., adm. May 27, 1847 dis. June 28, 1847 adm. July 9, 1847 adm. March 25, 1848 dis. Apr. 10, 1848

Port of Saint John: Alms House 1847   151

Dominic McCullogh, 40, R.C., Tyrone, Ire., adm. June 14, 1847, died July 20, 1847
Bernard McCullogh, 12, R.C., Tyrone, Ire., adm. June 14, 1847
Patrick McCullogh, 4, R.C., Tyrone, Ire., adm. June 14, 1847, died Sept. 6, 1847
Susan McCullough, 14, R.C., Tyrone, Ire., adm. June 14, 1847, died Aug. 17, 1847
Nancy McCullough, 8, R.C., Tyrone, Ire., adm. June 14, 1847 dis. Aug. 29, 1847
Thos. McCullough, 15, R.C., Tyrone, Ire., adm. June 15, 1847
Geo. O'Donell, 8, R.C., Donegal, Ire., adm. Dec. 30, 1848
Chas. O'Donell, 5, R.C., Donegal, Ire., adm. Dec. 30, 1848
Ellen O'Donell, 37, R.C., Donegal, Ire., adm. Dec. 30, 1848
Grace O'Donell, 1, R.C., Saint John, adm. Dec. 30, 1848. mo. came in *M. of Clydesdale*

Margaret Elizabeth, sailed from Youghal, Ire., arrived at Saint John June 28, 1847
John Finn, 40, R.C., Sligo, Ire., adm. June 29, 1847 died July 3, 1847
Mrs. Catherine Donovan, 30, R.C., Waterford, Ire., adm. June 30, 1847 dis. July 18, 1847
Mary Donovan, 8, R.C., Waterford, Ire., adm. June 30, 1847 dis. July 19, 1847
John Donovan, 2 years 6 mos., R.C., Cork, Ire., adm. June 30, 1847 died July 7, 1847
Michael Donovan, 1 year 6 mos., Waterford, Ire., adm. June 30, 1847 dis. July 19, 1847
Michl. Keoffe, 25, R.C., Waterford, Ire., adm. Aug. 3, 1847 died Aug. 29, 1847
Ellen Keefe, 22, R.C., Waterford, Ire., adm. Aug. 3, 1847 died Aug. 9, 1847
John Donovan, 30, R.C., Waterford, Ire., adm. Sept. 30, 1847

Mary, sailed from Cork, Ire., arrived at Saint John June 12 (19), 1847
Owen McCarthy, 25, R.C., Kerry, Ire., adm. June 21, 1847 dis. July 26, 1847
Michl. Mahoney, 35, R.C., Kerry, Ire., adm. June 22, 1847 dis. July 26, 1847
David Donane, 16, R.C., Cork, Ire., adm. June 24, 1847 dis. Aug. 21, 1847
Jane Taber, 18, R.C., Cork, Ire., adm. June 27, 1847 dis. July 24, 1847
Catherine Penney, 19, R.C., Cork, Ire., adm. June 27, 1847 dis. July 24, 1847
George Surl, 18, R.C., Cork, Ire., adm. June 30, 1847 dis. July 19, 1847
Denis Donovan, 26, R.C., Cork, Ire., adm. July 5, 1847 dis. July 22, 1847
Tim Waldram, 23, R.C., Galway, Ire. adm. July 9, 1847 died Sept. 11, 1847
Mrs. Mary Harrington, 30, R.C., Kerry, Ire., adm. July 15, 1847 dis. July 17, 1847
Tim Harrington, 12, R.C., Kerry, Ire., adm. July 15, 1847 dis. July

152   Irish Migration To New England: Port of Saint John

17, 1847
Peter Harrington, 4, Kerry, Ire., adm. July 15, 1847 dis. July 17, 1847
John Harrington, 1 year 6 mos., Kerry, Ire., adm. July 15, 1847 dis. July 17, 1847
John Regan, 22, R.C., Cork, Ire., adm. July 16, 1847 died July 28, 1847
Cornelius Crowley, 20, R.C., Cork, Ire., adm. July 17, 1847
Humphy Desmond, 32, R.C., Cork, Ire., adm. July 18, 1847 dis. Aug. 9, 1847
Michl. Hussey, 29, R.C., Cork, Ire., adm. July 19, 1847
John Griffin, 20, R.C., Cork, Ire., adm. July 27, 1841 dis. Aug. 3, 1847 adm. Emigrant Hospital June 1, 1848, fever, dis. Aug. 28, 1848
Betty Bresnahen, 15, R.C., Derry, Ire., adm. Aug. 3, 1847
Debora Bresnahan, 44, R.C. Kerry, Ire., adm. Aug. 5, 1847, died Aug. 28, 1847
Patt Bresnahan, 50, R.C. Kerry, Ire., adm. Aug. 5, 1847, died Sept. 5, 1847
Mary Bresnahen, 12, R.C. Kerry, Ire., adm. Aug. 5, 1847
Jerry Bresnahan, 10, R.C. Kerry, Ire., adm. Aug. 5, 1847
Dan Bresnahan, 8, R.C. Kerry, Ire., adm. Aug. 5, 1847
Michl. Bresnahan, 4, R.C. Kerry, Ire., adm. Aug. 5, 1847
Patk. Bresnahan, 2, R.C. Kerry, Ire., adm. Aug. 5, 1847
Catherine Penny, 18, R.C., Cork, Ire., adm. Aug. 16, 1847
John Griffin, 20, R.C., Cork, Ire.,

adm. Aug. 20, 1847
Ellen Donovan, 20, R.C., Cork, Ire., adm. Aug. 28, 1847
Ellen Cadogan, 24, R.C., Cork, Ire., adm. Aug. 28, 1847 died Sept. 3, 1847
Pat Jordan, 10, R.C., Mayo, Ire., adm. Sept. 1, 1847
James Jordan, 6, R.C., Mayo, Ire., adm. Sept. 1, 1847
Peter Jordan, 3, R.C., Mayo, Ire., adm. Sept. 1, 1847
Hanna Hussey, 18, R.C., Cork, Ire., admin. Sept. 2, 1847
Ellen Griffin, 18, R.C., Cork, Ire., adm. Sept. 23, 1847
Mary Griffin, 24, Cork, Ire., adm. March 20, 1848 dis. June 12, 1848
Ellen Griffin, 17, R.C., Cork, Ire., adm. Oct. 31, 1848 dis. Nov. 30, 1848

Mary Anne,
Mrs. Eliza Kemble (Eliza Kember), 42, R.C., Louth, Ire., adm. Aug. 30, 1847 dis. Sept. 8, 1847 adm. Sept. 14, 1847 dis. Sept. 17, 1847
Dennis Donovan, 24, R.C., Cork, Ire., adm. Sept. 27, 1847

Mary Dunbar, sailed from Cork, Ire., arrived at Saint John June 29, 1847
Michael Collins, 25, R.C., Cork, Ire., adm. July 2, 1847, dis. July 24, 1847
Daniel Hayes, 21, R.C., Cork, Ire., adm. July 5, 1847 dis. July 23, 1847
Johanna Donovan, 20, R.C., Cork, Ire., adm. July 3, 1847 died

Port of Saint John: Alms House 1847   153

July 5, 1847

Mary Grimmer, sailed from Cork, Ire., arrived June 12, 1847
Alex. McNutt, 16, Prot., Donegal, Ire., adm. Aug. 19, 1847 died Aug. 28, 1847
John McNutt, 14, R.C., Donegal, Ire., adm. Aug. 19, 1847 died Sept. 12, 1847

Mary Harrington, sailed from Donegal, Ire., arrived at Saint John May 12, 1847
James Folis, 36, Prot., Fermanagh, Ire., adm. May 18, 1847 dis. May 27, 1847, destitute, wife died in ho. with fever
Mrs. Catherine Folis, 23, Prot., Fermanagh, Ire., adm. May 18, 1847, died May 24, 1847
Anne Jane Folis, 4 mos., Prot., Fermanagh, Ire., adm. May 18, 1847, dis. May 27, 1847, taken away by father
Dennis Hilley, 30, R.C., Donegal, Ire., adm. May 21, 1847, dis. July 3, 1847
Anne Gallagher, 18, R.C., Fermanagh, Ire., adm. May 28, 1847 dis. July 12, 1847 adm. July 23, 1847
Mary Gallagher, 14, R.C., Donegal, Ire., adm. June 9, 1847
John Gallagher, 35, R.C., Fermanagh, Ire., adm. June 11, 1847 dis. June 23, 1847
Patrick Clancy, 26, R.C., Leitrim, Ire., adm. June 16, 1847 dis. July 1, 1847
Catherine Dealy, 10, R.C., Donegal, Ire., adm. June 26, 1847, dis. July 9, 1847

Biddy Dealy, 5, R.C., Donegal, Ire., adm. June 26, 1847, dis. July 9, 1847
Owen Daly, 8, R.C., Donegal, Ire., adm. June 26, 1847, dis. July 9, 1847
Bridget Ellice, 28, R.C., Donegal, Ire., adm. July 13, 1847
Francis Ellice, 28, R.C., Donegal, Ire., adm. July 13, 1847 dis. Sept. 20, 1847
John Harrington, 40, R.C., Kerry, Ire., adm. July 14, 1847 dis. July 17, 1847
James Slavin, 23, R.C., Donegal, Ire., adm. July 20, 1847 dis. July 27, 1847
Kitty Daly, 8, R.C., Donegal, Ire., adm. July 21, 1847 dis. Aug. 12, 1847
Biddy Daly, 4, R.C., Donegal, Ire., adm. July 21, 1847 died Aug. 7, 1847
John Slavin, 25, R.C., Donehal, Ire., adm. Aug. 24, 1847 dis. Sept. 2, 1847
Dennis Gallagher, 24, R.C., Leitrim, Ire., adm. Sept. 21, 1847
Mrs. Bridget Ellis, 26, Donegal, Ire., adm. March 20, 1848 dis. Apr. 19, 1848
Ann Conners, 15, Sligo, Ire., adm. March 20, 1848 dis. May 18, 1848

Mary Murray, sailed from Cork, Ire., arrived June 12, 1847
Mary Harrington, 14, R.C., Derry, Ire., adm. July 15, 1847 dis. July 17, 1847
Mary Brannen, 19, R.C., Kerry, Ire., adm. July 19, 1847
Mary Walsh, 21, R.C., Cork, Ire.,

adm. July 19, 1847 dis. July 22, 1847
Gubby Bresnahan, 14, R.C., Kerry, Ire., adm. Aug. 18, 1847

Matilda,
Mary McGlone, 20, R.C., Sligo, Ire., adm. Sept. 21, 1847
Tim Learey, 80, R.C., Cork, Ire., adm. Sept. 22, 1847

Mich. Heny Faning?, sailed from Waterford, Ire., arrived at St. John's, Nfld. Aug. 30, 1847
Patk. Keoffe, 56, R.C., Waterford, Ire., adm. Dec. 16, 1848

Midas, sailed from Galway, Ire., arrived at Saint John May 5, 1847
Biddy Connolly, 25, R.C., Galway, Ire., adm. May 11, 1847 dis. May 27, 1847 adm. June 3, 1847 dis. June 16, 1847 adm. June 29 1847 dis. 17 July 1847
Mary Keddy, 31, R.C., Galway, Ire., adm. June 22, 1847 dis. July 20, 1847
Edward Keady (Edwd. Keddie), 1, R.C., Galway, Ire., adm. June 22, 1847 dis. July 21, 1847, adm. Aug. 10, 1847 died Aug. 14, 1847
Catherine Donovan, 5, R.C., Cork, Ire., adm. June 23, 1847
Mary Roche, 19, R.C., Galway, Ire., adm. Aug. 3, 1847 dis. Aug. 26, 1847
Hanora Kidder, 5, R.C., Galway, Ire., adm. Aug. 9, 1847
Mary Kiddey, 24, R.C., Galway, Ire., adm. Aug. 9, 1847
Biddy Finny, 20, R.C., Galway, Ire., adm. Aug. 9, 1847
John Nevin, 22, R.C., Galway, Ire., adm. Sept. 5, 1847
Pat Mitchell, 15, R.C., Galway, Ire., adm. Sept. 14, 1847 adm. March 20, 1848 dis. May 29, 1848 adm. Emigrant Hospital May 1, 1848
John Casey, 14, R.C., Galway, Ire., adm. Sept. 8, 1847 adm. Emigrant Hospital June 1, 1848, fever

Midas, sailed from Galway, Ire., arrived at Saint John Sept. 4, 1847
Patrick Loughen, 26, R.C., Galway, Ire., adm. Sept. 6, 1847 died Sept. 8, 1847
Bridget Kelly, 16, R.C., Galway, Ire., adm. Sept. 6, 1847 died Sept. 29, 1847
John Coughlan, 26, R.C., Clare, Ire., adm. Sept. 7, 1847
John Seahill, 23, R.C., Galway, Ire., adm. Sept. 7, 1847 dis. Sept. 18, 1847
Michl. King, 3 mos., R.C., Galway, Ire., adm. Sept. 7, 1847 died Sept. 16, 1847
Hanora King, 28, R.C., Galway, Ire., adm. Sept. 7, 1847
Edward Fougum (Edward Tougum) 21, R.C., Galway, Ire., adm. Sept. 8, 1847
John Collins, 2 mos., R.C., Alms House, adm. Sept. 8, 1847
Mrs. Ellen Casey, 30, R.C., Galway, Ire., adm. Sept. 8, 1847
Mary Casey, 4, R.C., Galway, Ire., adm. Sept. 8, 1847 died Sept. 25, 1847
Catherine Conolly, 24, R.C., Galway, Ire., adm. Sept. 10, 1847 dis. Sept. 17, 1847

Port of Saint John: Alms House 1847   155

Mark Downes, 36, R.C., Galway, Ire., adm. Sept. 10, 1847 died Sept. 16, 1847
James Kenny, 16, R.C., Galway, Ire., adm. Sept. 11, 1847
Philip Geary, 27, R.C., Cork, Ire., adm. Sept. 11, 1847
Catherine Carey, 14, R.C., Galway, Ire., adm. Sept. 12, 1847
James Carey, 50, R.C., Galway, Ire., adm. Sept. 12, 1847
Biddy Jordan, 20, R.C., Galway, Ire., adm. Sept. 12, 1847 dis. Sept. 17, 1847
Biddy Madden, 21, R.C., Mayo, Ire., adm. Sept. 12, 1847 dis. Sept. 24, 1847
Pat Fahey, 24, R.C., Galway, Ire., adm. Sept. 12, 1847
John Hanley, 25, R.C., Galway, Ire., adm. Sept. 13, 1847
Martin Hanley, 40, R.C., Galway, Ire., adm. Sept. 13, 1847 died Sept. 15, 1847
Michl. Kenny, 45, R.C., Galway, Ire., adm. Sept. 13, 1847
John Heaney, 25, R.C., Galway, Ire., adm. Sept. 13, 1847 adm. March 20, 1848 dis. May 10, 1848 - adm. Emigrant Hospital May 1, 1848, destitute
Anthony McDonald, 38, R.C., Galway, Ire., adm. Sept. 13, 1847
James Keely, 25, R.C., Galway, Ire., adm. Sept. 13, 1847
John Hyne, 4 mos., R.C., Galway, Ire., adm. Sept. 14, 1847
Michael Hyne, 23, R.C., Galway, Ire., adm. Sept. 14, 1847
Mrs. Catherine Hyne, 30, R.C., Galway, Ire., adm. Sept. 14, 1847 dis. Sept. 24, 1847
Lawrence Mitchell, 13, R.C., Galway, Ire., adm. Sept. 14, 1847
John Mitchell, 11, R.C., Galway, Ire., adm. Sept. 14, 1847
Hugh Mitchell, 9, R.C., Galway, Ire., adm. Sept. 14, 1847
Marcus Conelly, 3, R.C., Galway, Ire., adm. March 20, 1848 dis. Apr. 28, 1848
Judy Mitchell, 46, R.C., Galway, Ire., adm. Sept. 14, 1847 adm. March 20, 1848, wid., dis. July 12, 1848
Thos. Mitchell, 15, R.C., Galway, Ire., adm. Sept. 14, 1847 adm. March 20, 1848 died Apr. 3, 1848
Michael Glynn, 20, R.C., Galway, Ire., adm. Sept. 15, 1847
Bridget Jinkins, 7, R.C., Galway, Ire., adm. Sept. 15, 1847
Sally Jinkins, 5, R.C., Galway, Ire., adm. Sept. 15, 1847
Michael Jenkins, 19, R.C., Galway, Ire., adm. Sept. 16, 1847 adm. March 20, 1848 dis. Apr. 10, 1848
Thos. Jenkins, 15, R.C., Galway, Ire., adm. Sept. 16, 1847 adm. March 20, 1848 dis. Apr. 10, 1848
Maurice Cusac, 22, R.C., Galway, Ire., adm. Sept. 16, 1847
Matt Guoin, 22, R.C., Galway, Ire., adm. Sept. 16, 1847
John Jenkins, 20, R.C., Galway, Ire., adm. Sept. 19, 1847 adm. March 20, 1848 dis. Apr. 10, 1848
Michael Quin, 19, R.C., Galway, Ire., adm. Sept. 19, 1847 adm. Emigrant Hospital June 1, 1848, fever, dis. Aug. 7, 1848 -
Cath. Curley, 22, R.C., Galway, Ire., adm. Sept. 23, 1847

Bridget Jenkins, 35, R.C., Galway, Ire., adm. Sept. 24, 1847 (Biddy Jenkins, wid.) adm. March 20, 1848 dis. Apr. 10, 1848
Darby Kilcannon, 40, R.C., Galway, Ire., adm. March 20, 1848 dis. Apr. 9, 1848
Mary Healey, 34, Galway, Ire., adm. March 20, 1848 dis. Apr. 14, 1848
Ann Lynch, 18, Galway, Ire., adm. March 20, 1848 dis. Apr. 29, 1848
Mrs. Ann Conolly, 33, Galway, Ire., adm. March 20, 1848 dis. Apr. 28, 1848
Cath. Curley, 26, Galway, Ire., adm. May 22, 1848 dis. Aug. 28, 1848
John Casey, 18, R.C., Galway,Ire., adm. May 30, 1848 dis. July 6, 1848
Jno. McDonough, R.C., Galway, Ire., adm. May 30, 1848 dis. June 26, 1848
Mic. Quin, 19, R.C., Galway, Ire., adm. May 30, 1848 dis. Aug. 7, 1848
Mic. McGowan, 38, R.C., Leitrim, Ire., adm. June 2, 1848 dis. July 2, 1848
Mary McGowan, 4, Sligo, Ire., adm. June 2, 1848 dis. July 31, 1848

Milton,
Dan Donahue, 38, R.C., Cork, Ire., adm. Aug. 3, 1847

Mountaineer, sailed from Liverpool, England landed at Halifax, Nova Scotia May 15, 1847

Michl. Gainsay (Michael Gancy), 34, R.C., Cork, Ire., adm. July 10, 1847, dis. Aug. 20, 1847 adm. Aug. 30, 1847
Jerry Connell, 32, R.C., Cork, Ire., adm July 20, 1847 dis. July 28, 1847 adm. Aug. 2, 1847 dis. Aug. 12, 1847
Thomas Fleming, 22, R.C., Mayo, Ire., adm. July 30, 1847 died Aug. 9, 1847
Owen Sweeney, 20, R.C., Cork, Ire., adm. Aug. 2, 1847
Daniel Donovan, 37, R.C., Cork, Ire., adm. Aug. 30, 1847

Nancy, sailed from Killala, Ire., arrived at Saint John June 9, 1847
Peter Jordan, 45, R.C., Mayo, Ire., adm., Sept. 1, 1847
Mrs. Anne Jordan, 45, R.C., Mayo, Ire., adm., Sept. 1, 1847 died Sept. 19, 1847
Mary Jordan, 7, R.C., Mayo, Ire., adm., Sept. 1, 1847
Biddy Jordan, 10 mos., R.C., Mayo, Ire., adm., Sept. 1, 1847 dis. Sept. 20, 1847

Nova Scotia, arrived 1847
Thos. Neal (not listed in Alms House Records) adm. May 22, 1848 Emigrant Hospital, bowel comp. dis. May 31, 1848

Ocean, sailed from Berehaven, Ire., arrived at Saint John June 9, 1847
Patk. Lowney, 24, R.C., Cork, Ire., adm. June 10, 1847
William Denish, 24, R.C., Cork, Ire., adm. June 10, 1847 died

July 22 1847
Jerry Murphy, 3, R.C., Cork, Ire., adm. June 11, 1847 dis. Aug. 26, 1847 adm. Aug. 27, 1847
Mary Murphy, 34, R.C., Cork, Ire., adm. June 11, 1847
Mary Sullivan, 14, R.C., Cork, Ire., adm. June 11, 1847 died June 30, 1847
Biddy Sullivan, 12, R.C., Cork, Ire., adm. June 11, 1847
Jeremh. Harrington, 20, R.C., Cork, Ire., adm. June 15, 1847
Mrs. Norry Sullivan, 22, R.C., Cork, Ire., adm. June 23, 1847 dis. Sept. 9, 1847
John Crolly, 25, R.C., Cork, Ire., adm. July 8, 1847 dis. July 24, 1847
Johanna Maley, 23, R.C., Kerry, Ire., adm. July 22, 1847
Narry Hurley, 1, R.C., Cork, Ire. adm. July 24, 1847 died Sept. 7, 1847
Hanora Hurley, 23, R.C., Cork, Ire. adm. July 25, 1847 dis. Sept. 17, 1847
Tim Hurley, 26, R.C., Cork, Ire. adm. July 25, 1847 dis. Sept. 17, 1847
James Delaney, 60, R.C., Cork, Ire., adm. Aug. 11, 1847
Margaret Keldiff, 18, R.C., Sligo, Ire., adm. Aug. 11, 1847
Mrs. Mary Murphy, 34, Cork, Ire., adm. Aug. 27, 1847
John Terple, 18, Halifax, N.S., adm. Aug. 27, 1847
Michael O'Donnell, 60, R.C., Cork, Ire., adm. Aug. 27, 1847 died Aug. 28, 1847
John Lee, 20, R.C., Cork, Ire., adm. Sept. 2, 1847

Catherine Crowley, 1, R.C., Cork, Ire., adm. Sept. 3, 1847 died Sept. 22, 1847
Hanora Crowley, 22, R.C., Cork, Ire., adm. Sept. 3, 1847 dis. Sept. 22, 1847
John Delany, 45, R.C., Cork, Ire., adm. Sept. 11, 1847 dis. Sept. 13, 1847
Norah Crowley, 20, Cork, Ire., adm. Apr. 28, 1848 dis. May 13, 1848

Pallas, sailed from Cork, Ire., landed at Saint John, June 21, 1847
Mrs. Kitty McArty, 26, R.C., Cork, Ire., adm. June 21, 1847
Mrs. Johanna Murphy, 24, R.C., Cork, Ire., adm. June 21, 1847 dis. Sept. 2, 1847
Patrick Savage, 26, R.C., Cork, Ire., adm. June 22, 1847 dis. July 5, 1847
Tim Allen, 24, R.C., Cork, Ire., adm. June 22, 1847 adm. March 20, 1848 died Apr. 3, 1848
Johanna Curran, 20, R.C., Cork, Ire., adm. June 29, 1847 dis. July 20, 1847
Owen McCarthy, 21, R.C., Cork, Ire., adm. June 30, 1847 dis. July 10, 1847
Peggy Dealy, 21, R.C., Cork, Ire., adm. July 5, 1847, dis. Aug. 21, 1847
Hanora Stack, 26, R.C., Cork, Ire., adm. July 5, 1847, died Aug. 19, 1847
Margaret Nailon, 8, R.C., Clare, Ire., adm. July 5, 1847, dis. Aug. 14, 1847
Cate Cain, 12, R.C., Cork, Ire.,

adm. July 5, 1847, dis. Aug. 3, 1847
Biddy Connors,30, R.C., Cork, Ire., adm. July 7, 1847
Anne Hartt, 16, R.C., Cork, Ire., adm. July 9, 1847 died Aug. 12, 1847
Norrie Quinlan, 27, R.C., Cork, Ire., adm. July 9, 1847 died Aug. 21, 1847
- Donnelly, 9, R.C., adm. July 9, 1847, died Aug. 2, 1847
James Fitzgerald, 25, R.C., Cork, Ire., adm. July 12, 1847, dis. July 20, 1847 adm. July 24, 1847 died Aug. 16, 1847
Thomas Carroll, 28, R.C., Cork, Ire., adm. July 12, 1847 dis. Aug. 14, 1847
John Roberts, 52, R.C., Cork, Ire., adm. July 13, 1847
James Daly, 26, R.C., Cork, Ire., adm. July 15, 1847 dis. July 17, 1847
Mary Daly, 24, R.C., Cork, Ire., adm. July 15, 1847 dis. July 17, 1847
Peggy Daly, 1 year 6 mos., R.C., Cork, Ire., adm. July 15, 1847 dis. July 17, 1847
Ellen Green, 60, R.C., Mayo, Ire., adm. July 22, 1847
Tom Farrel, 28, R.C., Cork, Ire., adm. July 24, 1847
Rich. Powers, 25, R.C., Cork, Ire., adm. July 24, 1847
Jerry Hennesy, 40, R.C., Cork, Ire., adm. July 27, 1847 died Sept. 6, 1847
Catherine Shearne, 23, R.C., Cork, Ire., adm. Aug. 22, 1847
Martin Murphy, 17, R.C., Clare, Ire., adm. Aug. 30, 1847 dis.

Sept. 6, 1847
Hanora Murphy, 16, R.C., Clare, Ire., adm. Aug. 30, 1847
Joanna Cremar, 18, Cork, Ire., adm. March 20, 1848 dis. May 13, 1848
Cath. O'Hearn, 26, Cork, Ire., adm. March 20, 1848 dis. Apr. 3, 1848

Pekin, sailed from Sligo, Ire., arrived Saint John
Sept. 24, 1847
John Radekin, 50, R.C., Sligo, Ire., adm. March 20, 1848 dis. Aug. 4, 1848
Frs. Murray, 26, R.C., Roscommon, Ire., adm. March 20, 1848 dis. March 30, 1848

Pero, sailed from Cork, Ire., arrived at Saint John Sept. 25, 1847
Wm Dealey, 18, R.C., Cork, Ire., adm. Sept. 25, 1847
Joanna Delaney, 32, R.C., Cork, adm. Sept. 25, 1847 died Sept. 30, 1847
Ann Ennis, 23, R.C., Galway, Ire., adm. Sept. 25, 1847
Ellen Dealey, 26, R.C., Cork, Ire., adm. Sept. 26, 1847
Honora Keohan, 25, R.C., Cork, Ire., adm. Sept. 27, 1847
Jno. Gearey, 40, R.C., Cork, Ire., adm. Sept. 27, 1847
Ellen Delaney, 32, R.C., Cork, Ire., adm. Sept. 29, 1847
Richd. Fitzgerald (Michl. Fitzgerald) 28, R.C., Cork, Ire., adm. March 20, 1848 died Apr. 3, 1848
Joanna Delaney, 32, Cork, Ire.,

Port of Saint John: Alms House 1847

adm. March 20, 1848 dis. Apr. 3, 1848

Perserverance, sailed from Derry, Ire., arrived at Saint John July 19, 1847
Margaret Walsh, 40, R.C., Cork, Ire., adm. June 25, 1847 dis. Sept. 17, 1847
John Curran, 24, R.C., Cork, Ire., adm. July 2, 1847, dis. July 21, 1847
Peggy Hardnett, 25, R.C., Cork, Ire., adm. June 26, 1847 dis. July 12, 1847
Johanna Walsh, 9, R.C., Cork, Ire., adm. June 26, 1847 dis. July 12, 1847
Judy McCarthy, 5, R.C., Cork, Ire., adm. June 26, 1847 dis. Aug. 2, 1847
Catherine Crowly, 17, R.C., Cork, Ire., adm. June 26, 1847 dis. July 12, 1847
Ellen Hardnett, 26, R.C., Cork, Ire., adm. June 28, 1847 died July 28, 1847
Jerry Haurihan, 34, R.C., Cork, Ire., adm. June 28, 1847 died July 4, 1847
Patrick Haurihan, 3, R.C., Cork, Ire., adm. June 28, 1847 dis. July 13, 1847
John Barrett, 24, R.C., Kerry, Ire., adm. June 29, 1847 dis. July 22, 1847
Michl. Hardnett, 22, R.C., Cork, Ire., adm. June 30, 1847 dis. July 9, 1847
Tim Hallahan, 26, R.C., Cork, Ire., adm. June 30, 1847
Hugh Connors, 24, R.C., Sligo, Ire., adm. July 1, 1847 dis. July 12, 1847
James Deady, 27, R.C., Cork, Ire., adm. July 1, 1847
Andrew Coleman, 33, R.C., Cork, Ire., adm. July 10, 1847, died July 20, 1847
Judy Haurihan, 6, R.C., Cork, Ire., adm. July 12, 1847 dis. Aug. 2, 1847
George Roberts, 22, R.C., Cork, Ire., adm. July 13, 1847 dis. July 20, 1847
Jerry Roberts, 10, R.C., Cork, Ire., adm. July 13, 1847 dis. July 21, 1847
John Roberts, 8, R.C., Cork, Ire., adm. July 13, 1847 dis. July 21, 1847
David Roberts, 6, R.C., Cork, Ire., adm. July 13, 1847 dis. July 21, 1847
Bess Roberts, 12, R.C., Cork, Ire., adm. July 13, 1847 died July 12, 1847
Patrick Danlley, 1, R.C., Cork, Ire., adm. July 16, 1847
Beckey Souce, 12, R.C., Cork, Ire., adm. July 16, 1847 dis. July 29, 1847
Mary Souce (Mary Collins), 50, R.C., Cork, Ire., adm. July 16, 1847 dis. July 29, 1847
Johanna Leary, 16, R.C., Cork, Ire., died Sept. 20, 1847
Jerry Donelly, 26, R.C., Cork, Ire., adm. July 20, 1847 dis. Aug. 12, 1847
Margt. Hickson, 9 years 6 mos., Kerry, Ire., adm. March 20, 1848 dis. Apr. 17, 1848
May Hickson, 5, Kerry, Ire., adm. March 20, 1848 dis. Apr. 17, 1848

Portland, sailed from Derry, Ire., arrived at Saint John, Aug. 3, 1847
Hugh McDade, 30, R.C., Galway, Ire., adm. Aug. 6, 1847
Wm Dolan, 34, R.C., Tyrone, Ire., adm. Aug. 11, 1847 adm. Apr. 10, 1848, age 35, died Apr. 24, 1848
Biddy Taylor, 22, R.C., Fermanagh, Ire., adm. Aug. 11, 1847
Ellen McCarthy, 15, R.C., Cork, Ire., adm. Aug. 12, 1847
Anne Murray, 23, R.C., Cork, Ire., adm. Aug. 12, 1847 dis. Sept. 14, 1847
John Woodburne, 21, Prot., Derry, Ire., adm. Aug. 14, 1847 died Sept. 2, 1847
Wm Stewart, 37, Prot., Derry, Ire., adm. Aug. 14, 1847 died Aug. 19, 1847
Nelly Dogherty, 25, R.C., Derry, Ire., adm. Aug. 16, 1847
Patrick Doherty, 8, R.C., Derry, Ire., adm. Aug. 16, 1847
Edward Doherty, 2 mos., R.C., Derry, Ire., adm. Aug. 16, 1847 died Aug. 30, 1847
Issabella Waide, 18, Derry, Ire., adm. Aug. 16, 1847
William Donelly, 19, R.C., Tyrone, Ire., adm. Aug. 16, 1847
Dan Doherty, 46, R.C., Derry, Ire., adm. Aug. 16, 1847 died Sept. 10, 1847
James McManus, 16, R.C., Tyrone, Ire., adm. Aug. 16, 1847 died Aug. 22, 1847
Mich. Gallagher, 20, R.C., Fermanagh, Ire., adm. Aug. 17, 1847 died Aug. 19, 1847
Mary Bowen, 22, R.C., Donegal, Ire., adm. Aug. 20, 1847
Nel Dogherty, 5?, R.C., Derry, Ire., adm. Aug. 20, 1847
Nancy Dogherty, 14, R.C., Derry, Ire., adm. Aug. 20, 1847
John Bonor, 55, R.C., Donegal, Ire., adm. Aug. 20, 1847 (died or discharged Sept. 10, 1847)
Danl. Bonor, 27, R.C., Donegal, Ire., adm. Aug. 20, 1847
Patrick Somers, 14, R.C., Donegal, Ire., adm. Aug. 20, 1847
Roger Doherty, 7, R.C., Kerry, Ire., adm. Ag. 20, 1847
Mary McHugh, 15, R.C., Tyrone, Ire., adm. Aug. 21, 1847 dis. Sept. 23, 1847
Sarah Sweeney, 26, R.C., Donegal, Ire., adm. Aug. 21, 1847 died Aug. 29, 1841
Margaret Gillan, 19, R.C., Donegal, Ire., adm. Aug. 22, 1847 dis. Sept. 20, 1847
John Warren, 30, R.C., Cork, Ire., adm. Aug. 23, 1847 dis. Aug. 30, 1847
Michael Nelson, 36, R.C., Donegal, Ire., adm. Aug. 23, 1847 dis. Aug. 30, 1847
John McNamara, 25, R.C., Tyrone, Ire., adm. Aug. 24, 1847
Anne Clarke, 15, Prot., Derry, Ire., adm. Aug. 24, 1847
James Blarney, 30, R.C., Donegal, Ire., adm. Aug. 28, 1847
Ellen McHugh, 14, R.C., Tyrone, Ire., adm. Sept. 9, 1847
Mary McHugh, 14, R.C., Tyrone, Ire., adm. Sept. 17, 1847
John Blaney, 40, R.C., Donegal, Ire., adm. March 20, 1848 dis. May 22, 1848 adm. Emigrant

Hospital May 1, 1848, dysentry
James Bratten, 20, R.C., Tyrone, Ire., adm. March 20, 1848 dis. March 22, 1848
Dan Bleurey, 1 year 3 mos., R.C., Donegal, Ire., adm. March 20, 1848 died May 11, 1848 adm. Emigrant Hospital May 1, 1848, delicate
Mrs. Ellen Bleurey, 30, Donegal, Ire., adm. March 20, 1848 died Apr. 3, 1848
Mrs. Mary King, 26, Galway, Ire., adm. May 4, 1848 confined May 9, 1848 of a son.
Martin Cahil, 50, R.C., Tipperary, Ire., adm. May 5, 1848 dis. May 14, 1848 adm. Emigrant Hospital May 5, 1848, fever

Prince Royal, sailed from Cork, Ire., arrived Saint John July 13, 1847
Thomas Murray, 27, R.C., Clare, Ire., adm. July 19, 1847

Princess Royal,
Mrs. Ellen Waul, 24, Limerick, Ire., adm. May 2, 1848 dis. May 15, 1848
Michl. Waul, 1 year 8 mos., R.C., Limerick, Ire., adm. May 2, 1848 dis. May 15, 1848 adm. Emigrant Hospital May 5, 1848, destitute

Princess,
John Buckley, 36, R.C., Kerry, Ire., adm. March 20, 1848 dis. May 9, 1848 adm. Emigrant Hospital May 1, 1848, destitute
John Buckley, 2 years 6 mos., R.C., Kerry, Ire., adm. March 20, 1848 dis. Aug. 2, 1848 adm.

Emigrant Hospital May 1, 1848, destitute
Ellen Buckley, 7, Kerry, Ire., adm. March 20, 1848 dis. Aug. 2, 1848
Murty Buckley, 5, Kerry, Ire., adm. March 20, 1848 dis. Aug. 2, 1848

Progress, sailed from Derry, Ire., arrived at Saint John June 8, 1847
Biddy Dever, 25, R.C., Donegal, Ire., adm. June 10, 1847
John Dever, 20, R.C., Derry, Ire., adm. June 10, 1847 dis. Aug. 16, 1847
Mary Dever, 15, R.C., Donegal, Ire., adm. June 10, 1847
Chas. Dever, 13, R.C., Derry, Ire., adm. June 10, 1847 dis. July 26, 1847
Celia Dever, 11, R.C., Donegal, Ire., adm. June 10, 1847 died July 8, 1847
Hugh Coyle, 14, R.C., Donegal, Ire., adm. June 11, 1847 dis. June 23, 1847
Thos. Phillips, 21, Prot., Wicklow, Ire., adm. June 7, 1848 dis. July 22, 1848 adm. Emigrant Hospital June 7, 1848, scarlet fever

Royal Mint, sailed from Liverpool, England, arrived in Saint John July 30, 1847
Peter McAbe, 40, R.C., Armagh, Ire., adm. Aug. 1, 1847 dis. Aug. 15, 1847
Eliza Gallagher, 20, R.C., Down, Ire., adm. Aug. 5, 1847 dis. Aug. 19, 1847
Mary Gallagher, 18, R.C., Down, Ire., adm. Aug. 5, 1847 dis. Aug.

19, 1847
Samuel Copland, 19, Prot., Fermanagh, Ire., adm. Aug. 13, 1847
Robert Burton, 30, Manchester, Eng., adm. Aug. 23, 1847 dis. Aug. 26, 1847
James Collins, 35, R.C., Cork, Ire., adm. Aug. 27, 1847
Nelly Lowrey, 20, R.C., Galway, Ire., adm. Aug. 27, 1847, died Sept. 8, 1847
Patt Harvey, 14, R.C., Leitrim, Ire., adm. Aug. 27, 1847 died Sept. 3, 1847
Denis Hurley, 25, R.C., Cork, Ire., adm. Aug. 27, 1847
Tom Fergus, 19, R.C., Mayo, Ire., adm. Aug. 28, 1847
Patrick Lee, 24, R.C., Leitrim, Ire., adm. Aug. 29, 1847 dis. Sept. 4, 1847
Pat Lowrey, 20, R.C., Galway, Ire., adm. Sept. 1, 1847
James Isbester, 56, Prot., Scotland, adm. Sept. 1, 1847
Maurice Broderick, 24, R.C., Cork, Ire., adm. Sept. 1, 1847
Pat Higgins, 37, R.C., Tyrone, Ire., adm. Sept. 4, 1847 dis. Sept. 8, 1847
Pat Higgins, 48, R.C., Tyrone, Ire., adm. Sept. 13, 1847
John O'Mara, 36, R.C., Tipperary, Ire., adm. March 20, 1848 dis. May 23, 1848 adm. Emigrant Hospital May 1, 1848

Ruby, sailed from Sligo, Ire., arrived at Saint John July 2, 1847
Mary Hanley, 24, R.C., Sligo, Ire., adm. July 3, 1847, died July 5, 1847
Johanna Maloney, 70, R.C., Roscommon, Ire., adm. July 10, 1847 died July 10, 1847
Thos. Murphey, 24, R.C., Sligo, Ire., adm. July 13, 1847
Catherine Caveny, 19, R.C., Sligo, Ire., adm. July 14, 1847
Patrick Kilpatrick, 20, R.C., Sligo, Ire., adm. July 14, 1847 died Sept. 25, 1847
Thomas Bruen, 24, R.C., Sligo, Ire., adm. July 14, 1847 dis. Sept. 18, 1847
John Loftus, 40, R.C., Sligo, Ire., adm. July 22, 1847 dis. Sept. 25, 1847
Mrs. Catherine Loftus, 40, R.C., Sligo, Ire., adm. July 22, 1847 dis. Sept. 24, 1847
Ellen Loftus, 14, R.C., Sligo, Ire., adm. July 22, 1847 dis. Sept. 24, 1847
Anne Loftus, 4, R.C., Sligo, Ire., adm. July 26, 1847 died Aug. 16, 1847
Margaret Loftus, 2, R.C., Sligo, Ire., adm. July 26, 1847 died Aug. 20, 1847
Mary Donoghue, 24, R.C., Cork, Ire., adm. July 27, 1847
And. Conway, 40, R.C., Sligo, Ire., adm. July 27, 1847 dis. July 27, 1847
Michl. Conway, 8, R.C., Sligo, Ire., adm. July 27, 1847 dis. July 27, 1847 adm. July 30, 1847
Margaret Walsh, 30, R.C., Cork, Ire., adm. July 27, 1847 died Aug. 15, 1847
Mary Kennedy, 24, R.C., Sligo, Ire., adm. July 27, 1847 died Aug. 15, 1847
And. Conway, 30, R.C., Sligo,

Ire., adm. July 30, 1847 died Aug. 31, 1847
Libby Conway, 3, R.C., Sligo, Ire., adm. July 30, 1847 died Sept. 9, 1847
Anne Conway, 1, R.C., Sligo, Ire., adm. July 30, 1847 died Aug. 14, 1847
Biddy Connell, 30, R.C., Sligo, Ire., adm. July 31, 1847
John Duffey, 24, R.C., Sligo, Ire., adm. Sept. 3, 1847
Pat Killpatrick, 21, R.C., Sligo, Ire., adm. Sept. 5, 1847
Mary Dogherty, 40, R.C., Mayo, Ire., adm. Sept. 15, 1847 died Sept. 19, 1847
Mary Dogherty, 17, R.C., Mayo, Ire., adm. Sept. 15, 1847
Biddy Dogherty, 5, R.C., Mayo, Ire., adm. Sept. 15, 1847
Michl. Dogherty, 12, R.C., Mayo, Ire., adm. Sept. 15, 1847 adm. Sept. 28, 1847
John Dogherty, 10, R.C., Mayo, Ire., adm. Sept. 15, 1847
Patrick Dogherty, 14, R.C., Mayo, Ire., adm. Sept. 15, 1847
Michael Walsh, 7, R.C., Galway, Ire., adm. Sept. 15, 1847
Pat Doherty, 14, R.C., Mayo, Ire., adm. Sept. 24, 1847 adm. March 20, 1848 dis. May 26, 1848 adm. Emigrant Hospital May 1, 1848, destitute
Jno. Divine, 40, R.C., Galway, Ire., adm. Sept. 24, 1847
Mich. McDade, 43, R.C., Louth, Ire., adm. Sept. 30, 1847
Peter McDade, 8, R.C., Louth, Ire., adm. Sept. 30, 1847
Mich. McDade, 6, R.C., Louth, Ire., adm. Sept. 30, 1847
Edward McDade, 3, R.C., Louth, Ire., adm. Sept. 30, 1847
Richd. Dogherty, 39, R.C., Mayo, Ire., adm. Sept. 30, 1847
And. Mangan, 30, R.C., Kilkenny, Ire., adm. Sept. 30, 1847
Mic. Sullivan, 3, R.C., Cork, Ire., adm. Sept. 30, 1847
Michl. Kavenagh, 28, R.C., Sligo, Ire., adm. March 20, 1848 dis. Apr. 16, 1848
Richd. Doherty, 17, R.C., Mayo, Ire., adm. March 20, 1848 dis. Apr. 17, 1848
Anthony Duffy, 20, R.C., Sligo, Ire., adm. March 20, 1848 dis. June 7, 1848 adm. Emigrant Hospital May 1, 1848, destitute
Mary Kevanagh, wid., 57, Sligo, Ire., adm. March 20, 1848 dis. Apr. 18, 1848
Mary Doherty, 40, Mayo, Ire., adm. March 20, 1848 dis. Apr. 18, 1848
Mary Dougherty, 7, Mayo, Ire., adm. March 20, 1848 dis. July 16, 1848
Bridget Dougherty, 5, Mayo, Ire., adm. March 20, 1848 dis. July 16, 1848

Sally, sailed from Cork, Ire., arrived at Saint John July 13, 1847
Mrs. Hanora Hickson, 36, Prot., Kerry, Ire., adm. July 12, 1847 adm. March 20, 1848 dis. Apr. 17, 1848
Robert Hickson, 11, Prot., Kerry, Ire., adm. July 12, 1847 adm. March 20, 1848 dis. March 23, 1848
Richard Hickson, 7, Prot., Kerry,

164 Irish Migration To New England: Port of Saint John

Ire., adm. July 12, 1847 adm. March 20, 1848 dis. Apr. 17, 1848
James Hickson, 3, Prot., Kerry, Ire., adm. July 12, 1847 adm. March 20, 1848 dis. Apr. 17, 1848
Margaret Hickson, 9 years 6 mos., Prot., Kerry, Ire., adm. July 12, 1847
Mary Hickson, 5, Prot., Kerry, Ire., adm. July 12, 1847
Johanna Hickson, 4 mos., Prot., Kerry, Ire., adm. July 12, 1847
Johanna Carey, 18, R.C., Cork, Ire., adm. July 15, 1847
Mary Ambrose, 9, R.C., Cork, Ire., adm. July 20, 1847 dis. July 21, 1847
Kit Quince (Kit Corkum), 30, R.C., Cork, Ire., adm. July 22, 1847 died Aug. 23, 1847
Johanna Quince, 6, R.C., Cork, Ire., adm. July 22, 1847 died Sept. 17, 1847
Pat Fitzgerald, 30, R.C., Kerry, Ire., adm. Aug. 4, 1847
Hanora Manning, 27, R.C., Kerry, Ire., adm. Aug. 4, 1847
Kitty Sullevan, 30, R.C., Kerry, Ire., adm. Aug. 13, 1847 dis. Sept. 9, 1847
Patrick O'Sullivan, 3, R.C., Kerry, Ire., adm. Aug. 13, 1847 died Aug. 13, 1847
John Sullivan, 30, R.C., Kerry, Ire., adm. Aug. 13, 1847 dis. Aug. 19, 1847
Johanna Coakley, 32, R.C., Cork, Ire., adm. Aug. 16, 1847 dis. Aug. 17, 1847
Thomas Coakley, 10, R.C., Cork, Ire., adm. Aug. 16, 1847 dis. Aug. 17, 1847
Tim Coakley, 32, R.C., Cork, Ire., adm. Aug. 16, 1847 dis. Aug. 17, 1847
Mary Coakley, 10, R.C., Cork, Ire., adm. Aug. 16, 1847 dis. Aug. 17, 1847
Jno. Sullivan, 21, R.C., Kerry, Ire., adm. Sept. 28, 1847

Sea,
sailed from Liverpool, England, arrived at Saint John Sept. 2, 1847
John Mooney, 22, R.C., Tipperary, Ire., adm. Sept. 6, 1847
John Sharp, 33, Prot., Staffordshire, Eng., adm. Sept. 7, 1847 dis. Sept. 12, 1847
John Roy, 23, R.C., Galway, Ire., adm. Sept. 7, 1847
John Donovan, 35, R.C., Cork, Ire., adm. Sept. 8, 1847
Pat Coughlan, 21, R.C., Cork, Ire., adm. Sept. 8, 1847
Mary Eagan, 18, R.C., Mayo, Ire., adm. Sept. 9, 1847
Michael McCarthy, 23, R.C., Cork, Ire., adm. Sept. 12, 1847 dis. Sept. 14, 1847
Johanna Sullivan, 30, R.C., Cork, Ire., adm. Sept. 13, 1847
Danl. Sullivan, 4, R.C., Cork, Ire., adm. Sept. 13, 1847
Michael Sullivan, 2, R.C., Cork, Ire., adm. Sept. 13, 1847
Michl. Sullivan, 40, R.C., Cork, Ire., adm. Sept. 13, 1847
Mrs. Catherine Lynch, 30, R.C., Kerry, Ire., adm. Sept. 13, 1847
Wm Lynch, 30, R.C., Kerry, Ire., adm. Sept. 13, 1847 died Sept.

Port of Saint John: Alms House 1847   165

20, 1847
Tim Lynch, 23, R.C., Kerry, Ire., adm. Sept. 13, 1847 died Sept. 17, 1847
Michl. Murphy, 8, R.C., Cork, Ire., adm. Sept. 13, 1847
Wm Mahoney, 30, R.C., Kerry, Ire., adm. Sept. 13, 1847
Matt Fye (Matt Tye) 28, R.C., Sligo, Ire., adm. Sept. 15, 1847
Denis Burke, 25, R.C., Kerry, Ire., adm. Sept. 16, 1847
Dennis McArty, 10, R.C., Cork, Ire., adm. Sept. 21, 1847 adm. March 20, 1848 dis. Apr. 15, 1848
Ellen Crofts, 20, Prot., Cork, Ire., adm. Sept. 23, 1847 dis. Sept. 27, 1847
Mary Healey, 40, R.C., Clare, Ire., adm. Sept. 23, 1847
Dan McArty, 29, R.C., Cork, Ire., adm. Sept. 28, 1847
Mary McArty, 21, R.C., Cork, Ire., adm. Sept. 28, 1847 died Oct. 1, 1847
Margt. McDade, 10, R.C., Cork, Ire., adm. Sept. 30, 1847
Wm Branley, 40, R.C., Sligo, Ire., adm. March 20, 1848 dis. June 14, 1848 adm. Emigrant Hospital May 1, 1848, destitute
And. Buckley, 40, R.C., Cork, Ire., adm. March 20, 1848 dis. May 1, 1848
Dan McArty, 15, R.C., Cork, Ire., adm. March 20, 1848 dis. Apr. 15, 1848
Jerry McArty, 24, R.C., Cork, Ire., adm. March 20, 1848 dis. March 23, 1848
John McArty, 16, R.C., Cork, Ire., adm. March 20, 1848 dis. Apr. 15, 1848
Norrie McArty, 40, Cork, Ire., adm. March 20, 1848 dis. Apr. 15, 1848
Mich. McArty, 23, R.C., Cork, Ire., adm. July 7, 1848 dis. July 22, 1848 adm. Emigrant Hospital July 7, 1848, fever, dis. July 22, 1848
Mary Faherty, 25, R.C., Galway, Ire., adm. July 29, 1848 dis. Aug. 12, 1848
Mrs. Biddy Magee, 52, R.C., Louth, Ire., adm. Nov. 22, 1848 died Dec. 5, 1848

Sea Bird, sailed from Newry, Ireland, arrived at Saint John
John Murphy, 50, R.C., Armagh, Ire., adm. June 8, 1847 died June 14, 1847
Mrs. Betty Murphy, 50, R.C., Armagh, Ire., adm. June 11, 1847
John McKee, 25, R.C., Down, Ire., adm. March 20, 1848 dis. March 27, 1848
Mrs. Cath. McKay, 26, Down, Ire., adm. March 20, 1848 dis. Apr. 3, 1848

Seraph, sailed from Cork, Ire., arrived at Saint John, July 23, 1847
Patk. Lynch, 20, R.C., Kerry, Ire., adm. Aug. 7, 1847
Margaret O'Connor, 14, R.C., Cork, Ire., adm. Aug. 16, 1847
Esther O'Connor, 24, R.C., Cork, Ire., adm. Aug. 16, 1847 died Aug. 17, 1847
Mathew Connor, 14, R.C., Cork, Ire., adm. Aug. 16, 1847
James Conners, 48, R.C., Cork, Ire., adm. adm. Aug. 17, 1847

166   Irish Migration To New England: Port of Saint John

dis. Aug. 19, 1847
Walker O'Conners, 15, R.C., Cork, Ire., adm. adm. Aug. 17, 1847 dis. Aug. 19, 1847

Shakespear, sailed from Liverpool, England, arrived at Saint John
John Gaveney, 20, R.C., Monaghan, Ire., adm. June 18, 1847 dis. July 12, 1847 adm. July 22, 1847, adm. July 22, 1847 died July 22, 1847
Mary Mills, 18, R.C., Louth, Ire., adm. June 23, 1847 died July 20, 1847
Mrs. Cath. Clancey, 40, R.C., Tipperary, Ire., adm. July 3, 1847 adm. March 20, 1848 dis. May 8, 1848
Peggy Clancey, 10, R.C., Tipperary, Ire., adm. July 3, 1847
Ellen Gregg, 18, R.C., Derry, Ire., adm. July 3, 1847, dis. July 22, 1847
Mary Hegarty, 8 mos., R.C., Cork, Ire., adm. July 16, 1847
Mary Clancey, 15, R.C., Tipperary, Ire., adm. July 16, 1847
Ellen Clancey, 14, R.C., Tipperary, Ire., adm. July 16, 1847
Norry Clancey, 12, R.C., Tipperary, Ire., adm. July 16, 1847
Judy Clancey, 9, R.C., Tipperary, Ire., adm. July 16, 1847
Catherine Clancey, 3, R.C., Tipperary, Ire., adm. July 16, 1847
Eliza Clancey, 1 year 6 mos., R.C., Tipperary, Ire., adm. July 16, 1847 died July 23, 1847
Wm Clancy, 35, R.C., Tipperary, Ire., adm. July 16, 1847 died Aug. 27, 1847
Patrick Haggirty, 37, R.C., Cork, Ire., adm. July 16, 1847 dis. July 27, 1847
Jerry Haggirty, 5, R.C., Cork, Ire., adm. July 16, 1847 died Aug. 27, 1847
Danl. Haggirty, 2, R.C., Cork, Ire., adm. July 16, 1847 died July 23, 1847
John Couchlin, 40, R.C., Cork, Ire., adm. July 16, 1847 died July 18, 1847
John Hesson, 9, R.C., Cork, Ire., adm. July 19, 1847
Michl. Hesson, 13, R.C., Cork, Ire., adm. July 19, 1847
Mary Hesson, 11, R.C., Cork, Ire., adm. July 19, 1847

Sir Charles Napier, sailed from Derry, Ireland, arrived at Saint John May 23, 1847
John Curran, 18, R.C., Tyrone, Ire., adm. June 19, 1847 dis. July 20, 1847
Anne Hazlet, 20, R.C., Tyrone, Ire., adm. June 24, 1847 dis. Aug. 6, 1847
Mary Allan, 25, R.C., Cork, Ire., adm. June 25, 1847 adm. March 20, 1848 dis. Aug. 1, 1848
Mary Ryan, 20, R.C., Leitrim, Ire., adm. June 26, 1847 died June 26, 1847
Ann Ryan, 3, R.C., Leitrim, Ire., adm. June 26, 1847 died Aug. 16, 1847
Cornelius Mulherrin, 57, R.C., Donegal, Ire., adm. July 20, 1847

Port of Saint John: Alms House 1847 167

died July 30, 1847
John Curran, 30, R.C., Cavan, Ire., adm. July 30, 1847 dis. Aug. 16, 1847
Anne Hazlett, 20, R.C., Tyrone, Ire., adm. Aug. 13, 1847 dis. Sept. 24, 1847
Anne Hazlett, 20, R.C., Tyrone, Ire., adm. Sept. 9, 1847
Henry Conners, 19, R.C., Donegal, Ire., adm. March 20, 1848 dis. Apr. 18, 1848
Eliza Carson, 23, Donegal, Ire., adm. Apr. 15, 1848 dis. May 14, 1848
Mrs. Mary Devlin, 33, R.C., Tyrone, Ire., adm. Nov. 29, 1848 dis. Dec. 4, 1848
Jane Devlin, 8, R.C., Tyrone, Ire., adm. Nov. 29, 1848 dis. Dec. 4, 1848 adm. Dec. 12, 1848
Barry Devlin, 10, R.C., Tyrone, Ire., adm. Nov. 29, 1848
Patrick Devlin, 4, R.C., Tyrone, Ire., adm. Nov. 29, 1848
Edward Devlin, 3 mos., Saint John, adm. Nov. 29, 1848, mo. came in *Sir Chas. Napier*
Mrs. Mary Devlin, 35, R.C., Tyrone, Ire., adm. Dec. 12, 1848
Charles Devlin, 50, R.C., Tyrone, Ire., adm. Dec. 12, 1848

Sir James McDonnell, sailed from Dublin, Ire., arrived in Saint John Aug. 17, 1847
Patrick McDermott, 27, R.C., Kings Co., Ire., adm. Aug. 17, 1847 dis. Aug. 21, 1847
Bridget McDermott, 20, R.C., Kings Co., Ire., adm. Aug. 17, 1847 dis. Aug. 21, 1847
Denis Rigney (Denis Regney) 28, R.C., Kings Co., Ire., adm. Aug. 17, 1847 dis. Aug. 21, 1847
James Holt, 58, R.C., Wicklow, Ire., adm. Aug. 18, 1847 dis. Aug. 19, 1847
John Holt, 17, R.C., Wicklow, Ire., adm. Aug. 19, 1847 died Aug. 22, 1847
Daniel Leary, 27, R.C., Cork, Ire., adm. Aug. 19, 1847
Thomas Seddie (Thomas Leddie), 54, Cavan, Ire., adm. Aug. 22, 1847 died Sept. 7, 1847
Mrs. Rose Seddie (Mrs. Rose Leddie), 54, Cavan, Ire., adm. Aug. 22, 1847 died Aug. 30, 1847
Catherine Seddie (Catherine Leddie), 19, Cavan, Ire., adm. Aug. 22, 1847 died Sept. 12, 1847
Betsey Seddie (Betsey Leddie), 18, Cavan, Ire., adm. Aug. 22, 1847 died Sept. 13, 1847
Thomas Kelly, 16, R.C., Westmeath, Ire., adm. Aug. 24, 1847 died Sept. 21, 1847
Biddy McLoughlan, 27, R.C., W. Meath, Ire., adm. Aug. 25, 1847 dis. Sept. 13, 1847
John McLoughlan, 5, R.C., Westmeath, Ire., adm. Aug. 25, 1847
Thomas McLoughlan, 3, R.C., Westmeath, Ire., adm. Aug. 25, 1847
Mrs. Anne Liddy, 30, R.C., Cavan, Ire., adm. Aug. 25, 1847 dis. Sept. 8, 1847
Danl. Leddie, 3, R.C., Cavan, Ire., adm. Aug. 25, 1847 died Aug. 29, 1847
Hanora Purcell, 18, R.C., Kings Co., Ire., adm. Aug. 25, 1847

168　Irish Migration To New England: Port of Saint John

John Purcell, 12, R.C., Kings Co., Ire., adm. Aug. 25, 1847
Julia Madden, 9, R.C., Galway, Ire., adm. Aug. 25, 1847 dis. Sept. 1, 1847
Pat Madden, 35, R.C., Galway, Ire., adm. Aug. 25, 1847 died Sept. 2, 1847
Tom Daly, 38, R.C., Meath, Ire., adm. Aug. 27, 1847 died Sept. 21, 1847
Mary Kelly, 11, R.C., Galway, Ire., adm. Aug. 30, 1847
Thomas Kelly, 55, R.C., Galway, Ire., adm. Aug. 30, 1847
John Kelly, 11, R.C., Galway, Ire., adm. Aug. 30, 1847
Patrick Kelly, 7, R.C., Galway, Ire., adm. Aug. 30, 1847
Thos. Kelly, 3 years 6 mos., R.C., Galway, Ire., adm. Aug. 30, 1847
Michl. Kelly, 2, R.C., Galway, Ire., adm. Aug. 30, 1847
Tom Purcell, 10, R.C., Dublin, Ire., adm. Aug. 30, 1847
James Purcell, 60, R.C., Dublin, Ire., adm. Aug. 30, 1847
Anny Purcell, 8, R.C., Quebec, adm. Aug. 30, 1847
John Murphy, 40, R.C., Cork, Ire., adm. Aug. 30, 1847 died Sept. 9, 1847
Ellen Dunn, 35, R.C., Mayo, Ire., adm. Aug. 30, 1847
Thomas Purcell, 20, R.C., Dublin, Ire., adm. Aug. 31, 1847
Patrick Wrinn, 40, R.C., Westmeath, Ire., adm. Aug. 31, 1847
John Bourke, 27, R.C., Galway, Ire., adm. Sept. 3, 1847
Margt. Dey, 19, R.C., Kings Co., Ire., adm. Sept. 3, 1847 died Sept. 6, 1847
John McHugh, 26, R.C., Roscommon, Ire., adm. Sept. 3, 1847 dis. Sept. 20, 1847
Mary Haloran, 32, R.C., Galway, Ire., adm. Sept. 4, 1847
Anne Maddin, 20, R.C., Galway, Ire., adm. Sept. 4, 1847
Murria Gately, 14, R.C., Kings Co., Ire., adm. Sept. 4, 1847
Peter Gately, 30, R.C., Kings Co., Ire., adm. Sept. 4, 1847
Thomas Kelly, 56, R.C., Westmeath, Ire., adm. Sept. 15, 1847
John Madden, 10, R.C., Galway, Ire., adm. Sept. 18, 1847
Michl. Madden, 5, R.C., Galway, Ire., adm. Sept. 18, 1847
Mary Madden, 3, R.C., Galway, Ire., adm. Sept. 18, 1847
John Boyle, 9 mos., R.C., Galway, Ire., adm. Sept. 18, 1847
Peggy Boyle, 32, R.C., Galway, Ire., adm. Sept. 18, 1847
Bridget Martin, 19, Galway, Ire., adm. March 20, 1848 dis. Apr. 6, 1848
Ann Coffey, 25, Kings Co., Ire., adm. March 20, 1848 dis. March 23, 1848
Pat Conners, 30, R.C., Kerry, Ire., adm. Sept. 14, 1848 dis. Sept. 30, 1848

Susan,
Richard Sullivan, 30, R.C., Cork, Ire., adm. Aug. 20, 1847
Catherine Sullivan, 14, R.C., Cork, Ire., adm. Sept. 10, 1847 dis. Sept. 27, 1847

Port of Saint John: Alms House 1847

Susan Anne,
Mary Harrington, 18, R.C., Cork, Ire., adm. Aug. 12, 1847 dis. Sept. 27, 1847
Jerry Sullivan, 25, R.C., Kerry, Ire., adm. Aug. 21, 1847 dis. Sept. 7, 1847
Cornelius Sullivan, 22, R.C., Cork, Ire., adm. Aug. 26, 1847 dis. Sept. 7, 1847
Michael Downey, 50, R.C., Cork, Ire., adm. Sept. 2, 1847
Denis Clearcy, 27, R.C., Cavan, Ire., adm. Sept. 10, 1847
Pat Clearcy, 6 mos., R.C., Cavan, Ire., adm. Sept. 10, 1847

Thorney Close,
John Cunningham, 24, Prot., Donegal, Ire., adm. June 22, 1847 dis. July 27, 1847
Wm Carr, 28, R.C., Fermanagh, Ire., adm. Aug. 5, 1847 died

Trafalgar, sailed from Cork, Ire., arrived at Saint John July 28, 1847
John Dehagan, 35, R.C., Cork, Ire., adm. July 26, 1847
John Donahue, 30, R.C., Cork, Ire., adm. July 27, 1847 died Aug. 10, 1847
Johanna Mahoney, 20, R.C., Cork, Ire., adm. July 28, 1847 dis. Aug. 18, 1847 adm. Aug. 30, 1847, age 21, dis. Oct. 1, 1847
Mary Driscoll, 24, R.C., Cork, Ire., adm. July 29, 1847 dis. Aug. 1, 1847 adm. Aug. 5, 1847
Morris McArty, 20, R.C., Cork, Ire., adm. July 30, 1847 dis. Aug. 18, 1847
Biddy Reily, 35, R.C., Louth, Ire., adm. July 30, 1847 dis. Aug. 4, 1847
Hanora Hurley, 26, R.C., Cork, Ire., adm. July 30, 1847 died Aug. 9, 1847
Nugent Spillane, 25, R.C., Killarney, Ire., adm. Aug. 3, 1847
Ellen Sullivan, 18, R.C., Kerry, Ire. adm. Aug. 5, 1847 dis. Sept. 11, 1847
John Sullivan, 22, R.C., Cork, Ire., adm. Aug. 5, 1847 dis. Aug. 23, 1847
Peter Hussey, 40, R.C., Waterford, Ire., adm. Aug. 5, 1847
Hanora Fitzgerald, 18, R.C., Cork, Ire., adm. Aug. 7, 1847
John Costello, 18, R.C., Cork, Ire., adm. Aug. 7, 1847

Very Rev. Theobold Matthew, sailed from Galway, Ire., arrived July 3, 1847
Hanora Thornton, 26, R.C., Galway, Ire., adm. Aug. 4, 1847 dis. Sept. 8, 1847

Ward Chipman, sailed from Cork, Ire., arrived at Saint John
Cornelius Harrington, 30, R.C., Cork, Ire., adm. July 31, 1847 dis. Aug. 12, 1847
Jerry Carty, 25, R.C., Cork, Ire., adm. Aug. 4, 1847
Mary Connors, 18, R.C., Cork, Ire., adm. Aug. 5, 1847 dis. Sept. 1, 1847
John Cahill, 25, R.C., Cork, Ire., adm. Aug. 4, 1847 dis. Sept. 8, 1847
Wm Lysight, 37, R.C., Cork, Ire., adm. Aug. 5, 1847 died Sept. 5,

1847
James Regan, 22, R.C., Cork, Ire., adm. Aug. 7, 1847 dis. Aug. 20, 1847
Wm Palmer, 23, R.C., Kerry, Ire., adm. Aug. 7, 1847
John Healey, 32, R.C., Cork, Ire., adm. Aug. 7, 1847
James Healy, 25, R.C., Cork, Ire., adm. Aug. 7, 1847 dis. Sept. 8, 1847
Jerry Noonan, 50, R.C., Kerry, Ire., adm. Aug. 7, 1847
John Collins, 24, R.C., Cork, Ire., adm. Aug. 8, 1847
Thos. Donovan, 15, R.C., Cork, Ire., adm. Aug. 8, 1847
Dan Shaughnison, 24, R.C., Kerry, Ire., adm. Aug. 8, 1847
Chas. Coughlin, 14, R.C., Cork, Ire., adm. Aug. 8, 1847
Michl. Crowley, 32, R.C., Cork, Ire., adm. Aug. 9, 1847
Mich Morarty, 32, R.C., Kerry, Ire., adm. Aug. 9, 1847
Patk. Triggs, 36, R.C., Cork, Ire., adm. Aug. 9, 1847
Owen Sullivan, 38, R.C., Cork, Ire., adm. Aug. 9, 1847
Bridget Sullivan, 6, R.C., Cork, Ire., adm. Aug. 9, 1847
Fanny Prating, 16, R.C., Cork, Ire., adm. Aug. 9, 1847
Jerry Sullivan, 33, R.C., Kerry, Ire., adm. Aug. 10, 1847 dis. Aug. 23, 1847
James Sullivan, 23, R.C., Kerry, Ire., adm. Aug. 10, 1847
Jerry Mahony, 13, R.C., Cork, Ire., adm. Aug. 11, 1847
Cornelius Mahony, 45, R.C., Cork, Ire., adm. Aug. 11, 1847
John Mahony, 12, R.C., Cork, Ire., adm. Aug. 11, 1847
Jno. Taunton, 30, Cork, Ire., adm. Aug. 11, 1847
Ellen Brien, 40, R.C., Cork, Ire., adm. Aug. 11, 1847 dis. Aug. 17, 1847
Ellen Brien, 12, R.C., Cork, Ire., adm. Aug. 11, 1847 dis. Sept. 7, 1847
Gubby Grady, 32, R.C., Kerry, Ire., adm. Aug. 12, 1847 died Aug. 17, 1847
Thomas Grady, 40, R.C., Kerry, Ire., adm. Aug. 12, 1847 dis. Aug. 18, 1847
Patrick Brine, 38, R.C., Kerry, Ire., adm. Aug. 12, 1847 died Aug. 25, 1847
John Keane, 23, R.C., Tipperary, Ire., adm. Aug. 14, 1847
Michael Hussy, 29, R.C., Cork, Ire., adm. Aug. 14, 1847 d. Aug. 19, 1847
David Noonan, 32, R.C., Tipperary, Ire., adm. Aug. 14, 1847 dis. Sept. 18, 1847
Catherine Collins, 32, R.C., Cork, Ire., adm. Aug. 14, 1847
Honora Murphy, 16, R.C., adm. Aug. 14, 1847 dis. Sept. 16, 1847
Mary Hurley, 16, R.C., Cork, Ire., adm. Aug. 15, 1847 dis. Aug. 24, 1847
Catherine Shaughereau, 20, R.C., Kerry, Ire., adm. Aug. 16, 1847
John Donovan, 35, R.C., Cork, Ire., adm. Aug. 16, 1847
Betty Hegarty, 10, R.C., Kerry, Ire., adm. Aug. 16, 1847 died Aug. 30, 1847
Mary Hegarty, 12, R.C., Kerry, Ire., adm. Aug. 16, 1847
Darby Hegarty, 35,, R.C., Kerry,

Ire., adm. Aug. 16, 1847
Denis Lynch, 30, R.C., Kerry, Ire., adm. Aug. 16, 1847 dis. Aug. 24, 1847
Conels Coffey, 30, R.C., Cork, Ire., adm. Aug. 16, 1847 dis. Sept. 7, 1847
Denis Dinneen, 35, R.C., Cork, Ire., adm. Aug. 16, 1847 dis. Aug. 19, 1847
Ellen Hegarty, 10, R.C., Kerry, Ire., adm. Aug. 17, 1847 died Sept. 4, 1847
John Healy, 29, R.C., Kerry, Ire., adm. Aug. 17, 1847
Tim Donovan, 25, R.C., Cork, Ire., adm. Aug. 18, 1847
Michl. McLoughlan, 30, R.C., Galway, Ire., adm. Aug. 18, 1847
Ellen Cavenagh, 18, R.C., Kerry, Ire., adm. Aug. 18, 1847 dis. Sept. 23, 1847
John Rearden, 20, R.C., Kerry, Ire., adm. Aug. 20, 1847
Abby Hegarty, 17, R.C., Kerry, Ire., adm. Aug. 21, 1847 adm. Sept. 2, 1847
Patrick Collins, 19, R.C., Cork, Ire., adm. Aug. 22, 1847
Mary Scanlan, 2, R.C., Limerick, Ire., adm. Aug. 22, 1847
Margt. Scanlan, 8 mos., R.C., Limerick, Ire., adm. Aug. 22, 1847
Catherine Scanlan, 29, R.C., Limerick, Ire., adm. Aug. 22, 1847 dis. Sept. 2, 1847
Mary Palmer, 40, R.C., Kerry, adm. Aug. 24, 1847
Mary Palmer, 16, R.C., Kerry, adm. Aug. 24, 1847 adm. Sept. 1, 1847
Lawrence Palmer, 10, R.C., Kerry, adm. Aug. 24, 1847
Michael Palmer, 6, R.C., Kerry, adm. Aug. 24, 1847
James Hooley, 23, R.C., Derry, Ire., adm. Aug. 24, 1847
Ellen Brown, 45, R.C., Cork, Ire., adm. Aug. 26, 1847
John Daly, 19, R.C., Cork, Ire., adm. Aug. 26, 1847
Edmond Collins, 12, R.C., Cork, Ire., adm. Aug. 27, 1847
James Collins, 8, R.C., Cork, Ire., adm. Aug. 27, 1847
Hanora Collins, 10, R.C., Cork, Ire., adm. Aug. 27, 1847 dis. Oct. 2, 1847
Ellen Murphy, 18, R.C., Cork, Ire., adm. Aug. 27, 1847 dis. Sept. 9, 1847
John Sullivan, 26, R.C., Cork, Ire., adm. Aug. 28, 1847
Murly Sullivan, 23, R.C., Kerry, Ire., adm. Sept. 1, 1847 dis. Sept. 7, 1847
Michl. Savage, 25, R.C., Cork, Ire., adm. Sept. 8, 1847
Tim O'Leary, 79, R.C., Cork, Ire., adm. Sept. 8, 1847
John Cahill, 20, R.C., Cork, Ire., adm. Sept. 15, 1847
Mary Hurley, 20, R.C., Cork, Ire., adm. Sept. 24, 1847
Pat McColiff, 33, R.C., Cork, Ire., adm. Sept. 27, 1847
John Healey, 21, R.C., Cork, Ire., adm. March 20, 1848 dis. Apr. 29, 1848
John Costello, 19, R.C., Cork, Ire., adm. March 20, 1848 dis. May 13, 1848 adm. Emigrant Hospital May 1, 1848, bowel comp.
Dennis Mahony, 8, R.C., Cork, Ire., adm. March 20, 1848 dis.

Apr. 16, 1848
John Mahan (John Mahar), 6, R.C., Cork, Ire., adm. March 20, 1848 dis. May 10, 1848 adm. Emigrant Hospital May 1, 1848
Pat Downey, 35, R.C., Kerry, Ire., adm. June 7, 1848 dis. Dec. 31, 1848 adm. Emigrant Hospital June 7, 1848, bruise
Jno. Downey, 11, R.C., Kerry, Ire., adm. June 7, 1848 dis. Dec. 31, 1848 adm. Emigrant Hospital June 7, 1848, destitute
Mary Downey, 30, Kerry, Ire., adm. June 7, 1848
Cath. Mahony, 35, Cork, Ire., adm. June 8, 1848 dis. July 9, 1848
Cecilia Coyne, 14, Cork, Ire., adm. June 12, 1848 dis. Sept. 15, 1848
Cath. Rairdon, 28, Cork, Ire., adm. July 20, 1848 dis. Oct. 13, 1848
Mrs. Mary Hooley, 35, R.C., Cork, Ire., adm. July 24, 1848 dis. Sept. 8, 1848
John Hooley, 3, R.C., Cork, Ire., adm. July 24, 1848 dis. Sept. 8, 1848 adm. Emigrant Hospital July 24, 1848, bowel comp., dis. Sept. 8, 1848
Michl. Hooley, 1 year 6 mos., R.C., Cork, Ire., adm. July 24, 1848 dis. Sept. 8, 1848 adm. Emigrant Hospital July 24, 1848, bowel comp., dis. Sept. 8, 1848
Wm Hooley, 3 mos., R.C., Cork, Ire., adm. July 24, 1848 dis. Sept. 8, 1848 adm. Emigrant Hospital July 24, 1848, St. John, destitute, dis. Sept. 8, 1848
Mary Conners, 20, R.C., Cork, Ire., adm. Oct. 28, 1848

Warrior, sailed from Belfast, Ire., arrived at Saint John Aug. 20, 1847
Arthur O'Neil, 50, R.C., Tyrone, Ire., adm. Sept. 4, 1847 died Sept. 12, 1847
Mary Magivern, 54, R.C., Antrim, Ire., adm. Sept. 14, 1847
James Donelly, 35, R.C., Derry, Ire., adm. March 20, 1848 dis. March 29, 1848
Margt. Cain, 13, Derry, Ire., adm. March 20, 1848 dis. March 29, 1848

Yeoman,
Mary Macwell, 19, R.C., Sligo, Ire., adm. Sept. 2, 1847 dis. Sept. 6, 1847
Eliza Gillhooley, 18, R.C., Sligo, Ire., adm. Sept. 2, 1847
Tim Fehily, 68, R.C., Sligo, Ire., adm. Sept. 5, 1847 died Sept. 7, 1847
Dominick Kivil, 27, R.C., Sligo, Ire., adm. Sept. 5, 1847
Peter Kelcorn, 34, R.C., Sligo, Ire., adm. Sept. 6, 1847 died Sept. 9, 1847
Edward McGuiniss, 56, R.C., Sligo, Ire., adm. Sept. 6, 1847 died Sept. 9, 1847
James Connelly, 18, R.C., Sligo, Ire., adm. Sept. 6, 1847
Mary Fehely, 10, R.C., Sligo, Ire., adm. Sept. 7, 1847 dis. Sept. 13, 1847
Mary Fehely, 50, R.C., Sligo, Ire., adm. Sept. 7, 1847 dis. Sept. 15, 1847
Margaret Fehely, 20, R.C., Sligo,

Port of Saint John: Alms House 1847   173

Ire., adm. Sept. 7, 1847 dis. Sept. 18, 1847
Mary Kevil (Mary Revil) 7, R.C., Sligo, Ire., adm. Sept. 7, 1847
John Brandy, 20, R.C., Sligo, Ire., adm. Sept. 8, 1847
Mary McGowan, 16, R.C., Sligo, Ire., adm. Sept. 9, 1847 dis. Sept. 18, 1847
James Killcoin, 30, R.C., Sligo, Ire., adm. Sept. 16, 1847 adm. March 20, 1848 dis. March 23, 1848
John Campbell, 25, R.C., Sligo, Ire., adm. Sept. 18, 1847
Mary McGuire, 4, R.C., Sligo, Ire., adm. Sept. 18, 1847
Biddy McGuire, 7, R.C., Sligo, Ire., adm. Sept. 18, 1847 died Sept. 21, 1847
Hanora McGuire, 2, R.C., Sligo, Ire., adm. Sept. 18, 1847
Cecilla McGuire, 9, R.C., Sligo, Ire., adm. Sept. 18, 1847
Mary McGuire, 40, R.C., Sligo, Ire., adm. Sept. 18, 1847
Mary McGuire, 32, R.C., Sligo, Ire., adm. Sept. 18, 1847
Biddy Foley, 31, R.C., Sligo, Ire., adm. Sept. 21, 1847
Mary McGlone, 17, R.C., Sligo, Ire., adm. Sept. 22, 1847
Margt. McMorris, 22, R.C., Sligo, Ire., adm. Sept. 22, 1847
Margt. McLaughlin, 20, R.C., Sligo, Ire., adm. Sept. 23, 1847
Cath. McGlown, 24, R.C., Sligo, Ire., adm. Sept. 24, 1847 died Sept. 30, 1847
James Pew, 26, R.C., Sligo, Ire., adm. Sept. 25, 1847
Biddy Clancy, 20, R.C., Sligo, Ire., adm. Sept. 27, 1847
Eliza Bartley, 11, R.C., Tyrone, Ire., adm. Sept. 27, 1847
Dan Gallagher, 37, R.C., Sligo, Ire., adm. Sept. 28, 1847
James Feehely, 25, R.C., Cork, Ire., adm. Sept. 28, 1847
Mic. Conelly, 16, R.C., Sligo, Ire., adm. Sept. 18, 1847
Phelix Conelly, 7, R.C., Sligo, Ire., adm. Sept. 18, 1847
John Branley, 20, R.C., Sligo, Ire., adm. March 20, 1848 dis. Apr. 14, 1848
John Campbell, 25, Prot., Sligo, Ire., adm. March 20, 1848 died March 26, 1848
Patk. Green, 40, R.C., Sligo, Ire., adm. March 20, 1847 dis. Apr. 27, 1848
Pat Kilmartin, 12, R.C., Sligo, Ire., adm. March 20, 1848 dis. May 17, 1848 adm. Emigrant Hospital May 1, 1848, destitute
Mary McGowan, 17, Sligo, Ire., adm. March 20, 1848 dis. July 3, 1848
Nancy McMahon, 25, Sligo, Ire., adm. March 20, 1848 dis. July 11, 1848
Mary Tague, 19, Sligo, Ire., adm. March 20, 1848 dis. July 26, 1848
Mary Morrow, 34, Sligo, Ire., adm. March 20, 1848 dis. July 13, 1848
Mary Kilmartin, 18, Sligo, Ire., adm. March 20, 1848 dis. May 16, 1848
Ann Rooney, 20, Sligo, Ire., adm. March 20, 1848 dis. Apr. 18, 1848
Mrs. Ellen Muloy, 30, Galway, Ire., March 20, 1848 dis. May 17,

174   Irish Migration To New England: Port of Saint John

1848
Ellen McGrath, 15, Sligo, Ire., adm. March 20, 1848 dis. May 13, 1848
Ellen Morrow, 12, Sligo, Ire., adm. March 20, 1848 dis. March 29, 1848
Mich. Gallagher, 19, R.C., Sligo, Ire., adm. May 13, 1848 dis. June 10, 1848 adm. Emigrant Hospital May 13, 1848, destitute

Vessel Not Identified,
Mary Martin, 17, R.C., Sligo, Ire., adm. June 21, 1847 dis. Aug. 24, 1847
Margaret Patten, 20, R.C., Donegal, Ire., adm. June 21, 1847 dis. Aug. 24, 1847
Johanna Fitzgerald, R.C., Alms House, adm. June 30, 1847
Mary Condon, 25, R.C., Cork, Ire., adm. July 8, 1847, dis. July 29, 1847
- Logure, R.C., Alms House, adm. July 11, 1847 dis. July 26, 1847
Johanna Cooney, 27, R.C., Cork, Ire., adm. July 13, 1847 dis. July 20, 1847
Margaret Butler, 25, R.C., Cork, Ire., adm. July 16, 1847 dis. Aug. 13, 1847
Mrs. Ellen Johnston, 40, R.C., Sligo, Ire., adm. July 17, 1847
Nancy Sweeny, 20, R.C., Cork, Ire., adm. July 26, 1847 dis. July 27, 1847, would not stay
Catherine Collins, adm. Aug. 14, 1847 died Aug. 21, 1847
Ellen Dogherty, 48, R.C., adm. Aug. 14, 1847 died Aug. 14, 1847
Anne Donovan, 21, adm. Aug. 21, 1847 died Sept. 12, 1847
Bridget O'Gara, 22, R.C., Sligo, Ire., adm. Aug. 30, 1847
Anne Barnan, 20, R.C., Sligo, Ire., adm. Aug. 30, 1847
Giln. Dysart, adm. Sept. 3, 1847 died Sept. 18, 1847
Mary Red, 22, R.C., Fermanagh, Ire., adm. Sept. 7, 1847 dis. Sept. 14, 1847
Mary Loachen, adm. Sept. 12, 1847
William Donnelly, 30, Prot., Derry, Ire., adm. Sept. 13, 1847 dis. Sept. 20, 1847
Mary Mahony, 5 mos., Saint John, adm. June 8, 1848 dis. July 9, 1848 [The dates of admission and discharge coincide with Cath. Mahony, 35, Cork, Ire. of the *Ward Chipman*, 1847]
Ed. Moran, 15, R.C., Tyrone, Ire., adm. March 20, 1848 died March 26, 1848
Margt. Glavin, 20, Kerry, Ire., adm. March 25, 1848 dis. May 29, 1848

Emigrants Admitted to the Alms House Saint John From Vessels Arriving in 1848

Agnes Jermyn, 1848
Tommy Lynch, 13, R.C., Kerry, Ire., adm. Aug. 11, 1848 died Aug. 25, 1848
Mary McAnartney, 8, R.C., Clare, Ire., adm. Sept. 26, 1848 died Oct. 24, 1848
Wm McAnartney, 30, R.C., Clare, Ire., adm. Sept. 26, 1848 dis. Oct. 31, 1848
Michl. McAnartney, 14, R.C., Clare, Ire., adm. Sept. 26, 1848 dis. Oct. 31, 1848
Lott McAnartney, 12, R.C., Clare, Ire., adm. Sept. 26, 1848 dis. Oct. 31, 1848
Mrs. McAnartney, R.C., Clare, Ire., adm. Oct. 21, 1848 dis, Oct. 31, 1848

Alexander, 1848
Betsy Dougherty, 20, R.C., Donegal, Ire., adm. Aug. 19, 1848 dis. Sept. 28, 1848

Anglo Saxon, arrived Saint John Dec. 1848
Jno. Williams (John Williams), 16, Meth., London, Eng., adm. Dec. 30, 1848 adm. Jan. 1, 1849 dis. Jan. 5, 1849 adm. Jan. 9, 1849 dis. Feb. 23, 1849

Atalanta, sailed from Dublin, Ire., arrived at Quebec May 1848
Edwd. Fitzpatrick, 26, R.C., Dublin, Ire., adm. Feb. 22, 1849 adm. Apr. 14, 1849

Bach McEvers, arrived March, 1848
Mary Barry, 24, R.C., Waterford, Ire., adm. March 26, 1849 died July 4, 1849

Blanche,
Margt. Meehan, 22, Donegal, Ire., adm. July 11, 1848 dis. July 27, 1848
Jane Mulderg, 24, Donegal, Ire., adm. July 14, 1848 dis. Aug. 23, 1848
Pat Quinn, R.C., 19, Donegal, Ire., adm. July 31, 1848 dis. Aug. 28, 1848
Bridget McMurray, 16, R.C., Leitrim. Ire., adm. Oct. 28, 1848 adm. Jan. 1, 1849 adm. March 20, 1849 dis. Apr. 30, 1849

British Queen, sailed from Derry, Ire., arrived at Saint John Aug. 27, 1848
Mrs. Eliza Dogherty, 24, R.C., Derry, Ire., adm. Jan. 4, 1849 adm. March 20, 1849 dis. May 8, 1849
Mary Ann Dogherty, 5, R.C., Derry, Ire., adm. Jan. 4, 1849 adm. March 20, 1849 dis. May 8, 1849
Margt. Dogherty, 1 year 6 mos., R.C., Derry, Ire., adm. Jan. 4, 1849 adm. March 20, 1849 dis.

May 8, 1849
John Dougherty, 30, R.C., Derry, Ire., adm. Jan. 4, 1849 adm. March 20, 1849 dis. Apr. 25, 1849

Charles, sailed from Youghal, Ire., arrived Saint John May 28, 1848
Tim McArty, 24, R.C., Cork, Ire., adm. June 3, 1848 dis. June 29, 1848 adm. July 8, 1848 dis. July 17, 1848
Ellen Foley, 20, Waterford, Ire., adm. June 5, 1848 dis. July 12, 1848
Patrick Foley, 25, R.C., Waterford, Ire., adm. June 5, 1848 died June 14, 1848
Michl. Harden, 17, R.C., Cork, Ire., adm. June 5, 1848 dis. July 24, 1848
John Scanlan, 25, R.C., Waterford, Ire., adm. June 5, 1848 dis. July 24, 1848
Jane Bochan, 25, Galway, Ire., adm. June 6, 1848 dis. Aug. 12, 1848
Ellen Bochan, 3 years 6 mos., adm. June 6, 1848 dis. Aug. 12, 1848
Richd. Harden, 29, R.C., Cork, Ire., adm. June 7, 1848 dis. July 24, 1848
Pat. Leahey, 22, R.C., Waterford, Ire., adm. June 7, 1848 dis. June 29, 1848
Wm Harden, 17, R.C., Cork, Ire., adm. June 9, 1848 dis. July 24, 1848
Wm Mullen, 22, R.C., Cork, Ire., adm. June 10, 1848 dis. June 29, 1848

Eli Scanlan, 60, Waterford, Ire., adm. June 10, 1848
Bridget Scanlan, 30, Waterford, Ire., adm. June 10, 1848 died Dec. 26, 1848
Cath. Scanlan, 7, Waterford, Ire., adm. June 10, 1848
Kitty Flynn, 18, Waterford, Ire., adm. June 11, 1848 dis. Aug. 17, 1848
Ellen Bryan, 30, Cork, Ire., adm. June 15, 1848 dis. Aug. 14, 1848
Jno. Murray, 25, R.C., Waterford, Ire., adm. June 16, 1848 died Nov. 15, 1848

Clare, sailed from Donegal, Ire., arrived at Saint John May 13, 1848
Margt. Donelly, 20, R.C., Tyrone, Ire., adm. Feb. 2, 1849 adm. March 20, 1849 died May 10, 1849

Commerce, sailed from Galway, Ire. arrived Saint John June 1848
Phelix Carrol, 35, R.C., Galway, Ire., adm. June 6, 1848 dis. July 24, 1848
Pat Carrol, 7, R.C., Galway, Ire., adm. June 6, 1848 dis. July 24, 1848
Biddy Potter, 20, Galway, Ire., adm. June 6, 1848 dis. July 24, 1848
Thos. Ryan, 21, R.C., Galway, Ire., adm. June 9, 1848 dis. July 31, 1848
Michl. Nailon, 22, R.C., Galway, Ire., adm. June 17, 1848 dis. July 31, 1848
Peggy Cainey, 26, R.C., Galway, Ire., adm. Jan. 3, 1849 adm.

Port of Saint John: Alms House 1848 177

March 20, 1849 dis. Apr. 28, 1849

Conqueror,
Michl. Higgan, 22, R.C., Clare, Ire., adm. July 29, 1848 dis. Aug. 15, 1848

Dealy (Daley), (no date given)
Mary Driscol, 16, Cork, Ire., adm. July 10, 1848 dis. Aug. 27, 1848

Dealy (Daley), sailed from Berehaven, Ire., arrived June 21, 1848
Jerry Sullivan, 19, R.C., Cork, Ire., adm. July 24, 1848 dis. Aug. 6, 1848

Fergus, sailed from Hull, England, arrived at Quebec May 18, 1848
Mrs. Ann Ibbison, 34, Prot., Yorkshire, Eng., adm. Nov. 1, 1848 adm. Jan. 1, 1849 adm. March 20, 1849 dis. Aug. 3, 1849 adm. Aug. 27, 1849 dis. Sept. 15, 1849
Margt. Ibbison, 4, Prot., Yorkshire, Eng., adm. Nov. 1, 1848 adm. Jan. 1, 1849 adm. March 20, 1849 dis. Aug. 3, 1849 adm. Aug. 27, 1849 dis. Sept. 15, 1849
Martha Ibbison, 4 mos., Prot., Yorkshire, Eng., adm. Nov. 1, 1848 adm. Jan. 1, 1849 age 5 mos. adm. March 20, 1849 age 8 mos. died June 2, 1849
John Ibbison, 33, Prot., Yorkshire, Eng., adm. Nov. 1, 1848 adm. Jan. 1, 1849 adm. March 20, 1849 died June 3, 1849
David Ibbison, 10, Prot., Yorkshire, Eng., adm. Nov. 1, 1848 adm. Jan. 1, 1849 adm. March 20, 1849 dis. Aug. 3, 1849 adm. Aug. 28, 1849 dis. Sept. 15, 1849
Thomas Ibbison, 7, Prot., Yorkshire, Eng., adm. Nov. 1, 1848 adm. Jan. 1, 1849 adm. March 20, 1849 dis. Aug. 3, 1849 adm. Aug. 28, 1849 dis. Sept. 15, 1849

Frederick, sailed from Cork, Ire., arrived at Saint John May 1848
John Casey, 22, R.C., Cork, Ire., adm. Apr. 30, 1849 died May 5, 1849

Fredericton, sailed from Plymouth, Eng., arrived 1848
John Casey, 23, R.C., Cork, Ire., adm. Aug. 10, 1848 dis. Aug. 14, 1848

Hannah, (no date given)
Margt. McGlone, 27, Mayo, Ire., adm. June 23, 1848 died Nov. 9, 1848

Hornet, sailed from Limerick, Ire., arrived July 5, 1848
John Meiny, 30, R.C., Clare, Ire., adm. July 12, 1848 dis. July 18, 1848
Bridget Bentley, 30, R.C., Clare, Ire., adm. Aug. 7, 1848 adm. Jan. 1, 1849 dis. Feb. 20, 1849
Robt. Bentley, 3, R.C., Clare, Ire., adm. Aug. 7, 1848 adm. Jan. 1, 1849 dis. Feb. 20, 1849
Pat Bentley, 6 mos., R.C., Clare,

Ire., adm. Aug. 7, 1848 adm. Jan. 1, 1849 dis. Feb. 20, 1849
Jno. Meeney, 32, R.C., Clare, Ire., adm. Aug. 8, 1848 dis. Aug. 16, 1848
Jno. Meeney, jr., 8, R.C., Clare, Ire., adm. Aug. 8, 1848 dis. Aug. 16, 1848
Jas. Reilley, 35, R.C., Limerick, Ire., adm. Aug. 11, 1848 died Sept. 17, 1849

Jno. Francis, sailed from Cork, Ire., arrived at Saint John May 27, 1848
Mary Coughlin, 20, Cork, Ire., adm. June 5, 1848 dis. July 12, 1848
Thos. Dohey, 18, R.C., Cork, Ire., dis. June 29, 1848
Tim McArty, 16, R.C., Cork, Ire., adm. June 9, 1848 dis. July 17, 1848
Dennis McArty, 14, R.C., Cork, Ire., adm. June 19, 1848 dis. July 17, 1848
Ed Fogarty, 5, R.C., Waterford, Ire., adm. June 19, 1848 dis. July 20, 1848
Mrs. Ann Fogarty, 42, Waterford, Ire., adm. June 19, 1848, dis. Aug. 14, 1848
Wm Cooney, 23, R.C., Tipperary, Ire., adm. June 27, 1848 dis. July 10, 1848
Mary Lyons, 14, Cork, Ire., adm. June 27, 1848 dis. July 31, 1848
Alice Lyons, 8, R.C., Cork, Ire., adm. June 27, 1848 dis. July 31, 1848

Jno. Hawkes, 1848
Mrs. Margt. Duig, 30, R.C., Limerick, Ire., adm. Aug. 23, 1848 dis. Nov. 20, 1848
Jno. Duig, 4, R.C., Limerick, Ire., adm. Aug. 23, 1848 dis. Nov. 20, 1848
Patt. Duig, 4 mos., R.C., Limerick, Ire., adm. Aug. 23, 1848 dis. Nov. 20, 1848

Leviathan, sailed from Baltimore, Ire., arrived at Saint John May 16, 1848
Ellen Sullivan, 20, Cork, Ire., adm. May 19, 1848 dis. June 14, 1848
Patk. Sullivan, 2, R.C., Cork, Ire., adm. May 26, 1848 dis. June 14, 1848. mo. in ho.
Mrs. Mellsop, 28, Cork, Ire., adm. June 14, 1848 dis. Oct. 17, 1848
Joseph Mellsop, 10, Prot., Cork, Ire., adm. June 14, 1848 dis. Oct. 17, 1848
Thomas Mellsop, 5, Prot., Cork, Ire., adm. June 14, 1848 dis. Oct. 17, 1848, sent to Boston
William Mellsop, 2 years 6 mos., Prot., Cork, Ire., adm. June 14, 1848 dis. Oct. 17, 1848, sent to Boston
Elizabeth Mellsop, 8, Cork, Ire., adm. June 14, 1848 dis. Oct. 17, 1848, sent to Boston

Linden, sailed from Galway, Ire., arrived Saint John June 21, 1848
Pat Conelly, 35, R.C., Galway, Ire., adm. June 22, 1848 dis. Dec. 31, 1848
Honor Sexton, 35, Clare, Ire., adm. June 24, 1848 dis. June 28, 1848
Honor Sexton, jr., 3, Clare, Ire.,

adm. June 24, 1848 died Aug. 15, 1848
Michl. Sexton, 20, R.C., Clare, Ire., adm. June 27, 1848 adm. Jan. 1, 1849 adm. March 20, 1849 dis. May 18, 1849
Pat Sexton, 6, Clare, Ire., adm. June 27, 1848 dis. June 28, 1848
Jenny Sexton, 13, Clare, Ire., adm. June 27, 1848 dis. July 6, 1848
Kitty Sexton, 11, Clare, Ire., adm. June 27, 1848 adm. Jan. 1, 1849 adm. March 20, 1849 dis. May 18, 1849
Nancy Sexton, 8, Clare, Ire., adm. June 27, 1848 adm. Jan. 1, 1849 adm. March 20, 1849 dis. May 18, 1849
Margt. Brown, 35, R.C., Clare, Ire., June 29, 1848, confined of a daughter Sept. 16, 1848 adm. Jan. 1, 1849, wid., adm. March 20, 1849
Honora Brown, 6, R.C., Clare, Ire., June 29, 1848 adm. Jan. 1, 1849
Mary Brown, 2, R.C., Clare, Ire., June 29, 1848, adm. Jan. 1, 1849 died Feb. 10, 1849
Michl. Brown, 50, R.C., Clare, Ire., June 29, 1848 died July 22, 1848
Mary Mahon, 20, Galway, Ire., adm. July 1, 1848 dis. Oct. 28, 1848
Teddy Kerley, 6, R.C., Clare, Ire., adm. July 6, 1848 dis. July 18, 1848
Conor Sexton, 55, R.C., Clare, Ire., adm. July 31, 1848 died Oct. 13, 1848
James Lawless, 35, R.C., Galway, Ire., adm. Aug. 28, 1848 died Oct. 17, 1848
Mrs. Cath. Lawless, 23, R.C., Galway, Ire., adm. Sept. 5, 1848, adm. Jan. 1, 1849, wid., dis. March 3, 1849
_ Brown, dau. of widow Brown, Alms House, adm. Sept. 16, 1848, mo. came in *Linden* adm. Jan. 1, 1849
Annie Brown, 6, R.C., Clare, Ire., adm. March 20, 1849
Margaret Brown, 6 mo., R.C., Alms House, adm. March 20, 1849 died Apr. 2, 1849 mo. came in *Linden*

Linden, (no date given)
John Coyne, 20, R.C., Galway, Ire., adm. Aug. 24, 1848 dis. Sept. 6, 1848

Lockwoods, sailed from Cork, Ire., arrived at Saint John Apr. 28, 1848
Margt. O'Neill, 19, Cork, Ire., adm. Apr. 26, 1848 dis. May 13, 1848
Mrs. Cath. Driscol, 27, Cork, Ire., adm. Apr. 27, 1848 adm. Jan. 1, 1849 adm. March 20, 1849
Dan Driscol, 3 years 6 mos., R.C., Cork, Ire., adm. Apr. 27, 1848 adm. 1 Jan. 1849 adm. March 20, 1849
Mary Dunavan, 28, Cork, Ire., adm. May 10, 1848, dis. June 8, 1848

Londonderry, sailed from Derry, Ire., arrived at Saint John Apr. 22, 1848
Dominick Gallagher, 22, R.C.,

Donegal, Ire., adm. Apr. 28, 1848 dis. July 24, 1848
Cath. Sweeney, 21, Donegal, Ire., adm. May 1, 1848 dis. Aug. 28, 1848
Biddy Sweeney, 19, Donegal, Ire., adm. May 8, 1848 died July 21, 1848
Cath. McCarron, 16, Tyrone, Ire., adm. May 9, 1848 dis. June 26, 1848
Mary McCarron, 13, Tyrone, Ire., adm. May 9, 1848 dis. June 26, 1848
Owen McCarron, 47, R.C., Tyrone, Ire., adm. May 10, 1848 dis. June 26, 1848
Lewis Blair, 21, Presby., Tyrone, Ire., adm. May 13, 1848 dis. June 20, 1848
Ellen Sexton, 24, Cork, Ire., adm. June 11, 1848 dis. July 9, 1848
James McGinn, 30, R.C., Tyrone, Ire., adm. June 22, 1848 died July 12, 1848
Mrs. Fanny Doherty, 45, Presby., Derry, Ire., adm. Dec. 1, 1848 adm. Jan. 1, 1849 dis. Jan. 9, 1849 taken by husband adm. Feb. 24, 1849 adm. March 20, 1849 dis. Apr. 30, 1849
Ann Doherty, 9, Presby., Derry, Ire., adm. Dec. 1, 1848 adm. Jan. 1, 1849 adm. March 20, 1849 dis. Apr. 30, 1849
Fanny Doherty jr., 6, Presby., Derry, Ire., adm. Dec. 1, 1848 adm. Jan. 1, 1849 died Feb. 9, 1849
Jane Doherty, 3 years 3 mos, Presby., Derry, Ire., adm. Dec. 1, 1848 adm. Jan. 1, 1849 dis. Jan. 9, 1843 adm. Feb. 24, 1849 adm. March 20, 1849 dis. Apr. 30, 1849
Eliza Doherty, 1, Presby., Derry, Ire., adm. Dec. 1, 1848 adm. Jan. 1, 1849 dis. Jan. 9, 1843 adm. Feb. 24, 1849 adm. March 20, 1849 dis. Apr. 30, 1849
Jos. Doherty (Jos. Dougherty), 39, Presby., Derry, Ire., adm. Feb. 24, 1849 adm. March 20, 1849 dis. Apr. 12, 1849
Mary Doherty, 12, Presby, Derry, Ire., adm. Feb. 24, 1849 adm. March 20, 1849 dis. Apr. 30, 1849

Lord Fitzgerald, arrived Jan. 1848
And. Crow, 23, R.C., Clare, Ire., adm. May 30, 1848 dis. June 22, 1848
John McNamara, 20, R.C., Clare, Ire., adm. May 30, 1848 dis. June 26, 1848

Lord Maidstone, arrived Saint John June 6, 1848
Rose McIntyre, 22, R.C., Tyrone, Ire., adm. Sept. 4, 1848 dis. Sept. 11, 1848
Wm Graham. Doctor, 38, Prot., Derry, Ire., adm. Oct. 17, 1848 dis. Dec. 2, 1848
Mrs. Jane Peacock, 36, Presby., Derry, Ire., adm. March 27, 1849 dis. Oct. 26, 1849
Martha Peacock, 8, Presby., Derry, Ire., adm. March 27, 1849 dis. Oct. 26, 1849
James Peacock, 39, Presby., Derry, Ire., adm. March 27, 1849 dis. Oct. 26, 1849
Wm Jno. Peacock, 14, Presby.,

Derry, Ire., adm. March 27, 1849 dis. Apr. 14, 1849
James Peacock, 11, Presby., Derry, Ire., adm. March 27, 1849 dis. May 30, 1849
David Peacock, 6, Presby., Derry, Ire., adm. March 27, 1849 dis. Oct. 26, 1849

Lord Sandon, sailed from Kinsale, Ire., arrived at Saint John May 16, 1848
Mrs. Bochan, 30, Cork, Ire., adm. June 8, 1848 dis. June 15, 1848, sent to Island
Ellen Bochan, 8, Cork, Ire., adm. June 8, 1848 dis. June 15, 1848, sent to Island
Mary Bochan, 3, Cork, Ire., adm. June 8, 1848 dis. June 15, 1848
Jno. Bochan, 6, R.C., Cork, Ire., adm. June 8 1848, dis. June 15, 1848, sent to Island
Tim Griffin, 40, R.C., Cork, adm. Oct. 19, 1848, adm. Jan. 1, 1849 adm. March 20, 1848
John Griffin, 5, R.C., Cork, adm. Oct. 19, 1848, adm. Jan. 1, 1849 adm. March 20, 1848
Joanna Griffin, 7, R.C., Cork, adm. Oct. 19, 1848, adm. Jan. 1, 1849 adm. March 20, 1848
Mary Learey, 40, R.C., Cork, adm. Feb. 14, 1849 adm. March 20, 1849 died May 10, 1849
Judy Leary, 1 year 3 mos., R.C., Cork, adm. Feb. 14, 1849 adm. March 20, 1849, age 1 year 6 mos.

Margaret, sailed from New Ross, Ire., arrived Saint John Oct. 1848
John Hennesy, 37, R.C., Wexford, Ire., adm. Nov. 14, 1848 adm. Jan. 1, 1849 adm. March 20, 1849 dis. Apr. 27, 1849 adm. Apr. 28, 1849 dis. May 2, 1849

Mary, arrived Jan. 1848
John Griffin, 20, R.C., Cork, Ire., adm. May 30, 1848 dis. Aug. 28, 1848

Mary, (no date given)
Jno. Murphy, 20, R.C., Cork, Ire., adm. June 17, 1848 dis. July 17, 1848

McDonnell, sailed from Cork, Ire., arrived at Saint John May 31, 1848
Tom Clifford, 40, R.C., Kerry, Ire., adm. June 2, 1848 dis. July 19, 1848
John Brannen, 25, R.C., Cork, Ire., adm. June 2, 1848 dis. June 29, 1848
Ellen Fleming, 19, Cork, Ire., adm. June 2, 1848 dis. Aug. 7, 1848
Cath. Morrison (Cath. Blake), 24, R.C., Cork, Ire., adm. Nov. 24, 1848 dis. Dec. 8, 1848 adm. Dec. 12, 1848 adm. Jan. 1, 1849 adm. March 20, 1849 dis. May 11, 1849
John Morrison, 1 month, R.C., Saint John adm. Nov. 24, 1848, mo. came in *McDonnell* adm. Jan. 1, 1849, age 2 mos., died Feb. 17, 1849
Kitty Dealey, 20, R.C., Cork, Ire., adm. Jan. 17, 1849 dis. Jan. 18, 1849
Michael Callaghan, 26, R.C., Kerry, Ire., adm. Feb. 5, 1849 dis.

Feb. 19, 1849
Kitty Driscol, 20, R.C., Cork, Ire., adm. Feb. 24, 1849
Kate Driscol (Kate Blake) 20, R.C., Cork, Ire., adm. March 20, 1848 dis. Aug. 14, 1849

Princess Royal, sailed from Cork, Ire., arrived at Saint John July 3, 1848
Mrs. Joanna Murphy, 30, R.C., Cork, Ire., adm. Jan. 18, 1849 dis. March 3, 1849
Eliza Murphy, 6, R.C., Cork, Ire., adm. Jan. 18, 1849 dis. March 3, 1849
Jane Murphy, 1 year 6 mos., R.C., Cork, Ire., adm. Jan. 18, 1849 dis. March 3, 1849
Wm Murphy, 8, R.C., Cork, Ire., adm. Jan. 18, 1849 dis. March 3, 1849
Michael Murphy, 4, R.C., Cork, Ire., adm. Jan. 18, 1849 dis. March 3, 1849

Redwing, sailed from Galway, Ire. arrived at Saint John 1848
John Burk, 30, R.C., Galway, Ire., adm. May 11, 1848 dis. June 30, 1848
Mary Fitzpatrick, 28, Galway, Ire., adm. May 19, 1848 dis. June 26, 1848
Ann Moohan, 20, Galway, Ire., adm. May 19, 1848 dis. Aug. 21, 1848
Michl. Glynn, 19, R.C., Galway, Ire., adm. May 22, 1848 died June 1, 1848
Jno. Riley, 12, R.C., Mayo, Ire., adm. June 8, 1848 dis. Aug. 7, 1848

Mary Reilley, 10, Mayo, Ire., adm. June 8, 1848 dis. Aug. 7, 1848
Michl. Noon, 25, R.C., Galway, Ire., adm. Oct. 18, 1848 dis. Nov. 4, 1848

Springhill, sailed from Donegal, Ire., arrived Saint John June 20, 1848
Margt. Miller, 20, Donegal, Ire., adm. June 20, 1848 dis. Aug. 23, 1848
Geo. Clark, 18, Prot., Donegal, Ire., adm. June 26, 1848 dis. Sept. 4, 1848
Thomas Clark, 20, Prot., Donegal, Ire., adm. June 27, 1848 dis. July 28, 1848

Steben Heath, 1848
Mrs. Ann Gallagher, 46, R.C., Waterford, Ire., adm. Oct. 24, 1848 adm. Jan. 1, 1849 dis. Jan. 5, 1849
Ann Gallagher, jr., 13, R.C., Waterford, Ire., adm. Oct. 24, 1848 adm. Jan. 1, 1849 dis. Feb. 19, 1849
Ellen Gallagher, 10, R.C., Waterford, Ire., adm. Oct. 24, 1848 adm. Jan. 1, 1849 dis. Jan. 5, 1849
Susan Gallagher, 6, R.C., Waterford, Ire., adm. Oct. 24, 1848 adm. Jan. 1, 1849 dis. Feb. 19, 1849
Michl. Gallagher, 62, R.C., Waterford, Ire., adm. Oct. 24, 1848 dis. Dec. 31, 1848 deserted

Triumph, sailed from Limerick, Ire., arrived at Saint John May 16, 1848

Anthony Grifin, 20, R.C., Clare, Ire., adm. May 16, 1848 dis. May 29, 1848
Bridget Byrnes, 20, Limerick, Ire., adm. June 6, 1848 dis. Aug. 21, 1848

Ward Chipman, arrived Spring, 1848
Honora McKenna (Hanora Guino), 19, R.C., Kerry, Ire., adm. Jan. 2, 1849 dis. May 23, 1849 adm. March 20, 1849 dis. May 23, 1849

Wm Kerry, sailed from Galway, Ire., arrived Sept. 1848
John Neagle, 26, R.C., Clare, Ire., adm. Oct. 24, 1848 dis. Nov. 3, 1848 adm. Nov. 6, 1848 dis. Nov. 7, 1848

Vessel Not Identified, 1848
Thos. Neall, 30, R.C., Tipperary, Ire., adm. May 22, 1848 dis. May 31, 1848 (Vessel sailed from Nova Scotia, arrived at Saint John)
Cath. Dunnegan, 33, Longford, Ire., adm. May 22, 1848 dis. Sept. 7, 1848

Mary Dunnegan, 4, Longford, Ire., adm. May 22, 1848 dis. Sept. 7, 1848
Pat Commons, 14, R.C., Galway, Ire., adm. May 30, 1848 dis. Aug. 8, 1848 (vessel arrived Jan. 1848)
Ellen Burk, 16, Sligo, Ire., adm. May 31, 1848 dis. July 12, 1848
Edward McGuest, 60, Prot., Armagh, Ire., adm. June 4, 1848, 15 years in the Province
Cath. Mangen, wid., 31, R.C., Kilkenny, Ire., adm. July 28, 1848 dis. July 28, 1848
Mary A. Moore, 14, R.C., Saint John, adm. July 29, 1848 died Oct. 28, 1848
Chas. Evans, 10, R.C., Cork, Ire., adm. Aug. 24, 1848 dis. Sept. 20, 1848
James Lawless, jr., 6 mos., R.C., Saint John, adm. Sept. 5, 1848 dis. Jan. 1, 1849
Jno. Farrel, 9, R.C., Galway, Ire., adm. Dec. 21, 1848
Jno. McAffrey, 10, R.C., Saint John, adm. Dec. 21, 1848 dis. Dec. 21, 1848

Emigrants Admitted to the Alms House Saint John From Vessels Arriving in 1849

Albion, sailed from Cork, Ire., arrived at Saint John May 30, 1849
Jerry Houran, 36, R.C., Cork, Ire., adm. June 2, 1849 dis. June 11, 1849
Mrs. Peggy Hourlihan, 35, R.C., Cork, Ire., adm. June 2, 1849 dis. June 6, 1849
Patrick Hourlihan, 19, R.C., Cork, Ire., adm. June 2, 1849 dis. June 6, 1849

Ann Hall, sailed from Liverpool, England, arrived Saint John July 9, 1848
Mary Grimes, 45, R.C., Monaghan, Ire., adm. Sept. 21, 1849 dis. Dec. 22, 1849
John Grimes, 7, R.C., Monaghan, Ire., adm. Oct. 12, 1849 dis. Dec. 22, 1849
Edward Grimes, 5, R.C., Monaghan, Ire., adm. Oct. 12, 1849 dis. Dec. 22, 1849
Mary Grimes, 12, R.C., Monaghan, Ire., adm. Dec. 6, 1849 dis. Dec. 22, 1849

Blanche, (no date given)
Mrs. Hagerty, R.C., adm. July 30, 1849 left Aug. 1, 1849, deliv'd child in street

Charlotte, sailed from Donegal, Ire., arrived Saint John Aug. 1, 1849

Mrs. Mary Slevin, 30, R.C., Donegal, Ire., adm. Dec. 3, 1849 adm. Jan. 1, 1850
Biddy Slevin, 1 year 3 mos., R.C., Donegal, Ire., adm. Dec. 3, 1849 adm. Jan. 1, 1850, age 1 year 6 mos.
Ned Slevin, 40, R.C., Donegal, Ire., adm. Dec. 3, 1849
Michael Slevin, 7, R.C., Donegal, Ire., adm. Dec. 3, 1849

Coronation, sailed from Liverpool, England, arrived Saint John June 16, 1849
James Clare, 24, Prot., Liverpool, Eng., adm. June 22, 1849 dis. June 30, 1849

Eliza Edward, sailed from Tralee, Ire., arrived at Saint John July 9, 1849
Patrick Brick, 32, R.C., Kerry, Ire., adm. July 11, 1849 dis. Aug. 5, 1849
Michael O'Donnell, 35, R.C., Kerry, Ire., adm. July 12, 1849 dis. July 26, 1849
Roger Crow, 48, R.C., Tipperary, Ire., adm. July 16, 1849 dis. July 30, 1849

Enterprise, sailed from Cork, Ire., arrived New York Oct. 1849
Michael Donahue, 39, R.C., Kerry, Ire., adm. Dec. 12, 1849

Georgiana, sailed from Liverpool, Eng., arrived Pictou, Nova Scotia June 1, 1849
Samuel Bingham, 14, Prot., Liverpool, Eng., adm. Jan. 11, 1850

Governor Douglas, sailed from Westport, Ire., arrived Saint John June 15, 1849
Thos. Grady, 19, R.C., Mayo, Ire., adm. June 20, 1849 dis. June 27, 1849
John Toole, 20, R.C., Mayo, Ire., adm. June 23, 1849 dis. June 27, 1849
Ellen Fallaher, 32, R.C., Mayo, Ire., adm. June 29, 1849 dis. Aug. 10, 1849
Ellen Fallaher jr., 11, R.C., Mayo, Ire., adm. June 29, 1849 dis. Aug. 10, 1849
James Fallaher, 6, R.C., Mayo, Ire., adm. June 29, 1849 died July 2, 1849
Philip McCail, 22, R.C., Mayo, Ire., adm. July 4, 1849 dis. Aug. 10, 1849
Peter O'Mealy, 16, R.C., Galway, Ire., adm. Aug. 2, 1849 dis. Aug. 28, 1847

Granville, sailed from Killala, Ire., arrived at Saint John Aug. 25, 1849
Michael Callahan, 9, R.C., Mayo, Ire., adm. Aug. 25, 1849 dis. Oct. 24, 1849
Cecilia Barnes, 24, R.C., Mayo, Ire., adm. Sept. 26, 1849 adm. Jan. 1, 1850
Mrs. Celia Loftus, 17, R.C., Mayo, Ire., adm. Dec. 6, 1849 adm. Jan. 1, 1850, age 18
Martin Loftus, 21, R.C., Mayo, Ire., adm. Dec. 6, 1849 adm. Jan. 1, 1850 dis. Jan. 9, 1850
Mary Cane, 32, R.C., Mayo, Ire. adm. Dec. 18, 1849

Londonderry, sailed from Derry, Ire., arrived at Saint John May 3, 1849
Robt. Saunders, 26, Prot., Fermanagh, Ire., adm. May 9, 1849 dis. May 11, 1849
Ann McAffry, 26, R.C., Fermanagh, Ire., adm. July 17, 1849 dis. Sept. 1, 1849 adm. Sept. 14, 1849 dis. Oct. 12, 1849
Margaret Salsberry (Margaret Salisbury), 3 mos., R.C., Saint John, adm. July 17, 1849 dis. Sept. 1, 1849, dau. of Ann McAffry adm. Sept. 14, 1849, age 5 mos., died Oct. 9, 1849
Walter Welsh, 71, R.C., Fermanagh, Ire., adm. Oct. 20, 1849

Nancy, sailed from Westport, Ire., arrived Saint John June 19, 1849
Anthony Cafferty, 20, R.C., Mayo, Ire., adm. June 23, 1849 died Aug. 3, 1849
Patrick Haligan, 24, R.C., Galway, Ire., adm. June 25, 1849
Thomas Hegarty, 20, R.C., Galway, Ire., adm. June 25, 1849 dis. Aug. 27, 1849
Patrick Welsh, 9, R.C., Galway, Ire., adm. June 25, 1849 dis.

July 13, 1849
Sally Cain, 33, R.C., Galway, Ire., adm. June 25, 1849 dis. Oct. 26, 1849 adm. Nov. 27, 1849 dis. Dec. 28, 1849
Biddy Gallagher, 13, R.C., Mayo, Ire., adm. June 25, 1849 dis. July 15, 1849
William Chambers, 9, R.C., Mayo, Ire., adm. June 30, 1849 dis. July 15, 1849
Peter Hagerty, 16, R.C., Galway, Ire., adm. Aug. 4, 1849 dis. Aug. 28, 1849
Peggy O'Donnell, 50, R.C., Mayo, Ire., adm. Aug. 4, 1849 dis. Sept. 6, 1849
Honor Garvy, 16, R.C., Mayo, Ire., adm. Aug. 4, 1849 dis. Sept. 6, 1849
Catherine Mitchell, 7, R.C., Mayo, Ire., adm. Nov. 14, 1849, fa. dead mo. in States adm. Jan. 1, 1850
Patrick Mitchell, 10, R.C., Mayo, Ire., adm. Nov. 14, 1849, fa. dead mo. away.

Pallas, sailed from Cork, Ire., arrived at Saint John May 4, 1849
Tim Hallisey, 45, R.C., Cork, Ire., adm. May 5, 1849, dis. June 6, 1849
Dennis Hallisey, 14, R.C., Cork, Ire., adm. May 5, 1849, dis. June 6, 1849 adm. June 12, 1849 dis. June 24, 1849 adm. Aug. 6, 1849 dis. Sept, 17, 1849
Tim Hallisey jr., 10, R.C., Cork, Ire., adm. May 5, 1849, dis. June 6, 1849 adm. June 12,

1849 dis. Nov. 14, 1849
Mrs. Hanora Hallisey, 44, R.C., Cork, Ire., adm. May 5, 1849, dis. June 6, 1849 adm. June 12, 1849 dis. Nov. 14, 1849
Mary Hallisey, 12, R.C., Cork, Ire., adm. May 5, 1849, dis. June 6, 1849 adm. June 12, 1849 dis. June 28, 1849 adm. July 23, 1849 dis. Nov. 14, 1849
Margt. Hallisey, 8, R.C., Cork, Ire., adm. May 5, 1849, dis. June 6, 1849 adm. June 12, 1849 dis. Nov. 14, 1849
Ann Hallisey, 6, R.C., Cork, Ire., adm. May 5, 1849, dis. June 6, 1849 adm. June 12, 1849 dis. Nov. 14, 1849
Hanora Hallisey jr., 4, R.C., Cork, Ire., adm. May 5, 1849, dis. June 6, 1849 adm. June 12, 1849 dis. Nov. 14, 1849
Mrs. Hanora Murphy, 40, R.C., Cork, Ire., adm. May 5, 1849, dis. June 6, 1849
Nancy Murphy, 11, R.C., Cork, Ire., adm. May 5, 1849, dis. June 6, 1849
Mary Murphy, 9, R.C., Cork, Ire., adm. May 5, 1849, dis. June 6, 1849
Tom Murphy, 7, R.C., Cork, Ire., adm. May 5, 1849, dis. June 6, 1849
Paddy Murphy, 5, R.C., Cork, Ire., adm. May 5, 1849, dis. June 6, 1849
Dan Murphy, 4, R.C., Cork, Ire., adm. May 5, 1849, dis. June 6, 1849
Dan Cadogan, 23, R.C., Cork, Ire., adm. May 5, 1849, dis.

Port of Saint John: Alms House Record 1849   187

June 6, 1849

Ruby, sailed from Westport, Ire., arrived Saint John Aug. 12, 1849
Catherine Kearney, 19, R.C., Mayo, Ire., adm. Sept. 10, 1849 dis. Nov. 13, 1849
Bridget Rody, 17, R.C., Mayo, Ire., adm. Sept. 11, 1849 dis. Sept. 16, 1849 adm. Oct. 1, 1849 dis. Nov. 7, 1849
Bridget Murray, 34, R.C., Mayo, Ire., adm. Sept. 29, 1849 dis. Dec. 12, 1849
Sarah Murray, 10, R.C., Mayo, Ire., adm. Sept. 29, 1849 dis. Dec. 12, 1849
Bridget Murray, jr., 8, R.C., Mayo, Ire., adm. Sept. 29, 1849 dis. Dec. 12, 1849
Catherine Murray, 4, R.C., Mayo, Ire., adm. Sept. 29, 1849 dis. Dec. 12, 1849
Mary Murray, 13, R.C., Mayo, Ire., adm. Oct. 12, 1849 dis. Dec. 12, 1849
Ann Murray, 5, R.C., Mayo, Ire., adm. Oct. 12, 1849 dis. Dec. 12, 1849
Thomas O'Hara, 36, R.C., Sligo, Ire., adm. Feb. 12, 1850

Sarah, sailed from Londonderry, Ire., arrived Saint John July 20, 1849
Mary Watson, 30, Prot., Derry, Ire., adm. Aug. 9, 1849 dis. Sept. 19, 1849
Mrs. Jane Anderson, 23, Prot., Tyrone, Ire., adm. Aug. 24, 1849 adm. Jan. 1, 1850
Mary Jane Anderson, 2, Prot., Tyrone, Ire., adm. Aug. 24, 1849 adm. Jan. 1, 1850
William Thomson, Prot., Alms House, son of Margt. Thomson, adm. Sept. 16, 1849
Margaret Thomson, 20, Prot., Tyrone, Ire., adm. Sept. 24, 1849 adm. Jan. 1, 1850

Sophia, sailed from Waterford, Ire., arrived Saint John June 14, 1849
Patrick Lawless, 10, Waterford, Ire., adm. June 15, 1849 dis. Aug. 10, 1849
James Lawless, 4, Waterford, Ire., adm. June 15, 1849
Alice Lawless, 9, Waterford, Ire., adm. June 15, 1849 dis. Aug. 24, 1849 adm. Nov. 27, 1849 adm. Jan. 1, 1850, age 10.
Lilly Lawless, 6, Waterford, Ire., adm. June 15, 1849 adm. Jan. 1, 1850, age 9
Mrs. Bridget Lawless, 41, R.C., Waterford, Ire., adm. Aug. 17, 1849 dis. Aug. 24, 1849 adm. Dec. 24, 1849 adm. Jan. 1, 1850
Mary Lawless, 11, R.C., Waterford, Ire., adm. Nov. 27, 1849, adm. Jan. 1, 1850, age 12

Standard, sailed from Limerick, Ire., arrived Saint John, Aug. 17, 1849
Mrs. Ellen Coleman, 27, Prot., Limerick, Ire., adm. Jan. 30, 1850 dis. Feb. 4, 1850

Unicorn, sailed from Liverpool, England, arrived Saint John

Oct. 2, 1849
Thomas Leonard, 29, Prot., Cork, Ire., adm. Oct. 18, 1849

Velocity, sailed from Waterford, Ire., arrived Saint John, Sept. 26, 1849
Ann Morissy, 24, R.C., Waterford, Ire., adm. Nov. 2, 1849 dis. Nov. 4, 1849

Waterford, sailed from Limerick, Ire., arrived at Saint John May 30, 1849
Catherine Kinney, 19, R.C., Limerick, Ire., adm. June 3, 1849 dis. July 2, 1849
Ellen Whalen, 23, 19, R.C., Limerick, Ire., adm. June 6, 1849 dis. July 8, 1849
Michael Connors, 40, R.C., Limerick, Ire., adm. Aug. 7, 1849 dis. Aug. 20, 1849 adm. Aug. 28, 1849 dis. Sept. 14, 1849
Catherine Connors, 34, R.C., Limerick, Ire., adm. Aug. 7, 1849 dis. Sept. 4, 1849
Honora Connors, 5, R.C., Limerick, Ire., adm. Aug. 7, 1849 dis. Sept. 4, 1849
Kitty Welsh, 18, R.C., Clare, Ire., adm. Aug. 17, 1849 dis. Sept. 10, 1849

Whitehaven, sailed from Sligo, Ire., arrived Saint John July 1849
Mrs. Kilmartin, 22, R.C., Guernsey, adm. Jan. 11, 1850 dis. March 5, 1850

No Vessel Identified,
James Mulherran, 7, R.C., adm. May 12, 1849, not an emigrant
Margaret Elliott, 5, R.C., Derry, Ire., adm. Sept. 13, 1849 dis. Sept. 14, 1849
Ann Welsh, 45, R.C., Mayo, Ire., adm. Sept. 28, 1849 (vessel sailed from Liverpool, Eng., arrived at Boston)
Ann Welsh jr., 9, R.C., Mayo, Ire., adm. Sept. 28, 1849 (vessel sailed from Liverpool, Eng., arrived at Boston)
Mrs. Sally Cane, 33, R.C., Galway, Ire., adm. Apr. 3, 1850 dis. Apr. 8, 1850

Sources For The Emigrant Vessel Tables

The **Alms House Records [A.H.]** contain the names of emigrants from vessels which landed at ports other than Saint John and are therefore not included in the following tables. In some cases Quebec or Halifax has been indicated as the port of arrival. Ship names are sometimes confused ie. the *Mary Kemble* (1846) should be the *Mary Campbell*; the *Adelaide* (1847) should be the *Adeline*.

Ship Returns [SR] contain the name of vessel, tonnage, place of departure, place of arrival, date of sailing, date of arrival, number of days on voyage, number of Adults admissible computed according to the Passenger Act, number of adults actually on board, Port at which the vessel touched, date of touching, days there, and if placed in quarantine for what cause. The returns also indicate the number of males and females categorized as adults, children between 14 and 7 and children under 7. Occasionally additional information may be found in the ship returns ie. (1842) the *Andover, Clyde* and *Westmorland* in which the cost of passage for some passengers was defrayed by the Emigrant Society. The ship returns, however, **do not** include the names of the passengers. The Emigrant Vessels of 1842 are listed in a *Catalogue of Vessels* compiled by Alexander Wedderburn *See Emigration Records RS8, Provincial Archives of New Brunswick, Fredericton, N.B. Microfilm F7890-7892*

The **New Brunswick Courier [NBC]**, a Saint John newspaper, contains two sources of information.: First, the **Emigration Office Reports** stated the names of the emigrant vessels, their masters, the date of their sailing from British ports and if passenger lists had been received. The reports were compiled from notices received by mail from Emigration officials in Ireland or England. Secondly, the **Marine Journal**, lists all vessels arriving at the Port of Saint John, stating the vessels' names, their masters, number of days passage, consignee of cargo, type of cargo or passengers. The ships were listed in the following tables (a) if a British port was stated as the place of departure and (b) if passengers were stated to be on board.

Appendix I - The Emigrant Vessels

Year-No. 1841	Vessel	Master	Port of Departure	Sailed	Arrived St. John	Source
1841-1	Agnes	Muir	Sligo		June 22	NBC
1841-2	Albert	Keith	Greenock		July 5	NBC
1841-3	Albion	W. Ebrington	Cork		May 25	SR
1841-4	Alexander	Pierce	Sligo		June 30	NBC
1841-5	Amazon	Fife	Cork		June 30	NBC
1841-6	Brothers	James Daniel	Newry		May 27	SR
1841-7	Caroline	Kirkpatrick	Ballyshannon		May 26	NBC
1841-8	Caroline	Kirkpatrick	Ballyshannon		Sept. 21	NBC
1841-9	Carrywell	Buchanan	Ballyshannon		June 26	NBC
1841-10	Cherub	Dougan	Londonderry		June 7	NBC
1841-11	Comet	Gilpin	Cork		June 21	NBC
1841-12	Dealy	M. Sterrat	Bantry		May 16	SR
1841-13	Dealy	Sterritt	Bantry		Sept. 15	NBC
1841-14	Edwin	Davis	Sligo		July 10	NBC
1841-15	Elizabeth	Sinclair	Liverpool		June 22	NBC
1841-16	Emerald	Sharp	Kinsale		June 29	NBC
1841-17	Friends	Allen McLean	Westport		May 29	SR
1841-18	George	Power	Cork		June 21	NBC
1841-19	Glengary	Hill	Liverpool		June 30	NBC
1841-20	Globe	James Parker	Belfast		May 25	SR
1841-21	Gratitude	Forret	Cork		May 25	NBC
1841-22	Harmony	Baillie	Dublin		June 10	NBC
1841-23	Industry	Allison	Cork		June 29	NBC
1841-24	Isadore	John Dunbar	Kinsale	Apr. 15	May 27	SR
1841-25	Jane	Rose	Limerick		June 27	NBC

1841-26	Jane Duffus	McDonald	Donegal		July 12	NBC
1841-27	John Wesley	David Davis	Cork	Apr. 19	May 29	SR
1841-28	Kangaroo	Prosser	Cork		June 7	NBC
1841-29	Kathleen	Robert Mills	Limerick	Mar. 12	May 2	SR
1841-30	Kentville	Hughes	Donegal		Sept. 13	NBC
1841-31	Larch	McAdam	Cork		June 19	NBC
1841-32	Lelia	McDonough	Galway		June 23	NBC
1841-33	Londonderry	McDonald	Londonderry		June 2	NBC
1841-34	Londonderry	Hattrick	Londonderry		Sept. 27	NBC
1841-35	Lord Sandon	George Feneron	Kinsale	Apr. 5	May 22	SR
1841-36	Louisa	Davies	Cork		May 26	NBC
1841-37	Macao	Millican	Londonderry		May 29	NBC
1841-38	Maria	Doran	Londonderry		June 22	NBC
1841-39	Mary	Nichols	Baltimore Ire		June 3	NBC
1841-40	Mary Campbell	Simons	Londonderry		June 1	NBC
1841-41	Minerva	Harrison	Belfast	June 30	Aug. 8	NBC
1841-42	Montreal Packet	Stewart	Dublin		May 26	NBC
1841-43	Pallas	Robert Hall	Cork	Apr. 5	May 21	SR
1841-44	Pons Ælii	Carroll	Cork		June 2	NBC
1841-45	Pons Albert	Jouett	Dublin		June 29	NBC
1841-46	Prudence	Christr. Bridger	Londonderry	Apr. 4	May 25	SR
1841-47	Rowena	R. Williams	Cork	Apr. 13	May 29	SR
1841-48	Royal William	Driscoll	Cork		May 27	NBC
1841-49	Sarah	Way	Sligo		June 30	NBC
1841-50	Sarah Jane	Muir	Donegal		July 5	NBC
1841-51	Thomas Hanford	McGrath	Cork		June 6	NBC
1841-52	Thyayirn	Cowlie	Londonderry		June 21	NBC
1841-53	Trusty	McCarthy	Belfast	June 18	Aug. 15	SR
1841-54	Volana	Foy	Greenock		May 16	SR
1841-55	Wilkinson	Banks	Belfast		May 26	NBC

Appendix I - The Emigrant Vessels

Year-No.	Vessel	Master	Port of Departure	Sailed	Arrived St. John	Source
1842-1	Agnes	Evans	Sligo		June 30	NBC
1842-2	Aisthorp	Warwick	Sligo		Aug. 11	NBC
1842-3	Albion	Thos. Meredith	Baltimore Ire	Apr. 18	June 1	NBC
1842-4	Albion	Wm Errington	Cork	Apr. 6	May 19	NBC
1842-5	Andover	Buckley	Cork	Apr. 5	May 14	NBC
1842-6	Argyle	Robert Power	Cork	Apr. 19	June 1	NBC
1842-7	Britannia	Coulthart	Liverpool		Aug. 18	NBC
1842-8	British Queen	A. Irvine	Cork	Apr. 19	May 26	NBC
1842-9	Caroline	Kilpatrick	Sligo (Ballys)		June 26	NBC
1842-10	Carrywell	Buchanan	Belfast	May 4	June 30	NBC
1842-11	Clifton	Bisson	Cork		July 8	NBC
1842-12	Clyde	Edwin Pentreath	Cork	Apr. 7	May 17	NBC
1842-13	Comet	Robert Gilpin	Dublin	May 7	July 2	NBC
1842-14	Cordelia	J. McMillan	Belfast	Apr. 30	June 18	NBC
1842-15	Creole	James Clark	Londonderry	May 7	June 15	NBC
1842-16	Dealys	Sterritt	Bantry	Apr. 8	May 27	NBC
1842-17	Defiance	Kitton	Cork		July 8	NBC
1842-18	Dykes	Harrison	Sligo	May 11	June 23	NBC
1842-19	Eliza[h] Grimmer	C.I. Frye	Liverpool	Apr. 20	June 6	NBC
1842-20	Envoy	Fra. Giffney	Londonderry	Apr. 17	May 25	NBC
1842-21	Friendship	Nichol	Londonderry		July 16	NBC
1842-22	Indemnity	Williamson	Cork		Sept. 6	NBC
1842-23	Jessie	Felix (Fittock)	Limerick	May 3	June 22	NBC
1842-24	Jessie	Duncan	Limerick	May 24	July 1	NBC
1842-25	John	McGraw	Waterford		June 19	NBC

Appendix I - The Emigrant Vessels

1842-26	John Francis	John Kent	Cork	Apr. 15	May 27	NBC
1842-27	John Wesley	D. Davis	Cork	Apr. 29	June 13	NBC
1842-28	John & Mary	Wright	Galway		May 31	NBC
1842-29	Kingston	Small	Cork	May 4	June 30	NBC
1842-30	Lady Milton	John Sinnott	Londonderry	May 4	June 24	NBC
1842-31	Lady Douglas	Serin	Drogheda		June 30	NBC
1842-32	Lavinia	Evans	Tralee		June 30	NBC
1842-33	Leila	John McDonagh	Galway	Apr. 26	June 6	NBC
1842-34	Londonderry	S. Hattrick	Londonderry	Apr. 4	May 19	NBC
1842-35	Londonderry	Hattrick	Londonderry		Sept. 14	NBC
1842-36	Lord Sandon	G. Feneron	Kinsale	Mar. 22	Apr. 28	SR
1842-37	Lord Sidmouth	Samuel Bryan	Port Glasgow	May 4	July 1	NBC
1842-38	Mabel	Nicholson	Liverpool		Oct. 14	NBC
1842-39	Maria	Doran	Londonderry	May 12	June 26	NBC
1842-40	Martha	John Linn	Cork	Apr. 26	June 15	NBC
1842-41	Martha Ann	Thos. Feran	Cork	Apr. 19	May 31	NBC
1842-42	Mary	Garde (Grade)	Cork	May 4	June 30	NBC
1842-43	Mary Caroline	Brewer	Liverpool	May 4	June 13	NBC
1842-44	Midas	Thomas Moore	Galway	Apr. 8	May 25	NBC
1842-45	Midas	Vaughan	Galway		Sept. 12	NBC
1842-46	Odessa	Vaughan	Londonderry		June 16	NBC
1842-47	Perthshire	S. Risk	Greenock	Apr. 1	May 11	NBC
1842-48	Pons Ælii	H. Wright	Cork	Apr. 24	July 1	NBC
1842-49	Portland	Robinson	Liverpool	Apr. 5	May 14	NBC
1842-50	Portland	Robinson	Liverpool		Oct. 10	NBC
1842-51	Promise	R. Bickford	Newry	Apr. 13	May 27	NBC
1842-52	Samuel	Flemming	Liverpool		Aug. 21	NBC
1842-53	Scotland	Johnston	Greenock		May 23	NBC

Appendix I - The Emigrant Vessels

Year-No. 1842	Vessel	Master	Port of Departure	Sailed	Arrived St. John	Source
1842-54	Silkworth	Meldrum	Cork	May 23	June 30	NBC
1842-55	South Esk	Nisbet	Liverpool	May 11	June 28	NBC
1842-56	Susan Jane	Strong	Sligo Dongeal		July 1	NBC
1842-57	Symmetry	Bryon	Liverpool		Aug. 18	NBC
1842-58	Thomas	Edmondon	Sligo	May 21	June 30	NBC
1842-59	Thomas Hanford	Herbert	Cork		June 23	NBC
1842-60	Trial	H. Bell	Dublin	May 13	July 2	NBC
1842-61	Westmorland	M.G. Walker	Cork	Apr. 9	May 22	NBC

Year-No. 1843	Vessel	Master	Port of Departure	Sailed	Arrived St. John	Source
1843-1	Don	O'Brien	Waterford		June 26	NBC
1843-2	Louisa		Cork		May 19	NBC
1843-3	Martha	Linn	Cork		July 7	NBC
1843-4	Sally	Ditchburn	Belfast		May 26	NBC
1843-5	Thomas Naylor	Gale	Cork		July 4	NBC
1843-6	Victory	Gloucester	Youghal		July 9	NBC

Appendix I - The Emigrant Vessels 195

Year-No. 1844	Vessel	Master	Port of Departure	Sailed	Arrived St. John	Source
1844-1	Asia	Hannah	Londonderry		June 10	NBC
1844-2	Blanche	White	Donegal		July 16	NBC
1844-3	British Queen	Card	Dingle		June 12	NBC
1844-4	Caroline	Kilpatrick	Ballyshannon		July 26	NBC
1844-5	Clio	Kelly	Cork		June 9	NBC
1844-6	Coxon	Morgan	Cork		May 26	NBC
1844-7	Envoy	Mason	Londonderry		June 16	NBC
1844-8	Fellowship	Armstrong	Londonderry		June 4	NBC
1844-9	Isadore		Cork		June 22	NBC
1844-10	John Francis	Deaves	Cork		May 30	NBC
1844-11	Kitty	Rex	Cork		July 20	NBC
1844-12	Londonderry	Hattrick	Londonderry		Oct. 24	NBC
1844-13	Mars	Flagg	Liverpool		June 2	NBC
1844-14	Martha	Lynn	Cork		May 30	NBC
1844-15	Midas	Oliver	Galway		Oct. 14	NBC
1844-16	Nero	Ellis	Limerick		May 30	NBC
1844-17	Normandy	Smales	Stockton		June 17	NBC
1844-18	Pallas	Hall	Cork		May 26	NBC
1844-19	Pearl	Ross	Liverpool		June 2	NBC
1844-20	Redwing	York	Galway		June 4	NBC
1844-21	Rose	Kelley	Belfast		June 18	NBC
1844-22	Sovereign		Newry		Sept. 2	NBC
1844-23	Thomas Hanford	Herbert	Cork		May 31	NBC
1844-24	Thorney Close		Dongegal		July 8	A.H.
1844-25	Wanderer	Raycraft	Baltimore Ire.		June 8	NBC
1844-26	Woodstock	Taber	Liverpool		June 22	NBC

Appendix I - The Emigrant Vessels

Year-No.	Vessel	Master	Port of Departure	Sailed	Arrived St. John	Source
1845-1	Agnes	Dougherty	Sligo		July 2	NBC
1845-2	Albion	Tardiff	Cork		May 29	NBC
1845-3	Ann	White	Donegal		June 27	NBC
1845-4	Ann	McFee	Limerick		Aug. 22	NBC
1845-5	Atlas		Cork			NBC
1845-6	Barbe McEver		Donegal			NBC
1845-7	Britannia	Couthard	Liverpool		June 5	NBC
1845-8	Brothers	Rowell	Cork		June 21	NBC
1845-9	Caroline	Lovett	Londonderry		June 13	NBC
1845-10	Caroline	Kilpatrick	Ballyshannon		June 4	NBC
1845-11	Champlain	Peneten	Cork		June 30	NBC
1845-12	Clyde		Liverpool		Jan. 2	A.H.
1845-13	Coxon	Morgan	Cork		May 27	NBC
1845-14	Cozen		Cork			NBC
1845-15	Creole	Clarke	Londonderry		May 28	NBC
1845-16	Cygnet	Hughes	Sligo		June 17	NBC
1845-17	Dealy	Starrett	Bantry		Sept. 4	NBC
1845-18	Dominica		Cork		June 4	A.H.
1845-19	Eliza Ann	Clarke	Cork		May 21	NBC
1845-20	Eliza Gillis		Galway		July 23	A.H.
1845-21	Ellen & Margaret		Cork			NBC
1845-22	Gov. Douglas	Hyde	Baltimore, Ire.		May 28	NBC
1845-23	Harriet	Wallace	Londonderry		July 4	NBC
1845-24	Henry Patterson	Keohan	Cork		June 15	NBC
1845-25	Hornet	Hodigan	Limerick		Aug. 16	NBC

Appendix I - The Emigrant Vessels   197

ID	Ship	Captain	Port	Date	Source
1845-26	Isadore	Walsh (Welsh)	Cork	May 21	NBC
1845-27	Jane	Casey	Cork	July 2	NBC
1845-28	John Wesley	Davis	Cork	May 23	NBC
1845-29	Lady Mary Fox	Dalton	Cork	June 3	NBC
1845-30	Levinthin	Roycraft	Baltimore, Ire.	May 19	NBC
1845-31	Londonderry	Hattrick	Londonderry	May 22	NBC
1845-32	Lord Fitzgerald	York	Galway	June 9	NBC
1845-33	Martha	John Mackay	Cork	June 3	NBC
1845-34	Mary	Dunbar	Cork	July 3	NBC
1845-35	New Zealand	P.R. Mackie	Londonderry	June 24	NBC
1845-36	Non Pareil		Cork		NBC
1845-37	Ocean	Power	Cork	May 22	NBC
1845-38	Pallas	Hatt	Cork		A.H.
1845-39	Pons Ælli	Mock	Cork	May 30	NBC
1845-40	Redwing	York	Galway	May 27	NBC
1845-41	Rose Macroom	Powers		May 21	NBC
1845-42	Sarah	Fletcher	Cork	June 23	NBC
1845-43	Sophia	Ballard	Waterford	May 28	NBC
1845-44	St. Lawrence	Robinson	Cork	May 21	NBC
1845-45	Sun		Donegal		NBC
1845-46	Thorney Close	Horan	Donegal	June 13	NBC
1845-47	Time	Driscoll	Cork	July 3	NBC
1845-48	Triumph	Scott	Baltimore, Ire.	May 27	NBC
1845-49	Velocity	McGrath	Waterford	June 2	NBC
1845-50	Venelia	Frink	Londonderry	May 23	NBC
1845-51	Wakefield		Newry	July 27	A.H.
1845-52	Warrior	Tiernan	Drogheda	June 13	NBC
1845-53	Woodland Castle	Williams	Cork	Aug. 7	NBC

198   Appendix I - The Emigrant Vessels

Year-No. 1846	Vessel	Master	Port of Departure	Sailed	Arrived St. John	Source
1846-1	Alanby	Leonard	Cork	May 11	May 12	NBC
1846-2	Alarm	Tardiff	Cork	Apr. 5	May 21	NBC
1846-3	Albion		Cork	Apr. 5	June 24	NBC
1846-4	Alexander	Weightman	Londonderry	Apr. 14	June 24	NBC
1846-5	Ann Wise	Allwood	Sligo		June 30	NBC
1846-6	Aulaby	Driscoll	Cork		July 31	NBC
1846-7	Blanche	Falconbridge	Donegal		July 18	NBC
1846-8	Bristol	Brinton	Londonderry			NBC
1846-9	Britannia		Baltimore Ire		June	NBC
1846-10	British Queen	Nowell	Newry	May 15	May 11	NBC
1846-11	Brothers		Bantry		Aug. 15	NBC
1846-12	Brothers		Newry		July	NBC
1846-13	Burman	Cann	Sligo		Aug. 2	NBC
1846-14	Caroline	Kirkpatrick	Ballyshannon		June 29	NBC
1846-15	Charles	McCarthy	Youghal		June 25	NBC
1846-16	Charlotte	Fowles	Ballyshannon		Aug. 1	NBC
1846-17	Chieftain	Hy. Duffy	Galway		June	NBC
1846-18	Coronation		Liverpool			NBC
1846-19	Coxon	Morgan	Cork	Apr. 10	May 20	NBC
1846-20	Creole	James Kirk	Londonderry	Apr. 23	May 30	NBC
1846-21	Cynthia Ann		Drogheda			NBC
1846-22	Danube	McNaghten	Donegal		Aug. 4	NBC
1846-23	Dealy	Sterratt	Bantry		May 12	NBC
1846-24	Duke Wellington		London			NBC
1846-25	Elizabeth	Young	Cork		July	NBC

Appendix I - The Emigrant Vessels   199

ID	Ship	Captain	Port	Date	Date	Code
1846-26	Ellen & Margaret	Jones	Cork	Apr. 13	June 1	NBC
1846-27	Emerald		Liverpool		Aug. 15	NBC
1846-28	Emigrant		Liverpool		Aug. 15	NBC
1846-29	Emulous		Newry			NBC
1846-30	Envoy	Hattrick	Londonderry	Apr. 14	May 22	NBC
1846-31	Fog-an-Bealse	Broughall	Dublin		June 30	NBC
1846-32	Garland	J. Robertson	Berehaven		June 24	NBC
1846-33	George Ramsay	Farrell	Kinsale		May 23	NBC
1846-34	Harriet	Wallace	Londonderry	Apr. 16	June 3	NBC
1846-35	Harry Kitty		Cork		July	NBC
1846-36	Hornet	Hedigan	Limerick	April	May 15	NBC
1846-37	Jane	Casey			June 4	NBC
1846-38	John Begg	Mackay	Galway	May	June 3	NBC
1846-39	John Francis	Deaves	Cork	Apr. 22	June 1	NBC
1846-40	Lady Napier	Stowe	Westport		May 20	NBC
1846-41	Leviathin	Roycraft	Baltimore Ire		May 12	NBC
1846-42	Lindon	Yorke	Galway		June	NBC
1846-43	Lord Fitzgerald	Yorke	Galway	May	June 6	NBC
1846-44	Lord Glenelg	Martin	Cork	Apr. 25	June 3	NBC
1846-45	Margt. Thompson	Lacey	Donegal	May	June 1	NBC
1846-46	Martha	Lynn	Cork	Apr. 18	June 3	NBC
1846-47	Mary	Dunbar	Cork	Apr. 5	May 20	NBC
1846-48	Mary Campbell	Berger	Londonderry		July 18	NBC
1846-49	Moy	O'Grady	Limerick	May 11	June	NBC
1846-50	Ocean		Cork	Apr. 15	June 6	NBC

Appendix I - The Emigrant Vessels

1846-51	Oregon		Liverpool		Aug. 15	NBC
1846-52	Pallas	Hall	Cork	Apr. 5	May 21	NBC
1846-53	Pearl	Rowles	Londonderry	July 1	Aug. 11	NBC
1846-54	Pons Ælii		Berehaven	May	June	NBC
1846-55	Princess	Vaughan	Cork	Apr. 5	May 12	NBC
1846-56	Princess Royal	Callaghan	Cork	Apr. 27	June 5	NBC
1846-57	Racer	Power	Dingle		June 29	NBC
1846-58	Recovery	Moore	Galway		June 20	NBC
1846-59	Regina	Reynolds	Baltimore Ire.	May	June 3	NBC
1846-60	Renewal	Cooper	Berehaven		June 26	NBC
1846-61	Richard N. Parker	Guest	Cork	May 6	June 29	NBC
1846-62	Rose Macroom	Power	Waterford	May	May 30	NBC
1846-63	Sir Jas McDonnell	Dunn	Tralee		May 21	NBC
1846-64	Sophia		Waterford		June	NBC
1846-65	St. Lawrence	Bullin	Baltimore Ire.		May 20	NBC
1846-66	Themis	Dobbin	bantry		June 20	NBC
1846-67	Thomas Hanford	Herbert	Cork	Apr. 16	May 30	NBC
1846-68	Triumph	Raycroft	Castletown	May	May 30	NBC
1846-69	Velocity	McGrath	Waterford		May 23	NBC
1846-70	Victoria	Price	Galway		May 18	NBC
1846-71	Victoria	Wheton	Youghal		June 28	NBC
1846-72	Virgilia	Cormack	Londonderry	Apr. 29	June 3	NBC
1846-73	Warner		Drogheda	May		NBC
1846-74	Warrior	Tiernan	Drogheda		May 30	NBC
1846-75	Wellington	Carey	Galway	May	June 3	NBC
1846-76	Woodland Castle	Williams	Cork	Apr. 23	June 3	NBC

Appendix I - The Emigrant Vessels 201

Year-No. 1847	Vessel	Master	Port of Departure	Sailed	Arrived St. John	Source
1847-1	Abeona	Attridge	Cork	May 31	July 6	NBC
1847-2	Adeline (Adelaide)	Neil	Cork	June 15	Aug. 1	NBC
1847-3	Aldebaran	Barres	Sligo	Mar. 22	May 16	NBC
1847-4	Alice		Galway	July 8	Aug. 20	NBC
1847-5	Amazon	Hays	Liverpool	Apr. 23	May 25	NBC
1847-6	Ambassadress	Bannerman	Liverpool	May 27	July 4	NBC
1847-7	Æneas		Cork	May 27	June 26	NBC
1847-8	Æolus	Michael Driscoll	Sligo		May 31	NBC
1847-9	Æolus	Driscoll	Sligo		Nov. 1	NBC
1847-10	Bach McEver	Betty	Cork	May 22	July 4	NBC
1847-11	Bethel	Mosher	Galway	July 15	Aug. 29	NBC
1847-12	Blanch	Green	Donegal		July 6	NBC
1847-13	Bloomfield	Patrick Beegan	Galway	May 30	Aug. 7	NBC
1847-14	British Queen	Bell	Londonderry	June 3	July 17	NBC
1847-15	British Merchant	Anderson	Cork	June 20	Aug. 4	NBC
1847-16	Caledonia		Cork	May 13	July 13	A.H.
1847-17	Caledonia		Liverpool		May 25	A.H.
1847-18	Caroline	Kirkpatrick	Ballyshannon	May 28	July 6	NBC
1847-19	Caroline	Honey	Limerick	Aug. 28	Oct. 1	NBC
1847-20	Chieftain	Wm McDonough	Galway	May 23	July 6	NBC
1847-21	Cushlamachree	Thomas	Galway	July 6	Aug. 16	NBC
1847-22	David	Yorke	Galway		May 31	NBC
1847-23	David	Yorke	Galway	Aug. 13	Oct. 10	NBC
1847-24	Dealy (Daley)	Stirratt	Bantry		May 27	NBC
1847-25	Eliza	Cheasty	Waterford	Apr. 20	June 22	NBC

Appendix I - The Emigrant Vessels

1847-26	Eliza	McCarthy		Youghal	July 10	NBC
1847-27	Eliza Ann	Wallace		Galway	June 11	NBC
1847-28	Eliza Parker			Waterford	June 21	A.H.
1847-29	Elizabeth Grimmer			Waterford	June 21	A.H.
1847-30	Ella	Small	Apr. 20	Cork	June 21	NBC
1847-31	Enterprise	Leonard		Kinsale	June 11	NBC
1847-32	Envoy	Laidler	June 19	Londonderry	July 23	NBC
1847-33	Fanny	Quinn	Aug. 28	Londonderry	Oct. 7	NBC
1847-34	Friends			Waterford	June 18	A.H.
1847-35	Garland		May 28	Cork	June 24	NBC
1847-36	Gem	Murray	May 28	Galway	June 30	NBC
1847-37	Glory			Cork	Aug. 12	A.H.
1847-38	Governor Douglas	Clark	Apr. 28	Baltimore, Ire	May 31	NBC
1847-39	Gowrie	Perkins	May 31	Cork	July 30	NBC
1847-40	Hannah	Shaw	Apr. 30	Sligo	July 3	NBC
1847-41	Helen Anna	Leonard		Galway	June 25	NBC
1847-42	Inconstant		Apr. 20	Cork	May 22	NBC
1847-43	James	Cochran	May 28	Cork		NBC
1847-44	James	Challis	Aug. 30	Limerick	Oct. 20	NBC
1847-45	Jane	Knox	June 2	Limerick	Aug. 3	NBC
1847-46	John	Robert Disbrow		Waterford	Sept 9	NBC
1847-47	John Clarke	Reed	May 21	Londonderry	June 30	NBC
1847-48	John S. DeWolfe	Mason		Killala	Aug. 9	NBC
1847-49	Kingston	Anderson	May 20	Cork	July 22	NBC
1847-50	Lady Bagot		May 27	Waterford	July 17	NBC

#	Ship	Captain	Port	Departed	Arrived	Source
1847-51	Lady Caroline	Malony	Newry	June 6	July 23	NBC
1847-52	Lady Dunblain	Brown	Killybegs	July 23	Sept 10	NBC
1847-53	Lady Sale	Anderson	Sligo	Aug. 10	Sept 9	NBC
1847-54	Leviathan	Roycraft	Baltimore, Ire	July 6	Aug. 12	NBC
1847-55	Linden	York	Galway		June 14	NBC
1847-56	Londonderry	Hattrick	Londonderry	July 4	Aug. 20	NBC
1847-57	Lord Fitzgerald	Yorke	Galway	July 23	Sep 9	NBC
1847-58	Magnes	S.. ell	Galway	June 3	July 24	NBC
1847-59	Malvinia	Chantley	Baltimore, Ire	May 9	July 3	NBC
1847-60	Marchioness of Clydesdale	Ferguson	Londonderry	Apr. 5	May 17	NBC
1847-61	Margaret Elizabeth	Stainstreet	Youghal		June 27	NBC
1847-62	Mary	Dunbar	Cork	Mar. 30	May 25	NBC
1847-63	Mary		Cork	Apr. 12	May 31	SR
1847-64	Mary	Sutton	Cork	May 28	June 17	NBC
1847-65	Mary Dunbar				June 29	A.H.
1847-66	Mary Harrington	Montgomer	Donegal	Mar. 30	May 10	NBC
1847-67	Mary Murray		Cork		June 12	A.H.
1847-68	Midas	Stitt	Galway	Mar. 31	May 5	NBC
1847-69	Midas	Stitt	Galway	July 17	Aug. 29	NBC
1847-70	Nancy		Killala	May 3	June 9	NBC
1847-71	Ocean		Baltimore, Ire	Apr. 28	May 28	NBC
1847-72	Orbit		Glasgow		May 30	SR
1847-73	Pallas	Hall	Cork	Apr. 5	May 22	NBC
1847-74	Pekin	Harvey	Sligo	Aug. 10	Sept 24	NBC
1847-75	Pero	Meredith	Cork	July 15	Sept 10	NBC

Appendix I - The Emigrant Vessels

1847-76	Perserverance	Callaghan	Cork	Apr. 30	June 24	NBC
1847-77	Portland	Stalker	Londonderry	June 9	July 31	NBC
1847-78	Prince Royal				July 13	A.H.
1847-79	Princess Royal	Driscoll	Limerick	Apr. 15	June 3	NBC
1847-80	Progress	Fegan	Londonderry	Apr. 5	June 3	NBC
1847-81	Rose		Cork	May 28	June 24	NBC
1847-82	Royal Mint	Williams	Liverpool	May 30	July 18	NBC
1847-83	Ruby	Ellingwood	Sligo	May 8	June 20	NBC
1847-84	Sally	Tooling	Cork	May 13	July 5	NBC
1847-85	Sea	Hubert	Liverpool	July 15	Aug. 28	NBC
1847-86	Sea Bird		Newry	Apr. 17		NBC
1847-87	Seraph	Mather	Cork		July 6	NBC
1847-88	Shakespear		Liverpool		May 30	NBC
1847-89	Sir Jas McDonnell	Dunn	Dublin		Aug. 11	NBC
1847-90	Sir Charles Napier	Sear	Londonderry	June 24	May 23	NBC
1847-91	St. Lawrence		Cork			NBC
1847-92	Susan		Berehaven	Aug. 19		NBC
1847-93	Susan Ann	Fox	Castletown		July 17	NBC
1847-94	Thorney Close	James Horan	Donegal		May 23	NBC
1847-95	Trafalgar	Younghusband	Cork	June 5	July 15	NBC
1847-96	Triumph	O'Brien	Sligo	Sept 25	Nov. 1	NBC
1847-97	Very Rev. Theobold Matthew	Yorke	Galway	June 12	July 3	NBC
1847-98	Ward Chipman	Bilton	Cork		July 22	NBC
1847-99	Warrior	Tiernan	Belfast	July 8	Aug. 20	NBC
1847-100	Yeoman	Purden	Sligo	July 13		NBC

Appendix I - The Emigrant Vessels   205

Year-No. 1848	Vessel	Master	Port of Departure	Sailed	Arrived St. John	
1848-1	*Alexander*					A.H.
1848-2	Adeline Cann	Cann	Waterford	May 18	June 28	NBC
1848-3	Agnes Jermyn	Hartt	Limerick	June 15	July 24	NBC
1848-4	*Æneas*	Cushman	Berehaven		Aug. 31	NBC
1848-5	Anglo Saxon				Dec.	A.H.
1848-6	*Bach Evers*		Cork	Mar. 25	May 9	NBC
1848-7	*Blanche*	Green	Donegal	May 28	July 9	NBC
1848-8	British Queen	Bell	Londonderry	Mar. 25	May 8	NBC
1848-9	British Queen	Bell	Londonderry		Aug. 27	NBC
1848-10	*Charles*	Hanlon	Youghal	April	May 28	NBC
1848-11	Clara (Clare)	Allan	Donegal	Apr. 7	May 12	NBC
1848-12	*Commerce*		Galway		June	NBC
1848-13	Concord	Thomas Bowler	Limerick		July 18	NBC
1848-14	*Dealy*	Dee	Bantry	June 5	June 21	NBC
1848-15	Exchange	Hewson	Sligo		May 24	NBC
1848-16	*Frederick*				May	A.H.
1848-17	Grace Darling	Hanratty	Newry	May 24	June 11	NBC
1848-18	*Hornet*	Michael Hedigan	Limerick	Apr. 20	July 5	NBC
1848-19	John Francis	Deaves	Cork		May 28	NBC
1848-20	*Jno. Hawkes*					A.H.
1848-21	Lady Lilford	Hughan	Limerick		Aug. 27	NBC
1848-22	*Leviathan*	McDowall	Skibbereen		May 16	NBC
1848-23	*Linden*	York	Galway		June 21	NBC
1848-24	*Lockwoods*	Errington	Cork		Apr. 22	NBC
1848-25	*Londonderry*	George Boyle	Londonderry	Mar. 16	Apr. 22	NBC

Appendix I - The Emigrant Vessels

Year-No.	Vessel	Master	Port of Departure	Sailed	Arrived St. John	
1848-26	Londonderry	Boyle	Londonderry		Aug. 27	NBC
1848-27	Lord Maidstone	Sheridan	Londonderry	May 11	June 17	NBC
1848-28	Lord Sandon	O'Brien	Kinsale	Apr. 9	May 15	NBC
1848-29	Margaret		New Ross		Oct.	A.H.
1848-30	McDonnell	H. McDonnell	Cork	Apr. 27	May 30	NBC
1848-31	Princess Royal	Driscoll	Cork	May 13	July 3	NBC
1848-32	Redwing	Isbister	Galway		May 1	NBC
1848-33	Spring Hill	Gunn	Donegal	Apr. 26	June 10	NBC
1848-34	Steben Heath					A.H.
1848-35	Themis	W. Leighton			May 16	NBC
1848-36	Triumph	Dudley	Limerick	Apr. 5	Spring	NBC
1848-37	Ward Chipman				Sept.	A.H.
1848-38	Wm Kerry					A.H.

Year-No. 1849	Vessel	Master	Port of Departure	Sailed	Arrived St. John	
1849-1	Albion	Daly	Cork		May 30	A.H.
1849-2	Alexander Stewart	Williams	Cork			NBC
1849-3	Æneas	Cardigan	Berehaven			NBC
1849-4	Ann Hall		Liverpool		July 9	A.H.
1849-5	Blanche	Green	Donegal			NBC
1849-6	British Queen	Bell	Londonderry			NBC

Appendix I - The Emigrant Vessels

1849-7	British Queen	Bell	Londonderry		NBC
1849-8	Charlotte		Donegal	Aug. 1	A.H.
1849-9	Coronation		Liverpool	June 16	A.H.
1849-10	Eliza	Couran	Sligo		NBC
1849-11	Eliza Edward	Walker	Tralee	July 9	A.H.
1849-12	Goliah	Slater	Liverpool		NBC
1849-13	Governor Douglas	Locke	Westport	June 15	A.H.
1849-14	Granville	Brown	Ballina	Aug. 25	A.H.
1849-15	Hibernia	Codd	Wexford		NBC
1849-16	Jane	Shea	Berehaven		NBC
1849-17	John	Knox	Westport		NBC
1849-18	Londonderry	Hattrick	Londonderry	May 3	A.H.
1849-19	Magog	Shank	Ayr		NBC
1849-20	Nancy	Brough	Westport	June 19	A.H.
1849-21	Ocean	Guest	Castletown		NBC
1849-22	Pallas	Harvey	Cork	May 4	A.H.
1849-23	Rover	Allen	Baltimore		NBC
1849-24	Ruby	Cook	Westport	Aug. 12	A.H.
1849-25	Sarah	Cook	Londonderry	July 20	A.H.
1849-26	Sophia		Waterford	June 14	A.H.
1849-27	Standard	Crosby	Limerick	Aug. 17	A.H.
1849-28	Unicorn		Liverpool	Oct. 2	A.H.
1849-29	Velocity		Waterford	Sept 26	A.H.
1849-30	Waterford	Robinson	Limerick	May 30	A.H.
1849-31	Whitehaven		Sligo	July	A.H.

Emigrant Vessel Footnotes

Vessel	Sailed	From	Arrived	Master
1841				
Kathleen[1]	March 12	Limerick	May 2	Robert Mills
Pallas[2]	Apr. 5	Cork	May 21	Robert Hall
1842				
Clyde[*3]	Apr. 7	Cork	May 17	Edwin Pentreath
Eliz^h Grimmer[*4]	Apr. 20	Lvr'pool	June 6	
C.I. Frye				

---

[1] On the 3rd April during a heavy gale Robert Smith, seaman, a foreigner, fell overboard from the fore rigging and was drowned, all efforts to save him being unavailing. The *Kathleen* experienced very heavy weather - had the wheel compasses and binnacle lamp broken - was supplied with compasses etc. by Captain Barrett of barque *George* from Hull. - New Brunswick Courier, Saint John, May 8, 1841, p.3 c.1

[2] Deaths on voyage of 2 unknown infants 5th & 6th July - Want of maternal nourishment and Inflammation of chest; two female births ... 1841 Ship Return, *Pallas*

[3] We understand that the passengers of the ship *Clyde* of this port from Cork on their arrival at the Wharf presented Capt. Pentreath of that vessel with an Address and a Snuff Horn having a silver top in token of his gentlemanly conduct towards them during the passage - New Brunswick Courier, Saint John May 21, 1842 p.2. c.7

[4] Died At sea, 7th May, on board barque *Elizabeth Grimmer* on the passage from Liverpool to St. John, Ann wife of Robert Norman of Bolton la Moors, Lancashire, England, age 28. - *New Brunswick Courier*, Saint John, June 18th, 1842 - Daniel F. Johnson, *Vital Statistics From New Brunswick Newspapers*

Appendix II - Footnotes to Vessels • 209

1845	Sailed	From	Arrived	Master
Martha Ann[*5]	Apr. 19	Cork	May 31	Thos. Feran
Pons Ælii[*6]	Apr. 24	Cork	July 1	H. Wright
Portland[7]		Lvrpool	Oct. 10	Robinson
Silkworth[8]	May 23	Cork	June 30	Meldrum

[5] One man killed on voyage. No complaint save of the unsafe state of the cooking place by which the death was occasioned. - *Martha Ann*, Ship Return, P.A.N.B., Emigration, F7891

[6] Landed at Halifax for Provisions - Ibid. Ship Return *Pons AElii*

[7] Died 31st Aug., on his passage from Liverpool, England to this port in the ship *Portland*, John L. Crane, age 22 son of John Crane, Esq. of Economy, N.S. - Ibid. *New Brunswick Courier*, October 15, 1842

[8] A melancholy accident occurred in our harbour on Sunday involving the death of five persons, emigrants who had lately arrived here in the brig *Silksworth* from Cork. It appears that eighteen of the passengers left the vessel in one of her boats for the purpose of landing in the city. It was very foggy at that time and the boat proceeded but a short distance when they suddenly descried the Carleton steam ferry boat coming towards them. The engine of the vessel was immediately stopped but the passengers in the ship boat, becoming alarmed and confused, unfortunately upset the boat. Every exertion was made on board the steamer and by boats from the shore to save the emigrants but five of their number found a watery grave. viz., Mrs. Coleman of City Cork, Ellen Hurley of Kennagh, County Cork, Mr. Morgan of Tipperary and his wife, and James Shay of County Kerry. - 8 July 1842 *Weekly Chronicle*, Saint John - Daniel F. Johnson, *Vital Statistics From New Brunswick Newspapers*

Irish Migration To New England: Port of Saint John

Champlain[9]	Cork	June 30	Penten
Cozen[10]	Cork		
Eliza Ann[11]	Cork	May 21	Clarke
Henry Patterson[12]	Cork	June 15	Keohan

---

[9] Barque Champlain in a state of mutiny put into Halifax 11th inst. - Ibid. Marine Journal, *New Brunswick Courier*, Saint John

[10] One man was lost overboard on voyage, Ibid. *New Brunswick Courier*

[11] Forty-five passengers left the *Eliza Ann* on her voyage when the vessel was beset with ice and went on board the *Countess of Durham* and the *Neptune*, both vessels of and from Newcastle, bound for Quebec. *Brig Lion*, Watson at Boston spoke 5th inst. lat. 42 26 long. 48 60 Brig *Countess of Durham* had been in the ice and received considerable damage. The *Neptune* arrived at Quebec May 16th and had on board 18 passengers taken from *Eliza Ann*, that vessel having struck the ice.- Marine Journal, *New Brunswick Courier*, Saint John

[12] Depositions by Passengers per Brigantine Henry Patterson sworn at City of Saint John June 19th, 20th, 1845 before M.H. Perley:
    Denis Lyon, late of Parish of Vintry Harbor in the County of Kerry, Labourer - That he paid Gregory O'Neil (broker at Cork) passage of himself, his wife, one child ten years of age, one child six years of age, his brother-in-law James Sheehy and a relative named Catherine Welahan
    John McCarthy, late of the Parish of Kilbritton in the County of Cork, Farmer and Butcher, with wife and child
    Edmond Kelly, late of Parish of Clany in the County of Kerry, Laborer, with a wife and Mary Sullivan (who is about 20 years of age), a relation for whom he paid passage money to Gregory O'Neil at Cork. [The deposition refers to the affidavit of another passenger, John Brosnehan]
    Bartholomew Donohue, late of the Parish of Clarney in the County of Kerry, Laborer
- *See Emigration Records P.A.N.B. Microfilm F16225*

New Zealand[13]   L'derry   June 24
P.R. Mackie
Velocity[14]   Waterfrd June 2   McGrath

1846
Albion[15]   Apr. 5   Cork   May 21   Tardiff
Alexander[16]   Apr. 14   L'derry   June 24   Weightman

---

[13] The passengers publicly acknowledge with gratitude attention provided by the captain and crew of "New Zealand", signed on behalf of the whole by Robert Fenton, John McKenna and Samuel Gordon. Ibid. *New Brunswick Courier*

[14] Monday, two sailors named Richard Burke and John Carey belonging to brig *Velocity* from Waterford, having quarrelled, a scuffle ensued, when Burke drew his knife and stabbed Carey which caused almost instantaneous death. A coroner's inquest held Tuesday returned a verdict of wilful murder. The murderer was arrested and is now lying in gaol awaiting trial. - June 7, 1845, *New Brunswick Courier*, Saint John, Ibid. *Vital Statistics From New Brunswick Newspapers*

[15] The Health Officer reports that Dennis Carty, age 25 and George Thomas, age 55, both passengers by *Albion* died at Partridge Island on 26th of fever of a very infectious nature. Ibid. *New Brunswick Courier*

[16] The brig *Alexander* was towed back into Londonderry on 21st April dismasted. The accident happened 15th April off Tory Island and upon the complaint of the passengers, the master has been dismissed. The Mate is bringing out the vessel and she will probably be ready to sail again 4th May, but the Government Agent thought many of the passengers will leave her. The Alexander sailed a second time from Londonderry on 7th May. The master of brig *Alexander* was prosecuted and fined at Saint John for the irregular and insufficient issue of provisions and water. - Ibid. *New Brunswick Courier*

Irish Migration To New England: Port of Saint John

Ann Wise[17]		Sligo	June 24	Allwood	
Burman[18]		Sligo	July	Cann	
Chieftain[19]		Galway	Aug. 1	Hyacinth Duffy	
Creole[20]	Apr. 23	L'derry	May 30	James Kirk	
Danube[21]		Donegal	Aug. 4	McNaghten	
Envoy[22]	Apr. 14	L'derry	May 22	Hattrick	

[17] The master of the *Ann Wise* was prosecuted and fined at Saint John for having a deficiency of provisions. Ibid. *Colonial Office Records*

[18] The master of the brig *Burman* was prosecuted and fined at Saint John for having a deficiency of provisions. - *Colonial Office Records*

[19] Lost mainmast 29th June. Public Letter addressed to Capt. Hyacinth Duffy of *Chieftain* from Moses H. Perley, Emigrant Officer at Saint John on behalf of the Lieutenant Governor praising his efforts in the management of the ship in her crippled condition. - Ibid. *New Brunswick Courier*

[20] There is one sick person aboard the *Creole* who will be landed at Partridge Island. Ibid. *New Brunswick Courier*

[21] The passengers of the *Danube* have been landed on Partridge Island, 23 of them very ill with fever; reported 8th Aug. Six cases of fever have occurred since landing - reported 15th Aug.
The master of Brig *Danube* from Ballyshannon was prosecuted at Saint John for not having a proper supply of provisions and water, for having made use of temporary hold-beams and for having sailed without proper medicines in breach of the Passengers Act. - *Colonial Office Records*, P.A.N.B.

[22] 42 sick persons with typhus fever from the *Envoy* have been landed at Partridge Island. Rose O'Neill, age 55, a passenger by the *Envoy* died in hospital, Partridge Island morning of June 6th.
Second Voyage of *Envoy*, Mason arrived Tuesday 15th Sept. after

Hornet[23]	by Apr.		Limerick	May 15	Hedigan
Leviathan[24]			Baltimor	May 12	Roycraft
Margt Thompson[25]			Donegal	June 1	Lacey
Ocean[26]	Apr. 15		Cork	June 6	
Pon Aelii[27]	May		Beerhvn	June 20	
Princess[28]	Apr. 5		Cork	May 12	Vaughan

voyage of 41 days. Ibid. *New Brunswick Courier*

[23] Second Voyage: The *Hornet*, Hedigan, Master, from Limerick with passengers for this port, sailed from Scattery Roads, Ireland on 7th July. Arrived Tuesday 18th Aug. after voyage of 41 days - Ibid. *New Brunswick Courier*

[24] Second Voyage: The *Leviathan*, Roycraft arrived Monday 14th Sept., after a voyage of 48 days; shipper James Kirk. Ibid. *New Brunswick Courier*

[25] The master of the *Margaret Thompson* was prosecuted and fined at Saint John for not having supplied the emigrants with the quantity or quality of provisions as required by the Passengers Act. - *Colonial Office Records* P.A.N.B. Microfilm

[26] There are several cases of measles aboard the *Ocean*. Ibid *New Brunswick Courier*

[27] Thirty-six persons from the *Pons Ælii* with malignant typhus fever, some in a very precarious state, have been landed on Partridge Island - one passenger died on board. All the other passengers by this vessel are being landed on the Island. On 15th August it was reported that a passenger by the *Pons Ælii* died at the Island on Tuesday 11th Aug. Ibid. *New Brunswick Courier*

[28] A child died on board the *Princess* while that vessel was lying at quarantine and was buried on Partridge Island. Ibid. *New Brunswick Courier*

Irish Migration To New England: Port of Saint John

Racer[29]		Dingle	June 29	Power
Renewal[30]		Beerhvn	June 26	Cooper
Richard N. Parker[31]		Cork	June 29	Guest
1847				
Abeona[32]	May 31	Cork	July 6	Attridge
Æolus[33]	-	Sligo	May 31	Michael Driscoll

---

[29] 15 cases of fever. The passengers of the *Racer* were landed on Partridge Island in consequence of the fever on board. The master of the brig *Racer* was prosecuted and fined at Saint John for having an excess number of passengers under the Passengers Act. Ibid. *Colonial Office Records*, P.A.N.B. Micro.

[30] The master of the barque *Renewal* was prosecuted and fined at Saint John for not supplying the proper quantity and quality of provisions and for excess number of passengers under the Passenger's Act. Ibid. *Colonial Office Records*

[31] The passengers of the *Richard N. Parker* were landed on Partridge Island in consequence of the fever on board. Ibid. *New Brunswick Courier*

[32] Arrived at quarantine during week prior July 10th; 1 death Ibid. New Brunswick Courier

[33] 5th June - The ship "Æolus" from Sligo with 17 sick - 26 deaths on the passage.
We the Committee of the Passengers of the ship *Æolus* of Greenock, Capt. Michael Driscoll, Commander, do send our thanks in the name of all passengers, to our ever-to-be remembered late Landlord, Sir Robert Gore Booth, Bart., Sligo; he was always kind to his tenants; it was not tyranny which forced us to emigrate - it was the loss of our crops for two years past and we hope to gain a living in America by strict industry and sobriety. We are thankful to Henry Gore Booth, Esquire, the owner of the *Æolus* for the ample stores put on board for the voyage and the good quality thereof. We are also thankful to Captain Driscoll for his upright conduct in the distribution of diet -

Appendix II - Footnotes to Vessels • 215

| Æolus[34] | - | Sligo | Nov. 1 | Driscoll |
| Alice[35] | July 8 | Galway | Aug. 20 | - |

---

giving all the same fair play - the widows and orphans and the sick were all kindly treated by him and his advice to all had a good effect, as there was not a single riot or blow struck during the voyage. Written by Mathias Ferguson, Head Manager,. Sanctioned by the Committee: Edward Johnston, Patrick Gilloon, Patrick Hart, John Mullowny, Thomas Gillan, Patrick McLoughlin, Adam Johnston, Bryan Feeny, Patrick Boyle, Thomas Keelty, Wm Johnston, Patrick Heraghty, Robert Gregg, Hugh Cristal, Dennis Gilloon, Charles Jones, Michael McDermott, Andrew Gilloon, James Munns, Patrick Feeney, Michael Smith, Wm Ferguson, Owen Toher, John Gillian, St. John May 31, 1847.
In the early part of the season the barque Æeolus arrived at this port with 500 emigrants from Sligo. These people had been tenants on the estate of Sir Robert Gore Booth, Bart. of Lissadell near Sligo and were sent out at his expense, in order to clear the estate of useless paupers, who could be chargeable upon it under the new Poor Law which has recently come into operation in Ireland. These emigrants were housed at the old Poor House, where some of them still remain who subsist chiefly by begging. Many have been sent to the Alms House and Infirmary and a large proportion will in all probability become a permanent charge upon this community. Ibid. *New Brunswick Courier*

[34] The Common Council has appointed a committee to make arrangements with the master of the *Æolus* respecting the unfortunate emigrants on board that vessel sent out by Lord Palmerston of whom every care will be taken consistent with public safety. - 6th Nov. Ibid. *New Brunswick Courier*

[35] At Quarantine Friday 20th August. 5 deaths. 15 cases of fever.
Information is wanted at this Office of Martin, James, Honor and Ellen Malone and of Thomas Hynes, all of whom arrived at this Port on the 20th of August 1847 in the Brig *Alice* from Galway (sgd) M.H. Perley. Ibid. *New Brunswick Courier*

216   Irish Migration To New England: Port of Saint John

Amazon[36]	Apr. 23	L'pool	May 25	Hays	
Ambassadress[37]		L'pool	July 4	Bannerman	
Bethel[38]	July 15	Galway	Aug. 29	Mosher	
Bloomfield[39]	May 30	Galway	Aug. 7	Patrick Beegan	

---

[36] 5th June - We understand that John Lawson and James Cullan, seamen and John Burns, a passenger, made their escape from barque *Amazon* at quarantine on Saturday night, 29th May. Ibid. *New Brunswick Courier*

[37] Arrived at Quarantine during week prior 10th July; 16 children and 3 adults died on passage. Ibid. *New Brunswick Courier*

[38] Died at Galway, Ireland, 10th July, John Blair, seaman on board barque "Bethel", age 25, native of Fredericton or Woodstock, New Brunswick. Ibid. *New Brunswick Courier*

[39] The schr. *Bloomfield* came to the Quarantine Ground yesterday morning, 6th August, and by the violence of the gale was driven from her anchors. She ran into a timber pond near Portland Point without damage. There were 74 passengers on board in a destitute and starving state with symptoms of fever. There were two deaths on the voyage. On Wednesday 18th August before B.L. Peters and Daniel Ansley, Esqs., upon the complaint of Mr. Perley, H.M. Emigration Agent, Patrick Beegan, Master, *Bloomfield* was convicted in full penalty of fifty pounds sterling and costs for not supplying the passengers by that vessel with sufficient water and provisions as required by the Passenger's Act. Return of money and effects of deceased emigrants received at Saint John Emigration Office during the season of 1847: Emigrant John Kennedy, ship *Bloomfield*, £1 7 6, with a chest containing articles of clothing to be sent to Cornelius Pelly, shop keeper, Galway, for brother of deceased. Yesterday a body was found floating in the harbor. From the fragments of his dress and his appearance, he seemed to have been a seaman of large stature. Kennedy, answering to the above description, was washed from the deck of the schr. *Bloomfield* during the gale on 6th inst. Ibid. *New Brunswick*

Appendix II - Footnotes to Vessels • 217

British Merchant[40]		Cork	Aug. 4	Anderson
British Queen[41]		June 3	L'derry	July 17
Bell				
Chieftain[42]	May 23	Galway	July 6	Wm McDonough
Ella[43]	Apr. 20	Cork	June 21	Small

Courier 21 August 1847.

[40] Arrived at Quarantine Thursday 5th Aug. 33 deaths occurred on board during the voyage and five more since her arrival at Quarantine. 50 of the passengers are very ill with fever. Return of money and effects of deceased emigrants received at Saint John Emigration Office during the season of 1847: ship *British Merchant*: Daniel Cleary, £2 15 6, claimed by two daughters of the deceased.; Ellen Dreslin, £8 4 0, claimed by only daughter of deceased who was a widow; John Corney, £11 10 6, remitted to Michael Corney, brother of the deceased, at Kinsale. Ibid. *New Brunswick Courier*

[41] Second Voyage: British Queen, Bell, sailed 25th September, 44 passengers. Arrived Monday 25th October after a voyage of 30 days. Shipper W. Howard. - Marine Journal, *New Brunswick Courier*

[42] (St. John) 12th July - To Capt. Wm. McDonough: We, the undersigned, on behalf of the ship *Chieftain* beg return you our sincere thanks for your attention during the passage from Galway to this port. (cabin): William Cavanagh, William Keane, Hugh Crean, Michael Higgins, Patrick Henessy, Patrick Reynolds. (steerage): Anne Mulheeny, James Flanagan, James Gready, Denis Mulheeny, William Staffle, Bryan King. - *Daily Morning News*, Saint John 14 July 1847

[43] On Tuesday 22nd June, an inquest was held before Dr. W. Bayard, Coroner on view of the body of John Flemming, a seaman on board Brig *Ella*, lying at the Breakwater. It appeared that the deceased, in attempting to get on board his vessel the previous night, somewhat intoxicated, in company with one of his

Irish Migration To New England: Port of Saint John

Envoy[44]	June	L'derry	July 23	Laidler
Fanny[45]	Aug. 28	L'derry	Oct. 7	Quinn

---

shipmates, John Connell, fell from the stage leading from the shore to the brig, and inflicted a wound on his head by striking upon the rocks. Connell, unable to get him to the brig, they both remained on the wharf during the night, Flemming made as comfortable as possible by his shipmate. He died about two hours after he was got on board in the morning. - Ibid. *New Brunswick Courier*

[44] 24th July at Quarantine. There are 8 cases of small pox on board the *Envoy*. One passenger died of the disease on the voyage and one other died of affection of the chest. By 31st July 17 cases of small pox were reported on board the *Envoy*. All the passengers were being landed on Partridge Island.

We the undersigned passengers on board the barque *Envoy* owned by Messrs. J.& J. Cook, merchants of Londonderry, Ireland do hereby offer to Capt. Laidler, Master of said vessel, and to his first mate, Mr. Gibson, our humble and sincere thanks for their great kindness during the passage from Londonderry to St. John, New Brunswick, and for the attention paid by them to our comfort, particularly to those of us who were sick; and we also bear testimony to the great care taken by them to prevent any infectious disease in the vessel, by enforcing cleanliness and order. Witness our hands this 23rd day of July 1847 (sgd) George Thomas Carey, William Gallagher, James Nelis, James Magirr, John Bradly, John Doherty, Samuel Porter, John Guay, Neal McCoy, Thomas Neely, Edward Little, Henry Glass, William Clarke, Hugh Mitchell, Thomas Silfridge, Edward Irwin, John Irwin, William Blair, William Kierans, James Gillogly, James Maguire, Charles Bustard, Edward Campbell, Phelix McElroy, Patrick Dougan, James Dougan, James Gallagher, Francis Gallagher, Bernard McGettigan, Nicholas Kearney, James Owens, Terence Conolly, Hugh Keane. Ibid. *New Brunswick Courier*
For passenger list refer to *Emigrants From Derry 1847-9* page 42

[45] Two infants died on passage, remainder are well. Ibid. *New Brunswick Courier*

Appendix II - Footnotes to Vessels • 219

Friends[46]	-	Waterford via Nfld.		
Governor Douglas[47]		Baltimor	May 31	Clark
Gowrie[48]	May 31	Cork	July 30	Perkins
John[49]	-	Waterfrd	Sept. 9	Knox
John Clarke[50]	May 21	L'derry	June 30	Robert Disbrow
Lady Dunblain[51]		Killybeg	Sept. 10	Brown
Lady Caroline[52]		Newry	July 23	Malony

---

[46] via St. John's, Nfld.

[47] The barque *Gov. Douglas* from Cork (reported June 5) with 236 passengers, 26 of whom and five of the crew ill of fever. Ibid *New Brunswick Courier*

[48] At Quarantine 31st July. 4 deaths on the voyage and 20 passengers now very ill. All on board are reported to be in a sickly and miserable state. The *Gowrie* came into port on the 12th Aug. having landed all her passengers on Partridge Island.

[49] Arrived at Quarantine during week prior 11th Sept., all in health. Ibid. *New Brunswick Courier*

[50] To Capt. Robert Disbrow of ship *John Clark* - Sir: I have received the instructions of His Excellency the Lieutenant Governor to communicate to you the high sense which His Excellency entertains of your conduct toward the passengers of the ship *John Clark* from Londonderry, whose preservation from sickness is ascribed to your kindness and great attention to them during the voyage. (sgd) M.H. Perley, Government Agent, St. John, N.B., 12th July Ibid. *New Brunswick Courier*
See Ibid. *Emigrants From Derry 1847-9* page 23 for passengers booking 13 April - 21 May 1847

[51] Arrived at Quarantine during week prior 11th Sept., all in health Ibid. *New Brunswick Courier*

[52] 24th July at Quarantine. The vessel is reported to be very clean and the passengers in good health. Neither sickness or death on the voyage. The vessel is reported to have come up

Irish Migration To New England: Port of Saint John

Lady Sale[53]	Aug. 10	Sligo	Sept. 9	Anderson	
Londonderry[54]		July 4	L'derry	Aug. 20	
Hattrick					
Lord Fitzgerald[55]		Galway	Sept. 9	Yorke	
Magnes[56]	June 3	Galway	July 24	S.. ell	
March. of Clydesdale[57]		L'derry	May 17	Ferguson	

from Quarantine 31st July Ibid. *New Brunswick Courier*

[53] A third division of 500 may be hourly expected by the *Lady Sale* from the estate of Sir Robert Gore Booth, Bart. of Lissadell near Sligo - 28th August. By official returns there are 176 adult females, of whom nine are widows having with them 57 children. - 4th Sept.: Arrived Quarantine during week prior 11th Sept. 3 died on passage 15 sick

[54] For passenger list refer to Ibid. *Emigrants From Derry Port 1847-49* page 44

[55] Arrived at Quarantine during week prior 11th Sept. - 4 died on passage 30 sick Ibid. *New Brunswick Courier*

[56] At Quarantine 31st July. There were ten deaths from fever during the voyage; 30 passengers and two of the crew are very ill. On 7th Aug. it was reported that the passengers by the *Magnes* were all landed before that vessel went on shore. Ibid. *New Brunswick Courier*

[57] Secretary's Office 22nd May 1847 - Sir, I am directed by His Excellency the Lieutenant Governor, to inform you that, having received a report from the Emigrant Agent of the testimony borne to the kind treatment which the passengers on board your ship had experienced from you during the voyage and the creditable state of the vessel, His Excellency is desirous of expressing to you his acknowledgements and the satisfaction with which he is assured of the health and comfort in which the passengers arrived. (signed) John S. Saunders - To Capt. Ferguson of ship *Marchioness of Clydesdale*
For passenger list refer to Dessie Baker, *Emigrants From Derry*

Appendix II - Footnotes to Vessels • 221

Mary[58]	-	Cork	May 25	Dunbar
Midas[59]	-	Galway	May 5	Stitt
Ocean[60]	Apr. 28	Baltimor	May 28	-
Pallas[61]	-	Cork	May 22	Hall
Pekin[62]	Aug. 10	Sligo	Sept. 24	Harvey
Pero[63]	July 15	Cork	Sept. 10	Meredith

Port 1847-49: Ship List from J.& J. Cooke's Line in cooperation with Derry Youth and Community Workshop Ltd. of Northern Ireland, Feb. 1985 page 3 - List of passengers booking 8 March - 2 April 1847 for voyage to Saint John, N.B.

[58] A case of small pox is reported on brig *Mary* Ibid. *New Brunswick Courier*

[59] Two adults and eight children died on the voyage - Ibid. *New Brunswick Courier*
The *Midas* made two voyages arriving at Port of Saint John 5th May and 29th August 1847.

[60] The *Ocean* from Beerhaven with 88 passengers, two sick Ibid. *New Brunswick Courier*

[61] Died Quarantine Station, Partridge Island (St. John) Friday eve., 25th June, of typhus fever, Capt. Robt. Hall of barque Pallas, age 51, native of Aberdeen, left wife, daughter. Ibid *New Brunswick Courier*, 3rd July 1847.

[62] We have but one passenger vessel arrived this week (25th Sept.) the "Pekin" from Sligo - 26 were sick. Ibid. New Brunswick *Courier*

[63] Arrived at Quarantine during week prior 11th Sept.; 21 died on passage, 3 children and 9 infants from small pox and 8 adults of fever. Ibid. *New Brunswick Courier*

222   Irish Migration To New England: Port of Saint John

Portland[64]	June 9	L'derry	July 31	Stalker
Progress[65]	-	L'derry	June 3	Fegan
Royal Mint[66]	May 30	L'pool	July 18	Williams
Seraph[67]	-	Cork	July 6	Mather
Sir Charles Napier[68]		L'derry	May 23	Sear

---

[64] At Quarantine 31st July. 4 deaths on the voyage; all well, except six in a feverish and debilitated state. Ibid. *New Brunswick Courier*
For passenger list refer to Ibid. *Emigrants From Derry Port 1847-49* page 31

[65] 5th June - 5 deaths on passage Ibid. *New Brunswick Courier*
For passenger lists refer Ibid. *Emigrants From Derry Port 1847-9* page 19 booking 30 March - 10 April 1847

[66] 24th July at Quarantine. The passengers with a few exceptions have been landed at Partridge Island, they being infected with a disease of an infectious nature. There were 19 deaths on board the *Royal Mint* during the voyage. The vessel is reported to have come up from Quarantine 31st July. Ibid. *New Brunswick Courier*

[67] Arrived at quarantine during week prior 10th July; 3 deaths 45 sick. The *Seraph* embarked her passengers for Boston, but finding on arrival there, that they would not be allowed to land unless bonds were given that they should not become chargeable upon the State, which the captain was not prepared to do, he proceeded with them to this port.; Came up from quarantine during week prior 24th July
Return of money and effects of deceased emigrants received at Saint John Emigration Office during the season of 1847: "Seraph", William Pine, £19 5 0, claimed by Mary Lonergan, sister of the deceased.; Month of July. Ibid *New Brunswick Courier*

[68] Return of money and effects of deceased emigrants received at Saint John Emigration Office during the season of 1847: Hugh Boyce, *Sir C. Napier*, Londonderry, £43 0 0, claimed

Susan[69]	Beerhaven	-
Thorney Close[70]	Donegal May 23	James Horan
Trafalgar[71] June 5	Cork July 15	Younghusband
Rev. Theobold Matthew	Galway July 3	Yorke

---

by Hugh Boyce, only surviving son of deceased, Rev. Robert Irvine, Trustee.
See Ibid. Emigrants From Derry Port 1847-49 page 11 for passenger list booking 17 March - 29 April 1847

[69] 24th July at Quarantine 18 ill, 3 deaths during voyage Ibid. *New Brunswick Courier*

[70] We, the undernamed passengers of the brig *Thorney Close* from Donegal to St. John, N.B., are deputed by the rest of our fellow passengers to return Capt. James Horan our heartfelt thanks for his kind and prompt attention to us during the time we were sea-sick; and when death spread his devouring shaft amongst us and carried away six children and one woman, by name Mrs. Magwood, there was he to be seen, comforting and consoling the invalids under their sad misfortune. We have also to return to each and every man who served him our grateful thanks for their civility and attention to us when sea-sick. (sgd) Farrel Brogan, Walter Long, Richard McGee, Billy McCownly, William Brogan, Francis Colgan, Robert McJunkin, Condy Breslin, St. John, June 17th, 1847. - Ibid. *New Brunswick Courier*

[71] 24th July at Quarantine. The passengers with a few exceptions have been landed at Partridge Island, they being infected with a disease of an infectious nature. The vessel is reported to have come up from Quarantine 31st July
Return of money and effects of deceased emigrants received at Saint John Emigration Office during the season of 1847: Michael Foley, ship *Trafalgar*, Cork, £4 1 0, remitted to Lt. Friend, Government Emigration Officer, Cork, and by him paid to Rev. Thos. O'Sullivan, P.P. , Killarney for father of the deceased.
Thomas Ritson, age 20, an apprentice on board Brig *Trafalgar* was drowned by falling from that vessel at the Breakwater on Tuesday night last. He was a native of Maryport, England. Ibid. *New Brunswick Courier* 31 July 1847

Ward Chipman[72]   Cork   July 22   Bilton
Yeoman[73]   July 13   Sligo   -   Purden

---

[72] 24th July at Quarantine. There were 23 deaths on board this vessel during the voyage and four since the vessel arrived at Quarantine. There are 40 passengers at present ill with fever. On 31st July it is reported that fever was increasing among the passengers and crew of the *Ward Chipman.* Ibid. *New Brunswick Courier*

[73] At quarantine 20th August. 2 deaths on passage. 30 cases of fever
During the past week (prior 28th August) The barque *Yeoman* from Sligo has landed 500 emigrants from Sir Robert Gore Booth estate (Lissadell near Sligo). The passengers by the *Yeoman* have been well fed and cared for on the voyage; a week's rations was furnished them on landing and they were then left to shift for themselves. Ibid. *New Brunswick Courier*

APPENDIX III

Emigrants of Charlotte County 1842

The following Petitions were obtained from the Journals of the House of Assembly for New Brunswick

To His Excellency Lieutenant Colonel Sir William McBean George Colebrooke K.H. Lieutenant Governor of the Province of New Brunswick &c &c &c [P.A.N.B. RS 8 Microfilm F7890]

The Petition of James M. Chandler, Peter Smith, Thomas Berry, Thomas Sime and John Parkinson, Commissioners of the Saint Andrews Alms and Poor House, and Overseers of the Poor for the Parish of Saint Andrews in the County of Charlotte, Humbly Sheweth,

That the Alms and Work House at Saint Andrews was originally intended for the benefit and devoted to the use of the Poor of the Parish of Saint Andrews, but that about fifteen years ago a practice began of receiving into the said Alms House Emigrant or foreign paupers, for the subsistence of whom the Legislature annually made provision to reimburse the Commissioners of the said Alms House.

That rents and other funds are appropriated to the support of the Parish Poor which would, with prudent management (and an occasional small assessment) be amply sufficient for their maintenance; but owing to the introduction of Emigrant Poor the expenses of the Alms House are much increased, and as the reimbursement for the latter is always long postponed, the effect has been to enhance the prices of supplies - occasion frequent assessments - and produce general dissatisfaction among the Parishioners.

That owing to this state of things your Petitioners are in debt about Five Hundred Pounds, of which the whole is due to them for the past support of Emigrant Poor.

That the duties thus devolving upon your petitioners (for which they receive no compensation) are so onerous that they cannot, without neglecting their own private business, perform them any longer, and compels them to call for a separation of the Emigrant from the Parish Poor.

Your Petitioners therefore respectfully beg leave to draw your Excellency's attention to the subject, and solicit you to devise some mode or system by which the Parish of Saint Andrews may be relieved from the care and maintenance of the Emigrant Poor, and that they may be placed in a separate Establishment, and under the exclusive control of suitable persons to be appointed for that purpose. But provided that your Excellency would order funds to be placed in the hands of the Treasurer, out of which your Petitioners could draw quarterly, to reimburse them for the advances as they accrue, then, the union of the Emigrant and Parish Poor would not be so severely felt, and the affairs of the Establishment would more smoothly on. The adoption of either of their two methods would relieve the embarrassments under which the Overseers of the Poor have to labor - but the system at present pursued cannot be longer endured - and your Petitioners with every respect beg leave to say that unless they can be aided by your Excellency in providing that one or other of the above named suggestions be carried into effect for their accommodation, in managing the Emigrants, and the affairs therewith connected, that your Petitioners will be compelled to decline the reception of any more Emigrants into the Poor House Establishment, and they will consequently be thrown upon the public for support. And your Petitioners as in duty bound will ever pray. - Saint Andrews, 11th January 1843

To His Excellency Lieutenant Colonel Sir William McBean George Colebrooke K.H. Lieutenant Governor of the Province of New Brunswick &c &c &c[P.A.N.B. RS 8 Microfilm F7890]

The Petition of J.M. Chandler, Peter Smith, Thomas Berry, Thomas Sime and John Parkinson, Commissioners of the Alms and Work House, and Overseers of the Poor for the Parish of Saint Andrews in the County of Charlotte, Humbly Sheweth,
   That by the accompanying accounts it will be seen that for the support of the Emigrant Poor, and other necessary outlays advanced on their behalf from the eleventh day of January 1842 to the tenth day of January, Instant, both days inclusive, your petitioners have expended the sum of Six hundred and thirty five pounds, twelve shillings and ten pence.
   That a large portion of these Emigrants were passengers in Vessels which arrived during the season, and became chargeable to the Parish in consequence of illness and indigent circumstances; and that of those who came by one vessel from Ireland in the month of June last, were upwards of Forty Individuals whose passages were defrayed by an extensive Landholder (to get quit of them off his Estate) and landed here in a state of absolute Pauperism: the major part without clothing of any kind suitable for the climate, and the whole destitute of both money and food. The immediate consequence was, that they became chargeable to the parish and your Excellency will see upon reference to our lists, from the 23rd day of June onwards, the names and numbers of those admitted into the poor house, and that three distinct families of the name of

Sheean compose twenty members thereof. Your petitioners are convinced that in the charge p. week they do not exceed the sum which it has cost to maintain each person, and therefore humbly pray that your Excellency would be pleased to take the premises into your favorable consideration and grant them the sum of Six hundred and thirty five pounds, twelve shillings and ten pence, to reimburse them for their expenditure. An as in duty bound will ever pray. - Saint Andrews, January 26th, 1843

Emigrants	Commence 1842	Terminate 1842	From Whence arrived
Lawrence Kerr	11 Jany.	5 July	Saint John
Fanny Kerr	11 Jany.	5 July	do
Daniel Mohany	11 Jany.	12 Jany	do
Kitty Mohany	11 Jany.	26 Sep.	do
Mary Mohany	11 Jany.	26 Sep.	do
Ellen Branagan	11 Jany.	18 July	do
Nancy McAlgar	11 Jany.	26 July	do
John McAlgar	11 Jany.	26 July	do
Mary Luin	11 Jany.	12 Dec.	do
Mary Luin Junr.	11 Jany.	12 Dec.	do
Margaret Luin	11 Jany.	12 Dec.	do
Ann Luin	11 Jany.	12 Dec.	do
Patrick Luin	11 Jany.	12 Dec.	do
Mary Morgan	11 Jany.	8 June	do
Mary Morgan Junr.	11 Jany.	8 June	do
William Morgan	11 Jany.	8 June	do
Ellen Morgan	11 Jany.	8 June	do
Dennis Morgan	11 Jany.	8 June	do
Terence Branagan	23 Jany.	18 July	do
Daniel McKay	7 Feby.	3 May	do
Elizabeth Mann	4 April	23 May	do
Joanna Mann	18 April	9 May	do
Daniel Mohany	16 April	26 Sep.	do
Charles Finnigan	24 May	23 June	do
Ellen Finnigan	24 May	23 June	do
Julia Finnigan	24 May	23 June	do
William Wallace	6 June	19 Sep.	Cork p. *Pallas*
Timothy Donahue	8 June	21 July	Saint John
Kitty Donahue	8 June	21 July	do
Kitty Donahue Junr.	8 June	21 July	do
Elizabeth Ash	15 June	10 July	do

Appendix III - Emigrants of Charlotte County • 229

Mary Ash	15 June	10 July	do
Bridget Sullivan	15 June	22 June	Cork
			p. *Pallas*
Humphrey Sullivan	15 June	22 June	do
Daniel Sheean Senr.	23 June	Remains	Cork
			p. *Eliza Ann*
Mary Sheean 1st	23 June	Remains	do
Ellen Sheean	23 June	Remains	do
Joanna Sheean Junr.	23 June	10 Sept.	do
Mary Sheean 2nd	23 June	Remains	do
Daniel Sheehan Junr.	23 June	Remains	do
Ellen Turnbull	24 June	21 July	do
Joseph Turnbull	24 June	21 July	do
Francis Turnbull	24 June	21 July	do
James Turnbull	24 June	21 July	do
William Finton	24 June	Remains	do
Mary Finton	24 June	Remains	do
Owen Finton	24 June	Remains	do
Margaret Finton	24 June	Remains	do
John Sheean	25 June	28 June	do
Judy Sheean	25 June	10 Sep.	do
Catherine Sheean 1st	25 June	10 Sep.	do
Jerry Sheean Senr.	27 June	28 June	do
Mary Sheean 3rd	27 June	Remains	do
Michael Sheean	27 June	Remains	do
Jerry Sheean Junr.	27 June	Remains	do
Thomas Sheean	27 June	Remains	do
Catherine Sheean 2nd	27 June	Remains	do
Patrick Sheean	27 June	Remains	do
Edward Sheean	27 June	Remains	do
Catherine Sheean 3rd	27 June	Remains	do
Barbara Sheean	27 June	30 June	do
Joanna Sheean	27 June	30 June	do
Catherine McCarty	27 June	12 July	do
John McCarty	27 June	12 July	do
Margaret Connell	28 June	1 Aug.	do
Patrick Connell	28 June	11 Sep.	do
Joanna Shay	29 June	10 Oct.	do
Catherine Shay	29 June	10 Oct.	do
William Shay	29 June	10 Oct.	do
Elizabeth Shay	29 June	10 Oct.	do
Ellen Shay	29 June	10 Oct.	do
John Moore	6 July	18 July	Saint John

230 • The Irish Emigrants

Bridget Clary	9 July	Remains	Cork
			p. *Eliza Ann*
Margaret Clary	9 July	Remains	do
Catherine Clary	9 July	Remains	do
Michael Clary	9 July	Remains	do
Garritt Fitzgerald	13 July	26 Sep.	Saint John
Jerry Sheean	2 Aug.	Remains	Cork
			p. *Eliza Ann*
Edward Sheean Senr.	19 July	2 May	do
James Ash	26 Aug.	10 Oct.	Saint John
Elizabeth Ash	26 Aug.	Remains	do
Mary Ash	26 Aug.	Remains	do
Catherine O'Brien	6 Sep.	4 Nov.	Jamaica
			p. *Volant*
Mary Ann O'Brien	6 Sep.	4 Nov.	do
Wheeney O'Brien	6 Sep.	4 Nov.	do
Margaret Stanton	6 Sep.	9 Dec.	do
Thomas Stanton	6 Sep.	9 Dec.	do
Mary Stanton	6 Sep.	9 Dec.	do
Bridget Stanton	6 Sep.	9 Dec.	do
Catherine Fleming	9 Sep.	Remains	do
Winnifred Ash	2 Nov.	Remains	Saint John
Patrick Stanton	18 Nov.	9 Dec.	Jamaica
			p. *Volant*
James McGowan	15 Dec.	Remains	Saint John

I certify that the foregoing list of Emigrants has been examined by me and that the number therein enumerated Fifty five came passengers in vessels which entered at this Port during the last season, Treasury Office, Saint Andrew (signed) 26 January 1843, David W. Jack, Dy. Treasurer & Act. Emigrant Agent.

To His Excellency Sir William MacBean George Colebrooke K.H. Lieutenant Governor and Commander in Chief of the Province of New Brunswick &c &c &c

To The Honorable the Legislative Council and To the Honorable the House of Assembly of New Brunswick

The undersigned Petitioners, Overseers of the Poor for the Parish of Saint George in the County of Charlotte, Humbly beg, that your Honorable Bodies will reimburse them from the Emigrant fund for advances made to a number of Emigrants, lately arrived in this Province and became sick and destitute in the Parish of Saint George the past year per the accompany Affidavits and Accounts, Amounting to Forty six pounds, two shillings and sixpence. And as in duty bound will ever pray - Saint George, N.B., February 10th, 1842 (signed) Justus Wetmore, John E. Messenette

Statement of Sundry Advances made to Emigrants by the Overseers of the Poor for thr Parish of Saint George per annexed receipts - Saint George, February 10th, 1842

Paid Charles Brawley for keeping Mary Daley and child from July to 4th February, 23 weeks
Dr. Robert Thomson's Bill for attending Mary Daley and child

Paid David Sturgeon for keeping Norah O'Leary and child, 5 weeks
Dr. Robert Thomson's Bill for attending Norah O'Leary and child in sickness
Cash advances Norah O'Leary to assist her and child to proceed to the United States

Cash advanced Jane Maginnis to assist her out of the County, being a distressed Emigrant

Provisions and clothing furnished Thomas Berry, wife and child
Paid John Jordan for attending the above partie
Dr. Robert Thomson's Bill for medical attendance on the above man, Thomas Berry

APPENDIX IV

Be Cautious With Passenger Lists

Be Cautious With Passenger Lists

by Terrence M. Punch, C.G.(C)

North Americans generally sigh with relief when they find the name of an ancestor on a ship's passenger list. There is a sense that the *Progenitor* has been found. Now they can look for his family in America after a certain date with confidence. They know the year of his arrival, the name of the ship, the port from which he sailed and possibly other details.

The purpose of this little homily is not so much to spoil your satisfaction as it is to warn you that passenger lists frequently provide misinformation, some of it mistaken enough to derail a genealogical search. Passenger lists are also guilty at times of creating non-existent persons, and misplacing real ones. If passenger lists have been published, there is the added danger of careless transcription, of compilers working with poor textual or microform material, of perpetuation of errors in the primary source.

Consider the perils that existed when the original document was being created. Perhaps the passengers spoke Gaelic or German and the recording clerk did not, or did so only very imperfectly. Perhaps the immigrants spoke English with an accent or a brogue through which the hapless clerk could not hear, so he wrote down what it *sounded like*. Of course, in the 1840 he wrote by hand and transcribers have to know when a certain squiggle conveyed an "n" and when a "u". Possibly the information was taken down in the open air or on a wharf or in an echoing warehouse, or conceivably in a rush, with the shipmaster pacing up and down waiting for the wind and tide to be just right. Perhaps there were throngs of noisy or frightened people milling about; in the Irish famine years that is easy to conceive. Was the immigrant reducing the declared age of his 14 year old to save on fare? Or, was the shipping clerk trying to squeeze a few more people aboard than by rights should have been carried. Given these circumstances, the accuracy of any list should be questioned by the researcher as a routine precaution.

[To illustrate, Mr. Punch compares the place names, personal names, and ages associated with the vessel Envoy" of 1847, drawn from three publications, namely, J. Elizabeth Cushing's, **A**

The Irish Emigrants: Port of Saint John, New Brunswick, Canada

Chronicle of Irish Emigration to Saint John 1847, a compilation of information drawn principally from the New Brunswick Courier; Mitchell's Emigrants From Derry Port 1847-9 and Baker's Irish Passenger Lists 1847-1871.]

To give some idea of the degree of difference, suffice it to say that only 168 entries agreed completely of the 259, 266 and 276 entries reported. Discrepancies amount to over 35 percent, ranging from minor errors to the more serious matter of omissions of entire family groups.

In some cases there are simple misspellings easily detected with a gazetteer. Thus Ballyconnoll turns out to be Ballyconnell and Duran is Durian. Drunon is found to be Dromen. In another case, Ballymoney may be a place in Antrim, or any of three communities in Derry or the one in Donegal; likewise Eden has three Derry locations, as well as one each in Donegal and Tyrone. Referring to the indexes of the Tithe Applotments or the Griffith Valuation might assist in identifying the relevant place name.

Mitchell and Harris are not in agreement on place names *per se*. Mitchell lists a William Brown from Newtownstewart and Eleanor Moore from Ballymagory, while Baker derives them from Limavady and Strabane, respectively. In eight places Mitchell gives a place name where Baker is blank, and in three cases the reverse is true. With regard to personal names, there are obvious differences in spelling, such as Mitchell's Nilly, Hannah and Ellan versus Baker's Nelly, Hannagh and Ellen.

Since those under 13 years of age travelled as children, only the ages of the young are given in the passenger list of the "Envoy" in 1847. Thomas Doyle and Mary McManus are not assigned an age in Mitchell, but in Baker appear aged 3 and 13 respectively. Hugh(y) McFadden and Terence Little are aged 1 in Mitchell, 1½ in Baker.

Mitchell's list has 266 passengers on board the "Envoy", seven more than given in Baker's version. On August 21, 1847, the *New Brunswick Courier* carries a card of thanks on behalf of the passengers of the "Envoy". Of the thirty-two men who signed

Appendix IV - Caution With Passenger Lists

the testimonial, four names appear in neither of Mitchell's nor Baker's lists. (see Appendix II Emigrant Vessel Footnotes) Possibly they had travelled as regular cabin passengers and as such, did not appear in the clerk's list. In any case, they account for some further part of the discrepancy in the overall figures reported in our three sources. If any of these four had been accompanied by a wife or child the total number would be affected yet again. The *New Brunswick Courier* reported the deaths of several "Envoy" passengers at the hospital on Partridge Island between August and November 1847 (see Chapter XIII). Four of the names are not found in any of our aforementioned lists. These omissions suggest an element of carelessness or haste.

To recaptulate
Names on the list reported by Baker   259
Additional names found in Mitchell   7
New names found on card of thanks   4
New names found among deaths on Partridge Island   4
Number of persons remaining unnamed   2

Total number of passengers alleged to have been aboard the "Envoy"   276

The purpose of this exercise has been to illustrate the imperfect nature of passenger lists. Those making use of such nominal rolls should approach them with caution.

INDEX

unknown
  Bridget 83
Adrian
  James 38
Aherrin
  Daniel 97
Aikin
  Francis 72
  Henry 12
  Martin 96
Allan
  Catherine 95
  Mary 166
Allen
  Catherine 137
  Margt A. 50
  Mary Ann 58
  Pat 126
  Patrick 27
  Tim 157
Ambrose
  Mary 164
Ames
  Bridt 50
Anderson
  Jane 187
  Mary Jane 187
  William 73
Anglin
  Timothy 17, 32
Ansley
  Daniel 216
Armstrong
  Diana 63
  Emily 79
  James 57
  Jane 17, 23, 28
  Jas 48
  John 21
  Mary 79
  Rachel 61
  Richd 34
  Robert 36
Ash

  Elizabeth 228, 230
  James 230
  Mary 229, 230
  Winnifred 230
Ashburn
  John 47
Atkins
  Harriet 64
Badger
  Pat 95
Baird
  Saml 77
Baker
  Margt 78
  Thomas 90
Balin
  Razo 97
Ballentine
  Eliza 74
Bamson
  Bridt 49
Bannon
  Mary 14
Bar
  Ellen 133
Baran
  Michael 98
Barber
  John 70
Barker
  Thos 102
Barnan
  Alli 118
  Anne 118, 174
  Biddy 118
  Catherine 118
  Libby 118
  Margaret 118
  Wm 118
Barnes
  Cecilia 185
  Mary 129
Barret

  Danl 51
  Ellen 81
  Julia 61
  Margt 41
  Patrick 48, 57
  William 97
Barrett
  Captain 208
  Edmund 89
  John 159
Barrey
  Catherine 68
  Ellen 67
  James 68
  Patrick 67
Barry
  Catherine 35
  Ellen 33
  Ellen 2d 35
  Ellen Jr 33
  James 35
  Joanna 49
  Mary 35, 46, 175
  Michael 125
  Patrick 33, 61
Bartley
  Eliza 173
Basset
  Danniel 59
Bateman
  Ann 46, 56
  Richd 78
Bates
  Nancy 19
Bazillon
  Ann 21
Beatty
  Eliza 48, 57
  Mary 95
  Mary J. 21
  William 103
Beck
  Matthew 23
Beegan

Patrick 216
Belford
  Anne 119
Bell
  James 22, 25
  Louisa 18
  Mary 12
Bennett
  Walter 126
Bentley
  Bridget 177
  ➤Pat 177
  Robt 177
  Samuel 17
Berne
  Ellen 121
  Sarah 120
Berry
  Thomas 231
Biggers
  Martha 18
Biggs
  John 21
Bingham
  Samuel 185
Bird
  Margaret 26, 29
Birmingham
  Sarah 61
Bishopson
  Bridt 38
Black
  Jane 11
  John 11
Blackson
  Thos 103
Blair
  John 216
  Lewis 180
  Sarah 18
  William 218
Blake
  Cath 181
  Catherine 24

Kate 182
  Margt 35, 46
  Mary 68
Blaney
  John 160
Blarney
  James 160
Bleurey
  Dan 161
  Ellen 161
Bloomfield
  Alex. 14
Bochan
  Bridget 123
  Ellen 176, 181
  Jane 176
  Jno 181
  Laurence 123
  Mary 123, 181
  Mrs 181
Bodkin
  Jno 132
Bohan
  Patrick 49
Boice
  Thomas 21
Bonor
  Danl 160
  John 160
Booth
  Henry Gore 214
  Sir Robert Gore 214, 220, 224
Bourke
  John 128, 132, 168
Bowen
  Mary 160
  William 23
Bowes
  Thos 116
Bowler
  ⁻ Mary 90
Bowles

Cathe 31
Boyce
  Ann 94
  Hugh 99, 222
  Thomas 28
Boyd
  James 65
  Jane 31, 60
  Margaret 65
Boyer
  Thos 99
  Will 99
Boyle
  Ann 52, 60
  Bridget 25
  Bridt 29
  Charles 27
  Henry 135
  Isabella 48, 57
  James 14, 135
  Jno 84
  John 135, 168
  Patrick 215
  Peggy 168
Br
  John 25
Bracken
  John 36
Braden
  Catherine 11
  Thomas 11
Bradley
  John 30, 38
  Sarah 150
Bradly
  John 218
Brady
  Mary 42
  Sarah 18, 19, 26
Branagan
  Ellen 228
  Terence 228
Brandon
  Timoy 41

Brandy
  John 173
Branley
  Ann 145
  John 173
  Wm 165
Branna
  Mary 135
Brannan
  Hanna 135
  Mary 135
  Sarah 94
Brannen
  Ann 143
  Cath 116
  James 116
  John 181
  Mary 143, 153
Bratten
  James 161
Brawley
  Charles 231
Bray
  Honora 94
Brecken
  George 37
Breen
  Michl 42
Brelian
  Michael 140
Brenen
  John 66
  Mary 66
Brennan
  Danl 42
  James 116
  Margt 19
  Mary 16
Brennen
  Cathe 26
  Catherine 16
  Michael 16
  Patrick 15, 25
Brennin

Catherine 135
Breslin
  Condy 223
  Constantia 97
Bresnahan
  Dan 152
  Debora 152
  Gubby 154
  Jerry 152
  Mary 48, 51, 57, 59
  Michl 152
  Patk 152
  Patt 152
Bresnahen
  Betty 152
  Mary 152
Brian
  Maurice 47, 56
Brick
  Patrick 184
Brickley
  David 30
Brickly
  Jeremh 27
Bridgeon
  Christr. 13
Brien
  Denis 42, 52
  Ellen 34, 170
  John 43
  Judy 138
  Mary 34
  Michl 56
  Patrick 18, 34, 43, 55
Brine
  Patrick 170
Briskley
  Thomas 22
Brochan
  Cath 123
Broderick
  Biddy 134

Ellen 133
Mary 39
Maurice 162
Patrick 139
Brogan
  Farrel 223
  William 223
Brosnehan
  John 210
Brown
  Annie 179
  Catherine 128
  David 21
  Eliza 31, 54
  Eliza J. 31
  Ellen 171
  Honora 179
  John 71, 140
  Kitty 141
  Margaret 179
  Margt 179
  Mary 78, 179
  Michl 179
  Penelope 32
  Sarah 32, 39
  widow 179
Bruen
  thomas 162
Bryan
  Catherine 59
  Ellen 104, 176
  Honoria 40
  John 104
  Mary 34
Bryant
  Bridget 89
  Harry 12
  Wm 81, 89
Bryen
  Cathe 50
Brymer
  Mary 68
Bryne
  Ellen 47

Bryson
  Jane 16
Buchanan
  Robert 62
  Robt 30, 39
Buckley
  And 165
  Bridget 54
  Daniel 104
  Ellen 161
  Hanora 42
  Jane 74
  John 74, 161
  Murty 161
  Nancy 74
Buke
  Margaret 42
Bulger
  Bridget 142
  Margaret 142
  Michl 142
Bunting
  Rowland 72
Burk
  Bridget 147
  Ellen 183
  John 47, 182
Burke
  Ann 144
  Catherine 33, 61
  Denis 165
  Ellen 52, 60, 140
  Jno 132
  John 34, 44, 45, 57, 102
  Margaret 114
  Margt 43
  Mary 37, 53
  Patrick 23, 33, 58
  Peter 13
  Richard 211
  Sarah 128
  Thomas 39, 54
Burne
  Mary 87
Burnes
  John 40
Burns
  John 102, 216
  Margaret 26, 29
  Margt 19
  Mary 51, 147
  Pat 149
  Unity 100
Burr
  C. 74
Burton
  Robert 162
Bustard
  Andrew 60
  Andrw 32
  Charles 218
  Frances 43, 57
  Margt 38, 49
Butin
  Mary 103
Butler
  John 117
  Margaret 174
Byrne
  Anthony 87
  Jno 84
  John 93
  Margaret 84
  Mary 84
  Mary Jr 87
  Pat 149
Byrnes
  Bridget 183
  Mrs 78
Cadogan
  Dan 186
  Ellen 152
Cafferty
  Anthony 185
Cagan
  Eliza 54
Cahal
Patrick 54
Cahall
  Patrick 41
Cahil
  Martin 161
Cahill
  John 169, 171
Cain
  Biddy 88
  Cate 157
  Ellen 85
  Julia 130
  Margt 172
  Mary 77
  Mary O. 36
  Michl 30
  Sally 186
Cainey
  Peggy 176
Cairnworth
  Ann 14
Call
  Bridget 56
  Bridt 46
Callaghan
  Edwd 50
  Francis 36
  Margt 48
  Mary 42, 107, 125, 131
  Michael 181
  Mick 102
  Stephen 44
  Thos 41
  Timothy 32
Callahan
  Denis 44
  Edward 59
  Francis 61
  J. 56
  Margt 52
  Mary 51, 59
  Michael 185
  Patk 33

Stephen 46
Callander
  Bridt 25
Callender
  Bridt 19
Calone
  Brian 114
  Denis 114
Calvin
  Sarah 102
Cameron
  Mary 95
Campbell
  Ann 85
  Biddy 110
  Bridget 138
  Cath 110
  Daniel 19
  Edward 218
  Geo 93
  Hugh 17, 21
  Jane 16, 24
  John 173
  Patk 99
  Robt 17
  Willm 22
Cane
  Gabriel 66
  Mary 185
  Sally 188
Capels
  Anne 138
Carberry
  John 74
Carey
  Adelaide 119
  Cath 77
  Catherine 43, 155
  Ellen 24
  George Thomas 218
  James 155
  Johanna 164
  John 211

Lewis 77
Carleton
  Sally 145
  Sarah A. 74
  Wid 145
Carlin
  Richd 39, 58
  Rosa 44
Carmoney
  Edwd 48
Carney
  Bridget 134
  Catherine 150
  Ellen 19
  James 100
  Johanna 137, 150
  Judy 134
  Mary 136, 137, 149
  Miche 53
  Nicholas 133
Carolane
  Dan 108
  Kitty 111
  Mary 111
  Peggy 112
  Roger 109
  Thomas 108
Carr
  Catherine 117
  James 18, 24, 26
  Mary 117
  Michael 1st 40
  Michael 2nd 40
  Peter 120
  Susan 25
  Wm 169
Carrel
  Nich 102
Carrick
  Patrick 39, 54
Carrigan
  Dorah 21
Carrington

Michael 105
Carrol
  Charles 74
  Ellen 81
  James 14
  John 41
  John 2d 23
  Pat 47, 176
  Patrick 57
  Phelix 176
  William 47, 48, 57
Carroll
  Thomas 158
Carry
  Michael 103
Carson
  Eliza 167
  George 23
  John 14
  Margt 36
Carter
  Alice 25, 28
  John 72
  Michl 43
Carthy
  Mary 125
  Paddy 114
  Patk 85
Carty
  Dennis 211
  Ellen 18, 33
  Honoria 41, 42
  Jerry 169
  Joanna 35, 46
  John 77
  Joseph 30
  Margaret 98
  Mary 36, 53, 98
  Patrick 35
Casey
  Ellen 154
  James 150
  John 150, 154, 156, 177

Kitty 150
Margaret 43
Margt 45
Mary 142, 154
Thomas 142
William 142
Cassidy
  Ann 12, 23, 62, 72
  Bernard 119
  Cornelius 17
  Cornelius Jr 17
  Corns 19
  Corns Jr. 17
  James 138
  Margaret 17
  Mary 145
  Pat 144
  Sarah 102
  Tom 145
Cassin
  John 44
Cassine
  T. 55
  Timothy 43
Catten
  Ellen 99
Caulfield
  James 27
  Peter 119
  Unity 76
Cavanagh
  Catherine 117
  Mary 117
  William 217
Cavenagh
  Ellen 171
Caveny
  Catherine 45, 56, 162
Cavil
  Ann 59
Chambers
  William 186

Cherry
  William 102
Chittick
  Catharine 11
  Thomas 11
Chute
  Bowen 50, 59
  Jane 58
Cilcannon
  Michael 103
Clance
  Mary 98
Clancey
  Cath 166
  Catherine 166
  Eliza 166
  Ellen 166
  Judy 166
  Mary 166
  Norry 166
  Pat 116
  Peggy 166
Clancy
  Biddy 173
  Bridget 136
  Cecilia 145
  Patrick 153
  Thos 130
  Wm 166
Clansey
  Margt 43
Clare
  James 184
  Thomas 119
Clark
  Daniel 103
  Geo 182
  Thomas 182
Clarke
  Ann 14
  Anne 160
  Bridt 21
  Jane 50
  Jas 32

  Margt 32
  Martin 94
  Patrick 50
  Peter 63
  Saml 71
  Samuel 16
  Thomas 14, 42, 50, 98
  William 218
Clary
  Bridget 230
  Catherine 230
  Margaret 230
  Michael 230
Clearcy
  Denis 169
  Pat 169
Cleary
  Cathe 36
  Catherine 49
  Daniel 217
  Denis 50, 58
  James 36
  John 22
  Thomas 36
Clelan
  Edward 89
  Mary 80
Clementy
  John 124
Clifford
  Edwd 24
  James 119
  Judy 120
  Mary 46, 56
  Michael 94
  Morgan 61
  Rosa 44
  Timothy 44
  Tom 181
Clougher
  John 13
Coakley
  Johanna 164

Mary 164
Thomas 164
Tim 164
Coan
  Dennis 120
  Dennis Jr 120
  John 91, 120
  Margaret 120
  Mary 107, 120
Coburt
  John 116
Cochrane
  Mary 100
Coff
  Mary 105
Coffee
  Catherine 41
  John 44, 96
  John 2d 47
  Julia 121
  Mary 42
  Michael 54
  Michl 40
Coffey
  Ann 168
  Catherine 120
  Conels 171
  Judy 120
Cogan
  Perez 62
  William 25, 28
Coil
  Bridget 94
  Cathe 18
  Jane 48, 57
Cole
  Edmond 146
Coleman
  Andrew 159
  Ann 95
  Eliza 130
  Elizabeth 24
  Ellen 187
  Hannah 130

James 75
Mary 47, 57
Mrs 209
Timothy 26
Timoy 29
Widow 133
William 64
Colgan
  Francis 223
Collings
  Catherine 69
Collins
  Abby 141
  Catherine 25, 63, 99, 170, 174
  Edmond 171
  Ellen 77
  Hanora 171
  Honoria 35
  James 162, 171
  Jno 82
  Joana 45
  John 49, 57, 154, 170
  Mary 23, 34, 52, 82, 159
  Mich 141
  Michael 152
  Norrie 82
  Patrick 171
Colman
  Mary Ann 73
Colter
  Julia 80
  William 17
Common
  Rebecca 34, 45, 56
Commons
  Pat 183
Condahy
  Bridget 59
Conden
  John 83

Condon
  Mary 174
Condray
  Jas 145
Conelly
  Marcus 155
  Mic 173
  Pat 178
  Phelix 173
Conley
  Patrick 94
  Winny 94
Conlie
  Biddy 115
Connel
  John 40
  Julia 82
  Margt 52
  Mary 52
  Michael 36
  Michl 18, 40, 46
Connell
  Anne 130
  Bartholomew 105
  Biddy 163
  Bridget 105
  Catherine 35
  Edwd 128
  Jerry 156
  Joana 19, 28
  John 80, 218
  Margaret 229
  Margt 42
  Mary 30, 35, 107
  Michael 35
  Michl 30
  Patrick 229
  Wm 150
Connelly
  Bridget 11
  Cathe 16
  D. 11
  Daniel 60
  Danl 124

Frances 11
James 172
John 146
Margaret 147
Margt 147
Tho. 11
Wm 11
Conner
  Catherine 24
  Ellen 30, 68
  James 56
  Margaret 82
  Mary 68, 86, 90
  Michl 91
  Roger 78
  William 100
Conners
  Ann 153
  Austen 121
  Austin 123
  Henry 167
  James 141, 165
  John 128, 146
  Mary 172
  Pat 168
  Sally 111
  Thomas 141
Connolly
  Biddy 154
  Brien 35
  Cathe 17
  Connolly 41
  Daniel 31
  Danl 31
  Ellen 34, 45
  Ellen Jr 34
  Frances 31
  Francis 31
  J. 54
  Joseph 31, 60
  Mary 34, 35
  Michl 18
  Pat 49
  Patrick 58

Peter 35, 46, 58
Thomas 31
Tim 77
William 31
Connor
  Bridget 104
  Denis 114
  Eleanor 19
  James 45
  Jeremh 45
  Jerry 47
  Julia 40
  Margaret 141
  Mary 59, 91, 141
  Mathew 165
  Michael 147
  Pat 101
  Pat] 101
  Timothy 97
Connors
  Biddy 158
  Catherine 188
  Honora 188
  Hugh 134, 159
  Mary 51, 169
  Michael 188
  Patrick 114
Connory
  Pat 148
Conny
  Bridget 99
Conohan
  Margt 88
  Tim 80, 81
Conolly
  Ann 156
  Catherine 154
  John 144
  Pat 148
  Terence 218
  Thomas 39
Conoroy
  John 117
Conray

James 143
Consader
  Darby 146
Consadin
  Darby 146
Consadine
  Michl 32
Constantine
  Jane 34, 40
Conway
  And 162
  Anne 163
  Cath 143
  Cathe 42, 51
  Honoria 33
  Johanna 119
  John 92
  Joseph 105
  Libby 163
  Mary 42, 55
  Michl 162
  Nailon 146
  Pat 149
  Sarah 19, 119
Cook
  Catherine 26
  Elizabeth 86
  Isabella 18
Cooke
  John 23, 122
Cooley
  Pat 40
Coomie
  Patrick 147
Cooney
  Johanna 174
  Pat 51
  Patrick 59
  Wm 178
Cooper
  Hannah 19
  Mary 10, 11, 37
  Peter 94
Copland

Samuel 162
Coram
  Charles 96
Corcannon
  Thomas 95
Corcoran
  Danl 53
  Ellen 42
  Thomas 57
  Thos 44
Cordey
  Margaret 131
Corigan
  Betty 110
Corker
  Mary 12
Corkeran
  Mary 129
Corkum
  Kit 164
Corney
  John 217
  Michael 217
Cornwall
  Mansfield 14
Corr
  George 96
Corragan
  Con 94
Corrigan
  John 97
  Owen 97
Corritt
  Margt 110
Corryan
  Mary 97
Cosh
  John 63
Coslin
  Patrick 146
Costello
  Ann 147
  Biddy 146
  Bridgt 146

John 169, 171
Margt 148
Mary 97
Michael 146
Pieacey 116
Terrence 144
Cotter
  James 126
  Mary 136
Cotton
  Charles 99
Couchlin
  John 166
Coughlan
  Catherine 33
  Cornelius 38
  Corns 32, 41, 55
  Ellen 33, 38
  James 24, 33
  John 33, 154
  Judy 47
  Julia 33
  Mary 32, 48
  Mary Jane 33
  Michl 82
  Pat 164
Coughlin
  Chas 170
  Margaret 99
  Mary 178
  Owen 95
Courtney
  Ellen 50, 58
  George 24, 28
Coveney
  Cathe 18
  John 18
Cox
  Mary 19
Coyle
  Catharine 13
  Hugh 161
Coyne
  Cecilia 172

John 179
Crade
  Patrick 100
Cradock
  Mary 43
Craig
  John 97
  Margaret 96
Crain
  Darby 135
Cramer
  Frances 23
Cranan
  John 46
Crane
  John 122
  John L. 209
Crann
  Catherine 115
  Hanna 135
  Kitty 135
  Mary 115, 135
Crawford
  Jas 92
  Robt 92
  Sarah 19
Crayon
  Corns 41
Creamer
  Margt 38
Crean
  Hugh 217
Creary
  William 19
Creighton
  Thomas 60
  Thos 52
Cremar
  Joanna 158
Cremins
  Thomas 125
Cremmins
  Patrick 125
Crimmins

John 17
Mary 22
Mary 2d 45
Cristal
  Hugh 215
Crocket
  William 34
Crofts
  Ellen 165
Crolly
  John 157
Cronan
  Libby 110
  Mary 110
Cronin
  Bridget 31
  Catherine 31, 61
  Elizabeth 31, 39, 54
  Francis 108
  Hanora 112
  Jerry 94, 98
  Margaret 82
  Margt 112
  Michael 99
  Richard 13
Crossin
  Margery 32
Crow
  And 149, 180
  Jane 29
  Roger 184
Crowley
  Catherine 61, 157
  Cornelius 73, 152
  David 89
  Hanora 157
  Honoria 39
  J. 54
  Jerry 136
  Johanna 122
  John 39, 78, 104
  Mary 14, 61
  Michael 26

Michl 18, 25, 122, 170
Norah 157
William 33, 60
Crowly
  Catherine 159
Crummins
  Jerry 98
  Timothy 98
Cudahy
  Bridt 50
Cue
  Richard 36
Cuff
  Cath 149
Culgin
  Patrick 94
Cullan
  James 216
Cullen
  J. 55
Cummidy
  Winfred 96
Cumming
  Biddy 114
  Dorah 93
  Mary 114
  Wm 93
Cummins
  Bridt 51
Cuningham
  Ellen 33
  James 33
  Mary 33
  Richd 33
Cunningham
  Catherine 103
  John 18, 83, 169
  Mary 61
  Norrie 76
  Thos 35
Curise
  Rose 50
Curley

Cath 155, 156
Mary 128
Sarah 26, 37
Thos 34
Curlin
  Patk 147
  Patrick 146
Curly
  Sarah 29
Curney
  Denis 114
Curran
  Curran 167
  Joanna 157
  John 159, 166
Curren
  Catherine 25
  D. 55
  Danl 44
  Maurice 45
Currey
  Elizabeth 66
Currie
  James 114
  Margaret 114
  Rose 53
  Sarah 21
Curry
  David 87
  John 87
Curryan
  Catherine 96
Curtain
  John 47
  Mary 40
Cusac
  Maurice 155
Cuthbert
  Mary I. 78
Dacey
  Helen 11
Dahy
  James 104
Daily

Edward 30
Julia 67
Mary 80
Daley
  Cornelius 15
  Daniel 42
  Edward 39, 54
  John 39, 54
  Margaret 2d 21
  Margt 1st 19
  Mary 231
  Mary A. 67
  Thomas 51, 59
Dalton
  Ellen 137
  Henry 64
  John 33, 74
Daly
  Ann 30
  Biddy 153
  Charles 124
  Danl 146
  Denis 150
  James 158
  John 30, 171
  John 2d 32
  Kitty 153
  Margaret 124
  Mary 30, 32, 128, 158
  Owen 153
  Peggy 158
  Tom 168
Danlinn
  Hugh 24
Danlley
  Patrick 159
Danner
  Will 96
Darcy
  Catherine 45
Daulton
  John 61
Day

J. 55
Jeremh 43
Mary 21
Deady
  James 159
Dealey
  Aeneas 81
  Dennis 150
  Ellen 158
  Kitty 181
  Wm 158
Dealy
  Biddy 153
  Bridget 146
  Catherine 153
  Owen 118
  Peggy 157
Dearness
  Maria 23
Dee
  Ann 16, 23
  Dennis 66
  Hannah 66
Deering
  Bridget 105
  James 105
  Susanh 18
Dehagan
  John 169
Delaney
  Edward 141
  Ellen 158
  James 157
  Jeremiah 128
  Joanna 158
  Margt 31
  Michl 31
  Patk 92, 93
Delany
  John 157
  Mrs 141
Delay
  Judith 43
  Margt 51

Maurice 34
Michl 92
Morris 61
Dele
  Eliza 19
Demery
  Thos 136
Demper
  Mary 27
Dempsey
  Jeremh 49
  Jerh 58
  John 38
  Margt 34, 44, 45
Denish
  William 156
Dennis
  Lucy 62
Dennish
  John 36
Dennison
  Ann 23
Densmore
  Jane 23
  John 65
  William 65
Dermond
  Timothy 105
Dervin
  Michael 18
Desmond
  And 137
  Catherine 106
  Denis 106
  Edward 137
  Ellen 106
  Humphy 152
  Johanna 106
  John 22
  Mrs 106
  Patrick 25, 28, 106
Devaly
  Mary 128

Deveney
  Catherine 83
Dever
  Biddy 161
  Celia 161
  Chas 161
  John 161
  Mary 84, 161
Devitt
  Andrew 94
  Hugh 118
Devlin
  Barry 167
  Charles 167
  Edward 167
  Henry 87
  Jane 167
  Mary 87, 167
  Patrick 167
Devon
  Elizabeth 21
Dey
  Margt 168
Dillan
  Mary 134
Dillon
  Ann 22
  Catharine 12
Dinneen
  Denis 171
Disbrow
  Robert 219
Divers
  Bridget 76
Divine
  Jno 163
  Mary 16, 19
  William 62
Dixon
  James 16, 29
Dogan
  Henry 95
  Tim 87
Dogherty

Barney 16
Biddy 163
Bridt 25, 51
Catherine 24
Chas 50
Eliza 175
Ellen 174
James 72
John 22, 53, 163
Margt 175
Martha 26
Mary 163
Mary Ann 175
Michl 163
Nancy 160
Nel 160
Nelly 160
Patrick 163
Rachl 37
Richd 163
Doherty
  Ann 180
  Biddy 133
  Bridget 94
  Dan 160
  Edward 160
  Eliza 180
  Fanny 180
  Fanny jr 180
  James 133
  Jane 180
  Jas 85
  John 218
  Jos 180
  Marjory 85
  Mary 139, 143, 163, 180
  Pat 102, 163
  Patrick 160
  Richd 163
  Roger 160
  Susan 144
Dohey
  Thos 178

Dolan
  Bridget 40
  John 47
  Margt 123
  Wm 160
Donaghue
  Ellen 99
Donahough
  Catherine 98
Donahue
  Dan 156
  Hannh 47
  Jerehm 44
  Jeremiah 84
  Jerry 55
  John 147, 169
  Kitty 228
  Kitty jr 228
  Martin 41
  Mary 21
  Michael 184
  Timothy 228
Donahy
  Dennis 137
Donald
  John 118
  Michl 118
Donaldson
  Elizh 36
  Mary 27
  Wm 52
Donaley
  Mary 137
Donane
  David 151
Donavan
  Joanna 60
Donavon
  Joanna 55
Donellan
  John 44
Donelly
  Dan 126
  Danl 127

James 172
Jane 127
Jerry 159
Margt 176
Michael 127
Michl 126
Peter 126, 127
William 160
Donnell
  Biddy 76
  Julia 118
  Margaret 118
  Mary 130
Donnellin
  John 55
Donnelly
  - 158
  Ellen 150
  Jane 126
  John 43
  Patrick 73
  William 174
Donoghue
  Mary 162
Donohue
  Bartholomew 210
Donoldson
  William 70
Donovan
  Alex 133
  Anne 174
  Bridget 122
  Cath 83
  Catherine 130, 151, 154
  Dan 107, 114, 132
  Daniel 156
  Danl 17
  Denis 125, 151
  Dennis 126, 152
  Ellen 152
  Hanora 122
  Honora 82

James 126
Jas 21
Jereh 23
Jeremiah 125
Jerry 122, 138
Jno 86
Joanna 27, 41, 52
Johanna 152
John 107, 131, 146, 151, 164, 170
Laurence 82
Margaret 56
Margt 39, 46, 51, 54
Mary 22, 24, 28, 42, 92, 122, 130, 141, 151
Michael 151
Patrick 125
R. 54
Richd 40, 58
Thos 170
Tim 146, 171
William 122
Dooley
  Judy 78
  Patrick 33, 61
  T. 55
  Thomas 44
Doran
  Judy 106
  Susan 133
Dorgan
  William 38
Dougan
  Bridget 81
  James 218
  Joanna 81
  John 94
  Mary 134
  Patrick 218
  Thomas 95
Dougherty

Bernard 68
Betsy 175
Bridget 163
Charles 58
John 176
Mary 163
Wm 85
Dowd
  Catherine 98
  James 66, 67
Dowds
  Bridget 66
  Margaret 66
  Mary 66
Dowling
  Allan 114
  Hazen 12
Downes
  Mark 155
Downey
  Eleanor 36
  Jno 172
  Mary 172
  Michael 169
  Pat 172
Doyle
  Bridt 31
  Brien 31
  Bryant 66
  Edwin 83
  Fanny 119
  Patk 91
Draper
  James 13
Drescool
  James 134
Dreslin
  Ellen 217
Driscol
  Cath 179
  Catherine 38
  Dan 179
  Honora 83
  Honoria 33

Jeremh 48
Jerh 58
John 17
Kate 182
Kitty 182
Mary 18, 25, 82, 177
Mary 2nd 23, 53
Patrick 61
Timothy 23
Driscoll
  John 29
  Mary 150, 169
  Michael 214
  Robert 104
  Tim 131
Driskil
  Mary A. 70
Duff
  P. 55
Duffey
  John 163
Duffy
  Anthony 163
  Betty 111
  Biddy 110, 111
  Bridget 17
  Charles 98
  Danl 85
  Eleanor 16
  Grace 112
  Hyacinth 212
  James 31, 39, 107
  John 109, 140
  Kitty 111
  Margaret 140
  Martin 108
  Martin jr 109
  Mary 39, 112
  Mary Ann 54
  Neill 85
  Peter 38
  Thos 109

Dugan
  Biddy 128
  Hugh 95
  Thomas 95
Duggan
  Ann 96
  Mary 142
Duig
  Jno 178
  Margt 178
  Patt 178
Dunahue
  Ewd 68
Dunane
  Ellen 88
Dunavan
  Mary 179
Duncan
  Robert 63
Dunion
  Catherine 68
  Elizabeth 68
  John 68
Dunlevy
  Denis 147
  Eleanor 84
Dunn
  Dunn 31
  Elizabeth 13
  Ellen 83, 168
  Hanora 122
  John 73
  Margaret 53
Dunnegan
  Cath 183
  Mary 183
Dunphy
  Margaret 25, 28
  Michael 22
Durigan
  Mary 97
Durkin
  James 140
  Pat 140

Dutley
  Ferguson 36
Dwyer
  John 38
  Sarah 19
Dyer
  Catherine 36
  James 94
Dynan
  Ellen 47
Dysart
  Giln 174
Eagan
  Ann 78
  Catherine 21
  Ellen 78
  Mary 164
Eastcock
  Thomas 69
Eaton
  Ellen 43
  Joseph 57
Edgett
  Melinda 14
Edmondstone
  Thos 14
Edwards
  Ann 85
Egan
  Elizabeth 36, 39
  Patrick 124
Ellice
  Bridget 153
  Francis 153
Elliot
  Robert 16
Elliott
  I. 11
  Margaret 188
Ellis
  Bridget 153
  Frs 136
Ellison
  William 72

Emslie
  William J. 73
Ennis
  Ann 158
Enright
  John 116
Evans
  Chas 183
  Sarah 53
  Thomas 38
  William 41
Ewing
  Mary I. 86
Fahan
  Debby 48
Faherty
  Mary 165
Fahey
  Lawrence 149
  Pat 155
  Winni 149
Fahy
  Bridget 52, 60
  Bridt 33
  Martin 13
  Mary 45
Fallaher
  Ellen 185
  Ellen jr 185
  James 185
Fallasy
  Ellen 105
Falvey
  Patrick 131
Falvy
  Michl 56
Farmer
  George 36
  Mary 48
Farnan
  Ann 13
Farrar
  John B. 59
Farrel
  George 38
  James 24, 119
  Jno 183
  John 23
  Martin 44
  Michl 55
  Tom 158
Farret
  Elleanor 32
Farrol
  John 27
Farry
  Thomas 11, 14
Fawcet
  George 64
  Isabella 64
Fee
  Margaret 56
  Margt 47
Feehely
  Dan 144
  James 173
Feeney
  Michl 145
  Patrick 215
Feeny
  Bryan 215
Fehely
  Margaret 172
  Mary 172
Fehily
  Tim 172
Fehin
  Bridget 143
Fennety
  Biddy 123
  Bridget 127
  Hannora 127
  Margaret 124
  Mary 124
Fenton
  Robert 211
Fergus
  Tom 162
Ferguson
  Capt 220
  Cath 128
  Jane 22
  Mary 128
  Mathias 215
  Wm 215
Ferrar
  John B. 51
Ferrer
  Rose Ann 35
Ferry
  Sally 81
Fevans
  Elizabeth 59
Fielding
  Eleanor 90
  Richard 63
Finan
  Jno 83
  John 116
  Widow 83
Finarty
  Martin 127
  Mathew 146
  Michael 127
Finigan
  Biddy 123
Finley
  Mary 105
Finn
  Bridget 14
  John 61, 151
  Margt 35, 51
  Mary 50, 52, 60, 135
  Mary jr 135
  Mich 144
  William 46, 56
Finnean
  Jas 42
Finnigan
  Charles 228
  Ellen 228

John 91
Julia 228
Mary 91
Pat 48, 144
Finny
  Biddy 154
  John 135
  Nelly 148
  Sally 147
Finton
  Margaret 229
  Mary 229
  Owen 229
  William 229
Fitzgerald
  Ann 20
  Bridget 36
  Edwd 88
  Ellen 36
  Garret 25, 28
  Garritt 230
  Hanora 169
  Hona 49
  Honor 104
  Honora 36
  Honoria 36
  James 158
  Jane 24, 43, 53, 60, 72
  Jas. 55
  Johanna 174
  John 90, 147
  Margaret 36, 90
  Margt 24
  Maria 20
  Mary 49, 58, 133
  Michl 91, 158
  Moris 90
  Pat 44, 164
  Richd 158
Fitzgibbon
  John 49, 58
  Miche 49, 57
Fitzpatrick

Edwd 175
Garret 30, 66
J. 54
John 41
Mary 128, 182
Timy 41
Fitzsimmons
  Edwd 93
  Jas 59
Fitzsimons
  Jas. 51
Flaghan
  John 43, 57
Flaherty
  Anthony 124
  Cathe 17, 28
  Catherine 24
  Elizabeth 117
  Jno 128, 148
  Margt 128
  Pat 128
Flanagan
  Dominick 107
  James 217
  Kitty 110
  Mary 83, 110
  William 105
Flanigan
  Ann 36
Flannegan
  Mary 140
Flavin
  Patrick 13
  Robert 55
  Robt 42
Fleming
  Catherine 230
  Ellen 181
  Thomas 117, 119, 156
Flemming
  John 217
  Margt 123
Fletcher

Elizabeth 14
Ellen 33, 49, 58
Flin
  Bridget 33
  Catherine 33
  Patrick 33
  Thomas 33
Flinn
  Catharine 14
  Cathe 50
  Catherine 37, 40, 59
  Honoria 13
  Martin 140
  Mary 40
  Mathew 116
  Matthew 18
  Matthias 25
  Owen 37
  Thomas 61
  William 45, 56
Flynn
  Charles 95
  Jane 136
  Kitty 176
  Matt 117
  Patt 130
Focher
  Mary 114
  Nancey 114
  Owen 114
  Pat 116
Fogarty
  Ann 178
  Ed 178
Folan
  Brian 147
  Tom 146
Folara
  Cath 88
Foley
  Ann 20, 112
  Biddy 144, 173
  Bidy 84

Bridget 120
Elizabeth 16, 29
Ellen 115, 176
James 120
James Jr 120
Jane 44
Jno 93
Joanna 45, 55, 81, 84
John 98, 120
Manus 144
Martin 129
Mary 33, 56, 144, 145
Michael 117, 223
Miche 33
Michl 46, 93, 120
Norrie 85
-Patrick 176
Tim 93
Folis
  Ann Jane 153
  Catherine 153
  James 153
Ford
  Barbara 16
  John 41, 102, 124
  Michl 44
  Pat 122
  Philip 94
  Robert 11
  Thomas 99
Forest
  Francis 52
Forester
  Margaret 130
Forker
  Mary 114
  Nancey 114
  Owen 114
  Pat 116
Forsythe
  Allecia 69
  Fanny 69, 70

George 69
Wm 69
Foster
  Catharine 10
Fougum
  Edward 154
Fowler
  Elisha 67
Fox
  Cath 110
  Catherine 94
  Mary 21
Foy
  Daniel 17, 29
  Dominic 17
Foy 23
  Laurence 95
  Martin 148
  Thomas 117
Frame
  Charles 54
  Christopher 39
Fraser
  Daniel 70
Frazer
  Frazer 18
Freal
  William 66
Freeborn
  James 22
Freeman
  Joana 20
  Joanna 28
Freil
  William 15
Fryer
  Mary 19
Fullerton
  Bridt 20
Furlong
  Martin 17, 24, 28
Fury
  Thos 32
Fye

Denis 122
Matt 165
Fyner
  Mary 136
Gafney
  John 43
Gahagan
  Mary 35, 72
Gainsay
  Michl 156
Gallagher
  Ann 111, 182
  Ann jr 182
  Anne 153
  Biddy 111, 186
  Bridget 145
  Dan 173
  Dennis 153
  Dominick 149, 179
  Eliza 161
  Ellen 145, 182
  Francis 218
  Gerald 137
  Henry 30, 121
  James 133, 218
  Jerald 137
  John 63, 108, 113, 153
  Lydia 20
  Margt 144
  Mary 121, 153, 161
  Mich 160, 174
  Michl 182
  Owen 46
  Patrick 11
  Susan 182
  William 218
Galone
  Bridget 143
Galoon
  John 115
  Martin 115

Mary 114
Nelly 115
Owen 115
Teady 114
Thomas 115
Galoone
  Peter 138
Gamage
  Mary 63
Gamblin
  Eliza 24, 62
Gamman
  Mary 32
Gancy
  Michael 156
Gannivan
  Mary 61
Gannon
  Miche 40
Garavan
  Dennis 134
Gardner
  James 144
  Mary 144
Garnet
  Daniel 98
Garr
  Ellen 102
Garret
  Michl 122
Garrity
  Ann 51, 59
Garvan
  Kitty 113
Garvin
  Daniel 13
Garvy
  Honor 186
Gately
  Bridt 40
  Mary 35, 70
  Murria 168
  Patrick 35, 70
  Peter 168

Thomas 37, 48, 70
Thos 32
Gavel
  Ann 52
Gaveney
  John 166
Gaveron
  Bridget 43
  Michl 37
Gavin
  John 40
Gaynor
  Mary 122
Geaney
  Wm 77
Gearey
  Jno 158
Geary
  Philip 155
Gelgowan
  Cathe 50
Gelson
  Hugh 35
Genley
  Mary 122
  Pat 122
Geohen
  Tom 139
George
  Elizabeth 66
Gibbon
  Ellen 22
  James 22
  Mary 27
  Pat 143
Gibbs
  George 18
Gibson
  James 96
  Matthew 25, 28
  Mr. 218
Gilgoure
  Cathe 58

Gill
  Ann 95
  James 96
  Margt 112
  Pat 109
  Peggy 145
  Timothy 13
Gillan
  Dora 36
  Dorah 36, 52, 72
  Elsi 110
  Jas 144
  John 62, 72
  Margaret 160
  Michael 94
  Thomas 215
Gillane
  Peter 138
Gillen
  Bridget 110
Gillespie
  Daniel 26
  Ellen 20, 28
  Francis 95
  John 95
  Margt 141
  Will 98
Gillespy
  Ellen 27
Gillhooley
  Eliza 172
Gillian
  John 215
Gilligan
  Catherine 103
Gillin
  Biddy 112
  Cath 112
  Catherine 115
  Eliza 114
  Ellen 115
  Jane 115
  Winni 114
  Wm 143

Gillis
  Sarah 52
Gillogly
  James 218
Gilloon
  Andrew 215
  Biddy 144
  Dennis 215
  Patrick 215
Gilmartin
  Dan 127
  Jno 143
  Thos 144
  Wm 144
Gilroy
  Biddy 115
  James 131
  Mary 115
  Peter 131
Glancy
  Margaret 98
  Mary 26, 29
Glass
  Henry 133, 218
Glassin
  M. 55
Glasson
  Miche 42
Glavin
  Margt 174
Gleeson
  Edwd 89
Glenhorn
  Ellen 92
Glenn
  Bridt 40
  Bridt 2d 49
  Jane 53
  Michl 47
Gloster
  William 50, 63
Glynn
  Michael 155
  Michl 182

Godfray
  Ann 136
Godsel
  Margt 47
Godsoe
  Nathan 72
Goggin
  David 129
Golderick
  Frs 144
  Owen 143
  Pat 143
Goldin
  John 139
Golding
  Cathe 44
  James H. 67
  John 67
Goodwin
  John 63
Gorcan
  John 140
Gordon
  Samuel 211
Gorman
  Bridget 31, 32
  Ellen 45
  J. 55
  John 43
  Margaret 142
  Mary 23
  Patrick 31, 60
  William 58
  Wm 49
Goslin
  Edwd 118
  Jane 118
  Pauline 118
Gough
  Thomas 26, 63
Gould
  William 25, 28
Grady
  Darby 149

Gubby 170
  Michael 43
  Thomas 170
  Thos 185
Graham
  Ann 22
  Francis 22
  Wm 180
Gray
  Elizabeth 13
  Unity 94
Gready
  James 217
Green
  Ellen 158
  John 94
  Mary 26
  Michael 134
  Michl 134
  Pat 113
  Patk 173
Greer
  Thomas 22
Gregg
  Ellen 166
  Robert 215
Greig
  Margaret 18
Grey
  Ellen 142
Griffin
  Biddy 149
  Ellen 152
  Joanna 181
  John 152, 181
  Julia 56, 90
  Julie 45
  Mary 33, 45, 152
  Tim 181
  William 133
Grifin
  Anthony 183
Grimes
  Cecelia 132

Edward 184
John 184
Margt 132
Mary 184
Terry 132
Grogan
  Pat 132
Guay
  John 218
Guiney
  Joanna 88
Guino
  Hanora 183
Gunnin
  Cath 145
  John 144
  Mary 145
Gunning
  Mary 94
Guoin
  Matt 155
Gurrel
  Rebecca 42, 55
Gwynn
  Andrew 103
Gypsum
  Rachel 96
Habertson
  Mary 19
Hachay
  Caroline 69
Hagarty
  John 16, 24, 28
  Richd 49, 53
Hagerty
  Mrs 184
  Peter 186
Haggarty
  Edwd 79
Haggerty
  Dan 139
  John 13
  Patk 150
Haggirty

Danl 166
Jerry 166
Patrick 166
Hahar
  Michl 130
Haik
  Bridget 105
Haley
  Brian 143
  Ellen 99
  Margaret 96
  Michael 122
  Patrick 29
Haligan
  Patrick 185
Hall
  Capt 98
  Robt 221
Hallahan
  Tim 159
Hallaron
  Margt 34
Hallisey
  Ann 186
  Dennis 186
  Hanora 186
  Hanora jr 186
  Margt 186
  Mary 186
  Tim 186
  Tim jr 186
Halloran
  Mary 48
Halnin
  Jeremh 34
  Mary 33
  William 33
Haloran
  Margt 47
  Mary 168
Haly
  John 122
  Mary 130
Hamilton

Margt 20
Haneberry
  Thos 127
Haney
  Edward 27
Hanigan
  Thomas 139
Hanley
  John 48, 57, 155
  Martin 155
  Mary 162
  Patk 86
  Thos 86
Hanna
  Ellen 87
  Nancy 20
Hannahan
  ~ John 34
Hannen
  Edwd 92
Hanney
  John 20
Hannifer
  Danl 40
Hannifin
  Danl 91
  Joanna 90
  Mary 91
Hanniming
  Patk 119
Hannon
  John 46, 56
  Michael 131
Hanover
  Thomas 26
  Thos 29, 30
Hanrahan
  John 46
Haragan
  Rose Ann 86
Harbour
  Elizabeth 55
  Elizh 44
Harden

Michl 176
Richd 176
Wm 176
Hardiman
  Patk 77
Hardnett
  Ellen 159
  Michl 159
  Peggy 159
Harkin
  Sarah 20, 24
Harkins
  Aneas 108
  Biddy 111, 112
  Bridget 145
  Jas 84, 109
  Margt 145
  Mary 111, 113
  Mich 109
  Pat 144
  Peggy 145
  Rose 84
  Wm 84
Harnet
  Hannah 38
  William 52
Harper
  David 139
Harragan
  Peggy 90
  Tim 90
Harrigan
  Jerry 98
  Joana 48
  Joanna 91
  Margt 43
  Mary 98
  Michl 136
Harrington
  Cath 74
  Cornelius 169
  Corns 34
  Eleanor 23
  Ellen 57

Hanora 125
J. 54
Jeremh 157
Jerry 98
John 26, 39, 152, 153
Mary 45, 74, 94, 98, 151, 153, 169
Peter 152
Tim 151
Harris
  Eleanor 13
  Rebecca 17, 29
Harrison
  Denis 139
  Ellen 139
  Mary 98, 109, 112
  Pat 109
Hart
  Patrick 215
  Timothy 52, 60
Hartt
  Allen 109
  Anne 158
  Bridget 112
  Cath 144
  Ellen 113
  Margt 141
  Martin 109
  Mary 100, 113, 115
Harvey
  Patt 162
Hassel
  Willm 28
Hassen
  Mary 58
  Rose Ann 48
  Sarah 49, 58
Hasset
  James 42
  Thomas 53
Hasted
  Mary 140

Hatherman
  Mary 34, 61
Haurihan
  Jerry 159
  Judy 159
  Patrick 159
Hautagan
  Cath 97
Havelin
  Mary 19
Hawkes
  John 91
Haxford
  Henry 13
Hay
  Mary 2nd 44
Hayes
  Daniel 152
  Dennis 91
  John 87
  Julia 81
  Mary 41, 55
Haynes
  Mary 103
Hays
  Cathe 22
  Denis 40
  Ellen 14, 42
  Frances 17, 27
  James 23
Hazell
  William 23
Hazen
  Ellen 10
Hazlet
  Anne 166
Hazlett
  Anne 167
Head
  Biddy 87
  Jno 87
Healey
  Anthony 141
  Biddy 112, 141

Cath 143
Ellen 81
Jeremiah 87
John 141, 170, 171
Kitty 141
Mary 110, 141, 156, 165
Nelly 110
Norah 103
Patk 81
Tim 140
Heally
  Catherine 62
  Eleanor 44
  Joanna 42
  Michl 40
  Michl 2nd 41
  Patrick 26
  Thomas 26
Healy
  James 170
  John 171
  Thomas 22, 29
  Thos 76
Heaney
  Hanora 77
  John 155
Hear
  Mary 105
Hearne
  Michl 121
  Patk 121
Hector
  Charlotte 72
Heffron
  Biddy 124
  John 124
Hegan
  John 132
  John Jr 132
  Pat 124
Hegarty
  Abby 171

Betty 170
Cate 139
Catherine 123
Dan 150
Darby 170
Ellen 171
Mary 150, 166, 170
Thomas 185
Heggarty
  John 150
Helland
  Chas 46
Henessy
  Patrick 217
Hennehey
  Michael 105
Hennessey
  Denis 35
Hennessy
  Cathe 41
  Honoa 23
  Jas 20
  Margt 53
Hennesy
  Catherine 125
  Jerry 158
  John 181
Hennigan
  Mary 114
Hennisay
  Catherine 97
Hennsessey
  James 30
Henrey
  Patrick 147
Henry
  David 100
Heraghty
  Patrick 215
Herbertine
  Ann 20
Herlin
  Ann 26, 29

Heron
  Joanna 84
  Martin 147
  Mary 127
Herren
  Morris 67
Herrick
  Ellen 83
  Jno 83
Herrin
  Mary 21, 34
Herring
  Mary 2nd 51
Herrington
  Joanna 53
Herron
  Biddy 118
  Corns 31
  Eliza 118
  John 117
  Mary 117
  Michl 117
  Patt 117
Hesson
  John 166
  Mary 166
  Michl 146, 166
Hester
  Biddy 140
  Mary 140
Hickey
  Charles 54
  Elizabeth 37
  Laurance 52, 60
  Mary 98
Hickson
  Edward 130
  ↘Hanora 163
  James 164
  Johanna 164
  Margaret 164
  Margt 159
  Mary 164
  May 159

Richard 163
Robert 163
Higgan
  Michl 177
Higgins
  Bernard 99
  Hannah 76
  James 76
  Margaret 60
  Margt 41
  Mary 30
  Mary Jr 30
  Michael 217
  Pat 113, 162
Hilley
  Dennis 153
Hilton
  Mary 27
Hines
  Catherine 47
Hiney
  Eliza 34, 43, 50, 59
  Maria 34
Hisan
  George 102
Hoar
  Mich 44
Hoare
  M. 55
Hober
  John 105
Hobin
  Mary 96
Hogan
  Daniel 43, 57
  Edward 131, 132
  Ellen 132
  Hanna 132
  Jno 132
  John 131
  Mary 101, 131
  Nancy 123
  Norry 131

Thomas 136
Holland
  Jeremh 37
  Jno 128
  Martin 128
  Michl 128
  Nancy 128
Hollin
  Jerry 96
Hollohan
  Margt 52
Holloran
  Mary 63
Holman
  Sarah 19
Holmes
  Elizabeth 17
  Thomas 25
Holohan
  Darby 43
Holt
  James 167
  John 167
Holtan
  John 125
Honlahan
  Dennis 100
Hood
  Nathl 115
Hooley
  Ann 81
  Ellen 81, 136
  James 171
  John 81, 125, 172
  Mary 172
  Michl 172
  Wm 81, 172
Hopkins
  Hanora 117
  Mary 147
Hopper
  Marian 62
Horan
  Bridt 46

James 223
Horgan
  Margaret 130
Horn
  Mary 92
Horne
  Danl 92
Hornett
  Margt 78
Hosey
  Paddy 140
  Pat 140
Houran
  Jerry 184
Hourlihan
  Patrick 184
  Peggy 184
Howard
  John 26, 28
Howe
  James 20
Howie
  Robert 79
Hues
  Robert 97
Hughes
  Ann 16
  Frederick 10
  John 24
  Mary 24, 28, 120
  Pat 139
Hunter
  Jane 22, 65
  Martha 62
Hurley
  Denis 162
  Ellen 209
  Hanora 157, 169
  Honora 84
  Johanna 85
  John 51
  Margt 34
  Mary 37, 45, 51, 150, 170, 171

Nancy 42, 137
Narry 157
Thomas 137
Tim 157
Hurly
  Bridget 99
Hussey
  Alice 87
  Hanna 152
  Joanna 87
  Mary 87
  Michl 152
  Molly 140
  Peter 169
  Thos 87
Hussy
  Michael 170
Hutchinson
  Wm 51, 59
Hyde
  Patrick 33, 60
  Patrick Jr 33
Hyne
  Catherine 155
  John 155
  Michael 155
Hynes
  Thomas 215
Ibbison
  Ann 177
  David 177
  John 177
  Margt 177
  Martha 177
  Thomas 177
Ingram
  Mary 50, 59
Irvin
  Elizh 41
  Irvin 37
  James 47
  Rosa 37, 52
Irvine
  Rev. Robert 222

Irving
  John 102
Irwin
  Edward 218
  John 218
Isaacs
  - 19
Isbester
  James 162
Jack
  David W. 230
Jackson
  Charlotte 86
  John 85
  Michael 105
  Sarah 105
  James
  Malvinia 73
Jenkins
  Biddy 156
  Bridget 156
  John 155
  Michael 155
  Thos 155
Jennings
  Michl 25, 28
  Pat 95
Jinkins
  Bridget 155
  Sally 155
  John
  John 229
Johnson
  Charles 115
  Eliza 115
  Margaret 116
  Robt 115
  Thos 115
Johnston
  Adam 115, 215
  Betsy 102
  Catherine 25
  Deborah 16
  Edward 215

  Eliz 112
  Ellen 109, 174
  James 15
  John 13, 116
  Margt 112
  Mary 39, 44
  Mary Anne 116
  William 63, 116
  Wm 215
Johnstone
  John 97
Jolly
  Martha 95
Jones
  Alex 27
  Charles 215
  Mary 65
  William 37, 47
Jordan
  Anne 156
  Biddy 155, 156
  James 152
  John 21, 231
  Mary 156
  Pat 152
  Peter 152, 156
Jordon
  Cathr 67
  Margaret 67
Joyce
  Margt 89
  Martin 76
  Mary 147
Judge
  Thomas 94
Kain
  Will 104
Kane
  Denis 51, 59
  Margaret 58
  Margt 47
Karan
  Eleanor 99
Kavanah

Patrick 56
Kavenagh
  Michl 163
Kavenah
  Pat 46
Keady
  Edward 154
Keane
  Hugh 218
  John 170
  William 217
Kearney
  Biddy 141
  Cathe 36
  Catherine 187
  Chas 144
  Mary 150
  Nicholas 218
  Patrick 36
  Peggy 123
Kearns
  Ann 145
  James 150
  Mrs 78
Kearny
  Ann 145
Keary
  Edward 116
Keating
  Catherine 127
  Elen 127
  James 88
  Mary 88
Keavlahan
  John 114
  Owen 115
Keddie
  Edwd 154
Keddy
  Mary 154
Keefe
  Arthur 41
  Bridget 61
  David 48, 57

  Elizabeth 36, 53
  Ellen 151
  Mrs 97
  Patrick 47, 56, 98
Keelty
  Thomas 215
Keely
  James 155
Keenan
  Thomas 103
Kehoe
  William 26
Keiley
  Mary 48
Keilley
  Jerry 83
Keily
  Mary 57
Kelcorn
  Peter 172
Keldiff
  Margaret 157
Kellahan
  Patrick 56
Kelleher
  Pat 46
Keller
  Bridget 120
  Catherine 120
  John 119
Kelley
  Bernard 94
  Catherine 67
  Danl 124
  Hugh 67
  John 67
  Mary 121
Kelly
  Alexander 76
  Alice 32
  Ann 50
  Anthony 76
  Bat 147
  Bridget 154

  Brien 50, 59
  Cath 140
  Catherine 2d 18
  Cornelius 80, 124
  Edmond 210
  Edward 26, 28, 38, 54
  Elizabeth 76
  Frances 32, 50
  Hanna 109
  Henry 76
  Hugh 30
  James 144, 150
  Jane 76, 133
  Jerry 134
  Joanna 1st 43
  Joanna 2nd 43
  John 50, 59, 168
  Julia 133
  Mary 26, 32, 35, 94, 101, 146, 168
  Matt 144
  Matt jr. 144
  Michl 149, 168
  Owen 144
  Pat 139, 140
  Patrick 168
  Peggy 139
  Philip 51
  Phillip 59
  Robt 76
  Thomas 167, 168
  Thos 168
  Tom 140
  William 16, 34, 35, 40, 49, 52, 58, 60, 70
  Wm 76
Kember
  Eliza 152
Kemble
  Eliza 152
Kenevan
  James 37

Kenna
  Bridt 33
  Rosa 11
Kennahan
  Margt 31
Kennan
  Patk 149
Kennedy
  Bridget 60, 76
  Cornelius 57
  Corns 48
  Danl 46
  Edward 57
  Edwd 48
  Ellen 90, 97
  James 91
  Jerry 107
  Joanna 90
  John 48, 57, 216
  Margt 42
  Mary 90, 91, 127, 162
  Mathew 143
  Pat 101, 140
  Patk 90
  Thos 22
  William 96
  Winfred 100
Kennevan
  Michael 61
Kennon
  Michael 94
Kenny
  James 103, 155
  John 40, 105
  Michl 155
Keoffe
  James 149
  Michl 151
  Patk 154
  Richd 81
Keohan
  Honora 158
Kerigan
  Patrick 95
Kerley
  Teddy 179
  Tim 148
Kerman
  Michl 21
Kermerson
  Ellen 18
  Patrick 18
  ridt 18
Kerr
  Fanny 228
  Lawrence 228
Keshane
  Catherine 126
Kevanagh
  Mary 163
Kevil
  Mary 173
Keyburn
  William 57
  Wm 48
Kidder
  Hanora 154
Kiddey
  Mary 154
Kidney
  Mary 131
Kierans
  William 218
Kilbride
  Biddy 100
  Jno 145
  John 113, 114
  Mary 115
  Nancy 114
  Pat 113, 145
  Patrick 131
Kilcannon
  Darby 156
Kilday
  James 90
Kilgallon
  John 108
  Mary 111
Kilkoyn
  Mary 51, 59
Killane
  Jno 83
  Mary 82
  Michl 83
  Nancy 82
Killcoin
  James 173
Killenan
  Dennis 93
Killigan
  Pat 95
Killmartin
  Anne 120
  Cate 138
  Judy 138
  Mich 150
  Peggy 138
Killpatrick
  Pat 163
Kilmartin
  Betty 112
  Biddy 110, 112
  Bridget 143
  Honor 111
  James 94
  Mary 110, 173
  Mich 107
  Mrs 188
  Owen 143
  Pat 107, 173
  Peggy 111, 145
  Sally 144
  Stephen 138
  Thos 107
  Winni 145
Kilney
  Dan 11
Kilpatrick
  John 16, 63
  Letitiae 34
  Patrick 162

Kilrayan
  Michl 135
Kilroy
  Anthony 51, 59
Kilryan
  Rose 135
Kindred
  Rosa 37
King
  Ann 129
  Brian 128
  Bryan 217
  Hanora 154
  John 95
  Margaret 123, 147
  Mary 123, 124, 161
  Mich 147
  Michael 146
  Michl 154
  Pat 124, 128
  Patk 123
  Rebecca I. 85
  Wm 123
Kingston
  Rachael 99
Kinneally
  Joanna 42
  Thomas 26
Kinnear
  Mary 63
Kinney
  Catherine 105, 188
Kirby
  Thos 92
  William 39, 105
Kircil
  Andrew 72
Kirk
  Anne 129
  Catherine 129
  James 213
  John 129
Kirkbride
  Davidson 27
Kirkbright
  Mary 21
Kivil
  Dominick 172
Knott
  Mary 44
Knowles
  Sarah 89
Kohan
  Jade 45
Krian
  Catharine 77
Lachey
  Enora M. 67
Lacky
  John 43
Laden
  Kitty 113
  Mary 113
  Michl 108
Lahey
  George 58
  Mary 59
  Michael 94
Lahy
  Eliza 51, 137
  George 49, 51
  Mary 51
Laidler
  Capt 218
Laing
  Cath 91
  James 20
Laird
  Isabella 64
Lalley
  Margt 78
Lalry
  Eliza 137
Land
  John 104
Landrigan
  Mary 89
Lane
  Alice 107
  Bridget 83
  Cath 83
  Jeremh 42
  John 104, 106
Langan
  Catherine 121
Langin
  Mary 135
Lantry
  Kearn 119
  Wenie 119
Larby
  John 14
Larken
  Margaret 140
Larkin
  John 45
  Mary 46, 56
  Peter 103
  Tim 142
Latta
  Eliza 101
Laughlin
  Eliz 143
  Johanna 127
  Kitty 109
  Mary 109
  Peggy 105
Lausay
  Patrick 97
Lavery
  Elizabeth 62
Lavis
  John 91
Lawler
  Bridget 76
Lawless
  Alice 187
  Bridget 187
  Cath 179

James 179, 183, 187
Lilly 187
Mary 187
Patrick 187
Lawlor
  Eli 76
Lawrence
  Alex 73
  Joseph 73
  Rebecca 73
Lawson
  John 216
Lawton
  John 77
Layman
  Charles 94
Leaden
  Biddy 111, 112
  Catherine 111
  Hanna 112
  Honor 111, 112
  Mary 112
Leahey
  Pat 176
Leahorn
  Ellen 92
Lean
  Eliza 104
Leane
  Allice 106
  Eliza 106
  Henry 106
  William 106
Learey
  Ellen 136
  Joanna 88
  Mary 94, 181
  Tim 154
Leary
  Daniel 167
  Ellen 87
  Hannah 67
  James 53, 134

Jno 84
Joanna 130
Johanna 99, 159
Judy 181
Mary 39
Matthew 53
Nancy 137
Patk 88, 122
Leavis
  James 91
Leddie
  Betsey 167
  Catherine 167
  Danl 167
  Rose 167
  Thomas 167
Lee
  Catherine 45, 56
  James 43, 58
  John 142, 157
  Margaret 32, 61
  Mary 32, 35, 60, 121
  Patrick 162
  Terrence 50, 58
  Thomas 38, 53
  Wm 121
Leekey
  John 56
Lehane
  John 141
Leighey
  James 56
  Patrick 27
Leighy
  George 59
  Hannah 31
  James 46
  Thomas 53
Lemon
  John 19
Lenahan
  Owen 144
Lenan

Francis 128
Lenehan
  - Sarah 31
Lennan
  Hannora 147
  Margt 76
  Mich 123
Lennehan
  Cathe 37
Lennihan
  Danl 25
Leonard
  Ned 108
  Thomas 188
Lewis
  Joanna 126
Liddy
  Anne 167
Liester
  Darby 131
Ligam
  Will 100
Linane
  Bridget 128
  Ellen 128
Linehan
  Daniel 98
Linesa
  John 97
Little
  Edward 218
  John 11
Livingston
  David 58
  John 21, 23
  John Jr 24, 28
  John Sr 28
Livingstone
  David 49
Lloyd
  J. 56
  John 46
  William 73
Loachen

Mary 174
Loftus
  Anne 162
  Catherine 162
  Celia 185
  Ellen 162
  John 162
  Margaret 162
  Martin 185
Logue
  Daniel 23
  Hugh 133
Logure
  - 174
London
  J. 55
Lonergan
  Mary 222
Lonevan
  Nancy 105
Long
  Ellen 125
  Jane 27
  Mary 101
  Matt 125
  Walter 223
Looney
  Cherry 47
  Edward 102
  James 97
  Margt 23
Loughan
  Wenifred 131
Loughen
  Catherine 124
  James 124
  John 124
  Judy 131
  Mary 124
  Michael 124
  Michl 124
  Pat 131
  Patrick 154
Loughery

Cathe 34
Henry 30
Loughlan
  John 124
Loughlane
  Batley 59
Loughnan
  Bartley 51
Loughnane
  Ellen 47
  Margt 42
Lovett
  Mary 41, 56, 77
Low
  Margaret 96
Lowery
  Michael J. 14
Lowney
  Patk 156
Lowrey
  John 104, 138
  Nelly 162
  Pat 162
Luin
  Ann 228
  Margaret 228
  Mary 228
  Mary jr 228
  Patrick 228
Lundon
  John 44
Lunney
  James 100
Lynch
  Ann 156
  Bridget 149
  Brien 46
  Catherine 164
  Daniel 40, 96
  Denis 171
  Ellen 126
  James 99
  John 51
  Margt 122

Pat 165
Patk 86
Tim 165
Tommy 175
Wm 164
Lynchigan
  Dennis 79
Lynn
  Francis 13, 63
  Jane 84
  Jno 84
  Thos 84
Lyon
  Corns 38
  Daniel 49, 58
  Denis 210
Lyons
  Alice 178
  Cate 146
  Mary 53, 178
  Pat 132
Lysight
  Wm 169
Mack
  Bridt 44, 55
  Mary 94
Mackie
  Sarah 21
MacMullen
  Jane 71
Macwell
  Mary 172
Madden
  Biddy 149, 155
  Bridget 129
  John 168
  Julia 168
  Mary 105, 168
  Michl 168
  Pat 129, 168
  Patrick 105
  Peggy 149
  Timothy 12
  William 40

Maddin
  Anne 168
Magan
  Pat 41
Magee
  Biddy 165
  Catherine 138
  Matilda 111
Maghan
  Mary 45
Maginnis
  Jane 231
Magirr
  James 218
Magivern
  Mary 172
Maglone
  Margaret 136
  Patrick 115
Magnor
  Eliza 35
  Mary 31, 37
  Mary 2d 38
Magowan
  Pat 144
Maguigan
  Arthur 121
Maguinas
  Patrick 124
Maguire
  Honora 107
  James 218
  John 103
Magwood
  Mrs 223
Mahan
  John 172
Mahaney
  Patrick 59
Mahany
  Corns 57
  John 27
  Margt 55
  Mary 28

Patrick 60
Mahar
  John 172
  M. 55
  Michl 44
Mahegan
  John 45, 57
Mahir
  Mahir 99
Mahon
  Cathe 49
  Mary 104, 179
  Michael 104
‑ Mahoney
  Cathe 48
  Johanna 169
  Margt 33
  Michl 151
  Wm 165
Mahony
  Cath 172, 174
  Catherine 23, 24
  Cornelius 170
  Corns 49
  Dan 90
  Dan jr 133
  Danl 21, 133
  Dennis 171
  Jerry 80, 170
  John 104, 170
  Judy 30
  Julia 80
  Margt 26, 43
  Martin 22
  Mary 26, 38, 92, 174
  Michl 127
  Nancy 118
  Patk 81
  Patrick 51
  William 84
  William Jr 84
Maine
  Margaret 118

Malady
  Matt 117
Maley
  Eliza 127
  Johanna 157
Malone
  Brid 128
  Ellen 215
  Honor 215
  James 132, 215
  John 135
  Martin 132, 215
  Mary 135
  Mich 116
  Michael 128
  Mrs 135
  Pat 48
  Patrick 57
  Thos 105
Maloney
  Johanna 162
  Martin 98
  Mary 94
  Pat 105
  Patrick 94
Maloone
  James 135
Mangan
  And 163
Mangen
  Cath 183
Manion
  Ellen 78
  Mary 146
  Peter 148
Mann
  Elizabeth 228
  Francis 97
  Joanna 23, 27, 228
  Mary 94
Mannen
  Peggy 131
Manni

Maurice 44
Mannian
  Andrew 98
Manning
  Hanora 164
  James 46
  Jas 40
  Johanna 131
  Saml 41
Manogue
  Mary 146, 148
Mansfield
  Patrick 37, 53
Mantan
  Bartley 94
Mantle
  Thomas 116
Manyon
  Patrick 40
  Thos 39
Mara
  Judith 42
Margt
  Margt 20
Marr
  John 147
Marrygan
  Mary 98
Marsters
  J. 70
Martin
  Bridget 168
  Edwd 123
  Emily 124
  John 94
  Joseph 96
  Mary 37, 174
  Sarah 12
  Thomas 15
Marven
  Briget 96
Mason
  J. 54
  James 41

Matcheson
  Bridget 58
  Bridt 49
Mathews
  Charlotte 117
  George 117
  Thos 117
Mathewson
  Elizh 16
Matthews
  Henry 51, 59
  Samuel 23
Maurice
  Bridget 139
Maxwell
  Margt 19
May
  Martin 139
  Patrick 15
  Thos 116
Maylone
  Patrick 115
McAbe
  Peter 161
McAffrey
  Ellen 87
  Jno 183
McAffry
  Ann 185
McAlgar
  John 228
  Nancy 228
McAllan
  James 38
McAllen
  Margt 61
McAlwee
  Henry 21
McAnarney
  Mich 90
McAnartney
  Lott 175
  Mary 175
  Michl 175

  Mrs 175
  Wm 175
McAneny
  John 42
McAneslin
  Ann 38, 54
  Florence 22
  James 27
McAnn
  Ed 107
  Mary 113
  Pat 109
McAnully
  Denis 62
McAnulty
  Denis 38
  James 18
  Jas. 29
  Pat 22
McArney
  Biddy 89
  Roseanna 86
McArron
  Rosa 79
McArthur
  Francis 104
  Mary 52, 59
McArty
  Cath 77, 137
  Chas 92
  Dan 165
  Dennis 165, 178
  Donald 67
  Ellen 82
  Jerry 126, 165
  John 165
  Kitty 157
  Margt 88, 92
  Mary 67, 91, 165
  Mich 165
  Morris 169
  Norrie 165
  Peggy 91
  Tim 176, 178

Wm 137
McAulay
  James 37, 53
  Mary 32
  Rodger 25
  Roger 29
McAvity
  James 124
  Rosanna 86
McBemore
  Ellen 128
McBride
  Elizabeth 74
  Heny 119
McBrine
  Henry 142
McC
  Elizabeth 18
McCabe
  Eliza 51
McCaffrey
  Cathe 37
  Elizh 16, 25, 28
  Saml 23
  Thos 23
McCahy
  Nancy 82
McCail
  Philip 185
McCalee
  John 94
McCallum
  Martha 18, 20, 28
  Mary 26
McCane
  Nancy 47
McCann
  Ellen 112
  Grace 22
  Jereh 25
  Jeremh 17, 28
  Mary 110
  Pat 113
McCardle

  Mary 51, 59
McCarlan
  Pat 97
McCarron
  Cath 180
  Mary 180
  Owen 180
McCarthy
  Dennis 80
  Ellen 117, 125, 160
  Fanny 125
  Jerry 124
  John 125, 141, 210
  Judy 150, 159
  Julia 125
  Margaret 125
  Margt 45, 56
  Michael 164
  Owen 134, 151, 157
  Patrick 134
McCarty
  Bridt 39, 54
  C. 55
  Callahan 22
  Catherine 229
  Danl 55
  Denis 40, 41
  Ellen 48, 68, 97
  Hanora 49
  Honoria 53
  Jeremh 32, 38
  Joanna 32
  John 46, 56, 97, 229
  Judith 34
  Margaret 101
  Margt 38
  Mary 20, 27, 32, 50
  Mary 2d 38
  Mary 3d 23

  Mary 4th 23
  Mary A. 68
  Mary Ann 14
  Mary E. 60
  Michl 32
  Mick 101
  Murty 42
  Patrick 37
  Ths. M. 69
McCluskey
  Michl 39
McClusky
  Martha 24
McCoane
  Catharine 11
  John 11
McColgan
  Ellen 82
  Neil 22
  Niel 16
  Thomas 148
  William 138
McColiff
  Pat 171
McColliff
  Bridget 81
  Jerry 81
McConnel
  Ann 72
  Frances 21
  John 22
McConnell
  Ann 31
  John 27, 148
  *Mary 20
McCormack
  Mary 105
McCormick
  Bernard 13
  Cathe 26, 29
  John 22
McCoughel
  Sarah 123
McCownly

Billy 223
McCoy
  Hugh 65
  John 65
  Neal 218
  Rosana 65
McCracken
  Grace 17, 25
McCue
  Larky 94
McCugle
  John 98
McCullogh
  Bernard 151
  Dominic 151
  Patrick 151
McCullough
  Nancy 151
  Rose 82
  Susan 151
  Thos 151
McCutcheon
  John 88
McDade
  Edward 163
  Hugh 138, 160
  Margt 165
  Mary 20, 148
  Mich 163
  Peter 163
McDermot
  Ann 31, 61
  Margt 31
  Pat 39, 42
  Patrick 54, 55
  Sarah 28
McDermote
  Patrick 94
McDermott
  Bridget 167
  Eliza 89
  Michael 215
  Patrick 167
  Sarah 24

McDivitt
  Hugh 18
McDonagh
  James 125
  John 147
  Patrick 96
McDonald
  Anthony 155
  Cather 65
  Edwd 65
  Robt 25, 28
  Sellia 65
McDonell
  Pat 132
McDonnel
  Jas 32
  Mary 45
McDonnell
  Bridget 116
  Randle 129
McDonough
  Bridget 82
  Jno 82, 156
  John 121, 148
  Margaret 96
  Mary 16, 45, 56
  Patrick 96
  Thos 132
  Wm 82, 217
McDougal
  Daniel 102
McDougald
  John 14
McE
  Mary 52
McElroy
  Barclay 37
  Phelix 218
McEwe
  Fanny 120
  Mary 60
McFarlan
  Maria 73
  Mary 12

McFarlin
  Mary 39
McFrederick
  James 12
McGachie
  Jane 20
  John 49, 58
  Rosanna 14
  Thomas 61
McGaffagan
  Mary 52
McGaffagon
  Mary 60
McGaloon
  James 115
McGantry
  Abigail 58
McGarigle
  Jane 86
  Mary 86
McGarragin
  Anne 117
McGarrahan
  Anne 117
  Mary 117
McGarrity
  Isaba 20
  Isabella 28
  Owen 30
McGarvey
  Ellen 37
McGaugh
  Cath 111
McGavan
  P. 55
McGaveron
  Brien 49
  Cathe 35, 49
  Francis 35
  J. 55
  James 43
  Thomas 35
  Willm 15
McGavigan

Philip 85
McGee
  Bridt 37
  Cathe 26, 29
  Elizabeth 62
  Honora 94
  James 94
  John 21
  John 2d 27
  Mary 94
  Pat 108
  Richard 223
McGettigan
  Bernard 218
McGilly
  Ann 85
McGiness
  Edward 99
McGinn
  James 180
  Jas 149
McGinnis
  Cathe 40
  Catherine 54
  James 96
McGlinche
  Pat 133
McGlone
  Margt 177
  Mary 114, 154, 173
  Michael 114
McGloun
  Hugh 115
  James 115
  Martin 135
McGlown
  Cath 173
  Frs 144
  Jno 144
  Margt 135
McGolderick
  Biddy 145
  Mary 145

McGolrick
  Mary 24
McGonigal
  Wm 85
McGourtry
  Abigl 50
McGoveren
  Willm 71
McGovern
  Patrick 143
McGowan
  Anne 143
  Ellen 50, 58, 109
  Grace 80
  James 115, 230
  Lawrence 11
  Margt 79
  Martha 20
  Mary 11, 98, 113, 156, 173
  Mic 113, 156
  Nancy 110
McGowen
  Cecilla 116
  Edward 116
  Ellen 116
  Margaret 116
  Mary 116
McGrade
  Michl 21
McGrath
  Ann 99
  Ellen 174
  Mick 97
McGraugh
  Susan 70
  Thomas 96
McGraw
  Sarah 20, 27
  Susan 17, 72
McGrory
  James 125
McGuest
  Edward 183

McGuigan
  Margt 121
McGuiggan
  Stephen 118
McGuiniss
  Edward 172
McGuire
  Ann 113
  Biddy 173
  Bridget 11, 31, 57
  Bridt 23, 45, 48
  Brien 49
  Cathe 32
  Cecilla 173
  Charles 96
  Corns 20, 51
  Hanora 173
  Isabella 17
  ⸱John 42
  Mary 112, 173
  Pat 47
  Patrick 56
McGunagle
  Margt 20
  Pat 22
  Susan 23
McHiggan
  Cathe 25
McHiggins
  Cathe 28
McHinch
  Jane 21, 25, 28
  Patrick 17
McHugh
  Chas 84
  Ellen 160
  James 119, 120
  John 168
  Martin 34, 60
  Mary 43, 160
  Thos 119
⸱ McHughes
  Lilly 119
  Mary 119

271

Rose 119
McInnes
  Biddy 83
McIntire
  Cathe 52
  Catherine 31
  Jas 20
  Mary 32
  Patrick 31
  Terence 32
  William 32
McIntyre
  Rose 180
  Turrents 66
  William 67
McIver
  Ann 26
  John 27
McJunkin
  Robert 223
McKay
  Cath 165
  Daniel 228
McKeane
  John 139
McKee
  John 165
McKelvey
  David 26
McKendra
  Ann 110
  Jno 109
  Mary 113
McKenna
  Bridget 31
  Cathe 53
  Cathe 1st 38
  Cathe 2d 38
  Honora 183
  John 120, 211
  Margaret 140
McKennah
  Bridget 61
McKever

Ann 111
Henry 108
Nelly 113
McKilline
  Mary 135
McKinny
  Margt 139
McLardy
  Elizabeth 73
McLauclan
  Ellen 68
  Hugh 68
McLaughlan
  Ann 26
  Bridt 25
  Cathe 49
  Edwd 21, 62
  Jno 31
  P. 57
  Pat 25
McLaughlin
  Hannah 80
  John 60
  Margt 173
  Mary 79
  Mich 143
  Pat 108
  Patrick 105
  Wm 82
McLean
  Mary 38
McLeary
  Francis 17
McLellan
  - 86
  Ann Jane 93
McLoon
  Bernd 126
  Mary 127
  Thos 126, 127
  Wilm 126, 127
  Wm 127
McLoughlan
  Biddy 167

John 167
Michl 171
Thomas 167
McLoughlin
  Mary 100
  Patrick 215
McLynch
  Pat 133
McLynn
  John 95
McMackie
  Ann 41
McMahan
  Cathe 61
  Margt 23
McMahon
  James 149
  Lawrence 147
  Margt 26, 28
  Mary 79
  Nancy 141, 173
  Tim 141
  Wm 79
McManaman
  Mary 37
McManus
  Ann 135
  Anne 100
  James 135, 160
  Jerry 94
  John 94
  Mary 38
  Nona 95
  Patk 135
McMaster
  Mary 53
McMonegal
  Beckey 150
McMorris
  Margt 173
McMorrisy
  Rody 95
McMorrow
  Denis 50, 58

McMullan
  Edward 97
McMullen
  Andw 30
  Wm 71
McMullin
  Alexander 116
  Ann 45
  Francis 117
  Isabella 116
McMurray
  Bridget 175
  Hugh 109
  James 107
  John 109
  Michl 109
  Nelly 110
  Pat 107
McNamara
  Bridget 36
  Bridt 52, 60
  Jno 149
  John 160, 180
  Margaret 11, 120
  Matth 120
  Nancy 50, 59
  Patk 119, 121
  Rosa 44
  Wm 123
McNeely
  Mary 96
McNulty
  Margt 144
McNutt
  Alex 153
  John 153
  Saml 131
McQuade
  Chas 85
McQuaid
  Mary 148
McQuid
  John 43
McQuidd

  J. 55
McRae
  Aaron 21
McShane
  Ann 22
  Sarah 18, 29
McShannon
  John 99
McSharry
  Barney 113
  Brian 113
  Cath 112
  Hanna 113
  James 108
  Mary 111
  Pat 109
  Tom 108
  Wid 111
McWade
  James 64
Mealey
  Mary A. 77
Meally
  Hugh 24
Meehan
  Margt 175
Meenan
  Ann 143
  Biddy 143
  Mich 143
Meeney
  Jno 178
  Jno jr 178
Mehan
  Thos 84
Meilen
  Patrick 33
Meiny
  John 177
Meirn
  Catherine 139
  Mary 139
Melerick
  Honoria 61

Mellin
  Ann 36
Mellsop
  Elizabeth 178
  Joseph 178
  Mrs 178
  Thomas 178
  William 178
Melowney
  David 123
Meloy
  Hannah 17, 23
  John 129
  Mary 50, 59
  Michl 108
Melvin
  Ellen 123
  Judy 123
  Mich 123
  Pat 123
  Peggy 123
Mendugh
  Thos 140
Mercer
  Robert 148
Merrick
  Saml 48
  Samuel 57
Merrin
  James 139
Messenette
  John E. 231
Milbrick
  Honora 34
Miles
  Mark 11
Millar
  James 11
Millen
  Ann 52
  Catherine 25
  Charles 27
Miller
  David 42

Elizabeth 17
Elizh 20
Isaac 73
John 74
Margt 182
Mary 20
Nancy 38
Robt 52
Mills
  And 118
  Mary 166
Milon
  Michael 128
Mitchel
  Biddy 121
  Cate 121
  John 99
  Margaret 120
  Mary 121
  Michl 121
Mitchell
  And 120
  Catherine 121, 186
  Hugh 155, 218
  James 39
  John 155
  Judy 155
  Lawrence 155
  Pat 120, 154
  Patrick 186
  Thos 133, 155
Mohan
  John 138
Mohany
  Daniel 228
  Kitty 228
  Mary 228
Monaghan
  Jeremh 34, 47
  Philip 40
  Rosa 40
Monday
  John 16

Monohan
  Michl 86
Montague
  Hugh 46
Montgomery
  Alexr 38
Moohan
  Ann 182
  Biddy 111, 113
  Jas 108
  Kitty 113
  Winni 111
Mooney
  Cath 112
  Cathe 26, 29
  John 164
  Mary Ann 112
  Tim 108
Moore
  Anne 140
  Betty 130
  Ellen 88, 93
  John 20, 53
  Mary A. 183
  Richd 93
Moran
  Ed 174
  John 96, 122, 135
  Mary 24, 107, 136, 145
  Nelly 111
  Nicholas 107
  Patk 90
  Thomas 97
Morarity
  Danl 47
Morarty
  Mich 170
Moreley
  James 88
Morgan
  Dennis 228
  Ellen 37, 228
  Mary 53, 228

  Mary jr 228
  Mr 209
  William 61, 228
Morin
  Bernard 96
  Lawrence 95
Morissy
  Ann 188
Morley
  Richard 105
Morris
  Ann 21, 85
Morrisey
  Mary 94
Morrison
  Cath 181
  Ellen 97
  John 95, 181
  Margaret 94
  Mary 142
Morrow
  Ellen 174
  Margt 75
  Margt jr 75
  Mary 173
  Matilda 35, 48, 52
Mulcahy
  Thomas 62
Mulderg
  Jane 175
Muldoon
  Ann 85
Muldown
  Muldown 36
Mulharon
  Mary 38
Mulheeny
  Anne 217
  Denis 217
Mulherran
  James 188
Mulherrin
  Cornelius 166
  Mary 130

Mulholland
  Andw 119
  Jane 119
  John 119
Mullane
  James 41
  Jerry 48
  Patrick 34
Mullaney
  Michael 94
Mullen
  Ann 112
  John 14, 109
  Martin 45
  Mary 111, 112
  Miche 39
  Michl 18
  Wm 176
Mullin
  Ann 133
  Francis W. 97
  Margaret 97
Mullins
  Margaret 93
  Mary 93
Mullowny
  John 215
Mulloy
  Ellen 111
Muloy
  Ellen 173
Munn
  Catherine 118
Munns
  James 215
Murdock
  Jane 126
  Margaret 126
Murkersu
  Robert 62
Murphey
  Thos 162
Murphy
  Abigail 37

Alia 142
Ann 39
Anne 120
Betty 90, 165
Biddy 139
Brid 140
Cathe 35, 45
Catherine 54, 142
Corns 45
Dan 136, 186
Daniel 33, 134
Denis 33
Edward 129
Eliza 182
Ellen 32, 35, 61, 142, 171
Hanora 134, 158, 186
Hona 49
Honora 170
James 83
Jane 182
Jeremh 35, 59
Jerh 42
Jerry 157
Jim 102
Jno 142, 181
Joana 41
Joanna 52, 60, 61, 182
Johanna 131, 157
John 31, 37, 41, 46, 56, 148, 165, 168
Judy 52
Laurence 142
Margaret 27
Margt 2d 43
Maria 43
Martin 158
Mary 16, 43, 52, 83, 131, 132, 134, 142, 157, 186
Mary 2nd 31

Mary 3d 33
Matt 117
Michael 18, 69, 134, 182
Michl 17, 142, 165
Nancy 186
Paddy 186
Pat 132
Patk 142
Patrick 30
Peggy 133, 134
Peter 149
Stephen 32
Timothy 32, 37
Tom 186
Wm 39, 77, 87, 182
Murray
  Ann 187
  Betsy 97
  Bridget 187
  Catherine 187
  Daniel 105
  Eliza 13
  Frs 158
  Jno 176
  John 94
  Libby 121
  Mary 23, 187
  Michl 83
  Murray 160
  Patrick 97
  Richd 89
  Sarah 187
  Susan 50
  Thomas 161
  Tim 122
Nagle
  Mary 37
Nailon
  Margaret 157
  Michl 176
  Nancy 149

Patrick 147
Nash
  Mary 27
Nathen
  Pat 101
Naughton
  Mary 101
Naulty
  Margt 133
  Michl 133
Neagle
  john 183
  Mary 121
Neal
  Thos 156
Neall
  Thos 183
Nealon
  Joanna 147
Neely
  Thomas 218
Nehel
  Maurice 121
Neil
  Elizabeth 121
  James 125
  Jerry 134
  John 96
  Margaret 103
  Michael 143
Nelis
  James 218
Nelson
  Elizabeth 20
  Michael 160
  Stephen 17
Neville
  Catherine 122
  Mary 122
  Michl 122
  Wm 81
Nevin
  Biddy 123
  Hanora 123

Joanna 148
John 154
  Mary 136
  Michael 122
  Pat 132
  Patrick 131
Newman
  Ellen 20
Nicholson
  John 96
  Mary 96
Nickolson
  Mary 96
Nighlin
  Peter 41
Noen
  James 127
Noon
  Mary 143
  Michl 182
Noonan
  Bridget 54
  Bridt 40
  Cathe 44
  David 170
  Denis 48
  Eliza 46, 101
  J. 55
  Jerry 170
  John 40
  Mary 24
  William 46, 56
Norman
  Ann 208
  Robert 208
Nowlan
  Bridget 23
Nowlen
  Murty 47
Nowlin
  Michael 58
  Michl 50
  Murty 56
Nuckley

Bridt 40
O'Brien
  Catherine 230
  D. 54
  Danl 39
  Eliza J. 60
  Fergus 130
  Hannah 77
  Honoria 53
  James 39, 122
  Jereh 30
  Jereh 2d 30
  Jeremh 60
  John 49, 52, 57, 60
  Mary 49, 59, 79, 140
  Mary Ann 230
  Pat 26
  Patrick 37
  Peter 92
  Sarah 83
  Wheeney 230
O'Bryan
  Thos 71
O'Cane
  Mary 52
O'Connell
  James 77
O'Conner
  Cath Ann 115
O'Conners
  Walker 166
O'Connor
  Denis 44
  Esther 165
  J. 55
  James 121
  Margaret 165
  Thos 98
O'Donell
  Chas 151
  Ellen 151
  Geo 151

Grace 151
O'Donnel
  James 48
  John 16, 29, 61
  M. 55
  Margaret 72
  Margt 51, 59
  Mary 39
  Michl 41
O'Donnell
  Michael 157, 184
  Peggy 186
  Sarah 87
O'Gara
  Bridget 174
  Mary 135
O'Hara
  Elizabeth 30
  John 139
  Margaret 11
  Mary 139
  Richard 139
  Sarah 85
  Thomas 187
O'Harran
  Daniel 97
O'Harrin
  Catherine 97
O'Harron
  Elizh 24
  Ellen 34
  James 56
  Jane 51, 59
  Jas 47
  Margt 34
O'Hearn
  Cath 158
O'Keefe
  Arthur 49, 58
O'Leary
  Jeremiah 31
  Joana 28
  Joanna 25
  Norah 231

Tim 171
O'Mara
  Bridget 142
  Brien 141
  Edward 141
  John 141, 162
  Murria 141
O'Mealy
  Peter 185
O'Neil
  Arthur 172
  Ellen 67
  Gregory 210
  Margaret 119
  Mary 118
  Phelix 140
O'Neill
  Ann 110
  Geo 118
  Jno 119
  Joanna 92
  Margt 179
  Mary 92
  Owen 118
  Patk 119
  Rose 212
O'Neils
  Rose 80
O'Rourk
  Brian 145
O'Sullivan
  Ann 74
  Patrick 164
  Rev. Thos. 223
Oakley
  Eliezer 69
  Emily 69
  Oakley 70
Oliphant
  Elizabeth 16
Olman
  Jerry 97
Operan
  Mary 94

Owen
  Catherine 96
  Mary 35
Owens
  James 218
Pain
  Mary 37
Palmer
  Lawrence 171
  Mary 171
  Michael 171
  Wm 170
Palmerston
  Lord 215
Parat
  Thomas 95
  Winney 95
Parish
  Eliza 27
Parker
  William 22
Parks
  Jane 20
  Robert 18
Partan
  Jane 97
Partelow
  Thomas 62, 69
Patten
  Margaret 174
Patterson
  Geo 106
Patton
  Dorah 71
  Elizabeth 71
  Joseph 71
Paul
  Jane 26
Payden
  Richd 32
Payton
  Joseph 36
Peacock
  David 181

James 180, 181
Jane 180
Martha 180
Wm Jno 180
Pelly
  Cornelius 216
Penney
  Catherine 151
Penny
  Catherine 152
Penrose
  Mary 12
Pentreath
  Capt 208
Perin
  Ann 143
Peters
  B.L. 216
Pew
  James 173
Phelan
  Harriet 133
Phillips
  Isabella 86
  Thos 161
Pine
  Will 103
  William 222
  Wm 81
Poland
  Zebulon 26
Pole
  Edwd 147
Porter
  Adam 30
  George 11
  John 79
  Samuel 218
Porthan
  John 98
Potter
  Biddy 176
Power
  Catherine 44

Eliz 78
Jane 20
John 45
John B. 63
Judy 33
Power 98
Powers
  Ally 142
  James 142
  Patrick 142
  Rich 158
Prating
  Fanny 170
Pratt
  Mary 16
  Mary 2nd 17
Preston
  Barbara 94, 99
Proctor
  James 86
  John G. 26, 63
Purcell
  Anny 168
  Hanora 167
  James 168
  John 168
  Thomas 168
  Tom 168
Pye
  Ann 110
  John 108
  Mary 37, 52, 60, 110
  Nancy 110
  Pat 107
  Thos 113
  Tom 107, 108
  Wm 107, 108
Quigly
  Catherine 142
Quillen
  Mary 41
Quillon
  Mary 34, 55

Quilly
  Mary 24, 28, 29
Quilty
  John 44
Quin
  John 10, 104
  Mary 31
  Mic 156
  Michael 155
  Owen 39
  Patrick 39, 70
  Thomas 17
Quince
  Johanna 164
  Kit 164
Quinlan
  Dennis 136
  James 73
  Johanna 136
  Norrie 158
Quinn
  Ann 26, 29
  Cath 149
  Charles 58
  Chas 46
  John 96, 100
  Julia 27
  Mary 24, 25, 28, 54
  Owen 54
  Pat 175
  Patrick 53, 54, 104
Radekin
  John 158
Rafter
  Catherine 94
  Ed 108
  Francis 109
  John 94
  Mary 96
  Thomas 94
  Thos 109
  William 94

Winni 111
Raidon
  Thomas 48
Rairden
  Danl 49
  Hanora 46
Rairdon
  Cath 172
  Daniel 57
  Denis 44
  Honoria 56
  John 39, 54
  Mary 16
  Mathew 70
  Rairdon 39
  Thomas 57
Ramsay
  Martha 16
  Mary 26
Ranney
  Patrick 96
Ratchford
  Thos 48
Ray
  William 63
Rearden
  John 171
Reardon
  Jane 100
Rearney
  Pat 140
Red
  Mary 174
Redmond
  Mary 117
  Thomas 119
Reed
  Ann 14
  Catherine 73
  Mary 20
Regan
  Danl 119
  Deborah 92
  Eleanor 30

Ellen 38
James 170
Jno 123
John 152
Michl 130
Timothy 30
Reiley
  Matt 131
Reilley
  Cath 91
  Jas 178
  Margt 75
  Mary 182
  Peter 120
Reilly
  Arthur 75
Reily
  Biddy 169
  John 138
  Mary 131
Revil
  Mary 173
Reynolds
  Patrick 217
Rhodes
  Mary 150
  Patrick 150
Richards
  James 16
Riggin
  Catherine 130
Riggs
  Jane 12
Righley
  Edward 47
  J. 55
  Judith 56
  Patrick 53, 54
  Timothy 41
  Timoy 47
Righly
  Judy 46
Rigney
  Denis 167

Riley
  Jno 182
  Julia 88
  Patrick 38
Ring
  Michael 148
  Timothy 15, 69
Riordan
  John 134
Risk
  Samuel 27
Ritson
  Thomas 223
Roach
  Cath 89
  Peggy 149
Roberts
  Bess 159
  David 159
  George 159
  Jerry 159
  John 158, 159
  Michl 43
Robinson
  Henry 24, 28, 73
  William 18
Robson
  Mercy 72
Roche
  John 118, 121
  Mary 154
Roden
  Francis 73
Rody
  Bridget 187
Rohan
  Judy 58
  Patrick 49, 58
Ronan
  Bridget 32
Roney
  William 66, 71
Rooney
  Ann 110, 173

Cath 109
Charles 140
James 97, 143
Margaret 102
Tim 143
Winni 143
Rourk
  Cath 110
  Martin 107
  Mary 110, 113
  Nicholas 27
  Nichs 20
  Pat 50
Rourke
  Nicholas 23
Roy
  John 164
Russel
  Frances 21
  Patrick 64
Russell
  John 63
Ryan
  Ann 166
  B. 54
  Barkley 39
  Bridget 126
  Catherine 102, 104
  Ellen 100
  Jno 130
  Joanna 17
  John 126
  Martin 126
  Mary 98, 166
  Michael 37
  Miche 53
  Michl 130
  Nancy 25, 28
  Patrick 17, 22, 34, 61
  Peter 98
  Richard 13
  Thomas 12

Thos 132, 176
Winni 126
Ryon
  Ellen 69, 71
  M.A. 70
  Mary A. 69
  Patrick 69
  Thomas 69, 70
Salisbury
  Margaret 185
Sallory
  John 129
Salsberry
  Margaret 185
Sampson
  Joseph 14
Saunders
  Robt 185
Savage
  Mary 146
  Michael 97
  Michl 171
  Owen 146
  Patrick 157
Scallan
  Martha 24
Scanlan
  Bridget 176
  Cath 176
  Catherine 171
  Eli 176
  Jerry 128
  Jno 143
  Joanna 93
  John 128, 176
  Margt 171
  Mary 171
  Patk 93
  Tim 128
Scanlen
  Brien 46
  Ellen 48
Scanlin
  Domenick 139

Ellen 57
Thomas 48
Scannel
  Timothy 34, 57
  Timoy 48
Scarlett
  Ann 11
Scobornia
  John 19
Seahill
  John 154
Seddie
  Betsey 167
  Catherine 167
  Rose 167
  Thomas 167
Sehey
  Robt 138
Selor
  Thos 147
Sexton
  Conor 148, 179
  Ellen 137, 180
  Honor 178
  Honor jr 178
  Jenny 179
  Kitty 179
  Michl 179
  Nancy 179
  Pat 179
  Patrick 105
Seymore,
  Benj 50
  Benjamin 72
Seymores
  Mary 71
Seymour
  Cathe 52
  Mary 36
Shanehan
  Ellen 37
Shannehan
  John 45
Shannohan

Wm 67
Shannon
  Ellen 150
  Mary 96
Sharp
  John 164
Sharpe
  Theresa J. 62
Shaughereau
  Catherine 170
Shaughereux
  Jas 135
Shaughnessy
  John 95
Shaughnesy
  Mary 121
Shaughnison
  Dan 170
Shay
  Catherine 229
  Elizabeth 229
  Ellen 229
  James 209
  Joanna 229
  William 229
Shea
  Joanna 90
  Judy 134
  Mary 90, 94
  Michael 134
  Patk 91
Sheals
  Frances 22
Shearne
  Catherine 158
Sheean
  Barbara 229
  Catherine 1st 229
  Catherine 2nd 229
  Catherine 3rd 229
  Daniel Sr 229
  Edward 229
  Edward Sr 230

Ellen 229
Jerry 230
Jerry Jr 229
Jerry Sr 229
Joanna 229
Joanna jr 229
John 229
Judy 229
Mary 1st 229
Mary 2nd 229
Mary 3rd 229
Michael 229
Patrick 229
Thomas 229
Sheehan
  Daniel 229
Sheehy
  James 210
Shefna
  Bridget 127
Shehan
  Alexr 34, 46, 56
  Cath 89
  Cornelius 27
  Danl 41
  Ellen 53
  Jeremh 51
  Jno 32
  John 42
  Nancy 24
Shehey
  Edmund 138
  Margt 138
  Mary 138
Sheley
  Edward 138
  James 138
Shelton
  Grace 73
Sheridan
  Bridget 11
  John 47, 56
  Mary 65
Sherridan

Jno 32
Sherry
  Thos 150
Shey
  Ellen 42, 56
  Ellen 2d 45
  Jeremh 46
  Jeremiah 63
  John 51, 59
  Margaret 37
  Mary 39, 52, 54
  Owen 53
  William 46
Sheyhey
  James 138
Shifna
  Bridget 127
Shoughereau
  James 134
Silfridge
  Thomas 218
Sinclair
  John 20
Slattery
  Mary 38
  Michl 61
Slavin
  James 153
  John 153
Slemons
  Cathe 25
  Catherine 16
Slevin
  Biddy 184
  Mary 184
  Michael 184
  Ned 184
Small
  John 38
Smeddy
  Honor 126
Smith
  Ellen 76
  Frances 20

James 30, 38, 53
John 114
Margaret 47
Margt 46
Michael 215
Mrs 114
Robert 208
William 73
Somers
  Bartholomew 135
  Mary 135
  Patrick 160
Souce
  Beckey 159
  Mary 159
Span
  - Margaret 118
Spann
  Michl 118
Speed
  Martin 102
Spellman
  Thos 138
Spillane
  Dennis 91
  Joana 18, 20
  Nugent 169
Spittle
  Ann 16
Splahan
  John 88
Spriggs
  Mary 40
Spring
  James 47, 56
Stack
  Hanora 157
  William 46, 56
Staffle
  William 217
Stanton
  Bridget 230
  Margaret 230
  Mary 230

Patrick 230
Thomas 230
Starrett
  Ann 20
Staunton
  Edmond 125
Steel
  Owen 107
Stephenson
  Margt 19
Sterling
  John 30, 61
Stevens
  Ellen 32
  George 31, 61
  Margt 31
  Mary 21
Stewart
  Ann 85
  James S. 73
  Maria 89
  Mary 65
  Sophia 89
  Thos 85
  Wm 160
Strattan
  Ellen 22
Stratton
  John 21
Strawbridge
  Cath 78
Strelin
  Alice 46
Stuart
  Jane 86
  Sarah 86
Stubs
  Thos 104
Sturgeon
  David 231
Sullevan
  Kitty 164
Sullivan
  - 78

Ann 49, 57, 88
Biddy 157
Bridget 119, 170, 229
Bridt 40
Carty 101
Cath 84, 92
Cathe 45
Catherine 168
Cornelius 169
Corns 37, 40
Daniel 98, 137
Danl 37, 43, 164
Denis 38, 53, 134, 136
Denis 2d 53
Ellen 45, 50, 53, 58, 90, 136, 169, 178
Eugene 85
Hannh 44
Honora 52
Honora 2d 45
Honoria 35, 61
Humphrey 87, 229
Hurly 96
J. 55
James 92, 170
Jane 137
Jerry 48, 79, 94, 125, 130, 134, 169, 170, 177
Jno 164
Jno Jr 136
Joanna 39, 54
Johanna 164
John 41, 43, 91, 106, 125, 136, 137, 164, 169, 171
Judy 137
Lawrence 88
Margaret 116

Margt 39, 45, 78, 89
Mary 25, 28, 35, 50, 58, 84, 88, 91, 101, 117, 125, 129, 137, 157, 210
Mary 2d 45, 58
Mary 3d 48
Mathew 148
Mic 163
Mich 91
Michael 164
Miche 59
Michl 43, 49, 51, 88, 122, 147, 164
Mick 102
Mrs 88
Murly 171
Nancy 37, 44
Norry 96, 157
Owen 40, 170
Pat 41
Patk 178
Patrick 33, 134, 146
Peggy 94
Peter 79
Richard 168
Thos 91
Tim 131
Supple
  A. 55
  Adam 41
  Cathe 35, 52
  Michael 35
Surahan
  Aaron 146
Surl
  George 151
Swadler
  Mary 21
Sweeney
  Biddy 180

Bridget 77
Cath 180
Hannh 44
Johanna 76
John 40
Margaret 130
Owen 156
Sarah 160
Sweeny
  Nancy 174
Sweetman
  Thomas 53
Swift
  Bridget 86
  Cath 86
Swinney
  Daniel 22, 47, 57
  Edwd 17
  John 52, 53, 59
  Mary 35
Taber
  Jane 151
Tague
  Mary 173
Tait
  Andrew 99
Talbot
  Margt 43
Talvey
  Daniel 124
Tape
  Annie 137
  Eliza 137
  Ellen 136
  Geo 136
  John 137
Tate
  Elizabeth 17
Taunton
  Jno 170
Taylor
  Agness 65
  Alexander 38, 97
  Biddy 160

Hugh 85
James 49, 57
Teat
  Matthew 62
Teavens
  Elizh 51
Terple
  John 157
Theall
  Charles 14
Thomas
  George 80, 211
  Jane 63
  Mary 36
  Mathl 53
  Nathe 60
Thompson
  Isabella 59
  Isabl 50
  Jane 25, 28
Thomson
  Jno 85, 86
  Margaret 187
  Margt 187
  Mary Jane 85
  Robert 231
  William 187
Thornton
  Hanora 169
Tierney
  Felix 50, 59
Tierny
  Patrick 130
Timms
  Mary 66
Timoney
  James 50
Tivnan
  John 117, 135
  Owen 135
Tobin
  Mary 89
  Wm 89
Todd

Elizabeth 13
Toher
  Owen 215
  Sally 100
Tole
  Matthias 12
Tolson
  Mary 14
Tolton
  John 16, 29
Toner
  Rose 148
Tonor
  John 85
Toole
  John 185
Toomey
  Catherine 130
Tougum
  Edward 154
Toy
  Thomas 117
Tracey
  Mary 11
Tracy
  Biddy 129
  Judy 129
  Mary 50, 58
  Michael 129
  Thomas 40
Trahee
  John 129
Treagh
  John 103
Triggs
  Patk 170
Trimble
  Jane 20
  Jane Jr 22
Trowe
  Geo 65
Trower
  Margt 50, 58
Tummany

Conly 94
Mary 99
Tumony
  And 107
Tuppen
  Jane 20, 26
Turdum
  Mary 127
Turnbull
  Ellen 229
  Francis 229
  James 229
  Joseph 229
Twoomay
  Mary 21
Tye
  Matt 165
Tyke
  John 73
Tyner
  Mary 136
Urquhart
  Grigor 39, 62
Vallely
  Jno 32
  John 37
Vance
  Sarah 47
  William 40
Vaughan
  Nancy 105
Vaul
  Jane 29
Vent
  Wm 35
Verise
  Catherine 44
Wade
  Mary 148
  Mich 118
  Michael 123
Waide
  Isabella 160
Waldram

Tim 151
Walker
  Alex 108
  Frances 18
  Thomas 13
Wallace
  Catherine 103, 120
  John 49, 57
  Judy 103
  Margaret 10
  Mary 103
  Patrick 103
  William 228
  Wm 31
Wallis
  Judy 103
Walsh
  Biddy 140
  Edmond 125
  Edward 147
  Johanna 137, 159
  John 128, 140
  Margaret 128, 159, 162
  Martin 95, 139
  Mary 105, 128, 148, 153
  Michael 122, 163
  Thomas 122, 140, 148
Ward
  Elizabeth 21
  Fanny 149
  Hugh 148
  John 47, 148
  Nancy 149
  Neil 148
  Rose 149
Warner
  Charlotte F. 13
Warrant
  Francis 114
Warren

Hanora 126
   John 126, 160
   Mary 76, 126
   Michael 117
Watkins
   Ann 21
Watson
   Ann 22
   Mary 187
Waul
   Ellen 161
   Michl 161
Way
   Elizabeth 22
Welahan
   Catherine 210
Welch
   Barthw 31, 38
   Biddy 148
   Bridget 124
   Ellen 18, 88
   Frances 48, 57
   Jno 124
   John 51, 60, 89
   Kate 150
   Margt 18
   Mary 28, 42
   Patrick 43, 55
   Richard 44
   Thomas 48, 57
Welsh
   Ann 188
   Ann jr 188
   Edward 105
   Kitty 188
   Mary 25
   Patrick 105, 185
   Walter 185
Westerberg
   L. Magnus 73
Wetmore
   Justus 231
Whalen
   Ellen 188

   Mary 13
Whelan
   Denis 38
   Jno 44
   Mary 52, 63
Whillehan
   Ellen 30
White
   Esther 22
   James 15, 29, 64
   James 2nd 35
   Johanna 125
   Jos 139
   Margaret 60
   Margt 51, 52
   Mary 46, 125
   Mary 2d 37, 50
   Mary 2nd 33, 58
   Mary Ann 56
Whooton
   Mary 47
Wier
   Thomas 20, 71
Wilby
   Elizabeth 35
Williams
   Charles 47
   John 175
   Mary 24
Williamson
   Cath 111
   Jas 108
Willis
   Michael 122
Wilson
   Andw 86
   Chas 86
   Elizabeth 21
   Grace 21
   Jane 86
   Mary 25
   Michael 64
   Wilson 19
Wise

   Nicholas 68
Wiseman
   Ellen 100
Wood
   George 21
   John 26, 29, 44
   William 47
Woodburne
   John 160
Wrenn
   Thomas 43
   Thos 55
Wrinn
   Patrick 168
Wynn
   Bridget 45, 56
   Elizabeth 45
Young
   James 74
   Rebecca 24

www.ingramcontent.com/pod-product-compliance
Lightning Source LLC
Chambersburg PA
CBHW061435300426
44114CB00014B/1693